Sunset

K·I·T·C·H·E·N
C·A·B·I·N·E·T

BY THE EDITORS OF SUNSET BOOKS

Sunset Publishing Corporation • Menlo Park, California

SUNSET BOOKS

PRESIDENT AND PUBLISHER
Susan J. Maruyama
DIRECTOR, FINANCE & BUSINESS AFFAIRS
Gary Loebner
DIRECTOR, SALES & MARKETING
Richard A. Smeby
MARKETING & CREATIVE SERVICES MANAGER
Guy C. Joy
PRODUCTION DIRECTOR
Lory Day
EDITORIAL DIRECTOR
Kenneth Winchester
EXECUTIVE EDITOR
Bob Doyle
COORDINATING EDITOR
Cornelia Fogle
RESEARCH AND TEXT
Cynthia Scheer
COPY EDITOR
Rebecca LaBrum
DESIGN
Sandra Popovich Graphic Design
COLOR ILLUSTRATIONS
Alice Harth

SUNSET PUBLISHING CORPORATION
CHAIRMAN
Jim Nelson
PRESIDENT/CHIEF EXECUTIVE OFFICER
Robin Wolaner
CHIEF FINANCIAL OFFICER
James E. Mitchell
PUBLISHER
Stephen J. Seabolt
CIRCULATION DIRECTOR
Robert I. Gursha
VICE PRESIDENT, MANUFACTURING
Lorinda B. Reichert
EDITOR, SUNSET MAGAZINE
William R. Marken
SENIOR EDITOR, FOOD AND ENTERTAINING
Jerry Anne Di Vecchio

COVER: Salmon Grill Diable (page 117) is served with Asparagus & Pasta Stir-fry (page 151) and Cheese & Bacon Corn Muffins (page 177). Cover design by Jacqueline Jones Design. Photography by Chris Shorten. Food styling by Sue White.

First printing July 1995
Copyright © 1995 Sunset Publishing Corporation, Menlo Park, CA 94025. First edition. All rights reserved, including the right of reproduction in whole or in part in any form.

Library of Congress Catalog Card Number: 95-67051
ISBN Hardcover edition: 0-376-02431-3
Softcover edition: 0-376-02432-1
Printed in the United States

printed on recycled paper

REAL FOOD FROM REAL PEOPLE

Enjoy with us this affectionate look back at Sunset's Kitchen Cabinet®, one of Sunset Magazine's most popular monthly features. Beginning in February 1929, thousands of cooks throughout the West have shared their creative cooking efforts with fellow Sunset readers. In this book, we've gathered nearly 600 of the best recipes for today's cooks, including an illustrated sampling of dishes from past decades.

Ever since the feature began, every recipe published in Kitchen Cabinet has been tested and approved by Sunset food editors—and often sampled enthusiastically and rated by other employees, too. For this book, we've retested the pre-1970 recipes and, if necessary, adjusted them slightly to reduce fat and sodium and to make instructions more specific. Nutritional data is provided for all recipes, except those appearing in our sampler of Kitchen Cabinet through the years.

For more than 65 years, Sunset and its readers have savored a warm rapport as we've shared new food discoveries. In this book, we're pleased to acknowledge some of the many Westerners who have enhanced our appreciation of Western foods.

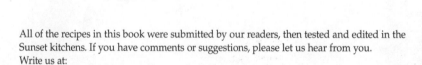

All of the recipes in this book were submitted by our readers, then tested and edited in the Sunset kitchens. If you have comments or suggestions, please let us hear from you.
Write us at:
Sunset Books
Cookbook Editorial
80 Willow Road
Menlo Park, CA 94025

If you would like to order additional copies of any of our books, call us at 1-800-634-3095 or check with your local bookstore. For special sales, bulk orders, and premium sales information, call Sunset Custom Publishing Services at (415) 324-5577.

Sunset's Kitchen Cabinet is a registered trademark of Sunset Publishing Corporation.

C·O·N·T·E·N·T·S

SUNSET'S KITCHEN CABINET THROUGH THE YEARS

A SAMPLING OF TYPICAL RECIPES AND ILLUSTRATIONS

Dear Reader,

Like so many families who moved West, we received a housewarming gift of Sunset from the resident relative. An incredible gardener who had become Westernized through its pages, she was almost evangelical in her enthusiasm for both the West and the magazine. It was at her home that I tasted my first rare hamburger—prepared from a Sunset recipe, grilled on a built-in brick barbecue made from a Sunset design, and served at a table-and-chair set built from barrels according to Sunset instructions. On her patio, I ate my first avocado, persimmon, and pomegranate—all enormously exotic to my Midwestern palate, but treated with comfort and familiarity in Sunset recipes.

This was just after World War II, and although still in grade school, I had already developed a burning passion for food and cooking. With the arrival of Sunset each month, I found myself turning to a feature called Kitchen Cabinet. The recipes weren't scary because they were short and looked easy, even to a 10-year-old. There was usually a little story about the contributor or the recipe, and there were endearing sketches that bridged my jump from comic books to cookbooks.

Time went on, and with hopes and dreams supported by the necessary training, I became a Sunset food writer in 1959. One of my first tasks was to retest recipes for an upcoming Kitchen Cabinet. I was thrilled to have such an old friend help me find my way as a budding journalist.

When we planned this book, leafing back through the years of Kitchen Cabinet was particularly nostalgic for me. This feature has mirrored our lives and our styles of entertaining, eating, and cooking over almost seven decades—a lifetime for many. Those few short pages each month have clearly reflected the ways we've changed—and the ways we've stayed the same.

Kitchen Cabinet came into being about 30 years after the first issue of Sunset was published in 1898. Founded by Southern Pacific Railroad, the magazine was named for the sleek Sunset Limited train that raced between St. Louis and Los Angeles. Its initial purpose was to lure travelers West to buy land and settle. Southern Pacific, of course, had lots of land to sell. The government, concerned that Sunset gave Southern Pacific an unfair advantage in such sales, pressed the company to divest the magazine. It did—and the staff, who dreamed of creating a literary journal like the Atlantic Monthly, took over. Financially, it was a faltering time, but luminaries such as Mark Twain and Bret Harte were among those who enriched the pages.

In the late 1920s, a salesman for Better Homes & Gardens—a man who spent a lot of time in the West doing business—began to question how a national publication could successfully serve a part of the country so different from other regions in its climate, geography, and foodstuffs. Laurence W. Lane made his move in October 1928, bought Sunset, and turned it into "The Magazine of Western Living": a magazine about the West for people who live in the West.

—— 1929 ——

Ruth Taylor White illustrated the first Kitchen Cabinet

—— 1930s ——

Cook in bobbed hair grates lemon peel for salad dressing

ZUCCHINI-CHEESE APPETIZER SQUARES

Here's another appealing vegetable-cheese custard. This one's made with shredded zucchini and topped with sesame seeds.

- ¼ cup sesame seeds
- ¼ cup salad oil
- 1 small onion, chopped
- 1 clove garlic, minced or pressed
- 2½ cups shredded zucchini
- 6 large eggs
- ⅓ cup fine dry bread crumbs
- ½ teaspoon *each* dry basil and dry oregano
- ¼ teaspoon *each* salt and pepper
- 3 cups (about 12 oz.) shredded Cheddar cheese
- ½ cup grated Parmesan cheese

Toast sesame seeds in a wide frying pan over medium-high heat, stirring often, until golden (2 to 4 minutes). Pour out of pan and set aside. Heat oil in pan; add onion and garlic and cook, stirring often, until onion is almost soft (about 4 minutes). Add zucchini and cook, stirring, until tender-crisp to bite (about 3 minutes). Remove from heat.

In a large bowl, beat eggs to blend. Stir in bread crumbs, basil, oregano, salt, pepper, Cheddar cheese, and zucchini mixture. Spread evenly in a greased 9- by 13-inch baking dish. Sprinkle with Parmesan cheese and sesame seeds.

Bake in a 325° oven until center of custard feels set when lightly pressed (about 30 minutes). Let cool in pan for about 15 minutes, then cut into about 1-inch squares. Serve warm, at room temperature, or cold. Makes about 120 appetizers. — *L. F., Concord, CA*

Per appetizer: 24 calories, 0.5 g carbohydrates, 1 g protein, 2 g total fat (1 g saturated), 14 mg cholesterol, 34 mg sodium

CHERRY TOMATO SALSA

Nippy with garlic and fresh jalapeños, this salsa tastes great with crisp cucumber slices or tortilla chips. For the prettiest presentation, use both red and yellow cherry tomatoes.

- 2 cups red or yellow cherry tomatoes (or use some of each color)
- 1 clove garlic, minced or pressed
- ⅓ cup lightly packed cilantro leaves
- 2 fresh jalapeño chiles, seeded and finely chopped
- 2 tablespoons *each* thinly sliced green onion and lime juice
- Salt and pepper
- About 3 cups cucumber slices
- Tortilla chips (optional)

Cut tomatoes into halves. In a food processor, combine tomatoes, garlic, cilantro, and chiles; whirl until tomatoes are coarsely chopped. (Or chop coarsely with a knife.) Transfer to a bowl and stir in onion and lime juice. Season to taste with salt and pepper.

Serve salsa with cucumber slices and, if desired, tortilla chips. Makes about 2 cups (about 6 servings). —*Nancy Fas, Cardiff, CA*

Per serving: 24 calories, 5 g carbohydrates, 1 g protein, 0.3 g total fat (0 g saturated), 0 mg cholesterol, 8 mg sodium

MARINATED MUSHROOMS

Tarragon, garlic, and shallots flavor these pickled mushrooms. Serve them with chilled white wine and toasted baguette slices for a simple before-dinner treat. (Be sure to provide wooden picks for spearing the mushrooms.)

- 4 cups water
- 6 tablespoons white wine vinegar
- 2 pounds small mushrooms (*each* about 1 inch in diameter)
- 4 or 5 small shallots, peeled and cut in half lengthwise
- 2 large cloves garlic, peeled and cut in half lengthwise
- 3 or 4 tarragon sprigs or ½ teaspoon dry tarragon
- 1 dry bay leaf
- ½ cup olive oil or salad oil
- ¼ teaspoon salt (optional)

In a 4- to 5-quart pan, bring water and 2 tablespoons of the vinegar to a rolling boil over high heat. Add mushrooms; cover, return to a boil, and boil for 5 minutes. Remove from heat and let cool; then cover and refrigerate in cooking liquid until next day.

The next day, drain mushrooms and pack in a glass jar (at least 1-quart size). Poke shallots, garlic, tarragon sprigs, and bay leaf down among mushrooms. Stir together oil, remaining ¼ cup vinegar, and salt (if used); pour over mushrooms. Cover and let stand at room temperature until next day.

Serve mushrooms; or refrigerate, covered, for up to 3 weeks (if oil thickens, bring mushrooms to room temperature before serving). Makes about 4 cups (12 to 16 servings). —*April Linton, Seattle*

Per serving: 89 calories, 4 g carbohydrates, 1 g protein, 8 g total fat (1 g saturated), 0 mg cholesterol, 3 mg sodium

Parmesan Zucchini Sticks

These easy oven-fried zucchini sticks make a crisp snack; they're good as a side dish at dinner, too.

- ⅔ cup grated Parmesan cheese
- ½ cup seasoned fine dry bread crumbs
- 1 teaspoon *each* ground sage and dry rosemary
- 2 large eggs
- 5 medium-size zucchini (about 1¾ lbs. *total*)
- 1 tablespoon olive oil or salad oil
     Salt
     Parsley sprigs (optional)

In a wide, shallow bowl, stir together cheese, bread crumbs, sage, and rosemary; set aside. In another bowl, beat eggs to blend.

Trim ends from zucchini. Cut each zucchini in half crosswise; then cut halves lengthwise into quarters. Add zucchini sticks to beaten eggs and mix gently. Lift out sticks, one at a time; drain briefly and roll in cheese mixture to coat evenly. Place sticks slightly apart in a greased shallow 10- by 15-inch baking pan. Drizzle with oil. Bake in a 450° oven until well browned and crusty (about 25 minutes). Sprinkle with salt to taste. Serve hot; garnish with parsley sprigs, if desired. Makes 6 servings.
—*B. L. Gonsalves, Sacramento*

Per serving: 143 calories, 12 g carbohydrates, 9 g protein, 7 g total fat (3 g saturated), 78 mg cholesterol, 456 mg sodium

Cheese & Bacon in a Bread Boat

Seasoned cream cheese mixed with sour cream and plenty of bacon heats in a hollowed-out French loaf.

- 1 pound bacon, diced
- 1 large round or oval loaf French bread (about 1½ lbs.)
- 1 large package (about 8 oz.) cream cheese, at room temperature
- 1 cup sour cream
- ½ cup *each* chopped green bell pepper and sliced green onions

Cook bacon in a wide frying pan over medium heat until crisp, stirring often. Remove bacon from pan with a slotted spoon and set aside. Reserve 3 tablespoons of the drippings; discard remaining drippings.

With a sharp knife, cut down through top of bread 1 inch from sides. Slide your fingers down along cut and pull bread out in one piece, leaving a shell about ½ inch thick. Cut bread chunk into ½-inch-thick rectangles about 1½ by 2 inches. Brush inside of shell with the reserved 3 tablespoons bacon drippings. Place shell and bread pieces in a single layer in 2 shallow 10- by 15-inch baking pans. Bake in a 350° oven for 20 minutes.

Meanwhile, in a bowl, mix cream cheese and sour cream until smoothly blended; stir in bell pepper, onions, and bacon. Remove bread shell from oven; spoon cheese mixture into shell. Return shell to oven and bake until filling is heated through (15 to 20 minutes). Place shell on a board; surround with bread pieces to dip into filling. Break up shell to eat with filling, too. Makes 10 to 12 servings. — *Marilyn Gibfried, Oakland, CA*

Per serving: 381 calories, 34 g carbohydrates, 11 g protein, 22 g total fat (11 g saturated), 44 mg cholesterol, 652 mg sodium

Cheesy Chestnut Tidbits

Get these little water chestnut–filled pastries all ready to bake—then chill or freeze them until needed. When company comes, you'll have fresh, hot appetizers ready to serve in half an hour or less.

- ½ cup (¼ lb.) butter or margarine, at room temperature
- 2 cups (about 8 oz.) shredded sharp Cheddar cheese
- ½ teaspoon garlic salt
- 1½ cups all-purpose flour
- 2 tablespoons sesame seeds
- ½ teaspoon paprika
     Dash of ground red pepper (cayenne)
     About 48 canned whole water chestnuts (two to three 8-oz. cans), drained

In a medium-size bowl, beat butter with an electric mixer until creamy. Beat in cheese until blended. Stir in garlic salt, flour, sesame seeds, paprika, and red pepper; mix until well blended. With your hands, gather mixture together and press into a smooth ball.

Pat water chestnuts dry on paper towels. Press about 1 level tablespoon of the pastry around each chestnut, covering it evenly with a coating about ⅛ inch thick. Place pastry-wrapped chestnuts on baking sheets. (At this point, you may cover and refrigerate until next day or freeze for up to 1 month; do not thaw before baking.)

To serve, bake pastries until lightly browned (15 to 20 minutes in a 425° oven if at room temperature or refrigerated; about 35 minutes in a 400° oven if frozen). Serve warm. Makes about 48 appetizers.—*T. M., Portland*

Per appetizer: 56 calories, 4 g carbohydrates, 2 g protein, 4 g total fat (2 g saturated), 10 mg cholesterol, 65 mg sodium

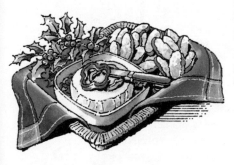

cheese and roasted peppers onto baguette slices. Makes 12 to 16 servings.—*Beverlee Holm, Sunnyvale, CA*

Per serving: 118 calories, 2 g carbohydrates, 7 g protein, 9 g total fat (6 g saturated), 32 mg cholesterol, 205 mg sodium

SHRIMP APPETIZER QUICHES

Bake these two-bite-size quiches in small muffin pans. If you like, you can freeze the cooled quiches after baking. To reheat, arrange them, still frozen, on a baking sheet and bake in a 375° oven until heated through (about 15 minutes).

- 1 package (about 10 oz.) refrigerated flaky buttermilk biscuits
- 4 ounces small cooked shrimp
- 1 large egg
- ½ cup whipping cream
- 2 tablespoons sliced green onion
- ¼ teaspoon *each* salt and dry dill weed
- ⅛ teaspoon ground red pepper (cayenne)
- ½ cup shredded Swiss cheese

Grease thirty 1¾-inch muffin cups. Separate dough into 10 biscuits. Then gently pull each biscuit apart to make 3 layers of equal thickness. Press each piece over bottom and sides of a muffin cup. Divide shrimp equally among pastry shells.

In a small bowl, beat egg, cream, onion, salt, dill weed, and red pepper until well blended. Divide mixture evenly among shells, using about 2 teaspoons for each; sprinkle evenly with cheese. Bake in a 375° oven until edges of quiches are browned and centers look set (15 to 20 minutes). Let cool for 5 minutes; serve warm. Makes 30 appetizers.—*I. R., North Sacramento, CA*

Per appetizer: 61 calories, 4 g carbohydrates, 2 g protein, 4 g total fat (2 g saturated), 21 mg cholesterol, 135 mg sodium

BAKED BRIE WITH ROASTED PEPPERS

Perfect for the holiday season, this whole cheese is baked until hot and spreadable on a bed of colorful roasted bell peppers.

- 1 *each* large red and green bell pepper (or 2 large red or green bell peppers), about 1¼ lbs. *total*
- 1 clove garlic, peeled and cut in half
- 1 round (about 1 lb.) ripe Brie cheese
  Plain or toasted baguette slices

Cut bell peppers in half crosswise. Cut 1 or 2 thin slices from each pepper for garnish; cover and refrigerate slices. Set pepper halves, cut sides down, in an 8- or 9-inch baking pan. Broil 6 inches below heat, turning occasionally, until charred on all sides (about 15 minutes). Cover peppers and let stand until cool. Pull off and discard skins, seeds, and stems; dice peppers.

Rub garlic over inside of an attractive shallow 9- to 10-inch baking dish; discard garlic. Spoon diced peppers into dish; set cheese on top. (At this point, you may cover and refrigerate until next day.)

Bake cheese, uncovered, in a 350° oven until edges are melted and center is hot and soft (15 to 20 minutes). Garnish cheese with reserved pepper slices. If desired, set cheese on an electric warming tray to keep hot. With a knife or spoon, scoop

SAVORY MUSHROOM TARTS

Cream of mushroom soup mixed with cheese, bacon, and sautéed fresh mushrooms makes a savory filling for these tiny tarts.

- 1 large egg
- ¼ cup dehydrated minced onion
- 1 can (about 10¾ oz.) condensed cream of mushroom soup
- ½ cup shredded jack, Swiss, or Gruyère cheese
- 2 tablespoons minced parsley
- ¼ cup dry sherry or milk
- 5 slices bacon
- 4 ounces small mushrooms, sliced
  Pastry for a double-crust 9-inch pie

In a medium-size bowl, beat egg, onion, soup, cheese, parsley, and sherry until well blended. Set aside. Cook bacon in a small frying pan over medium heat until crisp; drain, reserving 2 tablespoons of the drippings in pan. Crumble bacon and set aside.

To drippings in pan, add mushrooms and cook, stirring often, until soft. Stir bacon and mushrooms into soup mixture.

On a lightly floured board, roll pastry out to a thickness of 1/16 inch. Using a 2½-inch-round cutter, cut pastry into 36 rounds (reroll scraps as necessary). Line 1¾-inch muffin cups with pastry rounds, pressing pastry into cups to fit.

Spoon mushroom mixture evenly into pastry shells, using about 2 teaspoons for each. Bake in a 400° oven until edges of tarts are lightly browned (about 20 minutes). Serve warm. Makes 36 appetizers.—*C. E., Tolovana Park, OR*

Per appetizer: 82 calories, 6 g carbohydrates, 2 g protein, 6 g total fat (2 g saturated), 9 mg cholesterol, 149 mg sodium

CHEESE CRACKERS

Crispy cracker sticks are delicious for snacking or as an accompaniment to salads and soups. The zesty flavor comes from sharp Cheddar cheese and plenty of spice—black pepper, paprika, and cayenne in the dough, and cracked black pepper pressed into the sticks before baking.

    2 tablespoons butter or margarine, at room temperature
    1 large egg
    ½ teaspoon paprika
    ⅛ teaspoon ground black pepper
    ¹⁄₁₆ to ⅛ teaspoon ground red pepper (cayenne)
    2 cups (about 8 oz.) finely shredded extra-sharp Cheddar cheese
    1 cup all-purpose flour
       Cracked black pepper

In medium-size bowl, beat butter with an electric mixer until creamy. Add egg, paprika, ground black pepper, and red pepper; beat until blended. Beat in cheese, about ⅔ cup at a time, until combined. Stir in flour until thoroughly blended. With your hands, press dough into a smooth ball.

Divide dough in half. Place each portion of dough between 2 sheets of wax paper and roll into a 7- by 14-inch rectangle.

With a pastry wheel or sharp knife, cut each dough rectangle into ½- by 7-inch strips. Place strips slightly apart on large baking sheets. Sprinkle with cracked black pepper; lightly press pepper into dough.

Bake in a 400° oven until crackers are deep golden (6 to 8 minutes). Serve warm. Or, if made ahead, transfer to racks and let cool completely; then store airtight for up to 1 week. Makes 56 crackers. — *Gloria Danko, Bend, OR*

Per cracker: 29 calories, 2 g carbohydrates, 1 g protein, 2 g total fat (1 g saturated), 9 mg cholesterol, 30 mg sodium

ITALIAN SAUSAGE-STUFFED MUSHROOMS

Italian sausage and cheese make a savory filling for these hearty appetizers.

    16 medium-size mushrooms (*each about 2 inches in diameter*)
    8   ounces mild or hot Italian sausages, casings removed
    5   green onions, thinly sliced
    1   clove garlic, minced or pressed
    ½   teaspoon Italian herb seasoning (or ⅛ teaspoon *each* dry basil, marjoram, oregano, and thyme)
    1   teaspoon Worcestershire
    ¾   cup shredded jack cheese
        About 2 tablespoons olive oil or salad oil

Twist stems from mushroom caps; finely chop stems. Set all mushrooms aside.

Crumble sausage into a wide frying pan and cook over medium heat, stirring occasionally, until browned (8 to 10 minutes). Spoon off and discard fat from pan. Add mushroom stems, onions, garlic, herb seasoning, and Worcestershire. Cook, stirring occasionally, until all liquid has evaporated.

Remove sausage mixture from heat and stir in half the cheese. Generously brush mushroom caps with oil, then spoon about 1 rounded tablespoon of filling into each cap. Place caps, filled side up, in a shallow baking pan. Sprinkle with remaining cheese. (At this point, you may cover and refrigerate until next day.)

Bake, uncovered, in a 400° oven until filling is heated through (about 15 minutes; 18 to 20 minutes if refrigerated). Makes 16 appetizers. — *D. D., Lemon Grove, CA*

Per appetizer: 75 calories, 2 g carbohydrates, 4 g protein, 6 g total fat (2 g saturated), 14 mg cholesterol, 129 mg sodium

CRANBERRY APPETIZER MEATBALLS

These diminutive meatballs are cloaked in cranberry sauce—but that doesn't mean you must reserve them for the holidays. Guests will enjoy the spicy tidbits any time of the year.

    1½ pounds lean ground beef
    2   large eggs
    1   cup fine dry bread crumbs
    ⅓   cup *each* minced parsley, minced onion, and catsup
    1   tablespoon prepared horseradish
    1   clove garlic, minced or pressed
        Cranberry Sauce (recipe follows)

In a large bowl, combine beef, eggs, bread crumbs, parsley, onion, catsup, horseradish, and garlic. Mix until well blended. Shape into 1½-inch balls; set balls slightly apart in a 10- by 15-inch baking pan. Bake in a 450° oven until meatballs are lightly browned (about 15 minutes). Spoon off and discard fat.

While meatballs are browning, prepare Cranberry Sauce.

Pour sauce over browned meatballs. Reduce oven temperature to 350°; continue to bake, stirring occasionally, until sauce is bubbly (about 18 more minutes). Keep warm for serving in a chafing dish or on a warming tray. Makes about 50 meatballs (12 to 15 servings).—*T. Walker, San Francisco*

CRANBERRY SAUCE. In a bowl, mash 1 can (about 1 lb.) **jellied cranberry sauce** with 1 bottle (about 12 oz.) or 1¼ cups **tomato-based chili sauce** and 2 tablespoons firmly packed **brown sugar.**

Per serving: 68 calories, 8 g carbohydrates, 3 g protein, 3 g total fat (1 g saturated), 18 mg cholesterol, 143 mg sodium

WATER CHESTNUT APPETIZERS

Salty, smoky, and sweet, these bacon-wrapped bites taste best when made ahead, then reheated.

¼ **cup soy sauce**
16 **canned whole water chestnuts (from one 8-oz. can), drained**
4 **slices bacon**
¼ **cup sugar**

Pour soy sauce into a small bowl; add water chestnuts and let stand for 30 minutes. Cut each slice of bacon in half crosswise; then cut each piece in half again lengthwise.

Drain water chestnuts briefly. Roll each one in sugar, then wrap in a piece of bacon and secure with a wooden pick. Arrange bacon-wrapped chestnuts on a wire rack in a shallow baking pan lined with foil. Bake in a 400° oven until bacon is browned and crisp (20 to 25 minutes). Drain on paper towels. Serve hot. If made ahead, let cool; then cover and refrigerate for up to 8 hours. To reheat, arrange in a shallow baking pan and heat in a 350° oven for about 5 minutes. Makes 16 appetizers. — *E. S. E., Palo Alto, CA*

Per appetizer: 26 calories, 4 g carbohydrates, 1 g protein, 1 g total fat (0 g saturated), 1 mg cholesterol, 91 mg sodium

SPICY GRILLED SHRIMP

First drenched with an herbed marinade, then threaded on skewers, these succulent shrimp can be grilled or broiled. Try them as the lead-in to a pasta entrée, such as Paradise Pasta with Pine Nuts (page 137).

2 **pounds medium-size raw shrimp (about 36 per lb.), shelled and deveined**
1 **teaspoon chili powder**
1 **tablespoon white wine vinegar**
¼ **teaspoon pepper**
1 **clove garlic, minced or pressed**
1 **teaspoon dry basil**
½ **teaspoon salt**
1 **tablespoon finely chopped fresh mint**
¾ **cup salad oil**

Place shrimp in a large bowl or shallow dish. In another bowl (or in a jar), combine chili powder, vinegar, pepper, garlic, basil, salt, and mint. Add oil; stir (or shake) until well blended. Pour marinade over shrimp, cover, and refrigerate for at least 4 hours or until next day.

Meanwhile, soak about twenty-four 6- to 8-inch bamboo skewers in hot water to cover for at least 30 minutes.

Lift shrimp from marinade and drain briefly (discard marinade). Thread about 3 shrimp on each skewer.

Place on a lightly oiled grill about 6 inches above a solid bed of low coals. (Or place on a rimmed baking sheet and broil about 6 inches below heat.) Cook, turning once, until shrimp are just opaque in center; cut to test (about 4 minutes). Makes about 24 appetizers.—*K. G., Seattle*

Per appetizer: 64 calories, 0.4 g carbohydrates, 6 g protein, 4 g total fat (0.5 g saturated), 47 mg cholesterol, 69 mg sodium

APPETIZER MEATBALLS IN SPICY SAUCE

Bite-size meatballs in sweet-sour sauce are a nice choice for parties, since you can prepare them a day in advance.

⅓ **cup firmly packed brown sugar**
1 **can (about 8 oz.) tomato sauce**
3 **tablespoons lemon juice**
⅛ **teaspoon garlic salt**
½ **cup dry red wine**
About 1 small potato
1 **pound lean ground beef**
1 **small onion, finely minced**
1 **large egg**
½ **teaspoon salt**

In a 2- to 3-quart pan, combine sugar, tomato sauce, lemon juice, garlic salt, and wine. Bring to a boil over high heat, stirring; then reduce heat and simmer gently, uncovered, until sauce is thickened (about 20 minutes).

Meanwhile, peel potato and finely shred enough to make ⅓ cup. In a large bowl, combine shredded potato, beef, onion, egg, and salt; mix until well blended. Shape mixture into balls the size of large marbles.

Arrange meatballs slightly apart in a shallow 10- by 15-inch baking pan. Bake in a 500° oven until lightly browned (5 to 7 minutes). Then add browned meatballs and any pan juices to sauce. (At this point, you may let cool, then cover and refrigerate until next day.)

To serve, heat meatballs and sauce together over low heat, stirring gently. Makes about 60 meatballs (15 to 20 servings).—*M. R., Santa Barbara, CA*

Per serving: 30 calories, 2 g carbohydrates, 2 g protein, 2 g total fat (1 g saturated), 9 mg cholesterol, 51 mg sodium

1929 to 1933

Kitchen Cabinet recipes have always reflected the lives of Sunset readers. If trying economic times called for frugality, they found ingenious ways to employ every last slice of stale bread or cake, use pastry trimmings after making pies, and nourish the children on a rainy day with fresh spinach soup made from a single lamb shank bone.

Still, even when budgets were tight, entertaining at home could be a "dressy occasion," as a San Francisco contributor commented in 1930—and as artist Ruth Taylor White's drawings of cooks in chic frocks often suggest. Recipes for afternoon teas, luncheons, and bridge suppers were frequent, and readers enjoyed recreating the dishes they'd sampled in notable Western restaurants.

The earliest Kitchen Cabinet contributions are now over 60 years old, but the trends they illustrate still seem current today. Then, as now, Sunset readers delighted in seasonal produce and regional foods, learned the latest cooking techniques, devised menus to please family and friends, and planned the most efficient use of time in the kitchen.

BORSCH (RUSSIAN BEET SOUP)

- 6 medium-size beets
- 1 large onion, thinly sliced
- 1 teaspoonful of salt
- ¼ teaspoonful of pepper
- 3 tablespoonfuls of brown sugar
- 6 tablespoonfuls lemon juice
- 1 cupful of sour cream

Wash and peel the beets, and cut into ¼-inch slices. Into a soup kettle put 2 quarts of water. When boiling, add the beets, onion, salt, and pepper. Boil gently, uncovered, until beets are tender when pierced, 30 to 35 minutes; then add the sugar and lemon juice. You may add more sugar if you like.

Drain the liquid, and let it get ice cold, then add it slowly to the cupful of sour cream. Garnish with diced cucumbers, tiny green onions, and hard-cooked egg. This is delicious especially for warm weather. It may be kept in the refrigerator for up to 3 days, without the cream, adding it when needed. The beets may be pickled, or buttered, for use after the liquid is drained off. Makes 4 to 6 servings.— *L.K., Los Angeles (August 1929)*

SWEDISH PORK CHOPS

Select 4 center-cut **pork loin chops** (about 2 lbs. *total*). Place in a deep baking dish, and cover with about 2 tablespoonfuls of **fine, dry bread crumbs.** Sprinkle with **salt** and **pepper** to taste. Wash but do not peel 2 large, **tart cooking apples;** core and cut into quarters, and place on top of the chops. Peel and slice 2 small **onions** and arrange them also on the chops. Bake in a moderate oven (375 degrees) about 50 minutes. Garnish with **parsley** to serve. Makes 4 servings.—*Miss L. S., Nevada (April 1929)*

Borsch

Put 2 quarts of water in a soup kettle to boil—

Wash and peel 6 or 8 medium sized beets—

Put sliced beets and onion into boiling water

When tender add sugar and lemon juice—

It's a Good Idea

to serve piping hot cinnamon toast and cream cheese together with hot tea or coffee, for a light luncheon or afternoon tea.

Italian Pot Roast

1 to 2 ounces of Italian dried
  mushrooms

3 to 3½ pounds boneless beef bottom
  round or rump roast, trimmed of fat

2 tablespoonfuls of olive oil

2 large onions, chopped

4 cloves of garlic, minced

  Salt, pepper, and ground ginger

1 cupful of water

1 can (about 8 oz.) tomato sauce

1 cupful of ripe olives

Wash the mushrooms and put them to
soak in 1 cupful of hot water and let stand
for an hour. Wipe the meat. Heat the oil in
a kettle (a Dutch oven or waterless cooker
is best) and when hot, add the minced
onion and garlic. When the onions are yellow, put in the meat which has been well
seasoned with salt and pepper and a pinch
of ginger. Sear over a hot flame, turning
until brown on all sides. Add the 1 cupful
of water, then cover and let the meat simmer slowly for about 2 hours.

Drain mushrooms, reserving soaking
liquid. Add the soaked mushrooms, the
can of tomato sauce, and the ripe olives,
and cook 1 hour longer or until meat is
very tender when pierced. Whenever the
lid is lifted from the kettle, be sure to let
the moisture trickle over the meat; this
increases the quantity of gravy. Skim the
gravy before serving and thin with a little
of the reserved mushroom liquid if necessary. Noodles, spaghetti, macaroni, or
plain mashed potatoes make a delicious
accompaniment to this meat dish. Makes
10 to 12 servings.—*Mrs. B. S., San Francisco
(January 1930)*

Hamburger à la Brown Derby

2 pounds of ground round steak

  Salt and pepper

1 small onion, finely chopped

1 tablespoonful of butter

½ cupful of tomato catsup

2 tablespoonfuls of Worcestershire
  sauce

  A dash of Tabasco sauce

Season ground beef with salt and pepper
to taste; mix in onion. Pat into cakes and
fry in butter in a large skillet over medium-
high heat until well browned. Remove the
cakes to a hot platter (keep hot), pour off
all but 1 tablespoonful of the fat, and
return the skillet to the stove. Mix the catsup and other seasonings with the hot fat
in the skillet. Allow to simmer a few minutes and pour over the hamburger cakes.
Baked potatoes are delicious with these.
Makes 6 to 8 servings.—*Mrs. A. K., Hollywood, CA (February 1932)*

*Note: An accompanying menu, headlined
DELICIOUS!, suggested serving this recipe with
hashed brown potatoes, buttered broccoli, cornbread and honey, grapefruit halves, and coffee.*

Sour Cream Pie

2 large eggs

¾ cupful plus 2 tablespoonfuls of
  sugar

1 cupful of sour cream

1 cupful of raisins, chopped fine

1 teaspoonful of cinnamon

1 unbaked 8- or 9-inch pie shell

Beat the eggs and add the other ingredients; pour into the unbaked pie shell and
bake for 10 minutes in a hot oven (450 degrees). Then reduce the heat to 350 degrees
and finish baking, about 30 minutes, or
until a knife inserted in center comes out
clean. Serve plain or with whipped cream.
—*G. A., Starbuck, WA (January 1930)*

Drain off the liquid and chill—

When ice cold, add beet juice slowly to cream—

Garnish with diced cucumber, green onion, and hard-cooked egg.

This is delicious for warm weather.

Ruth Taylor White

It's a Good Idea

*to use wet scissors when
cutting dates for use in
cakes, muffins, date-and-
nut bread, and the like.*

S·O·U·P·S

There's something very soul-satisfying about a hearty bowl of soup," read the introduction to a 1961 recipe for Split Pea & Ham Soup. Indeed, pea soup recipes have been a Kitchen Cabinet staple since the late 1930s, when an Oregon contributor described her Split Pea Soup Superb as "practically a meal in itself." Sunset's editors designated a later example of the genre as "the revised old favorite of the month." • Some old favorites deserve revivals. You'll find more recent versions in Chunky Split Pea Soup with Ham Hocks (page 27) and Pistou Soup with Sausage (page 30). • Pea soup aside, until the 1960s, most soups were intended as traditional first courses or lunchtime fare for children home from school. Then, as dining at home became more relaxed, robust full-meal soups of meat, seafood, or poultry began to appear as frequent choices for informal entertaining and family meals. • "We like to accompany this clam bisque with toasted strips of raisin bread," wrote M.B.B. of Santa Cruz, California in 1929. Sixty-five years later, that suggestion still sounds tempting— but now you can try it with Spiced Purée of Carrot Soup (page 23) or Chile Clam Chowder (page 34).

Garden Gazpacho

Cold soups based on fresh vegetables became popular with Westerners in the 1950s. Of these, gazpacho—combining soup and salad in a single bowl—has long been a summertime favorite in California and the Southwest. The version below can take two forms. Made with chicken broth, it's light and mild; if you use nippy tomato cocktail, it has more substance. Serve it well chilled, with juicy lime wedges to squeeze into each serving.

- 1 large cucumber (about 12 oz.)
- 2 large ripe tomatoes (about 1 lb. *total*), peeled, seeded, and chopped
- 1 large red, green, or yellow bell pepper (about 8 oz.), seeded and chopped
- 1 can (about 2¼ oz.) sliced ripe olives, drained
- ¼ cup lime juice
- 4 cups chicken broth or spicy tomato cocktail
- 1 clove garlic, minced or pressed
- ½ cup thinly sliced green onions
- 1 tablespoon minced fresh thyme or 1 teaspoon dry thyme
  Liquid hot pepper seasoning
  Lime wedges

Peel cucumber and cut in half lengthwise; scrape out and discard seeds. Chop cucumber; place in a large bowl and add tomatoes, bell pepper, olives, lime juice, broth, garlic, onions, and thyme. Stir well; season to taste with hot pepper seasoning.

Cover and refrigerate for at least 1 hour or until next day. Before serving, stir well. Ladle into bowls and serve with lime wedges. Makes 8 servings.—*Linda M. Christensen, Albuquerque*

Per serving: 50 calories, 7 g carbohydrates, 3 g protein, 2 g total fat (0 g saturated), 0 mg cholesterol, 572 mg sodium

White Gazpacho

Garnish each serving of this cool, pale purée with a green onion "swizzle stick."

- 1 medium-size European cucumber (about 1 lb.), peeled and coarsely chopped
- 2 cups plain yogurt
- 2 tablespoons lemon juice
- 1 clove garlic, peeled
- 2 cups chicken broth
- 1 cup water
- 2 tablespoons minced cilantro
- 2 tablespoons thinly sliced green onion
- 4 whole green onions, ends trimmed; or 4 cucumber spears (*each* 4 to 6 inches long)

In a blender or food processor, combine chopped cucumber, yogurt, lemon juice, and garlic (if using a blender, also add about ½ cup of the broth). Whirl until smoothly puréed. Pour mixture into a 2-quart container and stir in broth and water. Cover and refrigerate for at least 2 hours or until next day.

Stir cilantro into soup; then pour soup into a serving bowl or pitcher and top with sliced green onion. Ladle or pour into bowls or glasses; garnish each serving with a whole green onion. Makes 4 servings. —*Lynne French, Aptos, CA*

Per serving: 105 calories, 11 g carbohydrates, 6 g protein, 4 g total fat (2 g saturated), 15 mg cholesterol, 556 mg sodium

Zucchini Vichyssoise

Western cooks are especially inventive when it comes to using zucchini, a perennial overachiever in summer vegetable gardens. Here, the sliced and simmered squash goes into a first-course soup with the rich, velvety texture of a vichyssoise. Enjoy it warm or cold, perhaps with a basket of crunchy breadsticks or a loaf of Onion Herb Batter Bread (page 187).

- 3 tablespoons salad oil
- 1 large onion, chopped
- 2 pounds zucchini, cut into about ¼-inch-thick slices
- 3 cups chicken broth
- 2 tablespoons chopped fresh basil or 1½ teaspoons dry basil
- ¼ teaspoon *each* ground nutmeg and ground white pepper
- 1 cup milk or half-and-half
  Basil sprigs (optional)

Heat oil in a 3- to 4-quart pan over medium heat. Add onion and cook, stirring often, until soft (about 5 minutes).

Add zucchini, broth, chopped basil, nutmeg, and white pepper. Bring to a boil; then reduce heat, cover, and simmer until zucchini is tender when pierced (about 10 minutes).

In a blender or food processor, whirl soup, about half at a time, until smoothly puréed. Return soup to pan and add milk; stir over medium heat just until heated through. If made ahead, let cool; then cover and refrigerate for at least 2 hours or until next day. Serve cold or reheated. To serve, ladle into bowls and garnish with basil sprigs, if desired. Makes 10 to 12 servings. —*Pati Lechner, Shepherd, MT*

Per serving: 74 calories, 6 g carbohydrates, 3 g protein, 5 g total fat (1 g saturated), 3 mg cholesterol, 283 mg sodium

Orange-Beef Broth

The flavor and aroma of fresh orange add interest to this clear beef broth. Offer it in cups or mugs, garnished with twists of orange peel. When we first printed the recipe in the 1960s, we suggested that readers serve the steaming-hot broth "in the living room to precede a winter dinner party."

  2 large navel oranges (1 to 1¼ lbs. *total*)
  3 tablespoons butter or margarine
  2 cans (about 10¾ oz. *each*) condensed beef broth
  1 soup can water
  ½ cup orange juice
  1 teaspoon sugar
  2 whole cloves

Using a vegetable peeler, cut 6 narrow strips, each about 1 inch long, from peel (colored part only) of oranges. Set aside. Then cut off and discard all remaining peel and white membrane from oranges.

Holding oranges over a 2-quart pan to catch juice, cut between membranes to release segments; drop segments into pan. Add butter to pan; bring to a simmer, then simmer for about 3 minutes. Add broth, water, orange juice, sugar, and cloves. Bring broth mixture to a boil; then reduce heat and simmer, uncovered, for about 10 minutes.

Pour broth mixture through a fine strainer set over a bowl; press oranges with the back of a spoon to extract all liquid. Discard residue. If made ahead, let cool; then cover and refrigerate until next day.

To serve, reheat broth. Pour into cups or small soup bowls; twist each strip of orange peel and add one twist to each cup. Serve hot. Makes 6 servings.—*G. H., Edmonds, WA*

Per serving: 106 calories, 11 g carbohydrates, 3 g protein, 6 g total fat (4 g saturated), 16 mg cholesterol, 793 mg sodium

Leek & Green Onion Chowder

Top this light, tangy soup with lemon slices and spoonfuls of sour cream.

  3 pounds leeks
  2 tablespoons butter or margarine
  2 tablespoons all-purpose flour
  ½ teaspoon ground white pepper
  1 large can (about 49½ oz.) chicken broth
  3 cups thinly sliced green onions
  ¼ cup lemon juice
     Salt
     Thin lemon slices
     Sour cream

Trim ends and all but about 3 inches of green tops from leeks; remove tough outer leaves. Split leeks lengthwise; rinse well, then thinly slice crosswise.

Melt butter in a 4- to 6-quart pan over medium-high heat. Add leeks; cook, stirring often, until soft (8 to 10 minutes). Stir in flour and white pepper; then stir in broth. Bring to a boil over high heat, stirring. Add onions; cook, stirring, just until onions turn bright green (about 2 minutes). Stir in lemon juice; season to taste with salt.

Ladle soup into bowls. Garnish each serving with lemon slices and a dollop of sour cream. Makes 6 servings.—*Betty Buckner, Port Angeles, WA*

Per serving: 151 calories, 21 g carbohydrates, 6 g protein, 6 g total fat (2 g saturated fat), 10 mg cholesterol, 1,087 mg sodium

Mexican Cauliflower Soup

Mild-mannered cauliflower, cooked and puréed, forms the base for this chile- and cumin-spiked soup. Serve it with cornsticks or hot corn muffins, if you like; Cheese & Bacon Corn Muffins (page 177) will do nicely.

  2 tablespoons butter or margarine
  1 medium-size onion, chopped
  1 can (about 4 oz.) diced green chiles
  1 teaspoon ground cumin
  2 cups chicken broth
  1 large head cauliflower (about 2 lbs.)
  4 stalks celery, chopped
  2½ to 3 cups milk (or use part or all chicken broth)
     Salt and pepper
  ¼ cup thinly sliced green onions

Melt butter in a 4- to 5-quart pan over medium-high heat. Add chopped onion, chiles, and cumin; cook, stirring often, until onion is soft (about 5 minutes). Add the 2 cups broth; reduce heat to low and cover pan.

Trim and discard leaves from cauliflower. Then coarsely chop cauliflower; add to broth along with celery. Bring to a boil over high heat; then reduce heat, cover, and simmer until cauliflower is tender when pierced (about 20 minutes).

Pour about half the soup into a blender or food processor and whirl until smoothly puréed. Return purée to pan. Thin to desired consistency with milk, then stir over medium-high heat until heated through. Season to taste with salt and pepper. Ladle into bowls and sprinkle with green onions. Makes 6 to 8 servings.—*Robin Saltonstall, Boulder, CO*

Per serving: 127 calories, 11 g carbohydrates, 6 g protein, 7 g total fat (4 g saturated), 22 mg cholesterol, 490 mg sodium

Orange Pumpkin Soup

Fall is the season for this colorful soup. Based on canned pumpkin and enriched with cream cheese, it goes together quickly.

    1   teaspoon salad oil
    1   large onion, chopped
    1   teaspoon ground coriander
    ¼   cup water
    1   can (about 1 lb.) pumpkin
    4   cups chicken broth
    1½ cups orange juice
    ½   cup dry white wine or chicken
        broth
    1   small package (about 3 oz.)
        cream cheese
        Salt and pepper
        Snipped chives or thinly sliced
        green onions

In a 3- to 4-quart pan, combine oil, onion, coriander, and water. Cook over high heat, stirring often, until liquid has evaporated and onion is very soft (5 to 7 minutes). Stir in pumpkin, broth, orange juice, and wine.

Bring to a boil; then reduce heat, cover, and simmer for 20 minutes. Cut cream cheese into ½-inch chunks; drop into a blender or food processor, add about 1 cup of the soup, and whirl until smooth. Return purée to soup in pan; stir until heated through. Season to taste with salt and pepper. Ladle into bowls and

sprinkle with chives. Makes 8 servings.—*Roxanne Chan, Albany, CA*

Per serving: 107 calories, 13 g carbohydrates, 4 g protein, 5 g total fat (2 g saturated), 12 mg cholesterol, 530 mg sodium

Spiced Purée of Carrot Soup

Watercress purée garnishes this tangy blend of carrots and potatoes.

    1   tablespoon olive oil
    1½ pounds carrots, thinly sliced
    2   medium-size onions, chopped
    1   cup chopped celery
    1   pound russet potatoes, peeled
        and cut into ½-inch cubes
    1   teaspoon *each* ground cumin
        and curry powder
    1   large can (about 49½ oz.) chicken
        broth
    1   cup lightly packed watercress
        sprigs
    ¼   cup plain yogurt
    3   tablespoons lemon juice

Heat oil in a 4- to 5-quart pan over medium-high heat. Add carrots, onions, and celery. Cover and cook, stirring often, until vegetables begin to brown (about 12 minutes). Add potatoes, cumin, curry powder, and broth. Bring to a boil over high heat; then reduce heat, cover, and simmer until potatoes are tender when pierced (10 to 15 minutes).

Meanwhile, whirl watercress and yogurt in a blender until puréed. Spoon into a small bowl; set aside.

Stir lemon juice into soup. In a food processor or blender, whirl soup, a portion at a time, until puréed. Return soup to pan; stir until hot. Ladle into bowls; drizzle with watercress purée. Makes 6 servings. —*Karil Frohboese, Park City, UT*

Per serving: 182 calories, 30 g carbohydrates, 7 g protein, 5 g total fat (0.5 g saturated), 1 mg cholesterol, 1,087 mg sodium

Soupe de Legumes

Dating from the 1960s, this mixed-vegetable purée is a light choice you can enjoy winter or summer. The contributor learned to make it in France—hence the recipe's name. Serve it in bowls or cups, topped with parsley or crisp croutons.

    2   leeks
    2   tablespoons butter or margarine
    1   large onion, chopped
    5   shallots, chopped
    2   cups cubed peeled russet or
        thin-skinned potatoes
    2   cups diced turnips
    1   medium-size carrot, sliced
    1   medium-size tomato (about 6 oz.),
        peeled and diced
    4   cups chicken broth or water
    3   tablespoons whipping cream
        Salt
        Minced parsley or croutons

Trim ends and all but about 3 inches of green tops from leeks; remove tough outer leaves. Split leeks lengthwise; rinse well, then thinly slice crosswise.

Melt butter in a 3½- to 5-quart pan over medium heat. Add leeks, onion, and shallots; cook, stirring often, until all vegetables are golden (8 to 10 minutes). Add potatoes, turnips, carrot, tomato, and broth. Bring to a boil over high heat; then cover, reduce heat, and simmer until all vegetables are very tender to bite (about 20 minutes).

In a blender or food processor, whirl soup, a portion at a time, until smoothly puréed. Return purée to pan, add cream, and stir over medium heat until heated through. Season to taste with salt. Ladle into bowls and sprinkle with parsley. Makes 6 servings.—*A. W., Ventura, CA*

Per serving: 178 calories, 25 g carbohydrates, 5 g protein, 7 g total fat (4 g saturated), 19 mg cholesterol, 747 mg sodium

TOMATO-POTATO SOUP

When your garden or the local farmers' market yields a bounty of red-ripe tomatoes, enjoy this thick and hearty purée. It's good hot or chilled, topped with a dollop of yogurt.

2 tablespoons butter or margarine

2 medium-size onions, minced

2 cloves garlic, minced or pressed

2 to 2½ pounds firm-ripe tomatoes, peeled

1 large russet potato (about 8 oz.), peeled and diced

¼ cup fresh basil leaves or 1 tablespoon dry basil

2 cans (about 14½ oz. *each*) chicken broth

Salt and pepper

Plain yogurt (optional)

Melt butter in a 4- to 6-quart pan over medium-high heat. Add onions and garlic; cook, stirring often, until onions are golden (about 15 minutes). Meanwhile, in a food processor or blender, whirl tomatoes until coarsely puréed.

Pour tomato purée into pan. Cook over medium-high heat, uncovered, stirring occasionally, until reduced by about a third.

Place potato and basil in food processor (if using a blender, also add ¼ cup of the broth); whirl until minced. Add to pan along with broth. Bring to a boil. Then reduce heat, cover, and simmer until potato is soft to bite (about 20 minutes). Season to taste with salt and pepper.

Serve hot or at room temperature. Or, to serve cold, let cool; then cover and refrigerate for up to 2 days. Ladle soup into bowls; offer yogurt to add to taste, if desired. Makes 4 servings.—*Jane A. Stone, Napa, CA*

Per serving: 203 calories, 29 g carbohydrates, 7 g protein, 8 g total fat (4 g saturated), 16 mg cholesterol, 981 mg sodium

SWEET POTATO SOUP

Thick, smooth sweet potato soup is a nice opener for a cool-weather dinner. Try it before an entrée of pork tenderloin or roast chicken.

3 pounds sweet potatoes or yams, peeled and diced

About 6 cups chicken broth

1½ tablespoons curry powder

¼ cup tomato paste

2 tablespoons lemon juice

¼ cup dry sherry (optional)

Salt and pepper

Cilantro leaves (optional)

In a 4- to 5-quart pan, combine sweet potatoes and 6 cups of the broth. Bring to a boil over high heat; then reduce heat, cover, and simmer until potatoes are soft enough to mash readily (about 20 minutes). With a slotted spoon, transfer potatoes to a food processor or blender; add curry powder and a little of the broth. Whirl until smoothly puréed.

Return purée to pan; add tomato paste, lemon juice, and sherry (if used). Stir over medium heat until heated through; thin with more broth, if desired. Season to taste with salt and pepper. Ladle soup into bowls and garnish with cilantro, if desired. Makes 8 to 10 servings. —*Dian Burke, Boulder Creek, CA*

Per serving: 143 calories, 29 g carbohydrates, 4 g protein, 1 g total fat (0 g saturated), 0 mg cholesterol, 731 mg sodium

SWISS CHARD BISQUE

Serve this creamy, bright green soup as a first course or a light lunchtime entrée with crusty bread and an assortment of cheeses.

1 large bunch (about 1 lb.) Swiss chard

1 can (about 14½ oz.) chicken broth

¼ cup butter or margarine

1 cup chopped mushrooms

3 tablespoons all-purpose flour

¼ teaspoon curry powder

2 cups half-and-half

Salt and pepper

4 slices bacon, crisply cooked, drained, and crumbled

Discard any tough stem ends from chard; then rinse chard and drain well. Thinly slice stems and leaves crosswise, keeping them in separate piles. Place stems in a wide frying pan, add 2 tablespoons of the broth, cover, and cook over medium heat until tender to bite (about 4 minutes). Add leaves (and 1 more tablespoon broth, if needed); cover and cook until wilted (about 3 minutes).

Turn chard mixture and remaining broth into a blender or food processor and whirl until smoothly puréed (you should have 3 to 3½ cups). Set aside.

Melt butter in a 2- to 3-quart pan over medium heat; add mushrooms and cook, stirring often, for 5 minutes. Stir in flour and curry powder; cook, stirring, until bubbly. Gradually add half-and-half; cook, stirring, until mixture is thickened. Stir in chard purée and stir until heated through. Season to taste with salt and pepper. Ladle into bowls and sprinkle with bacon. Makes 4 servings.—*T. W., Paradise, CA*

Per serving: 352 calories, 15 g carbohydrates, 10 g protein, 29 g total fat (17 g saturated), 81 mg cholesterol, 938 mg sodium

CREAM OF BROCCOLI SOUP

Sour cream, swirled into each bowlful, makes a pretty finish for hot broccoli-potato soup. (Stir the sour cream first to soften it.)

- 1 tablespoon salad oil
- 1 small onion, chopped
- 3 cups water
- 2 cups milk
- 4 chicken bouillon cubes
- 12 ounces thin-skinned potatoes, peeled and cut into 1-inch chunks
- 1½ pounds fresh broccoli
  Ground white pepper (optional)
  About 1 cup sour cream

Heat oil in a 4- to 5-quart pan over medium heat. Add onion; cook, stirring often, until lightly browned (8 to 10 minutes). Add water, milk, bouillon cubes, and potatoes. Bring to a boil; then reduce heat, cover, and simmer until potatoes are almost tender when pierced (about 10 minutes).

Meanwhile, trim and discard tough ends of broccoli stalks. Cut off broccoli flowerets; peel stems and cut crosswise into ⅛-inch-thick slices. Add sliced broccoli stems and flowerets to broth mixture. Cover and continue to simmer until all vegetables are tender when pierced (about 15 more minutes).

In a blender or food processor, whirl vegetable mixture, about half at a time, until smoothly puréed. Return soup to pan and stir over medium heat until heated through. Season to taste with white pepper, if desired. Ladle soup into bowls; offer sour cream to add to taste. Makes 6 to 8 servings.—*Paula Bohlman, Loma Linda, CA*

Per serving: 192 calories, 17 g carbohydrates, 6 g protein, 12 g total fat (6 g saturated), 24 mg cholesterol, 620 mg sodium

PESTO-ZUCCHINI SOUP

To build a light meal around this aromatic soup, accompany it with warm multigrain rolls and thin slices of baked ham.

- 3 pounds zucchini (about 10 medium-size)
- 3 tablespoons olive oil or salad oil
- 2 medium-size onions, chopped
- 1 large can (about 49½ oz.) chicken broth
- ¾ cup homemade or purchased pesto
- ⅓ cup matchstick-size pieces Parmesan cheese (or use grated Parmesan cheese)
  Basil sprigs (optional)

Cut one zucchini into matchstick strips; cover and refrigerate. Cut remaining zucchini crosswise into slices. Heat oil in a 5- to 6-quart pan over medium-high heat; add onions and cook, stirring often, until soft (8 to 10 minutes). Add sliced zucchini and 1 cup of the broth. Bring to a boil over high heat; then reduce heat, cover, and simmer until zucchini is very tender when pierced (about 15 minutes).

In a blender or food processor, whirl zucchini mixture, a portion at a time, until smoothly puréed. Return purée to pan along with remaining broth. Bring to a simmer over high heat, stirring. Remove from heat; stir in pesto. Ladle soup into bowls and top with reserved zucchini strips and cheese. If desired, garnish with basil

sprigs. Makes 6 to 8 servings.—*Libia Foglesong, San Bruno, CA*

Per serving: 274 calories, 13 g carbohydrates, 10 g protein, 22 g total fat (4 g saturated), 8 mg cholesterol, 1,153 mg sodium

A BIT O' EMERALD SOUP

Here's a new way to present the humble cabbage. Smoothed with a splash of sherry, this velvety blend of cabbage and fresh spinach is the perfect starter for a St. Patrick's Day dinner.

- 3 tablespoons butter or margarine
- 1 medium-size onion, chopped
- 1 clove garlic, minced or pressed
- 2 cans (about 14½ oz. *each*) chicken broth
- 8 ounces fresh spinach
- 1 small head cabbage (about 1 lb.)
- 2 cups milk
- ¼ cup dry sherry (optional)

Melt 2 tablespoons of the butter in a 5- to 6-quart pan over medium heat. Add onion and garlic; cook, stirring often, until onion is soft (about 5 minutes). Add broth and bring to a boil.

Meanwhile, discard stems and any yellow or wilted leaves from spinach; rinse spinach and drain well. Also halve and core cabbage. With a sharp knife, finely shred spinach and cabbage. Add cabbage and about half the spinach to broth. Cook, uncovered, just until cabbage is tender to bite (3 to 5 minutes).

In a blender or food processor, whirl soup, a portion at a time, until smoothly puréed. Return purée to pan. Add milk and remaining spinach; return to just below a boil. Stir in sherry (if desired) and remaining 1 tablespoon butter. Makes 8 servings. —*G. W., Monmouth, OR*

Per serving: 112 calories, 8 g carbohydrates, 5 g protein, 7 g total fat (4 g saturated), 20 mg cholesterol, 546 mg sodium

PASTA & BEAN SOUP

Colorful and quick, this healthful soup is thick with pasta and vegetables. Use any home-cooked or canned white beans—Great Northerns, cannellini, and navy beans all work well.

1 large red onion, chopped
1 teaspoon olive oil
1 cup chopped celery
4 cloves garlic, chopped
2½ quarts chicken broth
1½ cups dry small shell-shaped pasta
3 to 4 cups cooked or canned white beans, drained and rinsed
1 cup shredded carrots
1 package (about 10 oz.) frozen tiny peas
   Grated Parmesan cheese

Set aside ⅓ cup of the onion. In a 6- to 8-quart pan, combine remaining onion, oil, celery, and garlic. Cook over medium-high heat, stirring often, until onion is lightly browned (5 to 8 minutes). Add broth and bring to a boil. Stir in pasta and beans; reduce heat, cover, and simmer until pasta is tender to bite (5 to 7 minutes). Add carrots and peas; bring to a boil. Ladle soup into wide bowls and sprinkle with reserved ⅓ cup onion; offer cheese to add to taste. Makes 6 to 8 servings.—*Gina Stanziano Matthews, Palo Alto, CA*

Per serving: 284 calories, 47 g carbohydrates, 17 g protein, 4 g total fat (0.3 g saturated), 0 mg cholesterol, 1,491 mg sodium

ESCAROLE SOUP

Italians call this traditional pasta-dotted soup *zuppa di scarola*. It's made with the tender inside leaves of escarole (sometimes called broad-leaf endive).

1 large head escarole
2 tablespoons butter or margarine
2 tablespoons finely chopped onion
2 cans (about 14½ oz. *each*) chicken broth
⅛ teaspoon ground nutmeg
¼ teaspoon dry thyme
¼ cup dry small shell-shaped pasta or elbow macaroni, cooked and drained
   Salt and pepper
   Grated Parmesan cheese

Discard tough stem ends and coarse outer leaves from escarole, leaving tender green inner leaves. Rinse escarole and drain well. Stack leaves and cut crosswise into strips about ¼ inch wide; set aside.

Melt butter in a 3½- to 5-quart pan over medium heat. Add onion and escarole; cook, stirring, for about 3 minutes. Add broth, nutmeg, and thyme; bring to a boil. Stir in pasta and cook until heated through. Season to taste with salt and pepper. Ladle soup into bowls; offer cheese to add to taste. Makes 4 to 6 servings.—*H. N., San Francisco*

Per serving: 97 calories, 8 g carbohydrates, 4 g protein, 6 g total fat (3 g saturated), 12 mg cholesterol, 783 mg sodium

LEAFY BEAN SOUP

A bowl of spinach-and-bean soup, a crisp grilled cheese sandwich, and a juicy tomato salad add up to a satisfying lunch.

2 tablespoons butter or margarine
1 medium-size onion, finely chopped
1 clove garlic, minced or pressed
2 cans (about 14½ oz. *each*) chicken broth
1 dry bay leaf
8 ounces fresh spinach
1 can (about 15 oz.) cannellini (white kidney beans) or garbanzo beans
   Salt and pepper
   Grated Parmesan cheese

Melt butter in a 3½- to 5-quart pan over medium heat. Add onion and garlic; cook, stirring often, until onion is soft (about 5 minutes). Add broth and bay leaf. Bring to a boil; then reduce heat, cover, and simmer for 10 minutes.

Meanwhile, discard stems and any yellow or wilted leaves from spinach; then rinse spinach and drain well. Stack leaves and cut crosswise into ¼-inch-wide strips. Set aside.

Add beans and their liquid to broth mixture. Return soup to a simmer; add spinach and cook for 2 minutes. Remove and discard bay leaf. Season soup to taste with salt and pepper. Ladle into bowls; offer cheese to add to taste. Makes 4 to 6 servings.—*J. T., North Hollywood, CA*

Per serving: 149 calories, 16 g carbohydrates, 8 g protein, 6 g total fat (3 g saturated), 12 mg cholesterol, 1,058 mg sodium

COLORADO BEAN SOUP

To make this filling soup, just put all the ingredients in the pot and let them simmer away for hours, almost unattended. Serve the soup with warm, soft pretzels; offer juicy apples or pears for dessert.

1¼ cups (about 8 oz.) dried Great Northern beans
2 tablespoons salad oil

2 medium-size onions, chopped
1 medium-size turnip, diced
2 large stalks celery, cut into thin diagonal slices
3 quarts chicken or beef broth
2 pounds ham hocks, cracked
  Pepper

Sort through beans, discarding any debris. Rinse and drain beans; set aside.

Heat oil in a 6- to 8-quart pan over medium-high heat. Add onions and cook, stirring often, until soft (8 to 10 minutes). Add beans, turnip, celery, broth, and ham hocks. Bring to a boil over high heat; then reduce heat, cover, and simmer until beans mash easily and meat pulls readily from bones (about 3 hours).

Lift out ham hocks and let stand until cool enough to handle. Meanwhile, skim and discard fat from soup.

Pull ham from bones; discard skin, bones, and fat. Return ham to soup; reheat, then season to taste with pepper. If made ahead, let cool; then cover and refrigerate for up to 3 days. Reheat before serving. Makes 6 to 8 servings.—*B. T., Colorado Springs, CO*

Per serving: 275 calories, 28 g carbohydrates, 19 g protein, 10 g total fat (2 g saturated), 18 mg cholesterol, 2,145 mg sodium

LENTILS & HAM SOUP

Dried prunes and the distinctive spices used for flavoring pickles—among them mustard seeds, allspice, coriander, and cinnamon—give this soup its irresistible taste.

3½ to 4 pounds ham hocks, cut into 2-inch slices
2 dry bay leaves
1 teaspoon Italian herb seasoning (or ¼ teaspoon *each* dry basil, marjoram, oregano, and thyme)
1 teaspoon whole mixed pickling spices

⅛ teaspoon pepper
1 medium-size onion, chopped
1½ cups (about 12 oz.) lentils
6 to 8 small thin-skinned potatoes (*each* about 1½ inches in diameter), peeled; or 2 cups carrot chunks
12 to 16 pitted prunes
  Minced parsley

Place ham hocks in an 8- to 10-quart pan and add enough water to cover. Bring to a boil over high heat; drain, discarding liquid. Add 3 quarts water to pan; then add bay leaves, herb seasoning, pickling spices, pepper, and onion. Bring to a boil over high heat; reduce heat, cover, and simmer until meat begins to pull from bones (about 2 hours).

Pour ham hocks and broth through a strainer into a large bowl. Discard seasonings. Let ham hocks stand until cool enough to handle. Meanwhile, skim and discard fat from broth.

Pull ham from bones; discard skin, bones, and fat. Return ham and broth to pan and bring to a boil over high heat. Sort through lentils, discarding any debris; rinse lentils, drain, and add to soup. Reduce heat, cover, and simmer for 20 minutes. Add potatoes and prunes; cover and continue to simmer until potatoes are tender when pierced and lentils are tender to bite (about 25 more minutes). Ladle soup into bowls and sprinkle with parsley. Makes 6 to 8 servings.—*L. M., Everett, WA*

Per serving: 359 calories, 50 g carbohydrates, 26 g protein, 7 g total fat (2 g saturated), 35 mg cholesterol, 814 mg sodium

CHUNKY SPLIT PEA SOUP WITH HAM HOCKS

Full-meal soups have become real favorites with *Kitchen Cabinet* cooks. This traditional example is distinguished by its seasonings of rosemary and cloves.

1½ pounds ham hocks, cracked
1½ teaspoons whole black peppercorns
½ teaspoon whole cloves
1½ teaspoons dry rosemary
4 cups *each* beef broth and water
1 cup (about 8 oz.) green split peas
1 large onion, coarsely chopped
1 very large russet potato (about 12 oz.), peeled and diced
2 large carrots, thinly sliced
  Minced parsley

In a 5- to 6-quart pan, combine ham hocks, peppercorns, cloves, rosemary, broth, and water. Bring to a boil over high heat; then reduce heat, cover, and simmer, stirring occasionally, until meat pulls readily from bones (about 3 hours). Lift out ham hocks and let stand until cool enough to handle. Meanwhile, skim and discard fat from broth. Remove spices with a slotted spoon; discard. Continue to simmer broth, covered, over low heat.

Pull ham from bones; discard skin, bones, and fat. Add ham to broth. Sort through split peas, discarding any debris. Rinse and drain peas; add to broth along with onion, potato, and carrots. Simmer, uncovered, until peas are soft enough to mash easily (45 to 55 minutes). Ladle soup into bowls and sprinkle with parsley. Makes 6 servings.—*Lita J. Verts, Corvallis, OR*

Per serving: 267 calories, 41 g carbohydrates, 18 g protein, 4 g total fat (1 g saturated), 16 mg cholesterol, 952 mg sodium

MEATBALL MINESTRONE

For simmered-all-day flavor in under an hour, try this chunky minestrone. Simple spinach-beef meatballs, red kidney beans, and a hearty helping of macaroni add substance to the tomato-vegetable broth.

Spinach Meatballs (recipe follows)
1 tablespoon salad oil
1 large onion, chopped
7 cups water
7 beef bouillon cubes
1 can (about 14½ oz.) stewed tomatoes
1 can (about 15 oz.) red kidney beans
½ teaspoon *each* dry oregano and dry basil
1 cup *each* sliced carrots and celery
1 cup dry elbow macaroni or pasta bow ties

Prepare Spinach Meatballs. Heat oil in a 3½- to 5-quart pan over medium heat; add meatballs, a portion at a time, and cook until browned on all sides. When all meatballs have been browned, set them aside.

Add onion to pan and cook, stirring often, until soft (about 5 minutes). Stir in water, bouillon cubes, tomatoes, beans and their liquid, oregano, and basil. Bring to a boil; then reduce heat, cover, and simmer for 10 minutes.

Add carrots and celery; cover and simmer for 10 more minutes. Stir in macaroni; cover and simmer until tender to bite (about 10 more minutes). Return meatballs to soup and heat through. Skim and discard fat from soup. Makes 6 servings.
—*H. N., San Francisco*

SPINACH MEATBALLS. In a large bowl, combine 1 package (about 10 oz.) frozen chopped spinach, thawed and squeezed dry; 1½ pounds lean ground beef; ⅓ cup fine dry bread crumbs; 1 large egg; ½ teaspoon salt; and ¼ teaspoon pepper. Mix until well blended, then shape into 1-inch balls.

Per serving: 541 calories, 41 g carbohydrates, 31 g protein, 28 g total fat (10 g saturated), 121 mg cholesterol, 1,811 mg sodium

CABBAGE PATCH SOUP

Simple, homey flavors combine in this hearty soup-stew. If you like, top each bowlful with a mound of hot mashed potatoes accented with sautéed onion.

2 tablespoons butter or margarine
1 pound lean ground beef
1 medium-size onion, thinly sliced
½ cup thinly sliced celery
1 can (about 14½ oz.) tomatoes
2 cups water
1 can (about 15 oz.) red kidney beans
1 teaspoon chili powder
⅛ teaspoon pepper
2 cups finely shredded cabbage
Salt

Melt butter in a 3½- to 5-quart pan over medium-high heat. Crumble in beef; cook, stirring often, until browned. Add onion and celery and cook, stirring often, for about 5 more minutes.

Cut up tomatoes; add tomatoes and their liquid, water, beans and their liquid, chili powder, and pepper to pan. Bring to a boil over high heat; then reduce heat, cover, and simmer for 10 minutes. Add cabbage; cook until cabbage is tender to bite (about 3 minutes). Season to taste with salt. Makes 4 to 6 servings.—*J. T., North Hollywood, CA*

Per serving: 389 calories, 21 g carbohydrates, 22 g protein, 24 g total fat (10 g saturated), 81 mg cholesterol, 560 mg sodium

EGGPLANT SUPPER SOUP

A favorite among *Sunset* readers and staff since 1967, this soup serves up a full meal in a single bowl. The diced eggplant soaks up the broth like a sponge, absorbing all its rich flavors.

2 tablespoons butter or margarine
2 tablespoons olive oil or salad oil
1 medium-size onion, chopped
1 pound lean ground beef
1 medium-size eggplant (about 1 lb.), unpeeled, diced
1 clove garlic, minced or pressed
½ cup *each* chopped carrot and sliced celery
1 large can (about 28 oz.) tomatoes
2 cans (about 14½ oz. *each*) beef broth
1 teaspoon sugar
½ teaspoon *each* pepper and ground nutmeg
½ cup dry salad macaroni
2 tablespoons minced parsley
Salt
Grated Parmesan cheese

Melt butter in oil in a deep 4- to 5-quart pan over medium heat. Add onion; cook, stirring often, until soft (about 5 minutes). Crumble beef into pan; cook, stirring often, until meat is no longer pink. Add eggplant, garlic, carrot, and celery. Cut up tomatoes; add tomatoes and their liquid, broth, sugar, pepper, and nutmeg to pan. Bring to a boil over high heat; then reduce heat, cover, and simmer for about 30 minutes. Add macaroni and parsley; cover and continue to simmer until pasta is tender to bite (about 10 more minutes). Season to taste with salt.

Ladle soup into large bowls; offer cheese to add to taste. Makes 6 to 8 servings.—*H. N., San Francisco*

Per serving: 332 calories, 19 g carbohydrates, 16 g protein, 22 g total fat (8 g saturated), 58 mg cholesterol, 706 mg sodium

BEEF & BARLEY SOUP

A crusty loaf and a mixed green salad are good partners for this stick-to-your-ribs soup.

- ¾ cup (about 6 oz.) split peas
- ¾ cup (about 5 oz.) dried baby lima beans
  About 3 pounds beef short ribs, trimmed of fat
- 2 large onions, chopped
- ¼ cup chopped parsley
- 3 cloves garlic, minced or pressed
- 2 quarts water
- 3 beef bouillon cubes
- 1 tablespoon dry dill weed
- 4 ounces mushrooms, sliced
- ½ cup pearl barley
- 8 large carrots, cut into 1-inch-thick slices
  Salt and pepper

Sort through split peas and beans, discarding any debris. Rinse and drain peas and beans; set aside.

Place beef in a 6- to 8-quart pan and cook over medium-high heat, turning as needed, until browned on all sides. Add onions; cook, stirring often, until soft. Stir in peas, beans, parsley, garlic, water, and bouillon cubes. Bring to a boil over high heat; then reduce heat, cover, and simmer until meat is tender when pierced (about 2 hours).

Lift out meat and let stand until cool enough to handle. Meanwhile, skim and discard fat from broth. In a blender or food processor, whirl broth and vegetables, a portion at a time, until puréed. Return purée to pan; stir in dill weed, mushrooms, barley, and carrots. Tear meat into bite-size pieces; discard bones and fat, then return meat to pan.

Bring soup to a boil; then reduce heat, cover, and simmer until barley is tender to bite (about 45 minutes).

Season to taste with salt and pepper. Makes 6 to 8 servings.—*I. D., Seattle*

Per serving: 744 calories, 58 g carbohydrates, 35 g protein, 42 g total fat (17 g saturated), 92 mg cholesterol, 472 mg sodium

RAVIOLI & CABBAGE SOUP

For a quick, light supper or lunch, simmer purchased ravioli and shredded green cabbage in bacon-seasoned beef broth.

- 4 ounces sliced bacon, cut into ½-inch pieces
- 1 small onion, chopped
- 2 cloves garlic, minced or pressed
- 1 tablespoon chopped parsley
- 2 quarts beef broth
- 2 cups *each* water and shredded cabbage
- 1 large carrot, thinly sliced
- 1 pound purchased fresh or frozen ravioli
  Grated Parmesan cheese

Cook bacon in a 5- to 6-quart pan over medium heat until translucent and limp, stirring often. Add onion, garlic, and parsley. Continue to cook, stirring, until onion and bacon are lightly browned. Spoon off and discard fat from pan.

Add broth, water, cabbage, and carrot to pan. Bring to a boil over high heat. Separate any ravioli that are stuck together; then add ravioli to boiling broth.

Reduce heat to medium and boil gently, uncovered, stirring occasionally, until ravioli are just tender to bite (about 10 minutes for fresh pasta, about 12 minutes for frozen).

Ladle soup into bowls and offer cheese to add to taste. Makes 4 to 6 servings.—*V. H., Napa, CA*

Per serving: 368 calories, 35 g carbohydrates, 20 g protein, 17 g total fat (1 g saturated), 77 mg cholesterol, 1,820 mg sodium

BEEF & VEGETABLE SUPPER SOUP

If you like, top helpings of this lean, satisfying meal-in-a-bowl with sour cream or tart yogurt. Alongside, serve a crusty whole wheat loaf; complete the meal with a warm fruit dessert such as Fresh Pineapple Crisp (page 211).

- 1½ pounds lean boneless beef, trimmed of fat and cut into bite-size pieces
- 3 cups water
- 1 teaspoon salt
- ¼ teaspoon pepper
- 1 clove garlic, minced or pressed
- 1 dry bay leaf
- 3 tablespoons pearl barley or white rice
- 1 can (about 14½ oz.) tomatoes
- 2 stalks celery, sliced
- 2 large carrots, sliced
- 1 medium-size onion, cut into wedges
- ¼ small head cabbage, coarsely shredded
- 1 can (about 15 oz.) red kidney beans

In a 3½- to 5-quart pan, combine beef, water, salt, and pepper. Bring slowly to a boil, skimming off any foam that rises to the top. Add garlic and bay leaf. Reduce heat, cover, and simmer until meat is tender when pierced (about 1¼ hours).

Add barley to pan. Cut up tomatoes; add tomatoes and their liquid, celery, carrots, onion, and cabbage to pan. Bring to a boil; then reduce heat, cover, and simmer until all vegetables are tender to bite (about 20 minutes). Add beans and their liquid; cover and simmer just until heated through. Remove and discard bay leaf. Makes 6 servings.—*M. C., Salt Lake City*

Per serving: 285 calories, 26 g carbohydrates, 31 g protein, 6 g total fat (2 g saturated), 66 mg cholesterol, 819 mg sodium

PORK & SAUERKRAUT SOUP

After a football game or other fall outing, satisfy hearty appetites with this meaty soup. You might round out the meal with a big loaf of dark rye bread and Cool-as-a Cucumber Salad (page 44).

Meaty Soup Stock (recipe follows)
1 can (about 14½ oz.) sauerkraut, drained and rinsed
2 large carrots, sliced
1 large russet potato (about 8 oz.), peeled and diced
1 medium-size onion, chopped
½ teaspoon caraway seeds
1 teaspoon firmly packed brown sugar
4 ounces mushrooms, sliced
Salt and pepper

Prepare Meaty Soup Stock. In a 5- to 6-quart pan, combine stock, sauerkraut, carrots, potato, onion, and caraway seeds. Bring to a boil over high heat; then reduce heat, cover, and simmer until potato is very tender to bite (about 30 minutes).

Stir in meat (from Meaty Soup Stock), sugar, and mushrooms; cover and simmer for 15 more minutes. Season soup to taste with salt and pepper. Makes 6 to 8 servings.—*L. G., Bremerton, WA*

MEATY SOUP STOCK. Place 3 pounds **bone-in pork butt,** trimmed of fat, in a 5- to 6-quart pan. Cook over medium heat, turning as needed, until browned on all sides. Add 4 stalks **celery,** sliced; 2 large **onions,** sliced; 2 **whole cloves;** 1 clove **garlic,** minced or pressed; 1 **dry bay leaf;** 6 cups **water;** and 6 **chicken bouillon cubes.**

Bring to a boil over high heat; then reduce heat, cover, and simmer until meat is very tender when pierced (about 2 hours). Pour meat

and stock through a colander set over a large bowl; discard seasonings. Let meat stand until cool enough to handle; then cut or tear meat into bite-size pieces and set aside. Discard bone and fat. Skim and discard fat from stock.

Per serving: 295 calories, 17 g carbohydrates, 28 g protein, 13 g total fat (4 g saturated), 93 mg cholesterol, 1,039 mg sodium

PISTOU SOUP WITH SAUSAGE

Pistou, a thick and fragrant blend of basil, garlic, Parmesan cheese, and tomato paste, gives this supper soup its tantalizing flavor and aroma. Serve it with plain or toasted sourdough French bread.

1 pound leeks
8 ounces linguisa sausage, cut into ½-inch pieces
1 cup chopped carrots
½ cup (about 4 oz.) split peas
1½ cups diced thin-skinned potatoes
1 large can (about 49½ oz.) chicken broth
6 cups water
Pistou (recipe follows)
1 cup frozen cut green beans
⅔ cup 2-inch pieces dry spaghetti

Trim ends and all but about 3 inches of green tops from leeks; remove tough outer leaves. Split leeks length-

wise; rinse well, then thinly slice crosswise. Set aside.

Cook sausage in a 6- to 8-quart pan over medium-high heat, stirring often, until browned. Add carrots and leeks; cook, stirring, until leeks are soft (6 to 8 minutes). Spoon off and discard fat from pan.

Sort through split peas, discarding any debris. Rinse and drain peas; add to pan along with potatoes, broth, and water. Bring to a boil over high heat; then reduce heat, cover, and simmer until peas are soft to bite (about 1 hour).

Prepare Pistou; stir Pistou, beans, and spaghetti into soup. Increase heat to medium-high; then boil gently, uncovered, until spaghetti is just tender to bite (8 to 10 minutes). Makes 8 servings.—*Robin Warren, Fort Bragg, CA*

PISTOU. In a medium-size bowl, stir together 4 cloves **garlic,** minced or pressed; 1 can (about 6 oz.) **tomato paste;** ¾ cup grated **Parmesan cheese;** ¼ cup minced **parsley;** 1½ tablespoons **dry basil;** and ¼ cup **olive oil.**

Per serving: 319 calories, 33 g carbohydrates, 15 g protein, 15 g total fat (4 g saturated), 17 mg cholesterol, 1,259 mg sodium

ITALIAN SAUSAGE & BEAN SOUP

Looking for a speedy cold-weather supper? Here's one good choice: a spicy sausage-and-garbanzo soup. Serve it with a green salad, Cottage Cheese Pan Rolls (page 188), and fresh fruit.

About 1 pound mild Italian sausages, casings removed
1 clove garlic, minced or pressed
1 large onion, chopped
2 medium-size carrots, thinly sliced

1 cup thinly sliced mushrooms
⅓ cup chopped parsley
1 can (about 15 oz.) garbanzo beans
3 cups water
2 beef bouillon cubes
½ teaspoon rubbed sage
   Salt and pepper

Slice or crumble sausage into bite-size pieces; then cook in a 3-quart pan over medium-high heat, stirring often, until browned (8 to 10 minutes). Add garlic, onion, carrots, mushrooms, and ¼ cup of the parsley; cook, stirring often, until onion is soft. Spoon off and discard any fat from pan.

Add beans and their liquid, water, bouillon cubes, and sage. Bring to a boil over high heat; then reduce heat, cover, and simmer until beans are heated through and carrots are tender when pierced (about 10 minutes). Skim and discard any fat from soup, then season soup to taste with salt and pepper. Ladle soup into bowls and sprinkle with remaining parsley. Makes 4 servings.—*H. L., Napa, CA*

Per serving: 442 calories, 36 g carbohydrates, 24 g protein, 23 g total fat (8 g saturated), 65 mg cholesterol, 1,532 mg sodium

SPICED LENTIL-BARLEY SOUP

Nourishing lentils, garbanzo beans, and barley are at the heart of this winter soup, providing a robust base for a modest quantity of chicken and Italian sausage. Stir in bright spinach leaves just before serving.

8 ounces Italian sausages, casings removed
1 medium-size onion, chopped
3 cloves garlic, minced or pressed
⅓ cup pearl barley
1 cup (about 8 oz.) lentils

2 chicken breast halves (about 1 lb. *total*)
2 quarts chicken broth
½ cup minced parsley
1 can (about 15 oz.) garbanzo beans, drained and rinsed
1 jar (about 12 oz.) mild salsa
   About 1 pound fresh spinach

Crumble sausage into a 5- to 6-quart pan. Cook over medium-high heat, stirring often, until browned (8 to 10 minutes). With a slotted spoon, remove sausage from pan; set aside. To fat in pan, add onion, garlic, and barley. Cook, stirring often, until onion is soft and barley is toasted. Meanwhile, sort through lentils, discarding any debris; rinse and drain lentils.

Rinse chicken and pat dry; add chicken, lentils, broth, and parsley to pan. Bring to a boil over high heat. Then reduce heat, cover, and simmer until meat in thickest part of chicken breasts is no longer pink; cut to test (about 30 minutes).

Remove chicken from pan and let stand until cool enough to handle. Tear meat into shreds; discard skin and bones. Return meat to pan and stir in beans, salsa, and sausage. Bring to a simmer. Meanwhile, discard stems and any yellow or wilted leaves from spinach. Then rinse spinach, drain well, and chop. Stir spinach into soup; ladle soup into bowls. Makes 6 servings.—*Grace Kirschenbaum, Los Angeles*

Per serving: 464 calories, 47 g carbohydrates, 33 g protein, 16 g total fat (5 g saturated), 48 mg cholesterol, 2,323 mg sodium

HARVEST SOUP

Ground turkey has become a popular ingredient in the lighter cooking of the 1990s. In this warming soup, it combines with lots of fresh vegetables and a half-pound of herb-seasoned Italian sausage. Markets now offer the sausage made from turkey as well as the usual pork; either kind works well here. You might accompany the soup with Fall Fruit Platter (page 42).

8 ounces ground turkey
8 ounces mild Italian sausages, casings removed
½ cup chopped onion
6 cups beef broth
1 cup *each* tomato juice and dry red wine
3 large firm-ripe tomatoes (about 1¼ lbs. *total*), chopped
3 large carrots, sliced
2 cups coarsely chopped zucchini
1 tablespoon Worcestershire
2 teaspoons dry oregano
   Liquid hot pepper seasoning

Crumble turkey and sausage into a 3- to 4-quart pan; add onion. Cook over medium-high heat, stirring often, until meat is browned (8 to 10 minutes). With a slotted spoon, lift meat and onion from pan; set aside. Pour off and discard fat from pan; wipe pan clean.

Return meat and onion to pan; add broth, tomato juice, wine, tomatoes, carrots, zucchini, Worcestershire, and oregano.

Bring to a boil over high heat; then reduce heat, cover, and simmer until carrots are tender to bite (20 to 30 minutes). Season to taste with hot pepper seasoning. Makes 6 to 8 servings.—*Barbara Keenan, Fort Morgan, CO*

Per serving: 206 calories, 14 g carbohydrates, 15 g protein, 11 g total fat (3 g saturated), 35 mg cholesterol, 1,120 mg sodium

Quick Chicken–Vegetable Chowder

Braise-deglazing—a fat-free method of browning vegetables—was popularized in *Sunset* during the late 1980s. Soon readers, too, were using the technique to bring depth of flavor to satisfying dishes such as this creamy but low-fat soup.

1 cup *each* chopped onion, thinly sliced carrots, and diced celery
1¼ cups sliced mushrooms
4 cups chicken broth
2 cups dry pasta bow ties
1½ teaspoons dry tarragon
1½ pounds boneless, skinless chicken breasts, cut into 1-inch chunks
2½ cups milk blended with 1 tablespoon cornstarch
3 tablespoons chopped parsley
Salt and pepper

In a 5- to 6-quart pan, combine onion, carrots, celery, mushrooms, and ¼ cup of the broth. Bring to a boil over high heat; then boil, stirring often, until liquid evaporates and vegetables begin to brown (about 10 minutes). To deglaze, add ¼ cup more broth to pan and stir to scrape browned bits free. Continue to cook, stirring occasionally, until vegetables are well browned (3 to 5 more minutes).

Add remaining 3½ cups broth and bring to a boil. Stir in pasta and tarragon; reduce heat to medium-high, cover, and boil until pasta is barely tender to bite (about 6 minutes). Stir in chicken and milk mixture. Bring to a simmer. Simmer, stirring occasionally, until chicken is no longer pink in center; cut to test (about 6 minutes). Stir in parsley and season to taste with salt and pepper. Makes 4 to 6 servings.—*Bonnie E. Peterson, Tucson*

Per serving: 440 calories, 46 g carbohydrates, 44 g protein, 8 g total fat (3 g saturated), 96 mg cholesterol, 972 mg sodium

Turkey Barley Soup

A day or two after a roast turkey dinner, put the remains of the bird to use in a flavorful vegetable-barley soup.

1 turkey carcass (from a 12- to 20-lb. bird)
1 cup pearl barley
1 can (about 14½ oz.) tomatoes
2 cups sliced carrots
2 teaspoons poultry seasoning
½ teaspoon pepper
1 cup fresh or frozen peas
3 cups shredded cooked turkey
Salt

Break turkey carcass into easy-to-manage pieces and place in a 6- to 8-quart pan; add enough water to cover bones. Bring to a boil over high heat; then reduce heat and simmer, uncovered, until flavor has cooked out of bones (about 2 hours). Lift bones from pan and discard; skim and discard fat from broth. Add barley to broth and boil rapidly, uncovered, until barley is tender to bite and broth is reduced to 3 quarts (about 30 minutes; add water if broth boils down too far).

Cut up tomatoes; add tomatoes and their liquid, carrots, poultry seasoning, and pepper to broth. Cover and simmer for 20 minutes. (At this

point, you may let cool, then cover and refrigerate until next day; reheat before continuing.)

Stir peas and turkey into soup; cover and simmer until heated through (about 5 minutes). Season to taste with salt. Makes 8 to 10 servings.—*G. N., Portland*

Per serving: 226 calories, 25 g carbohydrates, 20 g protein, 5 g total fat (1 g saturated), 36 mg cholesterol, 192 mg sodium

Chicken Pozole

Flavors native to the Southwest mingle in this traditional hominy-enriched soup. Here, though, the dish is made in a lighter style, with chicken rather than the usual ham or fresh pork.

2 tablespoons salad oil
2 large onions, chopped
2 cloves garlic, minced or pressed
1 tablespoon dry oregano
½ teaspoon ground cumin
1 chicken (3 to 3½ lbs.), cut up, skinned, and trimmed of fat
1 large can (about 49½ oz.) chicken broth
2 cans (about 4 oz. *each*) diced green chiles
1 large can (about 30 oz.) yellow hominy, drained
1 can (about 2¼ oz.) sliced ripe olives, drained

Heat oil in a 5- to 6-quart pan over medium heat. Add onions, garlic, oregano, and cumin; cook, stirring often, until onions are soft (8 to 10 minutes). Rinse chicken and pat dry. Set chicken breasts aside; add remaining chicken pieces, broth, chiles, and hominy to pan.

Bring to a boil over high heat; then reduce heat, cover, and simmer for 10 minutes. Return to a boil; then add chicken breasts and immediately cover pan. Remove from heat and let stand until meat in thickest part is no longer pink; cut to test (about 20 minutes).

Lift all chicken from broth and let stand until cool enough to handle. Meanwhile, skim and discard fat from broth. Tear chicken into bite-size pieces; discard bones and fat. Return chicken to soup; add olives and bring to a boil over high heat. Makes 6 servings.—*Loretta Peña, Lakeside, AZ*

Per serving: 392 calories, 32 g carbohydrates, 32 g protein, 15 g total fat (3 g saturated), 78 mg cholesterol, 1,717 mg sodium

BASIL CHICKEN SOUP

You can use leftover cooked chicken or turkey in this aromatic main-dish soup. At the table, offer jarlsberg cheese to sprinkle into each bowlful.

- 1 tablespoon butter or margarine
- 1 large onion, chopped
- 1 clove garlic, minced or pressed
- 1 tablespoon all-purpose flour
- 2 cans (about 14½ oz. *each*) chicken broth
- 1 large russet potato (about 8 oz.), peeled and cut into ½-inch cubes
- 1 cup diced cooked chicken or turkey
- ½ cup chopped fresh basil (or use ½ cup chopped fresh spinach plus 2 tablespoons dry basil)
- ½ cup shredded reduced-fat or regular jarlsberg cheese

Melt butter in a 2- to 3-quart pan over medium heat. Add onion and garlic; cook, stirring occasionally, until onion is soft and lightly tinged with brown (about 10 minutes). Add flour and cook, stirring, until bubbly.

Gradually stir in broth. Increase heat to high; bring broth mixture to a boil. Add potato; reduce heat, cover, and simmer until potato is tender to bite (15 to 20 minutes). Add chicken; cover and simmer just until chicken is heated through (1 to 2 minutes).

Stir in basil. Ladle soup into bowls; offer cheese to add to taste. Makes 4 servings.—*Elizabeth K. Cooper, Kaneohe, Oahu, HI*

Per serving: 235 calories, 19 g carbohydrates, 19 g protein, 9 g total fat (4 g saturated), 46 mg cholesterol, 1,016 mg sodium

CHINESE CHICKEN & SHRIMP SOUP

This Asian-style soup is ready to serve almost as soon as it boils. Once you've prepared the wholesome ingredients—chicken, tiny shrimp, tofu, and vegetables—there's little left to do but combine and heat them.

- 1 large can (about 49½ oz.) chicken broth
- 2 tablespoons finely chopped fresh ginger
- 2 to 3 teaspoons soy sauce
- 2 boneless, skinless chicken breast halves (about 12 oz. *total*), cut into ½-inch cubes
- 2½ cups sliced mushrooms
- 3 cups thinly sliced bok choy
- 1 cup ½-inch cubes firm tofu
- ½ cup sliced green onions
- 8 ounces small cooked shrimp
- ¼ cup chopped cilantro
  Ground red pepper (cayenne) or hot chili oil (optional)

In a 4- to 5-quart pan, combine broth, ginger, and soy sauce; bring to a boil over high heat. Stir in chicken, mushrooms, bok choy, tofu, and onions. Then reduce heat and simmer, uncovered, until meat in thickest part is no longer pink; cut to test (about 2 minutes).

Remove pan from heat. Stir in shrimp and cilantro. Season soup to taste with red pepper, if desired. Makes 4 to 6 servings.—*Kristine Britton, Woodinville, WA*

Per serving: 247 calories, 7 g carbohydrates, 39 g protein, 8 g total fat (1 g saturated), 128 mg cholesterol, 1,576 mg sodium

RICE & SPINACH SOUP

Fresh spinach, tomato wedges, and shrimp add bright color to this lean rice soup. You might serve Soft Sesame Biscuits (page 181) alongside.

- 1 large can (about 49½ oz.) chicken broth
- 1 large onion, chopped
- ⅓ cup medium-grain white rice
- 2 cloves garlic, minced or pressed
- 2 small dried hot red chiles
- 4 cups lightly packed fresh spinach leaves
- 1 medium-size firm-ripe tomato (about 6 oz.)
- 4 ounces small cooked shrimp
- 2 tablespoons lime juice
  Lime wedges (optional)

In a 3- to 4-quart pan, combine broth, onion, rice, garlic, and chiles. Bring to a boil over high heat; then reduce heat, cover, and simmer until rice is tender to bite (20 to 30 minutes).

Meanwhile, cut spinach into thin shreds. Cut tomato into about ¾-inch-wide wedges. Stir spinach, tomato, and shrimp into simmering broth. Simmer, uncovered, just until spinach is wilted and tomato is heated through (about 1 minute). Stir in lime juice. Remove and discard chiles. Ladle s\into bowls; serve with lime wedges, if desired. Makes 6 servings.—*Mollie Minus, Milwaukie, OR*

Per serving: 123 calories, 17 g carbohydrates, 10 g protein, 2 g total fat (0.1 g saturated), 37 mg cholesterol, 1,103 mg sodium

CRAB & RICE CHOWDER

Corn, fresh broccoli, rice, and snowy flakes of crabmeat mingle in this creamy winter soup. For a warming lunch or supper, you might accompany the steaming chowder with crunchy carrot and jicama sticks and a basket of crisp-crusted rolls or your favorite crackers.

- 2 tablespoons salad oil
- 1 small onion, chopped
- 8 ounces mushrooms, thinly sliced
- 2 cups coarsely chopped fresh broccoli
- 1 small red bell pepper (about 5 oz.), seeded and chopped
- ½ teaspoon dry thyme
- 2 cups *each* chicken broth and milk
- 1 can (about 17 oz.) cream-style corn
- 5 to 6 ounces flaked cooked crabmeat
- 3 cups cooked long-grain white rice
  Salt and pepper

Heat oil in a 5- to 6-quart pan over medium-high heat. Add onion and mushrooms; cook, stirring often, until vegetables are tinged with gold (about 8 minutes). Add broccoli, bell pepper, and thyme; cook, stirring often, until broccoli is bright green and just tender to bite (about 4 minutes).

Reduce heat to medium and stir in broth, milk, and corn. Cook, uncovered, stirring occasionally, just until chowder is steaming (about 10 minutes; do not boil). Stir in crab and rice; simmer, uncovered, until crab and rice are heated through (about 2 minutes). Season to taste with salt and pepper. Makes 6 servings.—*Ellen S. Thomas, Portland*

Per serving: 347 calories, 53 g carbohydrates, 15 g protein, 9 g total fat (2 g saturated), 37 mg cholesterol, 687 mg sodium

SHRIMP SUPPER SOUP

Complement this simple soup with a salad of sliced beefsteak tomatoes and a loaf of crusty whole-grain bread.

- 2 tablespoons butter or margarine
- 2 green onions, thinly sliced
- 1 bottle (about 8 oz.) clam juice
- ½ teaspoon dry dill weed
- ½ cup frozen peas
- 1 pound medium-size raw shrimp (about 36 per lb.), shelled and deveined
- 1 to 2 cups cooked rice
- 2 cups half-and-half
  Salt and pepper
  Minced parsley

Melt butter in a 2½-quart pan over medium heat. Add onions and cook, stirring often, until soft (about 2 minutes). Stir in clam juice and dill weed; bring to a boil. Add peas; return broth to a boil. Add shrimp, rice, and half-and-half; adjust heat so soup simmers. Then cover and simmer until shrimp are just opaque in center; cut to test (about 3 minutes). Season soup to taste with salt and pepper; ladle into bowls and sprinkle with parsley. Makes 4 servings.—*M. B., Spanaway, WA*

Per serving: 421 calories, 31 g carbohydrates, 26 g protein, 21 g total fat (13 g saturated), 200 mg cholesterol, 396 mg sodium

CHILE CLAM CHOWDER

To bring new flavor to tomato-based clam chowder, try changing the seasonings. This zesty version is flavored Mexican-style, with chili powder, garlic, thyme, and bell pepper. Alongside, offer warm Cheese Biscuit Sticks (page 182).

- 1 large can (about 28 oz.) tomatoes
- 1 tablespoon olive oil or salad oil
- 1 medium-size onion, chopped
- 1 small clove garlic, minced or pressed
- 1 tablespoon all-purpose flour
- 2 cans (about 10 oz. *each*) baby clams
- 2 teaspoons sugar
- 2 to 3 teaspoons chili powder
- ½ teaspoon dry thyme
- 2 cups diced peeled potatoes
- ½ cup minced green bell pepper
  Salt and pepper

In a blender or food processor, whirl tomatoes and their liquid until puréed; set aside.

Heat oil in a 3½- to 5-quart pan over medium heat; add onion and cook, stirring often, until soft (about 5 minutes). Add garlic and flour; cook, stirring, until bubbly. Gradually stir in puréed tomatoes.

Drain liquid from clams and add to pan (reserve clams). Add sugar, chili powder, thyme, potatoes, and bell pepper. Bring to a boil over high heat; then reduce heat, cover, and simmer until potatoes are tender to bite (about 20 minutes).

Add clams to soup; then cover and simmer until clams are heated through (about 5 minutes). Season to taste with salt and pepper. Makes 4 to 6 servings.—*H. N., San Francisco*

Per serving: 224 calories, 28 g carbohydrates, 19 g protein, 5 g total fat (0.6 g saturated), 40 mg cholesterol, 342 mg sodium

Tuna Bean Soup

When you want to feed a crowd in a hurry, keep this hearty chowder in mind. It's quickly assembled with staples from the pantry cupboard—canned tuna, two kinds of beans, and tomatoes. If you keep cornmeal on hand as well, bake Cornmeal Bread (page 179) to serve with the soup.

1 large onion, chopped

4 ounces mushrooms, sliced

5 cups chicken broth

2 cans (about 15 oz. *each*) pinto beans, drained and rinsed

2 cans (about 15 oz. *each*) red kidney beans, drained and rinsed

1 large can (about 28 oz.) chopped tomatoes

1 can (about 8 oz.) tomato sauce

½ teaspoon dry oregano

1 large can (about 12½ oz.) water-packed solid white tuna, drained

Thinly sliced green onions (optional)

In a 5- to 6-quart pan, combine chopped onion and mushrooms. Cover and cook over medium-high heat until vegetables release their liquid (5 to 8 minutes). Uncover; bring to a boil over high heat. Then boil, stirring often, until liquid evaporates and vegetables begin to brown.

To deglaze, add ¼ cup of the broth to pan and stir to scrape browned bits free. Continue to cook, stirring occasionally, until vegetables begin to brown again.

Add pinto and kidney beans to pan along with remaining 4¾ cups broth, tomatoes, tomato sauce, and oregano. Bring to a boil over high heat; then reduce heat, cover, and simmer for 15 minutes. (At this point, you may let cool, then cover and refrigerate until next day. Reheat before continuing.)

Stir tuna into soup; heat through.

Ladle soup into bowls and top with green onions, if desired. Makes 8 to 10 servings.—*Ellen S. Thomas, Portland*

Per serving: 222 calories, 28 g carbohydrates, 21 g protein, 3 g total fat (0.3 g saturated), 15 mg cholesterol, 1,259 mg sodium

Mexican Oyster Stew

For a midwinter lunch, serve this soup with crusty bread and fruit.

3 tablespoons butter or margarine

1 medium-size onion, chopped

2 tablespoons chopped green bell pepper

2 tablespoons all-purpose flour

2 teaspoons chili powder

½ teaspoon *each* dry mustard and dry oregano

1 bottle (about 8 oz.) clam juice

2 cups milk

¼ cup dry sherry or milk

1 jar (about 10 oz.) small Pacific or other small oysters

About 10 pimento-stuffed green olives, sliced

Melt butter in a 3-quart pan over medium heat. Add onion and bell pepper and cook, stirring often, until soft (about 5 minutes). Stir in flour, chili powder, mustard, and oregano; cook, stirring, until bubbly. Gradually stir in clam juice, milk, and sherry and cook, stirring, until soup is bubbly.

Cut oysters into bite-size pieces; stir oysters and any liquid into soup. Cook, stirring occasionally, until oysters are firm and curled at edges (about 3 minutes). Ladle soup into mugs or small bowls and garnish with olives. Makes 2 to 4 servings. —*H. N., San Francisco*

Per serving: 368 calories, 24 g carbohydrates, 16 g protein, 21 g total fat (11 g saturated), 106 mg cholesterol, 802 mg sodium

Spinach Oyster Bisque

The special affinity of oysters and spinach has long been celebrated in classic dishes such as Oysters Rockefeller. Here, the popular duo is featured in a quick soup that's perfect for lunch or supper; try it with oyster crackers and a glass of crisp white wine.

2 tablespoons butter or margarine

1 large onion, chopped

2 tablespoons all-purpose flour

1 teaspoon Worcestershire

¼ teaspoon ground white pepper

5 cups chicken broth

½ cup dry white wine

1 package (about 10 oz.) frozen chopped spinach

1 jar (about 10 oz.) small Pacific or other small oysters

Whole nutmeg or ground nutmeg

Melt butter in a 4- to 5-quart pan over medium-high heat. Add onion; cook, stirring often, until onion begins to brown (8 to 10 minutes). Add flour and cook, stirring, until bubbly; then add Worcestershire and white pepper.

Remove pan from heat and stir in broth and wine. Add spinach; place pan over high heat. Stir until soup is boiling and spinach is thawed, breaking spinach up with a spoon as it thaws.

Cut oysters into bite-size pieces; stir oysters and any liquid into soup. Cook, stirring occasionally, until oysters are firm and curled at edges (about 3 minutes). Ladle soup into bowls. Offer a whole nutmeg to grate lightly over individual servings. Makes 4 servings.—*Helen Kennedy, Albuquerque*

Per serving: 217 calories, 16 g carbohydrates, 14 g protein, 9 g total fat (4 g saturated), 55 mg cholesterol, 1,436 mg sodium

1934 to 1937

Sunday Night Spaghetti

Fry minced onion, garlic, parsley and seasonings in the oil ~ ~

Add to tomatoes; add vinegar and simmer

In same frying pan, brown the cubed meat

Add to tomato mixture, cook a long time. Add mushrooms and heat again ~ ~ ~

Pour sauce over hot, cooked spaghetti on chop plate, and serve to delighted guests ~

RUTH TAYLOR

Sunset-style entertaining in the mid-1930s can be summed up by dinner menus entitled "Supper in the Patio" and "Good, and Not Too Expensive"—both from 1935. In addition to simple but elegant evening meals, Kitchen Cabinet contributors also shared recipes that helped them rise to the occasion "when company drops in and the larder is low" or when weekend house guests called for something special at breakfast.

Sunday night was a favorite time for low-key suppers with friends. In 1934, we featured Sunday Night Sandwiches toasted in a waffle baker; choices from 1935 included a Sunday evening menu planned around a puffy shrimp and cheese casserole. The 1937 Sunday Night Spaghetti reprinted below still makes a satisfying weekend repast.

The Kitchen Cabinet cook of this period probably spent more time in the kitchen than her modern counterparts. She might devote an afternoon to trying a treasured family recipe for homemade doughnuts, then stand by to stir together comforting Radio Special Supper Dish for late evening sustenance.

SUNDAY NIGHT SPAGHETTI

This is our favorite dish for Sunday night supper entertaining. We serve it in a large Chinese chop plate, with a plate of colorful raw vegetable salad on each side. Bowls of ripe olives that have been marinated in salad oil containing garlic, loaves of hot French bread, and plates of cheese complete the ensemble.

Here's the recipe, to serve 8:

- ¼ cupful of salad oil
- 1 large onion, chopped fine
- 1 clove of garlic, chopped fine
- ½ cupful of chopped parsley
- ½ teaspoonful of marjoram leaves, chopped
- ½ teaspoonful of sage leaves, chopped (powdered dried herbs may be substituted)
- ½ teaspoonful of powdered allspice
- 2 large cans (about 28 oz. *each*) of tomatoes
- ¼ cupful of cider vinegar
- 2 pounds of lean beef (boneless), cut into 1-inch cubes

Salt and pepper
- 1 to 1½ pounds of dry spaghetti
Large can (about 8 oz.) of mushroom

In a large frying pan heat about half of th oil, and in it fry the minced onion, garlic, and parsley, with the marjoram, sage, and allspice. Heat the tomatoes in a separate 3 to 4-quart saucepan. When the onion is golden brown, turn this mixture in with the tomatoes, and add the vinegar.

Next, to the same frying pan that the onion and herbs were cooked in, add a little more oil, and in it brown the cubed meat, salting and peppering it well while cooking. When browned, add it to the tomato mixture, and let simmer, covered, for at least an hour—3 or 4 will be better.

About 20 minutes before serving time, cook the spaghetti. Add the mushrooms (liquid and all) to the tomato sauce, add more seasonings if needed, and heat very hot. Put the drained spaghetti in the chop plate, pour the sauce over it, and serve.
—*Mrs. F. D. K., Hemet, CA (February 1937*

Green Bean Salad à la South Seas

My father, who was in the Navy, brought his recipe from the South Seas. Always when at home he mixed the seasonings himself at the family table. The salad is particularly delicious with cold roast beef.

> About 1 quart of cold cooked or canned cut green beans
> A pinch of salt
> ½ teaspoonful of pepper
> Juice of 2 small lemons (about ⅓ cupful of juice)
> 1 can (about 2 oz.) of anchovies
> 1 tablespoonful of salad oil
> 1 hard-cooked egg, sliced
> 1 red pimiento, cut small

Put the beans in a serving bowl. Put the salt and pepper in a large salad spoon, add the lemon juice, and sprinkle over the beans. Mash the anchovies to a paste with their own oil and the salad oil. Add to the beans and mix thoroughly but lightly. Lay the egg slices over the top, with the chopped pimiento in the center, and serve. —*Mrs. Y. O'D., Monterey, CA (April 1935)*

Radio Special Supper Dish

This dish was named in honor of my husband, who is a radio announcer. It is his supper favorite. It is quick to prepare, and delicious to eat if served immediately.

Melt a spoonful of **butter** in a small frying pan, and in it cook until soft a cut-up **tomato.** Remove from the fire and break in 2 **eggs,** then add 2 tablespoonfuls of **cream** or evaporated milk and a little **salt** and **pepper.** Put the pan back over the heat and cook, stirring constantly, until the eggs are barely set. Serve over a slice of **buttered toast.** —*Mrs. G. R. M., Santa Ana, CA (October 1936)*

Yellowstone Park Doughnuts

My mother won first prize in a cooking school contest more than 20 years ago, using this recipe. The prize was a trip through Yellowstone Park, hence our name for the doughnuts. They're plumper and more tender than any I've ever made.

> About 2 quarts of salad oil
> 3 large eggs, separated
> 1 cupful of sugar
> 4½ cupfuls of flour, sifted once before measuring
> 5 teaspoonfuls of baking powder
> 1 teaspoonful of salt
> 1 cupful of sweet milk
> 1 teaspoonful of grated nutmeg
> 3 tablespoonfuls of melted shortening

Heat the oil slowly in a deep, heavy kettle while preparing the dough, as follows:

Beat the egg whites stiff and dry, then add the yolks one at a time and beat very light after each addition. Beat in the sugar gradually. Sift the flour with the baking powder and salt, and add alternately with the milk, giving the batter a hard beating just before it is mixed stiff. Add the nutmeg and the melted shortening last. The dough must be just stiff enough to handle easily without sticking.

Turn out half the dough on a lightly floured board, roll out ½ inch thick, and cut with a doughnut cutter. Repeat, having all the doughnuts cut before frying them.

When the fat is moderately hot (380° to 390°F), drop in a few doughnuts, and turn them frequently until they are well puffed and beautifully browned, 2 to 2½ minutes for doughnuts, 1 to 1½ minutes for doughnut holes. Drain on paper toweling, and when cool roll in **granulated or powdered sugar** if desired. Makes about 22 doughnuts and 30 doughnut holes. —*Mrs. J.A.M., Mammoth Lakes P. O., CA (October 1937)*

~ Green Bean Salad ~
a la South Seas

Put salt and pepper in a salad spoon ~~~

Add lemon juice and sprinkle over beans ~~~~

Mash anchovies to a paste with the salad oil ~~~

Add to beans and toss until well mixed ~~~~

Decorate top with egg and pimiento and serve! ~~~~

S·A·L·A·D·S

They may seem to be casual creations, but distinctive salads and dressings have long been treasured by Kitchen Cabinet readers. "At a club convention, I saw three ladies picking this salad to pieces and jotting down their findings," reported Mrs. E. M. W. of Amity, Oregon in 1935. Her recipe for Unusual Apple Salad reappeared in 1980 in a slightly different form: Rosy Apple Teacup Salads (page 43), still intriguing after all these years. • "Be careful to make an artistic display of the separate colors," advised M. C. of Monterey, California in 1936. She could well have been describing our Tarragon-marinated Vegetable Platter from 1980 (page 45). Raw cauliflower salad proves to be a time-honored dish as well: it appears in Kitchen Cabinet as early as 1946, and Caesar-style Vegetable Salad (page 44) from 1981 gives the idea a fresh new twist. • Ample New Mexican Chili Bean Salad (page 50) came to us from an Albuquerque reader in 1994. But Mrs. H. M. F. of Oakland, California, writing in 1938, described it well: "I have had so many requests for this recipe when I've served it at buffet suppers, that I'm sure other readers of Sunset will treasure it as I do."

SPINACH SALAD ARMENIAN

This is a simple salad—just crisp fresh spinach and a marvelously zesty tomato dressing. You'll only need half a cup of the dressing for this recipe; serve the remainder over other vegetable salads.

Spicy Tomato Dressing or Egg-safe Spicy Tomato Dressing (recipes follow)

1 pound fresh spinach, stems removed, leaves rinsed and crisped
   Salt and pepper
2 hard-cooked large eggs, chopped

Prepare Spicy Tomato Dressing.

To serve, tear spinach into bite-size pieces and place in a large bowl. Add ½ cup of the dressing; mix gently, then season to taste with salt and pepper. Garnish with eggs. Makes 6 to 8 servings.—*Mrs. J. B., Elkton, OR*

SPICY TOMATO DRESSING. In a blender or food processor, combine 1 large **egg yolk,** ½ teaspoon **grated lemon peel,** ¼ teaspoon **dry mustard,** 1½ teaspoons *each* **paprika** and **Worcestershire,** 1 tablespoon **sugar,** ½ cup **canned tomato sauce,** and ¼ cup *each* **red wine vinegar** and **lemon juice.** Whirl until well blended. With motor running, add 1 cup **salad oil** in thin, slow, steady stream; continue to whirl until dressing is thickened. If made ahead, cover and refrigerate for up to 3 weeks. Makes about 2¼ cups.

EGG-SAFE SPICY TOMATO DRESSING. In a small bowl, mix 1 large **egg white** with 2 tablespoons **lemon juice.** Cover airtight and refrigerate for at least 48 hours or up to 4 days (upon longer standing, egg will begin to solidify). In a blender or food processor, combine egg white mixture with 1 tablespoon **sugar,** 2 tablespoons **lemon juice,** ½ teaspoon **grated lemon peel,** ¼ teaspoon **dry**

mustard, 1½ teaspoons *each* **paprika** and **Worcestershire,** ½ cup **canned tomato sauce,** and ¼ cup **red wine vinegar.** Whirl until well blended. With motor running, add 1 cup **salad oil** in thin, slow, steady stream; continue to whirl until dressing is thickened. If made ahead, cover and refrigerate for up to 2 weeks; stir before using. Makes about 2¼ cups.

Per serving of salad without dressing: 32 calories, 2 g carbohydrates, 3 g protein, 2 g total fat (0.5 g saturated), 61 mg cholesterol, 55 mg sodium

Per tablespoon of Spicy Tomato Dressing: 59 calories, 1 g carbohydrates, 0.1 g protein, 6 g total fat (1 g saturated), 6 mg cholesterol, 23 mg sodium

Per tablespoon of Egg-Safe Spicy Tomato Dressing: 57 calories, 1 g carbohydrates, 0.2 g protein, 6 g total fat (1 g saturated), 0 mg cholesterol, 25 mg sodium

CRISP SPINACH SALAD

This salad is a favorite for potlucks. Carry the salad and dressing separately, then mix just before serving.

1½ pounds fresh spinach, stems removed, leaves rinsed and crisped
8 ounces fresh bean sprouts
1 can (about 8 oz.) water chestnuts, drained and sliced
5 slices bacon, crisply cooked, drained, and crumbled
⅓ cup salad oil
2 tablespoons *each* sugar, catsup, and red wine vinegar
¼ cup finely chopped onion
1 teaspoon Worcestershire
   Salt and pepper
2 hard-cooked large eggs, sliced

Tear spinach leaves into bite-size pieces and place in a very large bowl. Add bean sprouts, water chestnuts, and bacon.

In a small bowl, combine oil, sugar, catsup, vinegar, onion, and Worcestershire; stir until sugar is dissolved. (At this point, you may

cover and refrigerate spinach mixture and dressing separately for up to 4 hours.)

To serve, stir dressing and pour over spinach mixture; mix gently. Season to taste with salt and pepper and garnish with eggs. Makes 8 to 10 servings.—*L. H., San Diego, CA*

Per serving: 151 calories, 9 g carbohydrates, 5 g protein, 11 g total fat (2 g saturated), 50 mg cholesterol, 163 mg sodium

SALAD ITALIANO WITH BASIL DRESSING

Another time, you might serve this basil dressing over sliced tomatoes.

3 tablespoons *each* red wine vinegar and grated Parmesan cheese
½ teaspoon dry mustard
¼ teaspoon *each* salt and pepper
6 tablespoons olive oil or salad oil
¼ cup thinly sliced green onions
½ cup chopped fresh basil
3 quarts bite-size pieces of rinsed, crisped lettuce
1 small cucumber (about 6 oz.), peeled and thinly sliced
1 small can (about 8 oz.) garbanzo beans, drained and rinsed
2 small tomatoes (about 8 oz. *total*), cut into thin wedges or slices
   About ½ cup croutons

In a small bowl, stir together vinegar, cheese, mustard, salt, pepper, oil, onions, and basil.

In a large bowl, layer lettuce, cucumber, and beans; arrange tomatoes on top. (At this point, you may cover and refrigerate dressing and salad separately for up to 2 hours.)

To serve, stir dressing and pour over salad; mix gently. Sprinkle salad with croutons and serve. Makes 6 servings.—*S. M., Vancouver, WA*

Per serving: 247 calories, 17 g carbohydrates, 6 g protein, 19 g total fat (3 g saturated), 2 mg cholesterol, 256 mg sodium

Romaine Salad with Creamy Garlic Dressing

This garlicky combination will remind you of a classic Caesar salad—with the addition of cherry tomatoes and creamy diced avocado. If you prefer not to use a raw egg, just follow our egg-safe variation.

- 2 cloves garlic, minced or pressed
- ½ teaspoon salt
- 1 tablespoon lime or lemon juice
- 1 large egg
- ⅓ cup mayonnaise
- 2 teaspoons Worcestershire or soy sauce
- 3 to 4 quarts rinsed, crisped romaine lettuce leaves
- 3 tablespoons grated Parmesan cheese
- 1 cup cherry tomatoes, cut into halves
- 1 avocado, pitted, peeled, and diced
- 2 green onions, thinly sliced
- ⅔ cup croutons

In a small bowl, mash garlic and salt together into a paste with the back of a spoon (or mash with a mortar and pestle and transfer to a bowl). Mix garlic paste with lime juice; then add egg and beat until foamy. Stir in mayonnaise and Worcestershire.

Tear lettuce into bite-size pieces; place in a very large bowl. Add cheese, tomatoes, avocado, onions, and croutons. Pour dressing over salad and mix gently. Makes 6 to 8 servings.—*L. H., Palm Springs, CA*

Per serving: 178 calories, 9 g carbohydrates, 5 g protein, 14 g total fat (3 g saturated), 38 mg cholesterol, 314mg sodium

Egg-Safe Romaine Salad with Creamy Garlic Dressing

Start by preparing this egg-safe dressing: In a small bowl, mix 1 large **egg white** with 2 tablespoons **lemon juice.** Cover airtight and refrigerate for at least 48 hours or up to 4 days (upon longer standing, egg will begin to solidify). In another small bowl, mash 2 cloves **garlic** (minced or pressed) and ½ teaspoon **salt** into a paste with the back of a spoon. Add egg white mixture and beat until foamy. Stir in ⅓ cup **mayonnaise** and 2 teaspoons **Worcestershire.**

To make salad, tear lettuce into a very large bowl as directed for **Romaine Salad with Creamy Garlic Dressing.** Add cheese, tomatoes, avocado, onions, and croutons as directed. Pour dressing over salad; mix gently. Makes 6 to 8 servings.

Per serving: 170 calories, 9 g carbohydrates, 5 g protein, 14 g total fat (2 g saturated), 8 mg cholesterol, 314 mg sodium

Warm Goat Cheese Salad

A modern first-course classic, this salad features crisp greens topped with broiled goat cheese, toasted walnut halves, and a mustard-based vinaigrette.

- ¾ cup walnut halves or pieces
- ¼ cup walnut oil or olive oil
- ¼ cup white wine vinegar
- 1 tablespoon Dijon mustard
  Salt and pepper
- 6 to 8 ounces round or log-shaped medium-firm goat cheese (chèvre)
- 12 ounces mixed salad greens (such as red leaf, oak leaf, and butter lettuce), separated into leaves, rinsed, and crisped

Spread walnuts in a large, shallow baking pan and toast in a 400° oven until dark golden brown (5 to 6 minutes). Set pan aside.

In a small bowl, stir together oil, vinegar, and mustard; season to taste with salt and pepper. Pour dressing into a small pitcher; set aside.

Cut cheese into 6 equal pieces and place in pan with walnuts. Broil about 3 inches below heat until cheese is speckled with brown and slightly melted (2 to 4 minutes). Meanwhile, tear lettuce leaves into large pieces and arrange on 6 individual plates.

Place one piece of cheese on each salad. Sprinkle walnuts over salads. Offer dressing to add to taste. Makes 6 servings.—*Jane Cross, Albuquerque*

Per serving: 274 calories, 5 g carbohydrates, 9 g protein, 25 g total fat (7 g saturated), 22 mg cholesterol, 211 mg sodium

Green & Orange Salad

This combination of greens and fresh orange segments is delicious with grilled beef or chicken; you might try it with Soy-Honey Barbecued Flank Steak (page 71).

- 2 large oranges (1 to 1¼ lbs. *total*)
- ⅔ cup salad oil
- 3 tablespoons white wine vinegar
- 1 teaspoon *each* salt and dry mustard
- 4 teaspoons sugar
  Dash of ground white pepper
- 1 small head romaine lettuce, separated into leaves, rinsed, and crisped
- 1 large head butter lettuce, separated into leaves, rinsed, and crisped
- 1 small cucumber (about 6 oz.), thinly sliced
- 3 green onions, thinly sliced

Grate enough peel (colored part only) from oranges to make 1 tablespoon; reserve for dressing. Cut off and discard all remaining peel and white membrane from oranges. Holding oranges over a bowl to catch juice, cut between membranes to release segments. Set segments aside; reserve juice in bowl.

In a small bowl, stir together oil, vinegar, salt, mustard, sugar, white pepper, the reserved 1 tablespoon orange peel, and 2 tablespoons of the reserved orange juice (if you did not collect enough juice, squeeze another orange).

Tear romaine and butter lettuces into bite-size pieces and place in a large bowl. Add cucumber, onions, and orange segments. Stir dressing to blend well; pour over salad and mix gently. Makes 6 servings.—*R. H., Scappoose, OR*

Per serving: 280 calories, 14 g carbohydrates, 2 g protein, 25 g total fat (3 g saturated), 0 mg cholesterol, 376 mg sodium

SUMMER SLAW

The light oil and vinegar dressing for this cabbage salad has a pleasing sweet-tart flavor.

- 1 large head cabbage (about 2 lbs.), finely shredded
- 2 medium-size mild white onions, thinly sliced and separated into rings
- ½ cup *each* sugar and cider vinegar
- 1 teaspoon *each* dry mustard and salt
- ⅛ teaspoon pepper
- 1 teaspoon celery seeds
- ½ cup salad oil
  Cherry tomato halves

In a large bowl, alternate layers of cabbage and onion rings. Set aside.

In a 1- to 1½-quart pan, stir together sugar, vinegar, mustard, salt, pepper, and celery seeds. Bring

to a boil, stirring until sugar is dissolved. Remove from heat, stir in oil, and pour over cabbage and onions. Let cool slightly; then cover and refrigerate for at least 4 hours or until next day, stirring several times.

Using a slotted spoon, lift cabbage and onions from dressing and heap into a serving bowl. Garnish with tomatoes. Makes 6 to 8 servings.—*E. M., San Diego, CA*

Per serving: 232 calories, 23 g carbohydrates, 2 g protein, 16 g total fat (2 g saturated), 0 mg cholesterol, 336 mg sodium

CONFETTI COLESLAW

Here's a cheerful addition to a fall buffet: a crisp slaw of red cabbage and tart apples in a tarragon-seasoned yogurt dressing.

- 1 cup plain yogurt
- ¼ cup mayonnaise
- 3 tablespoons white wine vinegar
- 1 tablespoon sugar
- ½ teaspoon dry tarragon
- 1 small head red or green cabbage (1 to 1¼ lbs.), shredded
- 2 large carrots, shredded
- 2 medium-size tart apples (about 12 oz. *total*), cored and coarsely chopped
- 4 green onions, thinly sliced
  Salt and pepper

In a small bowl, stir together yogurt, mayonnaise, vinegar, sugar, and tarragon. If made ahead, cover and refrigerate until next day.

In a large bowl, combine cabbage, carrots, apples, and onions; cover and refrigerate until serving time or for up to 2 hours.

To serve, pour dressing over cabbage mixture; mix gently. Season to taste with salt and pepper. Makes 6 servings.—*B. K., Fort Morgan, CO*

Per serving: 163 calories, 20 g carbohydrates, 3 g protein, 9 g total fat (2 g saturated), 10 mg cholesterol, 91 mg sodium

SPICY RED COLESLAW

Tossed with a celery seed–sprinkled vinaigrette, this salad seems lighter than many creamy coleslaws. It's good with grilled turkey sausages or plump bockwurst.

- 6 cups finely shredded red cabbage
- 1 cup *each* thinly sliced radishes and shredded carrots
- ¼ cup minced parsley
- 1 tablespoon finely chopped red onion
  Celery Seed Dressing (recipe follows)
  Salt and pepper
- 6 to 8 large green leaf lettuce leaves, rinsed and crisped

In a large bowl, combine cabbage, radishes, carrots, parsley, and onion. Prepare Celery Seed Dressing; pour over cabbage mixture and mix gently. Cover and refrigerate for at least 30 minutes or for up to 6 hours.

To serve, mix slaw again; season to taste with salt and pepper. Mound slaw in a lettuce-lined shallow bowl or platter. Makes 6 servings.—*Lisa Miller, Berkeley, CA*

CELERY SEED DRESSING. In a small bowl, stir together 3 tablespoons *each* **olive oil** and **lemon juice**, 2 tablespoons **red wine vinegar**, 2 teaspoons **sugar**, 1 teaspoon **Dijon mustard**, ½ teaspoon **celery seeds**, and ¼ teaspoon **ground cumin**.

Per serving: 97 calories, 8 g carbohydrates, 1 g protein, 7 g total fat (1 g saturated), 0 mg cholesterol, 40 mg sodium

Fall Fruit Platter

Show off a bright assortment of autumn fruits with this attractive salad. For the persimmons, choose either soft-ripe Hachiyas or the crisp Fuyu type; both taste good, though the latter will make neater slices.

- 2 medium-size grapefruit
- 2 large oranges (1 to 1¼ lbs. *total*)
- 2 medium-size persimmons, sliced
  Cinnamon Dressing (recipe follows)
- 2 medium-size red-skinned apples (about 12 oz. *total*)
- 1 large ripe avocado

Cut one each of the grapefruit and oranges in half crosswise; squeeze juice from one half of each fruit and reserve juice for dressing.

Cut off and discard all remaining peel and white membrane from all remaining grapefruit and oranges. Cut fruit crosswise into thin slices; arrange on a large rimmed platter along with persimmons. Then prepare Cinnamon Dressing. (At this point, you may cover and refrigerate sliced fruit and dressing separately for up to 4 hours.)

To serve, core and slice apples; pit, peel, and slice avocado. Arrange apples and avocado on platter with other fruits. Serve at once, with Cinnamon Dressing. Makes 6 to 8 servings.—*M. S., Seattle*

Cinnamon Dressing. In a small bowl, combine 1 small package (about 3 oz.) **cream cheese** (at room temperature) with 1 tablespoon **honey** and ½ teaspoon *each* **grated orange peel** and **ground cinnamon.** Beat until mixture is smoothly blended; then gradually beat in **reserved grapefruit and orange juice** until well blended.

Per serving: 189 calories, 26 g carbohydrates, 3 g protein, 10 g total fat (4 g saturated), 13 mg cholesterol, 40 mg sodium

Pear, Walnut & Blue Cheese Salad

To make a stylish first course for a winter dinner, start with a simple watercress-butter lettuce salad—then dress it up with thinly sliced pears, tangy blue cheese, and crunchy candied walnuts.

- Candied Walnuts (recipe follows)
- Shallot Dressing (recipe follows)
- 4 cups lightly packed watercress sprigs, rinsed and crisped
- 4 cups bite-size pieces of rinsed, crisped butter lettuce
- 2 small firm-ripe pears, cored and thinly sliced
  Salt
- ½ cup crumbled blue-veined cheese

Prepare Candied Walnuts and Shallot Dressing.

In a large bowl, combine watercress, lettuce, pears, and Candied Walnuts. Add Shallot Dressing and mix gently. Season to taste with salt. Spoon salad onto 6 individual plates; sprinkle with cheese. Makes 6 servings.—*Carmela Meely, Walnut Creek, CA*

Candied Walnuts. Pour 2 tablespoons **sugar** into a small frying pan. Cook over medium-high heat, shaking pan often, until sugar melts and turns amber in color. Add 1 tablespoon **water** (sugar will harden); cook, stirring, until sugar is melted again. Add ½ cup **walnut halves.** Stir until syrup clings to nuts. Spread nuts out on foil; let cool completely.

Shallot Dressing. In a small bowl, stir together 2 tablespoons **lemon juice,** ½ cup **olive oil** or salad oil, 1 large **shallot** (minced), and ½ teaspoon *each* **pepper** and **sugar.**

Per serving: 306 calories, 15 g carbohydrates, 5 g protein, 27 g total fat (5 g saturated), 8 mg cholesterol, 173 mg sodium

Tropical Jicama Salad

Jicama, previously little known outside Mexico, became a familiar sight in Western markets in the 1970s. Its crisp, slightly sweet flesh, reminiscent of water chestnuts in both texture and flavor, has made it a popular addition to salsas, relish trays, and refreshing salads like this one.

- 1 medium-size jicama (about 1¼ lbs.), peeled and cut into ⅛-inch-thick matchstick strips
- 2 cups small chunks pineapple
- 1 small firm-ripe papaya (about 12 oz.), peeled, seeded, and diced
- 1 cup thinly sliced celery
- ½ cup whole blanched almonds
- 2 teaspoons salad oil
- ½ cup dried currants or raisins
- 1 teaspoon curry powder
- 1 cup plain yogurt
  Salt

In a large bowl, combine jicama, pineapple, papaya, and celery. Set aside.

Toast almonds in a wide frying pan over medium heat, stirring often, until golden (about 5 minutes); pour out of pan and set aside. Add oil, currants, and curry powder; stir until currants are puffy (about 2 minutes). Remove pan from heat. In a bowl, combine currant mixture with almonds; let cool. Stir yogurt into currant-almond mixture; spoon over salad. Mix gently; season to taste

with salt. Makes 6 to 8 servings.
—*Joan MacDonald, Eugene, OR*

Per serving: 190 calories, 27 g carbohydrates, 5 g protein, 8 g total fat (1 g saturated), 4 mg cholesterol, 38 mg sodium

BUFFET ORANGE SALAD MOLD

Yogurt makes this pretty salad creamy, but not rich; a squeeze of orange is the dressing. For large parties, you can double or triple the recipe and use a 2- or 3-quart mold.

    1   package (about 3 oz.) orange-flavored gelatin
    1   cup boiling water
    2   tablespoons lemon juice
    ½   cup *each* finely shredded carrot and well-drained canned crushed pineapple
    2   tablespoons finely chopped celery
    1   tablespoon minced green onion (white part only)
    1   tablespoon finely minced fresh mint (optional)
    1   cup plain yogurt
        Lettuce leaves, rinsed and crisped, or mint sprigs
    1   orange, cut into 6 wedges

In a large bowl, stir together gelatin and boiling water until gelatin is completely dissolved. Stir in lemon juice and refrigerate until mixture is thick and syrupy. Stir in carrot, pineapple, celery, onion, and minced mint (if used). Stir in yogurt until well blended. Pour mixture into a 1-quart mold and refrigerate until firm (at least 6 hours).

To serve, unmold salad on a platter and garnish with lettuce. Surround salad with orange wedges; let guests squeeze a little orange juice over their servings. Makes 6 servings.—*H. N., San Francisco*

Per serving: 95 calories, 19 g carbohydrates, 3 g protein, 1 g total fat (0.8 g saturated), 5 mg cholesterol, 60 mg sodium

ROSY APPLE TEACUP SALADS

Use small Golden Delicious or Newtown Pippin apples for these cunning little salads. The apples are first simmered in a rosy-red cinnamon syrup, then filled with a mixture of crisp almonds and crushed pineapple.

    8   small apples (*each* about 2 inches in diameter)
    3   cups water
    1¼ cups sugar
    ¼   cup tiny red cinnamon candies
    1   can (about 8 oz.) crushed pineapple, drained
    3   tablespoons slivered almonds
    1   envelope unflavored gelatin
    1   cup apple juice
    2   tablespoons lemon juice

Peel and core apples. If necessary, pare sides of apples so each fits in a wide, deep teacup. In a 5- to 6-quart pan, combine water, sugar, and cinnamon candies. Bring to a simmer, stirring to dissolve sugar. Set apples upright in syrup and simmer gently until just tender when pierced (about 10 minutes); turn apples often so they cook evenly. Lift apples from syrup and set in teacups. Reserve 1 cup of the syrup.

Combine pineapple and almonds. Spoon mixture into cavities of apples; scatter any leftover mixture over apples.

In a small pan, sprinkle gelatin over apple juice and let stand until softened; then stir over low heat until completely dissolved. Add dissolved gelatin to the reserved 1 cup syrup; stir in lemon juice. Spoon syrup mixture over apples. Cover and refrigerate until firm (at least 4 hours). Makes 8 servings.—*L. K., Bigfork, MT*

Per serving: 243 calories, 58 g carbohydrates, 2 g protein, 2 g total fat (0.2 g saturated), 0 mg cholesterol, 5 mg sodium

AVOCADO WITH GAZPACHO

A good-looking choice for a summer meal, this salad features avocado shells filled with a tangy, garlic-spiked mixture of tomatoes, cucumber, bell pepper, and green onion.

    3   medium-size ripe avocados
    3   tablespoons lemon juice
    1½ cups peeled, seeded, chopped tomatoes
    ½   cup diced peeled cucumber
    ¼   cup *each* chopped green bell pepper and thinly sliced green onions
    1   small clove garlic, minced or pressed
    1   tablespoon red wine vinegar
    2   tablespoons olive oil
    ⅛   teaspoon liquid hot pepper seasoning
        Salt
        Shredded lettuce
        Sour cream

Halve avocados and remove pits. Spoon out flesh from avocado halves in large pieces, leaving a ¼-inch-thick layer of avocado in each avocado shell. Brush insides of avocado shells with about 1 tablespoon of the lemon juice; cover. Dice avocado flesh; place in a bowl and add remaining lemon juice, tomatoes, cucumber, bell pepper, onions, garlic, vinegar, oil, and hot pepper seasoning. Season to taste with salt. Mix lightly; cover. (At this point, you may refrigerate avocado shells and avocado-tomato mixture for up to 4 hours.)

Arrange a bed of lettuce on each of 6 individual plates. Place an avocado shell on each plate; heap avocado-tomato mixture in each shell. Offer sour cream to add to taste. Makes 6 servings.—*H. N., San Francisco*

Per serving: 218 calories, 11 g carbohydrates, 3 g protein, 20 g total fat (3 g saturated), 0 mg cholesterol, 20 mg sodium

Cool-as-a-Cucumber Salad

Fresh mint contributes to the frosty flavor of this refreshing green-and-white salad.

- 3 large cucumbers (about 2 lbs. *total*)
- ½ teaspoon salt
- 2 cups plain nonfat yogurt
- 3 cloves garlic, minced or pressed
- 2 tablespoons lemon juice
- 1 tablespoon minced fresh dill or 1½ teaspoons dry dill weed
- 1 tablespoon minced fresh mint or 1½ teaspoons dry mint
  About 2 teaspoons extra-virgin olive oil
- 8 to 16 large butter lettuce leaves, rinsed and crisped

Peel and halve cucumbers; scrape out and discard seeds. Coarsely chop cucumbers, place in a colander, and mix in salt; let drain for 15 minutes. In a large bowl, combine cucumbers, yogurt, garlic, lemon juice, and dill. Cover and refrigerate for at least 3 hours or until next day.

Pour cucumber mixture into a serving bowl; sprinkle with a third of the mint, then drizzle with 2 tea-spoons of the oil. Serve salad on a lettuce-lined platter or individual plates; sprinkle with remaining mint and a few drops of oil. Makes 8 serv-ings.—*Laurie Wilcox, Palm Desert, CA*

Per serving: 65 calories, 9 g carbohydrates, 4 g pro-tein, 2 g total fat (0.3 g saturated), 1 mg cholesterol, 134 mg sodium

Tri-mustard Tomato Salad

If you want to take this salad to a picnic, combine all the ingredients but the tomatoes—carry them whole, then cut them up and add to the bowl just before serving. We call for Dijon mustard in the dressing, but you might want to experiment with other types as well.

- Tri-mustard Vinaigrette (recipe follows)
- 1 medium-size cucumber (about 8 oz.)
- 1 medium-size green bell pepper (about 6 oz.)
- 1 medium-size red onion, cut crosswise into ¼-inch-thick slices and separated into rings
- 4 large firm-ripe tomatoes (about 2 lbs. *total*), cut into ½-inch-thick wedges
  Salt and pepper

Prepare Tri-mustard Vinaigrette and set aside.

Score cucumber lengthwise with tines of a fork (or peel cucumber). Cut cucumber crosswise into ¼-inch-thick slices. Cut bell pepper in half lengthwise; discard stem and seeds, then cut each half crosswise into ¼-inch-thick slices.

In a salad bowl, combine cucum-ber, bell pepper, onion, tomatoes, and vinaigrette. Mix gently; season to taste with salt and pepper. Makes 6 to 8 servings.—*Sandra Shogerson, Boise, ID*

TRI-MUSTARD VINAIGRETTE. In a small bowl, stir together ¼ cup **salad oil**; 2 tablespoons *each* **white wine vinegar, Dijon mustard**, and **mustard seeds**; 2 teaspoons **dry mustard**; and ½ to 1 teaspoon **liquid hot pepper seasoning**.

Per serving: 135 calories, 11 g carbohydrates, 3 g protein, 9 g total fat (1 g saturated), 0 mg choles-terol, 131 mg sodium

Sliced Tomato Salad

Make the most of late summer's rich, ripe tomatoes with this simple, gingery salad. It's a nice partner for juicy grilled sausages.

- 1-inch-long piece fresh ginger
- 2 large or 4 small ripe tomatoes (about 1 lb. *total*), peeled and cut into ¼-inch-thick slices
- ½ medium-size mild white onion, thinly sliced
- 1 tablespoon sugar
- ⅛ teaspoon pepper
- ½ teaspoon salt
- 2 tablespoons red wine vinegar
  Red or green leaf lettuce leaves, rinsed and crisped, and minced parsley (optional)

Peel ginger and cut it into very thin slices; then cut each slice into thin strips. In a shallow serving bowl, alternate tomato and onion slices; distribute ginger evenly over top. In a small bowl, stir together sugar, pepper, salt, and vinegar until sugar is dissolved; pour over vegetables. Cover and refrigerate for about 2 hours.

Just before serving, spoon some of the dressing from bowl up over tomatoes and onion. Garnish with lettuce and sprinkle with parsley, if desired. Makes 4 servings.—*D. Y., Seattle*

Per serving: 45 calories, 10 g carbohydrates, 1 g protein, 0.4 g total fat (0 g saturated), 0 mg choles-terol, 285 mg sodium

Caesar-style Vegetable Salad

Mix crunchy raw vegetables with a Caesar-style dressing to make this lively salad. The raw egg called for here is traditional in Caesar salads, but you may omit it if you prefer. The salad is a good choice for summer picnics, since there's no fragile lettuce to wilt in the heat. Carry the egg (if you're using it), dressing, and cheese separately, then mix the salad just before serving.

Caesar Dressing (recipe follows)
About 1 pound fresh broccoli
1 small head cauliflower (about 1 lb.)
1 small zucchini (about 3 oz.)
2 large carrots
4 ounces mushrooms, thinly sliced
1 small red or green bell pepper (about 5 oz.), seeded and diced
1 large egg, beaten (optional)
¾ cup grated Parmesan or Romano cheese

Prepare Caesar Dressing and set aside.

Trim and discard tough ends of broccoli stalks. Cut off flowerets, then cut them into bite-size pieces. Peel stalks and cut diagonally into paper-thin slices. Trim and discard leaves from cauliflower, then cut cauliflower into bite-size pieces. Cut zucchini and carrots into paper-thin slices.

In a large bowl, combine broccoli, cauliflower, zucchini, carrots, mushrooms, and bell pepper. Add egg (if used) and mix gently to coat vegetables. Drizzle salad with Caesar Dressing and sprinkle with cheese; mix gently, then serve immediately. Makes 6 to 8 servings.—C. J., San Anselmo, CA

CAESAR DRESSING. In a small bowl, stir together ⅔ cup **olive oil** or salad oil; 6 tablespoons **lemon juice;** 2 cloves **garlic** (minced or pressed); 6 to 8 **canned anchovy fillets** (chopped); ¾ teaspoon **pepper;** and 1½ teaspoons **Worcestershire.**

Per serving: 276 calories, 10 g carbohydrates, 7 g protein, 24 g total fat (5 g saturated), 9 mg cholesterol, 347 mg sodium

CHILLED VEGETABLE SALAD PLATTER

Try this appealing combination of green beans, tomatoes, red onion, and artichokes with barbecued ribs or poultry; or serve it with Oven-fried Chicken & Spareribs (page 105).

1 pound green beans (ends trimmed), broken or cut into 2-inch lengths
2 large tomatoes (about 1 lb. *total*), peeled and sliced
1 medium-size mild red or white onion, thinly sliced and separated into rings
1 can (about 14 oz.) water-packed artichoke hearts, drained
½ cup white wine vinegar
¼ cup olive oil or salad oil
2 cloves garlic, minced or pressed
1 teaspoon dry basil
½ teaspoon dry oregano
Salt and pepper

In a 3½- to 5-quart pan, cook beans, uncovered, in about 2 quarts boiling water until just tender to bite (3 to 5 minutes). Drain, immerse in cold water until cool, and drain again. Set aside.

Arrange tomatoes in a single layer on a large rimmed platter; distribute onion rings over tomatoes. Cut artichokes into halves; arrange artichokes and beans over onion.

In a small bowl, stir together vinegar, oil, garlic, basil, and oregano; season to taste with salt and pepper, then pour evenly over vegetables.

Cover and refrigerate for at least 1 hour or up to 4 hours, tipping platter and spooning dressing up over vegetables several times. Makes 6 to 8 servings.—G. J., San Luis Obispo, CA

Per serving: 126 calories, 13 g carbohydrates, 3 g protein, 8 g total fat (1 g saturated), 0 mg cholesterol, 12 mg sodium

TARRAGON-MARINATED VEGETABLE PLATTER

This vegetable quartet is ideal for the buffet table. Make it a day in advance, if you like; the flavor improves with longer marinating.

1 medium-size to large head cauliflower (1½ to 1¾ lbs.)
4 large carrots, cut diagonally into ¼-inch-thick slices
1 package (about 9 oz.) frozen artichoke hearts, thawed
2 cups cherry tomatoes
Tarragon Dressing (recipe follows)

Trim and discard leaves from cauliflower. Then break cauliflower into small flowerets; cut any large flowerets in half lengthwise, if necessary, so that all flowerets are about the same size. Steam cauliflower, carrots, and artichokes separately: arrange each vegetable on a steamer rack and steam over about 2 inches boiling water until barely tender to bite (allow 7 to 10 minutes for cauliflower, 4 to 6 minutes for carrots and artichokes). As each vegetable is cooked, immerse it in cold water until cool, then drain well.

Arrange steamed vegetables and tomatoes in separate rows in a 9- by 13-inch dish or on a platter. Prepare Tarragon Dressing and pour over all. Cover and refrigerate for at least 4 hours or until next day. Makes 6 to 8 servings.—T. S., Tacoma, WA

TARRAGON DRESSING. In a small bowl, stir together ⅔ cup **olive oil** or salad oil; ⅓ cup **tarragon wine vinegar;** 1 clove **garlic**, minced or pressed; 1½ tablespoons **Dijon mustard;** ½ teaspoon **salt;** 1 tablespoon minced **fresh tarragon** or 1 teaspoon dry tarragon; and ¼ teaspoon **pepper.**

Per serving: 248 calories, 14 g carbohydrates, 3 g protein, 21 g total fat (3 g saturated), 0 mg cholesterol, 282 mg sodium

CHILLED BROCCOLI CHEESE SALAD

This broccoli dish works well as either a salad or a cold vegetable. Try it with grilled chicken or a broiled steak such as Barbecue Steak Western (page 71).

1½ pounds fresh broccoli
¼ cup salad oil
3 tablespoons lemon juice
2 tablespoons thinly sliced green onion
¼ teaspoon *each* garlic salt and dry mustard
⅛ teaspoon pepper
Red oak leaf or butter lettuce leaves, rinsed and crisped
3 tablespoons crumbled blue-veined cheese
2 hard-cooked large eggs, finely chopped
Sliced radishes

Trim and discard tough ends of broccoli stalks. Peel stalks; then cut broccoli into bite-size (2- to 3-inch-long) pieces. Arrange broccoli on a steamer rack and steam over about 1 inch boiling water until barely tender when pierced (about 5 minutes). Immerse broccoli in cold water until cool, then drain well. Cover and refrigerate until cold or until next day.

In a small bowl, stir together oil, lemon juice, onion, garlic salt, mustard, and pepper. If made ahead, cover and refrigerate until next day.

About an hour before serving, divide broccoli equally among 6 lettuce-lined individual plates.

Stir dressing and spoon evenly over broccoli. Sprinkle salads evenly with cheese and eggs and garnish with radishes. Makes 6 servings. —*K. S., Los Angeles*

Per serving: 143 calories, 5 g carbohydrates, 5 g protein, 12 g total fat (3 g saturated), 74 mg cholesterol, 159 mg sodium

GREEN BEAN SALAD WITH YOGURT-DILL DRESSING

Flowers found their way into salads in the 1980s. Nasturtiums, we've discovered, make a vivid, delicately spicy accent for green salads or cold vegetable combinations like this one—a mixture of tender green beans and tomatoes in a tart yogurt dressing.

1½ pounds green beans, ends trimmed
Dill Dressing (recipe follows)
1 can (about 3½ oz.) pitted ripe olives, drained
1 large firm-ripe tomato (about 8 oz.), cut into wedges
⅓ cup chopped walnuts
Salt
Nasturtium blossoms (pesticide-free), rinsed and gently patted dry; or dill sprigs

In a 5- to 6-quart pan, cook beans, uncovered, in about 3 quarts boiling water until just tender to bite (3 to 5 minutes). Drain, immerse in cold water until cool, and drain again. Then cut beans diagonally into 3-inch lengths.

Prepare Dill Dressing.

Place beans in a large bowl and add olives, tomato, walnuts, and dressing. Mix gently, then season to taste with salt. Garnish with nasturtiums. Makes 6 to 8 servings.—*Karen Lohmann, Olympia, WA*

DILL DRESSING. In a small bowl, stir together ½ cup **plain yogurt,** 2 tablespoons **olive oil** or salad oil, 3 tablespoons chopped **fresh dill** or 1 tablespoon dry dill weed, 2 tablespoons **lemon juice,** and ½ teaspoon **pepper.**

Per serving: 132 calories, 11 g carbohydrates, 3 g protein, 10 g total fat (1 g saturated), 2 mg cholesterol, 142 mg sodium

THREE-BEAN SALAD

Nearly 40 years old, this recipe is the simple, classic three-bean salad many of us remember from childhood. To make it, you just mix canned green, wax, and kidney beans with a sweet-sour vinaigrette, then chill to blend the flavors. The original suggests, "You may like to add a little sliced celery for additional crunchiness." (In keeping with modern tastes in salad dressings, we've decreased the quantities of sugar and oil in this recipe.)

1 can (about 15 oz.) cut green beans
1 can (about 15 oz.) cut yellow wax beans or garbanzo beans
1 can (about 15 oz.) red kidney beans
1 small green bell pepper (about 5 oz.), seeded and finely chopped
1 small onion, finely chopped
¼ cup *each* sugar and salad oil
⅓ cup distilled white vinegar
½ teaspoon salt
¼ teaspoon pepper

Pour green beans, wax beans, and kidney beans into a colander to drain; rinse well. Drain again, then place in a large glass (or other nonmetallic) bowl. Add bell pepper and onion; mix gently until ingredients are evenly combined.

In a small bowl, stir together sugar, oil, vinegar, salt, and pepper until sugar is dissolved; pour dressing over bean mixture and mix gently. Cover and refrigerate until ready to serve. For best flavor, prepare salad a day in advance to give vegetables time to absorb flavor. To serve, use a slotted spoon to lift salad from dressing in bowl and spoon onto individual plates. Makes 10 to 12 servings.—*J. W. D., Winthrop, WA*

Per serving: 105 calories, 13 g carbohydrates, 3 g protein, 5 g total fat (0.6 g saturated), 0 mg cholesterol, 262 mg sodium

JICAMA-PEA SALAD

Just four ingredients—jicama, green peas, seasoned vinegar, and mint—go into this refreshing salad. Make it with either fresh or frozen peas.

1½ cups peeled, diced jicama
¾ cup seasoned rice vinegar (or ¾ cup unseasoned rice vinegar plus 2 tablespoons sugar)
About 1½ pounds unshelled peas; or 1 package (about 10 oz.) frozen tiny peas, thawed
¼ cup finely chopped fresh mint
8 to 16 large butter lettuce leaves, rinsed and crisped
Mint sprigs

In a bowl, combine jicama and vinegar; let stand for at least 15 minutes or up to 5 hours.

If using fresh peas, shell them; you need 2 cups. In a 2- to 3-quart pan, cook shelled peas in about 1 inch boiling water, uncovered, stirring occasionally, just until peas are bright green and heated through (2 to 3 minutes). Drain, immerse in cold water until cool, and drain again. (Don't cook frozen peas.)

Mix peas and chopped mint into jicama mixture. To serve, use a slotted spoon to lift salad from dressing in bowl and spoon onto 8 lettuce-lined individual plates. Garnish with mint

sprigs. Spoon any extra dressing over salads, if desired. Makes 8 servings.—*Gloria Thomasson, Tucson*

Per serving: 54 calories, 11 g carbohydrates, 2 g protein, 0.2 g total fat (0 g saturated), 0 mg cholesterol, 448 mg sodium

GREEN PEA SALAD

A crisp red apple, some onion, and a touch of horseradish transform a package of frozen peas into a delicious and unusual salad. If you like, use plain yogurt in place of the sour cream (sweeten the yogurt with ½ teaspoon honey or sugar, if desired).

1 package (about 10 oz.) frozen tiny peas
1 tart red-skinned apple, cored and chopped
3 green onions, thinly sliced
½ cup sour cream
½ to 1 teaspoon prepared horseradish
¼ teaspoon salt
⅛ teaspoon pepper
2 teaspoons lemon juice
Salad greens of your choice, rinsed and crisped

Turn peas out of package into a colander or strainer; run hottest tap water over them just until they're thawed. Rinse peas with cold water, then drain well. (To speed up draining, you might roll the peas on paper towels to absorb extra moisture.) In a large bowl, combine peas, apple, and onions.

In a small bowl, stir together sour cream, horseradish, salt, pepper, and lemon juice; pour dressing over pea mixture and mix gently. To serve, mound salad in a bowl lined with greens. Makes 4 to 6 servings.—*A. L., Aptos, CA*

Per serving: 106 calories, 12 g carbohydrates, 4 g protein, 5 g total fat (3 g saturated), 10 mg cholesterol, 199 mg sodium

CRISP KRAUT SALAD

To make this crunchy, sweet-tart salad even more colorful, top it with ripe tomato wedges or slices just before serving.

1 can (about 14½ oz.) sauerkraut
1 jar (about 2 oz.) sliced pimentos, drained
½ cup chopped onion or thinly sliced green onions
¾ cup sliced celery
1 cup coarsely shredded carrots
1 medium-size green bell pepper (about 6 oz.), seeded and sliced
¼ cup cider vinegar
½ cup sugar
¾ teaspoon salt
⅛ teaspoon pepper
Iceberg lettuce leaves and chopped parsley (optional)

Pour sauerkraut into a strainer and drain, pressing out all liquid. Then place sauerkraut in a large bowl and add pimentos, onion, celery, carrots, and bell pepper. In a small bowl, stir together vinegar, sugar, salt, and pepper until sugar is dissolved; pour dressing over sauerkraut mixture. Mix gently. Cover and refrigerate for at least 30 minutes or up to 6 hours. If desired, serve salad in a lettuce-lined bowl and sprinkle with parsley. Makes 8 servings.—*H. S., Bishop, CA*

Per serving: 71 calories, 18 g carbohydrates, 0.7 g protein, 0.1 g total fat (0 g saturated), 0 mg cholesterol, 338 mg sodium

POTATO SALAD WITH OREGANO VINAIGRETTE

If you prefer your potato salad without distracting elements, you'll relish this pristine interpretation—just cubed red-skinned potatoes in an herbed vinaigrette with sweet red onion. It's a good partner for beef burgers, Sesame Flank Steak (page 71), or Oven-barbecued Chicken (page 99).

2 **pounds medium-size red thin-skinned potatoes, scrubbed**
⅓ **cup olive oil or salad oil**
¼ **cup white wine vinegar or lemon juice**
1 **tablespoon minced fresh oregano or 1½ teaspoons dry oregano**
1 **tablespoon minced parsley**
   Salt and pepper
⅓ **cup diced red onion**
   Oregano sprigs (optional)

Place unpeeled potatoes in a 5- to 6-quart pan and add enough water to cover. Bring to a boil over high heat; then reduce heat, partially cover, and boil gently until potatoes are tender when pierced (25 to 30 minutes). Drain and let stand until cool enough to handle, but still warm; then peel potatoes and cut into about ½-inch chunks.

In a large bowl, stir together oil, vinegar, minced oregano, and parsley. Add warm potatoes and mix gently; season to taste with salt and pepper. Mound onion in center of salad; then garnish salad with oregano sprigs, if desired. If made ahead, cover and let stand for up to 4 hours. Mix onion into salad before serving. Makes 4 to 6 servings.—*Jackie Tieger, Buena Park, CA*

Per serving: 266 calories, 31 g carbohydrates, 3 g protein, 15 g total fat (2 g saturated), 0 mg cholesterol, 14 mg sodium

RED POTATO SALAD WITH YOGURT

A creamy, thyme-scented yogurt dressing flavors this simple salad.

2 **pounds large red thin-skinned potatoes, scrubbed**
½ **cup *each* plain yogurt and mayonnaise**
3 **tablespoons unseasoned rice vinegar (or 3 tablespoons white wine vinegar plus 1 teaspoon sugar)**
2 **cloves garlic, minced or pressed**
1 **tablespoon minced fresh thyme or 1 teaspoon dry thyme**
½ **cup *each* thinly sliced green onions and thinly sliced celery**
   Salt and pepper

Place unpeeled potatoes in a 5- to 6-quart pan and add enough water to cover. Bring to a boil over high heat; then reduce heat, partially cover, and boil gently until potatoes are tender when pierced (25 to 30 minutes). Drain, immerse in cold water until cool, and drain again. Then cut potatoes into ¾-inch cubes.

In a large bowl, stir together yogurt, mayonnaise, vinegar, garlic, thyme, onions, and celery. Add potatoes and mix gently. Season to taste with salt and pepper. If made ahead, cover and refrigerate until next day. Makes 6 servings.—*Kathy Cooper, Ashland, OR*

Per serving: 279 calories, 32 g carbohydrates, 4 g protein, 16 g total fat (3 g saturated), 13 mg cholesterol, 284 mg sodium

CRUNCHY POTATO SALAD

The potatoes, eggs, and onions are traditional for potato salad—but for extra crunch, this recipe also includes cubes of jicama and a garnish of salted peanuts.

2 **large white thin-skinned potatoes (about 1 lb. *total*), scrubbed**
6 **hard-cooked large eggs, chopped**
1 **medium-size green bell pepper (about 6 oz.), seeded and chopped**
½ **cup sliced green onions**
⅔ **cup peeled, cubed jicama**
6 **to 8 radishes, sliced**
   Creamy Dressing (recipe follows)
   Salt and pepper
   Chopped salted peanuts

Place unpeeled potatoes in a 4- to 5-quart pan and add enough water to cover. Bring to a boil over high heat; then reduce heat, partially cover, and boil gently until potatoes are tender when pierced (25 to 30 minutes). Drain, immerse in cold water until cool, and drain again.

Peel potatoes, cut into ½-inch cubes, and place in a large bowl; mix in eggs, bell pepper, onions, jicama, and radishes.

Prepare Creamy Dressing and pour over potato mixture; mix gently. Season to taste with salt and pepper. Cover and refrigerate for at least 2 hours or until next day. Just before serving, sprinkle salad with peanuts. Makes 6 servings.—*M. S., China Lake, CA*

CREAMY DRESSING. In a small bowl, stir together ½ cup **sour cream,** ¼ cup **mayonnaise,** ¼ cup drained **sweet pickle relish,** 1 teaspoon **Dijon mustard,** and ¼ teaspoon **liquid hot pepper seasoning.**

Per serving: 273 calories, 22 g carbohydrates, 9 g protein, 17 g total fat (5 g saturated), 226 mg cholesterol, 231 mg sodium

MINTED POTATO SALAD

This salad is a perfect complement for a leg of lamb roasted in a covered barbecue, and for simple grilled lamb chops, too. Pour the dressing—a tart blend of lemon, green onion, garlic, and mint—over the potatoes while they're still warm, so they'll absorb all the flavors.

- 4 pounds medium-size white thin-skinned potatoes, scrubbed
- ½ cup thinly sliced green onions
- 1 clove garlic, minced or pressed
- 6 tablespoons lemon juice
- ½ cup olive oil or salad oil
- 3 tablespoons chopped fresh mint or 1 tablespoon dry mint
- ½ teaspoon *each* sugar and pepper
- 1½ teaspoons salt
  About 1 cup thinly sliced radishes

Place unpeeled potatoes in a 6- to 8-quart pan and add enough water to cover. Bring to a boil over high heat; then reduce heat, partially cover, and boil gently until potatoes are tender when pierced (25 to 30 minutes). Drain and let stand until cool enough to handle, but still warm.

Meanwhile, in a small bowl, stir together onions, garlic, lemon juice, oil, mint, sugar, pepper, and salt.

Peel potatoes, cut into ½-inch cubes, and place in a large bowl. Pour dressing over warm potatoes and mix gently. Cover and refrigerate for at least 4 hours or until next day, stirring gently several times.

About 45 minutes before serving, add radish slices to salad and stir gently until evenly combined. Let stand at room temperature until serving time. Makes 8 to 10 servings.
—E. D., Saugus, CA

Per serving: 261 calories, 35 g carbohydrates, 4 g protein, 12 g total fat (2 g saturated), 0 mg cholesterol, 386 mg sodium

GINGER-SWEET POTATO SALAD

A spicy sherry-honey dressing complements this sweet potato salad. Crunchy with celery and roasted almonds, it's sure to perk up a day-after-Thanksgiving turkey supper.

- 2 pounds medium-size sweet potatoes or yams, scrubbed
- 1 cup *each* sliced green onions and thinly sliced celery
- ½ cup chopped dry-roasted almonds
- ⅓ cup *each* cream sherry and lemon juice
- ¼ cup salad oil
- 1 tablespoon honey
- 1 tablespoon minced fresh ginger or ½ teaspoon ground ginger
  Salt and pepper

Place unpeeled sweet potatoes in a 4- to 5-quart pan and add enough water to cover. Bring to a boil over high heat; then reduce heat, partially cover, and boil gently until potatoes are tender when pierced (25 to 30 minutes). Drain, immerse in cold water until cool, and drain again. Peel potatoes and cut into ½-inch cubes.

In a large bowl, stir together onions, celery, almonds, sherry, lemon juice, oil, honey, and ginger. Add potatoes and mix gently; season to taste with salt and pepper. If made ahead, cover and refrigerate for up to 6 hours. Makes 6 to 8 servings.
—Gladys Kent, Port Angeles, WA

Per serving: 258 calories, 31 g carbohydrates, 4 g protein, 13 g total fat (1 g saturated), 0 mg cholesterol, 34 mg sodium

WHITE BEAN SALAD

This salad, of Turkish origin, is best served at room temperature.

- 1¼ cups (about 8 oz.) dried small white beans
  Salt
- ¼ cup *each* olive oil and white wine vinegar
- 1 bunch green onions (ends trimmed), thinly sliced
- ¼ cup finely chopped parsley
- ⅛ teaspoon pepper
- 1 medium-size green bell pepper (about 6 oz.), seeded and cut into thin strips
- 1½ cups halved cherry tomatoes
- 2 hard-cooked large eggs, sliced
  About 8 pitted ripe olives

Sort through beans, discarding any debris. Rinse and drain beans. In a 4- to 5-quart pan, bring 4 cups water to a boil. Add beans; boil for 2 minutes. Remove from heat, cover, and let stand for 1 hour. Drain and rinse, discarding water.

In pan, dissolve 1 teaspoon salt in 3 cups water. Bring to a boil; add soaked beans, reduce heat, cover, and boil gently until beans are tender to bite (1 to 1½ hours). If necessary, add more water during cooking to keep beans submerged. Drain well.

Place beans in a large bowl; add oil, vinegar, onions, parsley, and pepper. Mix gently, then season to taste with salt. Cover and let stand for at least 2 hours or until next day.

With a slotted spoon, lift beans and onions from dressing (reserve dressing) and transfer to a serving bowl. Arrange bell pepper, tomatoes, eggs, and olives attractively over beans. Just before serving, drizzle some of the dressing over salad and mix gently. Makes 6 to 8 servings.
—M. B., Portola Valley, CA

Per serving: 236 calories, 27 g carbohydrates, 11 g protein, 10 g total fat (2 g saturated), 61 mg cholesterol, 304 mg sodium

Lentil & Black Bean Salad

Chinese fermented black beans bring pungent flavor to this East-meets-West salad. Dress the simple combination of lentils and ripe tomatoes with a fragrant raspberry vinaigrette.

- 1½ cups (about 12 oz.) lentils
- 3 cups chicken broth
  Raspberry Vinaigrette (recipe follows)
- 3 tablespoons fermented salted black beans or drained capers
- 2 medium-size firm-ripe tomatoes (about 12 oz. *total*)
  Salt and pepper
- ⅓ cup cilantro leaves

Sort through lentils, discarding any debris. Rinse and drain lentils. In a 2- to 3-quart pan, bring broth to a boil over high heat. Add lentils, reduce heat, cover, and simmer until lentils are tender to bite (about 30 minutes). Drain and let cool. Meanwhile, prepare Raspberry Vinaigrette.

Place black beans in a fine strainer and rinse thoroughly with cool water; drain. Cut a few thin slices from one of the tomatoes and set aside; then chop remaining tomatoes and place in a 2- to 3-quart bowl. Add black beans, lentils, and Raspberry Vinaigrette; mix gently. Season to taste with salt and pepper. Top with cilantro leaves and tomato slices. Makes 6 to 8 servings.—*Mary Harvey, Huntington Beach, CA*

RASPBERRY VINAIGRETTE. In a small bowl, stir together ⅓ cup *each* **raspberry vinegar** and **olive oil**; 2 cloves **garlic,** minced or pressed; and 2 teaspoons *each* minced **fresh thyme** and minced **fresh marjoram** (or ¾ teaspoon *each* of the dry herbs).

Per serving: 262 calories, 27 g carbohydrates, 13 g protein, 12 g total fat (1 g saturated), 0 mg cholesterol, 624 mg sodium

New Mexican Chili Bean Salad

Made with canned beans and corn, this generous dish is quick to put together when you need a salad for a party or potluck.

- New Mexican Dressing (recipe follows)
- 1 can (about 15 oz.) *each* garbanzo beans, red kidney beans, and pinto beans
- 1 can (about 17 oz.) whole-kernel corn
- ½ cup thinly sliced green onions
- ⅓ cup chopped cilantro
- 1 large red bell pepper (about 8 oz.), seeded and chopped
- 1 can (about 4 oz.) diced green chiles

Prepare New Mexican Dressing and set aside. Pour garbanzo beans, kidney beans, pinto beans, and corn into a colander to drain; rinse well. Drain again and pour into a large bowl. Mix in onions, cilantro, bell pepper, chiles, and New Mexican Dressing. Cover and refrigerate for at least 1 hour or until next day, stirring occasionally. Makes 10 to 12 servings. —*Jane E. Cook, Albuquerque*

NEW MEXICAN DRESSING. In a small bowl, stir together ¼ cup **red wine vinegar,** 2 tablespoons **salad oil,** ¼ teaspoon **pepper,** and 1 teaspoon *each* **chili powder, dry oregano,** and **ground cumin.**

Per serving: 143 calories, 23 g carbohydrates, 6 g protein, 4 g total fat (0.4 g saturated), 0 mg cholesterol, 339 mg sodium

Golden Couscous Salad

Here's a good-looking accompaniment for Roast Pork with Soy-Garlic Baste (page 83) or grilled pork tenderloin. Orange slices encircle a mound of spiced couscous studded with raisins, crisp cucumber, and green onions.

- 1¼ cups chicken broth
- 1 cup couscous
- ½ cup golden raisins
- 2 tablespoons finely chopped crystallized ginger
- 1 teaspoon grated orange peel
- ½ teaspoon ground cumin
- 3 tablespoons seasoned rice vinegar (or 3 tablespoons unseasoned rice vinegar plus 2 teaspoons sugar)
- 3 tablespoons orange juice
- ½ cup finely chopped cucumber
- ¼ cup thinly sliced green onions
- 4 large oranges (2 to 2½ lbs. *total*)
- 1 to 2 tablespoons chopped salted roasted almonds

In a 3- to 4-quart pan, bring broth to a boil over high heat. Stir in couscous, raisins, ginger, orange peel, and cumin; cover pan and remove from heat. Let stand until all liquid has been absorbed (about 5 minutes). Fluff couscous lightly with a fork; then stir in vinegar, orange juice, cucumber, and onions. (At this point, you may cover and let stand for up to 4 hours. Stir before using.)

Cut off and discard peel and all white membrane from oranges; thinly slice oranges crosswise. Arrange orange slices in a ring around edge of a rimmed platter; mound couscous mixture in center. Sprinkle salad with almonds. Makes 4 to 6 servings.—*Sally Vog, Springfield, OR*

Per serving: 315 calories, 67 g carbohydrates, 8 g protein, 3 g total fat (0.3 g saturated), 0 mg cholesterol, 462 mg sodium

Curried Rice Salad

This easy-to-make salad starts with a mix. For a heartier dish, you might stir in bite-size pieces of cooked chicken, ham, beef, or cheese.

- 1 package (about 7 oz.) chicken-flavored rice-and-vermicelli mix
  Butter or margarine and water called for on package of mix
- ½ teaspoon curry powder
- 1 jar (about 6 oz.) marinated artichoke hearts
- 10 pimento-stuffed green olives, sliced
- ½ cup chopped green bell pepper
- 4 green onions, sliced
- ¼ cup mayonnaise
  Lettuce leaves, rinsed and crisped
- 4 to 6 hard-cooked egg halves or deviled egg halves

Check rice-and-vermicelli mix instructions; measure out quantities of butter and water called for on package. Discard seasoning packet. Melt butter in a wide frying pan; stir in curry powder, then add rice mix and brown it according to package directions. Add water and cook as directed until rice is tender to bite. Remove from heat and let cool.

Meanwhile, drain artichokes, reserving marinade; cut artichokes into bite-size pieces. Stir artichokes, olives, bell pepper, and onions into cooled rice mixture.

Stir together artichoke marinade and mayonnaise; gently stir dressing into rice mixture. Transfer to a bowl, cover, and refrigerate for at least 6 hours or until next day.

To serve, mound rice mixture on a lettuce-lined platter; garnish with egg halves. Makes 4 to 6 servings. —D. T., Honolulu

Per serving: 382 calories, 34 g carbohydrates, 12 g protein, 23 g total fat (6 g saturated), 232 mg cholesterol, 1,099 mg sodium

Broccoli, Pasta & Bean Salad

Offer this sturdy salad as a side dish with barbecued chicken or ribs.

- 1 pound fresh broccoli
- 2 cups dry large shell-shaped pasta
- 1 can (about 15 oz.) red kidney beans, drained and rinsed
- ½ cup olive oil
- ¼ cup red wine vinegar
- 1 tablespoon Dijon mustard
- ½ teaspoon dry basil
  Salt and pepper

Trim and discard tough ends from broccoli stalks. Peel stalks, then thinly slice crosswise. Cut flowerets into bite-size pieces. Set broccoli aside.

In a 5- to 6-quart pan, cook pasta in about 3 quarts boiling water until just tender to bite (10 to 12 minutes); or cook according to package directions. Add broccoli; cook just until broccoli turns bright green (1 to 2 minutes). Drain pasta and broccoli; rinse with cold water until cool, then drain again. In a large bowl, mix pasta, broccoli, and beans.

In a small bowl, stir together oil, vinegar, mustard, and basil. Add to pasta mixture and mix gently. Season to taste with salt and pepper. If made ahead, cover and refrigerate for up to 2 hours. Makes 6 to 8 servings.—J. Heflin, Kirkland, WA

Per serving: 292 calories, 29 g carbohydrates, 8 g protein, 16 g total fat (2 g saturated), 0 mg cholesterol, 139 mg sodium

Hot Garbanzo & Pasta Salad

For a full-meal salad, spoon warm pasta in a chunky garbanzo sauce over a bed of crisp, cold romaine lettuce. Round out the menu with a crusty whole-grain loaf and glasses of iced tea or a fruity red wine.

- 8 to 10 large romaine lettuce leaves, rinsed and crisped
- 3 tablespoons olive oil, butter, or margarine
- 4 ounces cooked ham, finely diced
- ½ cup chopped onion
- 3 large cloves garlic, minced or pressed
- 1 can (about 15 oz.) garbanzo beans, drained and rinsed
- 2 beef bouillon cubes
- 1 cup water
- 2 to 3 cups cooked gnocchi-shaped pasta or macaroni
- ¼ cup minced parsley
- 2 to 4 lemon wedges
- ½ cup grated Parmesan cheese

Sliver enough stem ends of lettuce to make 2 cups; set aside. Then line a wide, shallow bowl with lettuce leaves, overlapping leaf tips around rim. Mound cut lettuce in center of leaves; cover and refrigerate.

Heat oil in a wide frying pan over medium heat. Add ham, onion, and garlic; cook, stirring often, until onion is soft (8 to 10 minutes). Add beans and bouillon cubes. With the back of a large spoon, mash beans slightly. Add water and bring to a boil, stirring to dissolve bouillon cubes. Add pasta and parsley; mix until pasta is heated through.

Spoon pasta mixture over cut lettuce in serving bowl. Offer lemon wedges and cheese to season salad to taste. Makes 2 to 4 servings.—Vera Hemphill, Napa, CA

Per serving: 661 calories, 78 g carbohydrates, 31 g protein, 25 g total fat (6 g saturated), 33 mg cholesterol, 1,560 mg sodium

TUNA NOODLE SALAD

Crusty rolls and iced tea go well with this crunchy whole-meal salad.

Relish Dressing (recipe follows)

4 ounces dry rotini or other small spiral-shaped pasta

1 large can (about 12½ oz.) water-packed chunk-style tuna, drained

1 package (about 10 oz.) frozen peas, thawed

½ cup *each* chopped green bell pepper, thinly sliced radishes, thinly sliced celery, thinly sliced mushrooms, and thinly sliced green onions

2 medium-size tomatoes (about 12 oz. *total*), cut into wedges

3 hard-cooked large eggs, sliced or cut into wedges

Prepare Relish Dressing and set aside.

In a 3½- to 5-quart pan, cook pasta in about 2 quarts boiling water until just tender to bite (8 to 10 minutes); or cook according to package directions. Drain well, rinse with cold water until cool, and drain again; then pour into a large bowl.

Break tuna into large chunks and distribute over pasta. Then add peas, bell pepper, radishes, celery, mushrooms, and onions. Spoon Relish Dressing over salad; mix gently until ingredients are evenly combined. Cover and refrigerate for at least 1 hour or up to 6 hours.

To serve, mix salad again; then garnish with tomatoes and eggs. Makes 6 to 8 servings.—*E. H., Sunnyvale, CA*

RELISH DRESSING. In a small bowl, stir together ¾ cup **mayonnaise,** ½ cup **tomato-based chili sauce,** ⅓ cup drained **sweet pickle relish,** and ½ teaspoon **prepared horseradish.** Season to taste with **salt** and **pepper.**

Per serving: 409 calories, 31 g carbohydrates, 22 g protein, 22 g total fat (4 g saturated), 139 mg cholesterol, 729 mg sodium

ANTIPASTO PASTA SALAD

Inspired by a typical Italian antipasto selection, this tempting salad combines vegetables, prosciutto, cheese, and pasta in a fruity vinaigrette.

Cooked Artichoke Hearts (recipe follows); or 1 can (about 14 oz.) water-packed artichoke hearts, drained and cut into quarters

5 cups cooked, cooled rotini or other small spiral-shaped pasta

1 cup pitted ripe olives

3 cups cooked, cooled fresh broccoli flowerets

4 ounces mushrooms, thinly sliced

1 cup quartered cherry tomatoes

2 ounces prosciutto or cooked ham, cut into thin strips

1 cup (about 4 oz.) finely shredded Asiago or Parmesan cheese

Raspberry-Basil Vinaigrette (recipe follows)

Prepare Cooked Artichoke Hearts.

In a large bowl, mix artichokes, pasta, olives, broccoli, mushrooms, tomatoes, prosciutto, and cheese. Prepare Raspberry-Basil Vinaigrette; pour over salad and mix gently. If made ahead, cover and refrigerate until next day. Makes 8 to 10 servings.—*Lee McGill, Lake Almanor Peninsula, CA*

COOKED ARTICHOKE HEARTS. You will need 10 small **artichokes** (*each* about 2 inches in diameter). Break off tough outer leaves from each artichoke until you reach the pale, edible inner leaves. Trim thorny tips from leaves; peel artichoke bottoms. In a 4- to 5-quart pan, cook artichokes in about 2 quarts boiling water, uncovered, until tender when pierced (about 20 minutes). Drain and let cool; cut into quarters.

RASPBERRY-BASIL VINAIGRETTE. In a small bowl, stir together ½ cup **raspberry vinegar,** ⅔ cup **olive oil,** 1½ teaspoons **dry basil,** and ¼ teaspoon **pepper.**

Per serving: 395 calories, 35 g carbohydrates, 14 g protein, 23 g total fat (5 g saturated), 14 mg cholesterol, 483 mg sodium

SOBA NOODLE SALAD

If you can't find soba—slender Japanese buckwheat noodles—make this cool Asian salad with capellini.

8 ounces dry soba noodles or capellini (angel hair pasta)

1½ cups julienne slivers of red or green bell peppers

½ cup *each* thinly sliced celery and thinly sliced green onions

1 teaspoon Oriental sesame oil

2 tablespoons *each* oyster sauce, soy sauce, and lemon juice

½ cup salted roasted cashews

In a 4- to 5-quart pan, cook pasta in about 2 quarts boiling water until just tender to bite (about 5 minutes for soba, about 3 minutes for capellini); or cook according to package directions. Drain well, rinse with cold water until cool, and drain again. In a serving bowl, mix pasta, bell peppers, celery, and onions.

In a small bowl, stir together oil, oyster sauce, soy sauce, and lemon juice; pour over salad and mix gently. Sprinkle with cashews. Makes 4 servings.—*Maureen Valentine, SeaTac, WA*

Per serving: 346 calories, 54 g carbohydrates, 12 g protein, 10 g total fat (2 g saturated), 0 mg cholesterol, 994 mg sodium

Tortellini Salad

Cheese- or meat-filled tortellini, shiny ripe olives, and a variety of colorful vegetables go into this hearty entrée salad.

- 4 cups fresh broccoli flowerets
- 1 jar (about 6 oz.) marinated artichoke hearts
  Basil-Mustard Dressing (recipe follows)
- 4 cups cooked, cooled cheese- or meat-filled tortellini
- 1½ cups *each* sliced mushrooms and quartered cherry tomatoes
- 1 can (about 6 oz.) medium-size pitted ripe olives, drained
  Salt

In a 4- to 5-quart pan, cook broccoli in about 2 quarts boiling water until tender-crisp to bite (2 to 3 minutes). Drain, immerse in cold water until cool, and drain again. Set aside.

Drain artichokes, reserving marinade for Basil-Mustard Dressing; then prepare dressing. In a large bowl, combine artichokes, tortellini, mushrooms, tomatoes, olives, and Basil-Mustard Dressing. (At this point, you may cover and refrigerate broccoli and tortellini mixture separately until next day.)

To serve, mix broccoli into tortellini mixture; season to taste with salt. Makes 4 to 6 servings.—*Donna Shapiro, Phoenix*

BASIL-MUSTARD DRESSING.
Measure **reserved artichoke marinade** and add enough **salad oil** to make ⅓ cup. Pour into a small bowl and stir in ⅓ cup **red wine vinegar**, 1 tablespoon *each* **Dijon mustard** and **dry basil**, 2 teaspoons **lemon juice**, and ½ teaspoon **pepper.**

Per serving: 431 calories, 59 g carbohydrates, 21 g protein, 14 g total fat (1 g saturated), 51 mg cholesterol, 993 mg sodium

Spinach Pesto Pasta Salad

When fresh basil is hard to find, whirl together a pungent spinach dressing to cloak a salad of linguine, black olives, and halved cherry tomatoes. The dish makes a delicious vegetarian entrée, and it's just as good as an accompaniment for a platter of thin-sliced deli meats.

- 1 pound dry linguine
- 1 cup firmly packed chopped fresh spinach
- 3 tablespoons dry basil
- 1 or 2 cloves garlic, peeled
- ⅓ cup *each* grated Parmesan cheese and olive oil
- ½ cup drained, chopped dried tomatoes packed in oil (optional)
- 1 can (about 2¼ oz.) sliced ripe olives, drained
- 2 cups cherry tomatoes, cut into halves
  Salt and pepper

In a 6- to 8-quart pan, cook linguine in about 4 quarts boiling water until just tender to bite (8 to 10 minutes); or cook according to package directions. Drain, rinse with cold water until cool, and drain again. Set aside.

In a food processor or blender, combine spinach, basil, garlic, cheese, and oil. Whirl until smoothly puréed, scraping down sides of work bowl as needed.

In a large bowl, combine linguine, spinach pesto, dried tomatoes (if

used), olives, and cherry tomatoes. Mix gently; season to taste with salt and pepper. Makes 8 to 10 servings. —*Lois Dowling, Tacoma, WA*

Per serving: 291 calories, 41 g carbohydrates, 8 g protein, 11 g total fat (2 g saturated), 2 mg cholesterol, 132 mg sodium

Taco Salad

This old favorite combines a hot meat sauce and shredded Cheddar cheese with cold, crisp lettuce. If you prefer a spicier flavor, you might add diced fresh or canned chiles to the beef mixture.

- 1 pound lean ground beef
- ¼ cup finely chopped onion
- ½ teaspoon salt
- 2 teaspoons chili powder
- 1 can (about 8 oz.) tomato sauce
- 1 medium-size head iceberg lettuce, shredded
- ⅓ cup shredded Cheddar cheese
- 2 medium-size tomatoes (about 12 oz. *total*), peeled and cut into wedges
- 1 avocado, pitted, peeled, and sliced (optional)
- 1½ to 2 cups corn chips or tortilla chips

Crumble beef into a wide nonstick frying pan; add onion. Cook over medium-high heat, stirring often, until meat is no longer pink and onion is soft (about 7 minutes). Stir in salt, chili powder, and tomato sauce. Bring to a simmer; keep hot.

Divide lettuce equally among 4 individual plates. Top lettuce evenly with hot meat mixture; sprinkle with cheese. On each salad, arrange a fourth each of the tomato wedges and avocado slices (if used). Arrange corn chips around salads and serve immediately. Makes 4 servings. —*A. R., Alhambra, CA*

Per serving: 496 calories, 24 g carbohydrates, 27 g protein, 33 g total fat (12 g saturated), 95 mg cholesterol, 894 mg sodium

Chicken & Avocado Salad

Since the glamour days of Hollywood's Brown Derby Restaurant in the 1930s, Cobb Salad has been a Western favorite. No wonder, then, that decades later it's still inspiring variations such as this one, made with gently steeped chicken breasts.

- 4 **chicken breast halves (about 2 lbs. total)**
  Blue Cheese Dressing (recipe follows)
- 3 **quarts bite-size pieces of rinsed, crisped romaine lettuce**
- 1 **firm-ripe avocado, pitted, peeled, and sliced**
- 1 **hard-cooked large egg, chopped**
- 6 **slices bacon, crisply cooked, drained, and crumbled**

In a 5- to 6-quart pan, bring 3 quarts water to a boil over high heat. Rinse chicken and add to water; return to a boil. Then cover pan tightly, remove from heat, and let stand until meat in thickest part is no longer pink; cut to test (about 20 minutes). If chicken is not done after 20 minutes, return it to water, cover pan, and let stand longer, checking at 2- to 3-minute intervals.

Remove chicken from water and let stand until cool enough to handle. Then discard skin and bones and tear meat into thin shreds. (At this point, you may cover and refrigerate until next day.)

Prepare Blue Cheese Dressing. Place lettuce in a large bowl; mound chicken over lettuce. Scatter avocado, egg, and bacon over chicken. Pour dressing over salad; mix gently. Makes 6 servings.—*Kelly McCabe, Portland*

BLUE CHEESE DRESSING. In a small bowl, stir together ½ cup **olive oil** or salad oil, ¼ cup **white wine vinegar,** 1 teaspoon **Dijon mustard,** ¼ teaspoon **pepper,** and ¼ cup crumbled **blue-veined cheese.**

Per serving: 421 calories, 6 g carbohydrates, 29 g protein, 32 g total fat (6 g saturated), 106 mg cholesterol, 275 mg sodium

Chicken Salad with Sesame Dressing

Toasted sesame seeds, lemon peel, and lemon juice make a refreshing dressing for this entrée salad. Enhancing the tender chicken are crisp celery, sweet kiwi fruit, and creamy avocado.

- **Sesame Dressing (recipe follows)**
- 3 **quarts bite-size pieces of rinsed, crisped leaf lettuce**
- 4 **large kiwi fruit**
- 2 **cups shredded cooked chicken**
- 1 **large firm-ripe avocado, pitted, peeled, and sliced**
- 1 **cup thinly sliced celery**
- ⅓ **cup thinly sliced green onions**

Prepare Sesame Dressing; set aside.

Place lettuce in a wide serving bowl. Peel kiwi fruit with a sharp knife; then thinly slice crosswise. Arrange kiwi fruit, chicken, avocado, celery, and onions on top of lettuce. Pour Sesame Dressing over salad and mix gently. Makes 4 to 6 servings.—*R. A. Ross, Sonora, CA*

SESAME DRESSING. In a small frying pan, combine 3 tablespoons **sesame seeds** and ⅓ cup **salad oil.** Cook over low heat, stirring often, until seeds are golden (5 to 8 minutes). Remove from heat and let cool. Then stir in ½ teaspoon *each* **grated lemon peel** and **dry mustard,** ¼ cup **lemon juice,** and 1 tablespoon *each* **sugar** and **soy sauce.** Season to taste with **salt.**

Per serving: 434 calories, 25 g carbohydrates, 21 g protein, 30 g total fat (5 g saturated), 50 mg cholesterol, 300 mg sodium

Tarragon Hazelnut Chicken Salad

The orange-accented dressing for this main-dish salad is lightened with nonfat yogurt and reduced-calorie mayonnaise.

- 1 **cup hazelnuts**
  Tarragon Dressing (recipe follows)
- 3 **cups bite-size pieces of cooked chicken**
- ½ **cup thinly sliced green onions**
  Salt
  Large lettuce leaves, rinsed and crisped

Spread hazelnuts in a shallow baking pan and toast in a 350° oven until pale golden beneath skins (about 10 minutes). Let nuts cool slightly; then rub off as much of skins as possible with your fingers. Coarsely chop nuts and set aside.

Prepare Tarragon Dressing. To dressing, add chicken, onions, and ⅔ cup of the hazelnuts; mix gently, then season to taste with salt. Spoon salad onto lettuce-lined individual plates and sprinkle with remaining ⅓ cup hazelnuts. Makes 4 to 6 servings.—*Emily Bader, Bothell, WA*

TARRAGON DRESSING. In a large bowl, stir together ½ cup **plain nonfat yogurt;** ¼ cup **reduced-calorie or regular mayonnaise;** 2 tablespoons *each* **frozen orange juice**

concentrate (thawed) and **white wine vinegar;** 1 tablespoon minced **fresh tarragon** or 1 teaspoon dry tarragon; and ½ teaspoon **ground white pepper.**

Per serving: 367 calories, 10 g carbohydrates, 29 g protein, 24 g total fat (4 g saturated), 79 mg cholesterol, 157 mg sodium

CHICKEN-CURRY SALAD

To heighten the flavors of this delicate salad, prepare it several hours before serving. The original recipe notes: "For a women's luncheon, you might arrange 1 or 2 canned peach halves on each plate with the salad, and serve with hot crescent rolls and coffee or orange-flavored tea."

  4 to 5 cups large chunks of cooked chicken or turkey
  2 teaspoons grated onion
  1 cup *each* diagonally sliced celery and finely chopped green bell pepper
  ¼ cup half-and-half
  ⅔ cup mayonnaise
  ½ teaspoon salt
  ⅛ teaspoon pepper
  1 teaspoon curry powder
  2 tablespoons white wine vinegar
     Salad greens of your choice, rinsed and crisped

In a large bowl, combine chicken, onion, celery, and bell pepper. In a small bowl, stir together half-and-half, mayonnaise, salt, pepper, curry powder, and vinegar. Add dressing to chicken mixture; mix lightly. Cover and refrigerate for at least 1 hour or up to 4 hours. To serve, spoon salad into a serving bowl or onto individual plates; surround with greens. Makes 6 to 8 servings. —*K. P., Lewiston, ID*

Per serving: 342 calories, 3 g carbohydrates, 27 g protein, 24 g total fat (5 g saturated), 96 mg cholesterol, 372 mg sodium

STIR-FRIED TURKEY SALAD

Contrast hot-from-the-skillet turkey with cold lettuce and a pungent dressing to make this supper salad.

     Creamy Mustard Dressing (recipe follows)
  3 quarts bite-size pieces of rinsed, crisped butter lettuce
  1 large firm-ripe tomato (about 8 oz.), cut into wedges
  1 large firm-ripe avocado, pitted, peeled, and sliced
  ¼ cup thinly sliced green onions
  4 slices bacon, cut into thin slivers
  1 pound turkey thigh, skinned, boned, trimmed of fat, and cut into thin strips
  ¼ cup grated Parmesan cheese

Prepare Creamy Mustard Dressing; set aside.

In a large bowl, arrange lettuce, tomato, avocado, and onions.

Cook bacon in a wide frying pan or wok over medium-high heat, stirring often, until crisp (about 4 minutes). With a slotted spoon, lift out bacon and set aside. Pour off and discard all but 1 tablespoon drippings from pan.

Increase heat to high. Add turkey to pan and stir until lightly browned (3 to 4 minutes); pour turkey and any pan juices over lettuce mixture. Pour Creamy Mustard Dressing over salad; add cheese and bacon, then mix gently. Makes 4 to 6 servings.—*Mary Benham, Spokane, WA*

CREAMY MUSTARD DRESSING.
In a small bowl, stir together ¼ cup **olive oil,** 3 tablespoons *each* **mayonnaise** and **white wine vinegar,** 1 tablespoon **Dijon mustard,** and 1 teaspoon **dry thyme.**

Per serving: 446 calories, 10 g carbohydrates, 25 g protein, 35 g total fat (7 g saturated), 82 mg cholesterol, 378 mg sodium

COOL CURRY TURKEY SALAD

Accompanied by slender wedges of honeydew melon, a piquant turkey-rice salad makes a tempting light dinner for a warm evening. Another time, you might prepare it with chicken.

  2   tablespoons butter or margarine
  1   tablespoon *each* minced fresh ginger and curry powder
  2   cups diced cooked turkey or chicken
  2½ cups cold cooked rice
  1   cup plain nonfat yogurt
  ¾   cup thinly sliced green onions
  ½   cup thinly sliced water chestnuts
  ¼   teaspoon salt
      Dash of pepper
  1   small honeydew melon (about 2½ lbs.), seeded, cut into slender wedges, and peeled
      Romaine lettuce leaves, rinsed and crisped

Melt butter in in a medium-size frying pan over medium heat. Add ginger and curry powder. Cook, stirring, just until seasonings are lightly browned (about 1 minute). Remove from heat and let cool slightly.

In a large bowl, combine ginger–curry powder mixture, turkey, rice, yogurt, ½ cup of the onions, water chestnuts, salt, and pepper; mix gently to blend. Cover and refrigerate turkey mixture and remaining ¼ cup onions separately for at least 1 hour or up to 3 hours.

Just before serving, arrange melon wedges on one side of a platter. Line other side of platter with lettuce leaves; mound turkey mixture atop lettuce. Garnish with remaining ¼ cup onions. Makes 6 servings.—*Geri Ellen Howard, Portland*

Per serving: 262 calories, 32 g carbohydrates, 19 g protein, 7 g total fat (3 g saturated), 47 mg cholesterol, 207 mg sodium

TURKEY-GRAPE SALAD

Grate a little fragrant nutmeg over servings of this hot-weather salad.

- ½ cup slivered almonds
- 4 cups cubed cooked turkey
- 3 stalks celery, cut into thin slanting slices
- ½ cup *each* mayonnaise and sour cream
- 3 tablespoons lemon juice
   Romaine lettuce leaves, rinsed and crisped
- 2 cups seedless grapes
- 1 whole nutmeg

Toast almonds in a wide frying pan over medium heat, stirring often, until golden (about 5 minutes). Pour out of pan and set aside.

In a large bowl, combine turkey and celery. In a small bowl, stir together mayonnaise, sour cream, and lemon juice. Pour dressing over turkey mixture; mix well. (At this point, you may cover and refrigerate until next day.)

To serve, line each of 6 individual plates with 3 or 4 lettuce leaves. Spoon turkey salad equally onto plates; top each serving with ⅓ cup of the grapes, then sprinkle salads evenly with almonds. Pass nutmeg with a grater to grate over individual servings. Makes 6 servings.—*J. B., Santa Rosa, CA*

Per serving: 440 calories, 14 g carbohydrates, 31 g protein, 29 g total fat (7 g saturated), 92 mg cholesterol, 206 mg sodium

SMOKED SALMON & CHEESE SALAD

This striking combination may remind you of a sophisticated Caesar salad. Mixed greens are tossed with pungent Gorgonzola, pine nuts, slivers of smoked salmon—and freshly toasted French bread croutons that taste so good they're worth the extra trouble!

- 2 tablespoons pine nuts
- 1 cup (about 1¼ oz.) ½-inch cubes French bread
- 6 tablespoons olive oil
- 2 ounces sliced smoked salmon
- 3 ounces Gorgonzola cheese, crumbled
- 2 quarts bite-size pieces of rinsed, crisped romaine lettuce
- 2 cups bite-size pieces of rinsed, crisped Belgian endive
- ½ cup thinly sliced green onions
- 3 tablespoons white wine vinegar
- 1 teaspoon Dijon mustard
   Salt and pepper

Toast pine nuts in a medium-size frying pan over medium heat, stirring often, until golden (3 to 5 minutes). Pour out of pan and set aside. Add bread cubes and 1 tablespoon of the oil to pan. Cook, stirring often, until bread is golden (about 5 minutes). Remove from pan and set aside.

Cut salmon into ½-inch-wide strips and place in a large bowl. Add pine nuts, bread cubes, cheese, lettuce, endive, and onions.

In a small bowl, stir together remaining 5 tablespoons oil, vinegar, and mustard until well blended; pour over salad and mix gently but thoroughly. Season to taste with salt and pepper. Makes 6 servings. —*Susie Cabell, Boulder, CO*

Per serving: 233 calories, 7 g carbohydrates, 8 g protein, 20 g total fat (5 g saturated), 15 mg cholesterol, 335 mg sodium

CRAB LOUIS WITH CREAMY DRESSING

If you have leftover dressing, store it in the refrigerator for several days; it's delicious with salads of shrimp or other seafood, chicken, or mixed greens.

   Louis Dressing (recipe follows)
- 1 large head iceberg lettuce
- 1½ to 2 pounds cooked crabmeat
- 4 hard-cooked large eggs, cut into slices or wedges
   About 12 large pitted ripe olives
   Paprika

Prepare Louis Dressing.

Remove outside leaves of lettuce and divide equally among 6 individual plates. Then shred remaining lettuce and pile inside lettuce leaves on each plate.

Arrange crab equally atop lettuce, placing the nicest leg pieces on top. Arrange eggs and olives on each serving and dust lightly with paprika. If made ahead, cover and refrigerate for up to 2 hours. At the table, offer dressing to add to taste. Makes 6 servings.—*L. W., Albany, CA*

LOUIS DRESSING. In a medium-size bowl, stir together 1 cup **mayonnaise;** 3 tablespoons **tomato-based chili sauce;** 1 tablespoon *each* **Worcestershire** and **lemon juice;** ½ **green bell pepper**, seeded and finely chopped; 1 **canned pimento,** diced; and ⅛ teaspoon **salt.**

In a small bowl, beat ½ cup **whipping cream** until softly whipped; fold into dressing. Cover and refrigerate while you prepare salad. Makes about 1¾ cups.

Per serving of salad: 187 calories, 5 g carbohydrates, 27 g protein, 7 g total fat (1 g saturated), 245 mg cholesterol, 417 mg sodium

Per tablespoon of Louis Dressing: 74 calories, 1 g carbohydrates, 0.2 g protein, 8 g total fat (2 g saturated), 10 mg cholesterol, 87 mg sodium

MINTED TUNA SALAD

Fresh mint and lime give a refreshing flavor to this whole-meal salad. Serve it with a selection of your favorite crisp crackers and a pitcher of lemonade.

½ teaspoon grated lime peel
3 tablespoons lime juice
2 tablespoons chopped fresh mint
1 large can (about 12½ oz.) water-packed chunk-style tuna, drained
1½ cups cold cooked rice
1 cup *each* frozen peas (thawed) and thinly sliced celery
2 tablespoons *each* thinly sliced green onion and chopped parsley
   Tangy Dressing (recipe follows)
   Salt and pepper
   Salad greens of your choice, rinsed and crisped
   Mint sprigs

In a small bowl, stir together lime peel, lime juice, and chopped mint; set aside. In a large bowl, combine tuna, rice, peas, celery, onion, and parsley. Pour in lime-mint mixture, stir well, cover, and refrigerate for at least 2 hours or up to 4 hours. Meanwhile, prepare Tangy Dressing.

To serve, pour Tangy Dressing over tuna mixture and mix gently. Season to taste with salt and pepper. Spoon salad into a serving bowl lined with greens; garnish with mint sprigs. Makes 6 servings.—*H. N., San Francisco*

TANGY DRESSING. In a small bowl, stir together 1 teaspoon **Dijon mustard,** 2 teaspoons **sugar,** and ½ teaspoon **liquid hot pepper seasoning.** Gradually add ½ cup **mayonnaise** and ¼ cup **buttermilk,** stirring until well blended. Cover and refrigerate.

Per serving: 281 calories, 17 g carbohydrates, 18 g protein, 15 g total fat (2 g saturated), 33 mg cholesterol, 376 mg sodium

SHRIMP & CUCUMBER TOMATO SALAD

For summer meals, what could be easier than this: a salad of tiny shrimp spilling over crisp watercress sprigs and ripe, juicy tomatoes! Complete your menu with iced tea and crusty French rolls.

1 medium-size cucumber (about 8 oz.)
1 pound small cooked shrimp
½ cup thinly sliced green onions
2 tablespoons minced cilantro
½ cup reduced-calorie or regular mayonnaise
   Salt and pepper
   About 2 cups lightly packed rinsed, crisped watercress sprigs
4 medium-size firm-ripe tomatoes (about 1½ lbs. *total*), cut into quarters
1 lemon, cut into 8 wedges

Peel and halve cucumber; scrape out and discard seeds. Finely dice cucumber, place in a large bowl, and mix in shrimp, onions, and cilantro. (At this point, you may cover and refrigerate for up to 2 hours.)

Just before serving, stir mayonnaise into shrimp mixture; season to taste with salt and pepper. Divide watercress equally among 4 individual plates; top each plate with 4 tomato quarters. Spoon shrimp mixture evenly over watercress and tomatoes; garnish salads with lemon wedges. Makes 4 servings.—*Betty Cornelison, Portland*

Per serving: 247 calories, 15 g carbohydrates, 27 g protein, 10 g total fat (2 g saturated), 231 mg cholesterol, 446 mg sodium

BROILED AVOCADO SALAD

Heat this broiled first-course salad just long enough to melt the cheese.

   Anchovy Dressing (recipe follows)
3 medium-size ripe avocados
4 teaspoons grated Parmesan cheese
8 ounces small cooked shrimp
¼ cup shredded jack cheese
   Salt

Prepare Anchovy Dressing and set aside.

Halve and pit avocados. With a small, sharp knife, score through avocado flesh just to—not through—shells, dividing surfaces into about ½-inch squares.

In a small bowl, mix Parmesan cheese, shrimp, and Anchovy Dressing; mound equally into avocado shells. Set avocado shells, filled side up, side by side in an 8- or 9-inch baking pan. Sprinkle with jack cheese; broil about 4 inches below heat until cheese is melted and flecked with brown and avocados are partially warmed (5 to 6 minutes). Serve hot; season to taste with salt. Makes 6 servings.—*Corky Jones, San Anselmo, CA*

ANCHOVY DRESSING. In a small bowl, stir together ¼ cup **salad oil,** 3 tablespoons **red wine vinegar,** 1 tablespoon **lemon juice,** 2 teaspoons **Dijon mustard,** 1 teaspoon **anchovy paste** or drained minced canned anchovies, and ¼ teaspoon **pepper.**

Per serving: 308 calories, 8 g carbohydrates, 12 g protein, 27 g total fat (5 g saturated), 80 mg cholesterol, 218 mg sodium

Chicken Tchakhokbelli

Melt butter and fry chicken till golden brown.

Remove chicken and fry onion in butter ~ ~ ~

Place chicken in roasting pan; add other ingredients

Bake, uncovered, in a hot oven, turning once ~ ~ ~

Serve with Rice Pilaff!

As early as the 1930s, recipes from restaurant chefs found their way into Kitchen Cabinet indirectly, as readers adapted favorite dishes, then passed their creations along. But Sunset's first celebrity chef was probably George Mardikian, proprietor of the popular Omar Khayyam's restaurants in San Francisco and Fresno (the San Francisco establishment endured well into the 1960s). Two of Mardikian's Armenian specialties appeared in Kitchen Cabinet in 1941, and additional contributions were featured during the World War II years. Chef Mardikian's success may have been due in part to his exuberant talent for making appetizing, exotic-sounding dishes from simple, readily available ingredients. The savory selections reprinted here, for example, require little more than chicken, rice, broth, butter, and a few staple seasonings.

Circus Baked Potatoes, a recipe from 1938, displays the talents of a much different sort of showman chef—the cook in a traveling circus! This is the kind of comforting food also exemplified by La Salsa con Queso (a hot cheese dip to pour over tortilla chips) and practical Quick Cherry Pudding, both from 1939.

CHICKEN TCHAKHOKBELLI (also known as "Prince Mdivani Special")

2 small chickens (2 to 2½ lbs. *each*)
½ cup butter
1 onion, sliced
⅓ cup sherry
½ cup tomato juice
1 cup water
1 teaspoon paprika
1 teaspoon salt
Pepper

Cut the chickens into quarters; then rinse the pieces and pat them dry. Melt the butter in a frying pan and fry the chicken until light brown. Remove the chicken to a baking pan, leaving the drippings in the frying pan. Fry the onion in these drippings until limp and golden, then pour over the chicken. Add the remaining ingredients. Bake uncovered in a hot oven (400°) for one hour, turning the chicken over after the first half hour. The juices in the pan make a delicious gravy. Serve with Rice Pilaff. Makes 8 servings.—*Chef George Mardikian, San Francisco (May 1941)*

RICE PILAFF (every grain is separate and the flavor is superb)

1½ cups raw rice
¼ cup butter
3 cups broth (chicken, lamb or beef)
Salt and pepper

Rinse the rice well and dry with paper towels or a clean cloth. Melt the butter in a heavy skillet or Dutch oven, add the rice, and braise until the butter begins to bubble. Add the broth and seasonings and bring to a boil. Cover and bake for 30 minutes in a hot oven (400°); then remove, stir well, and bake 10 minutes longer. Mold servings of pilaff in a teacup and invert onto a platter with the Chicken Tchakhokbelli. Makes 8 servings.—*Chef George Mardikian, San Francisco (May 1941)*

CIRCUS BAKED POTATOES

My husband, when a boy of 18, ran away with a circus to play in the band. He used to regale me with stories of circus life, and would dwell lovingly on the many excellent dishes the circus cook served. Here is one simple but unusual one that I've tried and found really good.

Using a metal sponge, scrub large russet potatoes thoroughly, dry, and rub lightly with **salad oil** or drippings. Pierce each potato with a fork in several places, then arrange the potatoes in a shallow baking pan. Bake in a fairly hot oven (400°) for 40 to 45 minutes, then remove from oven and, protecting the hands with a cloth, carefully make a hole lengthwise through each potato, using an apple corer or a knife. Into each cavity insert a **wiener,** and return the potatoes to the oven for 15 minutes longer, or until well done. Serve immediately. The juices of the wieners go all through the potatoes, giving them a delicious flavor.

Other adaptations of this same idea that I have tried and liked are: (1) bore holes in the potatoes before baking, fill with **pork sausage meat,** plug up the holes with bits of potato, place in a pan, and bake as usual; (2) fill the holes with **hamburger** or ground round, well-seasoned with **salt** and **pepper** and **onion.**—*Mrs. P. G. E., Huntington Beach, CA (March 1938)*

LA SALSA CON QUESO *(a lively dish from Mexico)*

This Mexican "sauce with cheese" is just the thing for a cold night's supper. *La salsa* is served over crisp tortilla chips or corn crisps, which come in bags and are all ready to serve.

- ½ **small onion, chopped**
- 1 **teaspoonful of butter**
- 1 **can (about 14½ oz.) of diced tomatoes**
- ¼ to ½ **small fresh red chile pepper, seeded and cut fine**
- 1 **cupful of diced longhorn or pasteurized process American cheese**

Fry the chopped onion in the butter for 2 or 3 minutes, then pour in the tomatoes and add the finely cut chile pepper. Simmer together for 10 to 15 minutes, or until the mixture is slightly reduced and thickened. Then add the diced cheese and take the pan up just as the cheese begins to melt into the sauce.

Pour immediately over a stack of the chips on a dinner plate, and eat while still crisp and hot.—*M. K. C., Elk Grove, CA (January 1939)*

QUICK CHERRY PUDDING *(hurry-up dessert for a busy day)*

Here's my wash-day favorite. I assemble the ingredients while the last tubful of clothes is washing, and have the whole thing ready to bake by the time the oven's heated.

- 1 **can (about 1 lb.) pitted tart red cherries, undrained**
- 2 **tablespoonfuls of quick-cooking tapioca**
- ½ **cupful of sugar**

Mix the cherries and their juice with the tapioca and sugar, and pour into a buttered 1- to 1½-quart baking dish. Then make the topping:

- ¾ **cupful of flour**
- ½ **cupful of sugar**
- ¼ **cupful of butter or margarine**

Work the flour, sugar, and butter together until the mixture is evenly crumbly. Sprinkle thickly over the cherry mixture and bake in a moderate oven (350°) for about 45 minutes, or until lightly browned. Serve warm at Monday lunch, or chill and serve with whipped cream at dinner.—*Mrs. J. M., Independence, OR (February 1939)*

CIRCUS BAKED POTATOES

~Scrub and oil large baking potatoes; bake 45 minutes~

~Using apple corer, bore holes lengthwise ~ ~ ~

~Insert wieners in holes, and finish baking ~ ~ ~

~Serve immediately ~ ~ ~ and ARE THEY GOOD!

E·G·G·S & C·H·E·E·S·E

Scrambled eggs, omelets, soufflés—the ways we cook eggs in Kitchen Cabinet haven't changed much over the years. "Scramble as usual, being careful not to cook too long," cautioned a Hawaiian contributor in 1933, discussing the preparation of Scrambled Eggs with Green Onions. That advice is equally valid when you make South-of-the-Border Brunch Eggs, Eggs Ramona, or Greek Scrambled Eggs (recipes on the facing page). • Brunch might seem a fairly recent innovation, but it was a familiar occasion for entertaining as long ago as 1937. That's when a Washington reader offered a recipe for scrambled eggs with bacon and fresh corn, suggesting that it be served "for late Sunday breakfast or brunch." • Thanks to H. N. of San Francisco, we published a recipe for Broccoli Frittata in 1945. "Translated, this is a broccoli omelet, which can be served either as a vegetable or as a light main dish," she explained. Much the same can be said of contemporary cousins such as Zucchini Omelets (page 62), Ratatouille Frittata (page 64), and Sicilian Ricotta Frittata (page 63).

South-of-the-Border Brunch Eggs

Pan-fried sausages go well with this version of scrambled eggs.

White Sauce (recipe follows) or ¾ cup canned white sauce
- ½ cup thinly sliced green onions
- 1 can (about 4 oz.) whole green chiles, seeded and chopped
- 1 cup milk
- 8 large eggs
- ¼ cup butter or margarine
- 2 tablespoons salad oil
- 6 corn tortillas (*each* about 6 inches in diameter), cut or snipped into short, thin strips
- 3 medium-size tomatoes (about 1 lb. *total*), peeled, seeded, and chopped
- 1 can (about 2¼ oz.) sliced ripe olives, drained
- 2 cups (about 8 oz.) shredded jack cheese

Prepare White Sauce. Pour sauce into a large bowl. Mix in onions and chiles; gradually stir in milk. Add eggs; beat until blended. Set aside.

Melt 2 tablespoons of the butter in oil in a wide frying pan over medium-high heat (or use an electric frying pan set at 350°). Add tortilla strips and cook, stirring often, until crisp (about 5 minutes). Reduce heat to medium-low (or reduce temperature to 250°); add remaining 2 tablespoons butter. When butter is melted, pour in egg mixture. Cook, lifting cooked portion with a wide spatula to let uncooked eggs flow underneath, until eggs are softly set.

Distribute tomatoes, olives, and cheese evenly over eggs. Cover pan, remove from (or turn off) heat, and let stand until cheese is melted. Makes 6 servings.—*J. W., Santa Monica, CA*

WHITE SAUCE. Melt 1½ tablespoons **butter** or margarine in a small pan over medium heat. Blend in 1½ tablespoons **all-purpose flour** and cook, stirring constantly, until bubbly. Season to taste with **salt** and **paprika.** Remove from heat and gradually stir in ⅔ cup **milk;** return to heat and continue to cook, stirring, until sauce boils and thickens (2 to 3 minutes). Remove from heat; let cool slightly.

Per serving: 515 calories, 23 g carbohydrates, 22 g protein, 37 g total fat (18 g saturated), 361 mg cholesterol, 583 mg sodium

Greek Scrambled Eggs

For scrambled eggs with a Mideastern flavor, add toppings of feta cheese and tangy Greek olives.

- 12 large eggs
- ¼ cup water
- ¾ teaspoon dry oregano
- ⅛ teaspoon pepper
- 2 tablespoons butter or margarine
- 6 to 8 ounces feta cheese
- 1 medium-size tomato (about 6 oz.), diced
- ¼ cup chopped parsley
- 10 to 12 calamata olives or pitted ripe olives

In a large bowl, beat eggs with water, oregano, and pepper to blend. Melt butter in a wide frying pan with an ovenproof handle over low heat. Pour in egg mixture. Cook, lifting cooked portion with a wide spatula to let uncooked eggs flow underneath, until eggs are just softly set.

Break cheese into about ½-inch chunks and sprinkle evenly over eggs. Then broil 4 to 6 inches below heat just until cheese is hot (1 to 2 minutes). Sprinkle evenly with tomato and parsley; garnish with olives. Cut into wedges to serve. Makes 6 servings.—*C. S., Portland*

Per serving: 293 calories, 5 g carbohydrates, 18 g protein, 23 g total fat (11 g saturated), 465 mg cholesterol, 682 mg sodium

Eggs Ramona

When you're preparing to make this speedy main dish for brunch or supper, get out two wide frying pans—one for the sautéed vegetable mixture, another for the eggs. Serve the dish with grilled ham slices and fresh pineapple spears.

- 2 tablespoons salad oil
- ½ medium-size green bell pepper, seeded and diced
- ½ cup minced onion
- 6 medium-size mushrooms, thinly sliced
- 2 tablespoons minced parsley
- ½ teaspoon salt
- ¼ teaspoon pepper
- ½ teaspoon Italian herb seasoning (or ⅛ teaspoon *each* dry basil, marjoram, oregano, and thyme)
- ½ teaspoon Worcestershire
- 8 large eggs
- 2 tablespoons butter or margarine
- 2 large tomatoes (about 1 lb. *total*), peeled, seeded, and diced

Heat oil in a wide frying pan over medium heat. Add bell pepper and onion; cook, stirring often, until vegetables are soft but not browned (about 5 minutes). Add mushrooms, parsley, ¼ teaspoon of the salt, ⅛ teaspoon of the pepper, herb seasoning, and Worcestershire. Cook, stirring occasionally, for about 15 minutes. Remove from heat.

In a large bowl, beat eggs to blend; beat in remaining ¼ teaspoon salt and remaining ⅛ teaspoon pepper. Set aside. Melt butter in another wide frying pan over medium-low heat; add eggs and cook, stirring, until eggs begin to set. Add mushroom mixture and tomatoes; cook, stirring gently, until eggs are softly scrambled. Makes 4 servings.—*A. H., San Francisco*

Per serving: 302 calories, 10 g carbohydrates, 14 g protein, 23 g total fat (8 g saturated), 441 mg cholesterol, 479 mg sodium

milk, and wine until well blended. Pour egg mixture evenly over cheese.

Bake in a 375° oven until top of pie is golden brown and center feels set when lightly pressed (25 to 30 minutes). Let stand for 5 minutes before serving. Makes 6 to 8 servings.—*Fran Washko, Aurora, CO*

Per serving: 390 calories, 29 g carbohydrates, 20 g protein, 22 g total fat (12 g saturated), 151 mg cholesterol, 420 mg sodium

sauce and remaining 2 tablespoons cilantro. Season to taste with salt and pepper. Makes 4 servings.—*Karen E. Bosley, Lake Oswego, OR*

Per serving: 219 calories, 9 g carbohydrates, 14 g protein, 15 g total fat (5 g saturated), 433 mg cholesterol, 174 mg sodium

GRUYÈRE CHEESE PIE

Filled with an abundance of slow-cooked, sweetly caramelized onions, this custardy casserole is reminiscent of traditional Swiss, Alsatian, and German cheese tarts—but it's made with sliced sourdough bread rather than a pastry crust. Serve it for brunch or supper with applesauce, grilled sausages, and a fruity white wine such as Gewürztraminer.

- 2 tablespoons butter or margarine
- 2 large onions, thinly sliced
- 9 slices sourdough or French bread (*each* about 2½ by 4 inches, and ½ inch thick)
- 1 teaspoon caraway seeds
- 2½ cups (about 10 oz.) shredded Gruyère or Swiss cheese
- 3 large eggs
- ⅓ cup all-purpose flour
- ¼ teaspoon ground nutmeg
- ¾ cup *each* milk and dry white wine

Melt butter in a wide frying pan over medium-low heat. Add onions and cook, stirring occasionally, until very soft and golden (20 to 25 minutes). Remove from heat and set aside.

Fit bread slices snugly together in a single layer over bottom of a buttered shallow 2½-quart baking dish. Evenly distribute onions, caraway seeds, and cheese over bread. In a bowl, beat eggs with flour, nutmeg,

INDIAN-SPICED SCRAMBLED EGGS

A spicy, cilantro-laced tomato sauce enlivens these scrambled eggs.

- 1 teaspoon olive oil
- 1 small onion, chopped
- 2 cloves garlic, minced or pressed
- 1½ teaspoons chili powder
- ½ teaspoon ground turmeric
- 3 large pear-shaped (Roma-type) tomatoes (about 12 oz. *total*), chopped
- 3 tablespoons chopped cilantro
- 8 large eggs
- ¼ cup water
- 1 tablespoon butter or margarine
   Salt and pepper

In a wide nonstick frying pan, combine oil, onion, and garlic. Cook over medium-high heat, stirring often, until onion is lightly browned (3 to 5 minutes). Stir in chili powder and turmeric. Add tomatoes and 1 tablespoon of the cilantro; cook, stirring often, until almost all liquid has evaporated (8 to 10 minutes). Spoon sauce into a bowl; keep warm. Rinse and dry pan.

In a large bowl, beat eggs with water to blend. Melt butter in frying pan over medium heat. Add egg mixture; cook, lifting cooked portion with a wide spatula to let uncooked eggs flow underneath, until eggs are softly set. Top eggs with tomato

ZUCCHINI OMELETS

These little shredded-zucchini omelets, lightly seasoned with nutmeg, taste delicious with crisp bacon.

- 3 small zucchini (about 8 oz. *total*)
- 4 large eggs
- 1½ tablespoons minced parsley
- ⅛ to ¼ teaspoon *each* ground nutmeg, pepper, and salt
- 4 teaspoons butter or margarine
- ½ cup shredded Swiss cheese (optional)

Finely shred zucchini. With your hands, squeeze as much liquid from zucchini as possible. Then measure zucchini; you should have 1 cup. Place zucchini in a bowl and add eggs and parsley; beat until blended. Beat in nutmeg, pepper, and salt.

Set an 8- to 9-inch omelet pan over medium heat. Swirl 1 teaspoon of the butter in pan until melted. Add a fourth of the zucchini mixture and spread over pan bottom with a spatula. Cook until omelet is lightly browned on bottom, but top is still moist. Remove pan from heat. Fold one-third of the omelet over center; then slide unfolded edge onto a plate and flip folded portion over on top. Keep warm.

Repeat to make 3 more omelets, using remaining butter and zucchini mixture. Sprinkle omelets with cheese, if desired; serve at once. Makes 4 servings.—*Judith A. Gaulke, Menlo Park, CA*

Per serving: 118 calories, 2 g carbohydrates, 7 g protein, 9 g total fat (4 g saturated), 223 mg cholesterol, 207 mg sodium

CHILE & CHEESE TOSTADAS

Baked or shirred eggs are a time-honored breakfast dish—but in this recipe, there's a new twist. Each egg bakes in the center of a crisp flour tortilla, encircled by Cheddar and jack cheeses, mushrooms, and tomatoes.

    4 flour tortillas (*each* 7 to 9 inches in diameter)
    1 tablespoon salad oil
    1 medium-size onion, chopped
 1½ cups sliced mushrooms
    1 cup chopped green bell pepper
    1 can (about 4 oz.) diced green chiles
    1 teaspoon dry oregano
 1½ cups (about 6 oz.) *each* shredded Cheddar cheese and shredded jack cheese
  12 large, thin slices firm-ripe tomato
    4 large eggs

Place 2 tortillas in each of 2 shallow 10- by 15-inch baking pans. Bake in a 450° oven until tortillas are golden (5 to 10 minutes). Set aside.

Heat oil in a wide frying pan over medium-high heat. Add onion, mushrooms, bell pepper, chiles, and oregano; cook, stirring often, until onion is browned (about 10 minutes). Spread tortillas with onion mixture, leaving an inch-wide circle uncovered in center of each tortilla. Then sprinkle onion mixture with Cheddar and jack cheeses.

Return tortillas to oven and bake until cheese is barely melted (about 3 minutes). Top evenly with tomatoes, leaving centers of tortillas open; break one egg into center of each tortilla. Continue to bake until eggs are set (about 10 more minutes). Makes 4 servings.—*Harriet Barker, Meadview, AZ*

Per serving: 598 calories, 32 g carbohydrates, 32 g protein, 38 g total fat (19 g saturated), 302 mg cholesterol, 903 mg sodium

BLUEBERRY-TOPPED FRENCH TOAST

For a weekend breakfast or homey dessert, try topping hot French toast with warm blueberry sauce. Dress up dessert servings with dollops of whipped cream, if you like.

  ⅓ cup sugar
    1 tablespoon cornstarch
    2 cups fresh blueberries
    2 tablespoons lemon juice
  ⅓ cup water
    3 large eggs
  ¼ cup half-and-half or milk
       About 2 tablespoons butter or margarine
    6 slices firm-textured white bread (crusts trimmed, if desired)
       Whipped cream (optional)

In a 1- to 1½-quart pan, mix sugar and cornstarch. Add blueberries, lemon juice, and water. Cook over medium heat, stirring often, until mixture is thickened. Pour into a bowl or sauce boat; keep warm.

In a shallow bowl, beat eggs with half-and-half to blend. Heat a griddle or wide frying pan over medium heat until a drop of water sizzles on it. Lightly coat griddle with butter. Dip bread into egg mixture, saturating thoroughly; place bread slices on griddle and cook, turning once, until browned on both sides. As toast is cooked, transfer it to a warm platter and keep warm.

To serve, spoon blueberry sauce and whipped cream (if desired) over toast. Makes 3 main-dish or 6 dessert servings.—*B. M., Ontario, CA*

Per main-dish serving: 453 calories, 65 g carbohydrates, 12 g protein, 17 g total fat (8 g saturated), 241 mg cholesterol, 427 mg sodium

SICILIAN RICOTTA FRITTATA

Ricotta cheese adds extra protein to this simple frittata. Serve it for breakfast or a light supper.

    4 large eggs
    1 cup ricotta cheese
  ¼ cup grated Parmesan or Romano cheese
    3 tablespoons minced parsley
  ¼ teaspoon salt
  ⅛ teaspoon pepper
  ¼ cup olive oil or salad oil
    6 tomato slices; or 1 can (about 8 oz.) marinara sauce

In a large bowl, beat eggs and ricotta cheese until well blended. Stir in Parmesan cheese, parsley, salt, and pepper.

Heat oil in a wide frying pan over medium heat. When oil is hot, reduce heat to medium-low and add egg mixture. Cook, lifting cooked portion with a wide spatula to let uncooked eggs flow underneath, until bottom of frittata is set and lightly browned. Cut frittata into sixths with spatula; then turn each section over and cook until lightly browned on other side.

Garnish frittata with tomato slices; or heat marinara sauce in a small pan over low heat and offer to spoon over frittata. Makes 6 servings.—*M. C., North Hollywood, CA*

Per serving: 220 calories, 3 g carbohydrates, 10 g protein, 19 g total fat (6 g saturated), 165 mg cholesterol, 231 mg sodium

RATATOUILLE FRITTATA

In 1965, we described how to make the Provençal vegetable stew called *ratatouille*—and our readers have been requesting the recipe ever since. In this *Kitchen Cabinet* favorite from 1988, the now-familiar ratatouille ingredients brighten an egg dish.

1   small eggplant (about 12 oz.)

6   tablespoons olive oil

2   cloves garlic, minced or pressed

1   medium-size red onion, sliced

3   small zucchini (about 8 oz. *total*), thinly sliced

1   cup chopped red bell pepper

4   medium-size firm-ripe tomatoes (about 1½ lbs. *total*), peeled, seeded, and chopped

¼   cup minced fresh basil

6   large eggs, lightly beaten

1   cup (about 4 oz.) shredded Parmesan cheese

Quarter unpeeled eggplant lengthwise, then thinly slice crosswise. Heat ¼ cup of the oil in a wide frying pan over medium heat. Add eggplant, cover, and cook for 10 minutes, stirring once or twice. Increase heat to medium-high. Add remaining 2 tablespoons oil, garlic, onion, zucchini, and bell pepper. Cook, uncovered, stirring often, until zucchini is tender-crisp to bite (about 5 minutes). Add tomatoes and basil; cook, stirring, until tomatoes are soft (about 2 minutes).

Reduce heat to medium. Pour eggs into pan, cover, and cook until eggs are softly set (about 5 minutes). Sprinkle cheese over eggs; cover and cook until cheese is melted (about 2 minutes). To serve, spoon from pan. Makes 6 servings.—*Carol Braswell, Fresno, CA*

Per serving: 329 calories, 15 g carbohydrates, 16 g protein, 24 g total fat (7 g saturated), 225 mg cholesterol, 382 mg sodium

GOLD COUNTRY SPECIAL

Sharp Cheddar enhances the traditional Hangtown fry—scrambled eggs with oysters, a dish from California's Gold Rush days.

1   jar (about 10 oz.) small Pacific or other small oysters

3   tablespoons butter or margarine

6   large eggs

⅓   cup half-and-half

2   tablespoons *each* finely chopped green bell pepper and thinly sliced green onion

½   cup shredded sharp Cheddar cheese

    Salt and pepper

4   slices bacon, crisply cooked, drained, and crumbled

    Lemon wedges and catsup

Drain oysters and cut into bite-size pieces. Melt butter in a wide frying pan with an ovenproof handle over medium heat; add oysters and cook until edges curl (about 3 minutes). Meanwhile, in a large bowl, beat eggs with half-and-half, bell pepper, onion, and 2 tablespoons of the cheese until blended. Season to taste with salt and pepper.

Pour egg mixture over oysters. Reduce heat to medium-low and cook, lifting cooked portion with a wide spatula to let uncooked eggs flow underneath, until eggs are just softly set.

Sprinkle bacon and remaining 6 tablespoons cheese over eggs; then broil about 4 inches below heat until cheese is melted and bubbly (about 3 minutes). Cut into wedges and serve at once. Offer lemon wedges and catsup to season eggs to taste. Makes 4 to 6 servings.—*H. N., San Francisco*

Per serving: 293 calories, 5 g carbohydrates, 18 g protein, 22 g total fat (11 g saturated), 327 mg cholesterol, 364 mg sodium

BACON & EGG BURRITOS

Hearty and casual, these burritos are easy to make. While the tortillas warm in the oven, you prepare a filling of eggs scrambled with bacon, cheese, and chiles.

10   flour tortillas (*each* 7 to 9 inches in diameter)

8   ounces sliced bacon

10   large eggs

¼   cup water

    Salt and liquid hot pepper seasoning

1   can (about 4 oz.) diced green chiles

¼   cup sliced green onions

1½   cups (about 6 oz.) shredded Cheddar cheese

2   ripe avocados, pitted, peeled, and sliced

Brush tortillas lightly with hot water; stack tortillas, wrap in foil, and heat in a 350° oven until warm (10 to 15 minutes).

Meanwhile, cook bacon in a wide frying pan over medium heat until crisp; lift from pan, drain, crumble, and set aside. Pour off and discard all but 3 tablespoons drippings from pan.

In a large bowl, beat eggs with water to blend; season to taste with salt and hot pepper seasoning. Add egg mixture to drippings. Cook over medium heat, lifting cooked portion with a wide spatula to let uncooked eggs flow underneath, until eggs are almost set. Remove from heat; sprinkle with bacon, chiles, onions, and cheese. Cover and let stand until cheese is melted. Spoon a tenth of the egg mixture into each tortilla; top with avocado slices and roll up, tucking in sides. Eat out of hand. Makes 5 servings.—*S. B., Lake Havasu City, AZ*

Per serving: 764 calories, 48 g carbohydrates, 32 g protein, 50 g total fat (17 g saturated), 475 mg cholesterol, 1,019 mg sodium

PUFF PANCAKE WITH MANGOES

When mangoes are at their peak in early summer, team the golden, juicy-ripe fruit with fresh raspberries to make a luscious topping for this billowing oven pancake.

- 4 large eggs
- 1 cup *each* all-purpose flour and milk
- 6 tablespoons butter or margarine
- 2 medium-large firm-ripe mangoes (about 1½ lbs. *total*)
- 3 tablespoons orange marmalade
- 1 tablespoon lemon juice
- 1½ cups fresh raspberries

Preheat oven to 425°. In oven, warm a wide frying pan with an ovenproof handle or a shallow 3-quart baking dish.

While oven is preheating, combine eggs, flour, and milk in a blender or food processor. Whirl until smoothly blended.

When oven reaches 425°, remove frying pan and add ¼ cup of the butter; swirl and tilt pan to coat with butter. Pour batter evenly into pan; return pan to oven. Bake until pancake is golden brown and crisp around edges (about 20 minutes).

Meanwhile, peel mangoes and cut fruit from pits in ½-inch-thick slices. Melt remaining 2 tablespoons butter in a wide frying pan over high heat. Stir in marmalade and lemon juice. Add mangoes; stir gently, turning to coat with butter mixture, just until heated through (about 5 minutes).

Spoon mangoes into center of pancake; sprinkle with raspberries. Cut into wedges to serve. Makes 6 servings.—*Carole Van Brocklin, Port Angeles, WA*

Per serving: 343 calories, 42 g carbohydrates, 8 g protein, 17 g total fat (9 g saturated), 178 mg cholesterol, 187 mg sodium

CINNAMON–APPLE DUTCH BABY

To make this family-size pancake, you pour a thin, egg-rich batter over cinnamon-spiced apples, then bake for just 15 to 20 minutes. Serve the golden pancake immediately, while it's still hot and puffy.

- 6 tablespoons butter or margarine
- 2 teaspoons ground cinnamon
- ¼ cup granulated sugar
- 2 large Gravenstein or Granny Smith apples (about 1 lb. *total*), peeled, cored, and thinly sliced
- 4 large eggs
- 1 cup *each* all-purpose flour and milk
- Powdered sugar

Melt butter in a wide frying pan with an ovenproof handle over medium-high heat. Stir in cinnamon and granulated sugar. Add apple slices and cook, turning often, until translucent (about 5 minutes). Place pan, uncovered, in a 425° oven for about 5 minutes.

In a blender or food processor, combine eggs, flour, and milk; whirl until smoothly blended. Pour batter evenly over apples in pan. Bake until pancake is puffy and golden (15 to 20 minutes). Dust pancake with powdered sugar; then cut into wedges and serve. Makes 6 servings.—*Lyn Proctor, Chandler, AZ*

Per serving: 323 calories, 37 g carbohydrates, 8 g protein, 17 g total fat (9 g saturated), 178 mg cholesterol, 180 mg sodium

RANCHERO SOUFFLÉ

Sliced oranges go well with this hearty, company-size casserole.

- Spicy Tomato Sauce (recipe follows)
- About three-fourths of a 1-pound loaf sourdough bread
- 1 pound Cheddar cheese, shredded
- 1 pound sliced bacon, crisply cooked, drained, and crumbled
- 6 large eggs
- 3 cups milk
- 2 teaspoons dry mustard

Prepare Spicy Tomato Sauce.

Cut enough bread into ½-inch-thick slices to make 2 single layers in a greased 9- by 13-inch baking dish. Arrange half the slices in a single layer in dish, cutting or overlapping slices to fit. Spread with half the Spicy Tomato Sauce; top with half each of the cheese and bacon. Repeat layers, using remaining bread, sauce, cheese, and bacon.

In a bowl, beat eggs with milk and mustard to blend; pour over casserole. Cover and refrigerate for at least 8 hours or until next day.

Bake, uncovered, in a 350° oven until casserole is heated through and center is puffy (about 55 minutes). Let stand for 20 minutes before serving; cut into squares to serve. Makes 8 to 10 servings.—*Irene McPherrin, Redwood City, CA*

SPICY TOMATO SAUCE. Pour 1 can (about 14½ oz.) **tomatoes** into a 1½- to 2-quart pan. Mash tomatoes. Add 3 tablespoons **tomato paste;** 1 large **onion,** finely chopped; 1 clove **garlic,** minced or pressed; 1 can (about 4 oz.) **diced green chiles;** 1 teaspoon **dry oregano;** and ⅛ teaspoon **ground red pepper** (cayenne). Bring to a rolling boil over high heat, stirring.

Per serving: 518 calories, 31 g carbohydrates, 28 g protein, 31 g total fat (16 g saturated), 218 mg cholesterol, 1,046 mg sodium

FOOLPROOF SOUFFLÉ SQUARES

Unlike most soufflés, this one won't fall when it's cut into servings. It's filled with a colorful blend of mushrooms and packaged mixed vegetables; for a heartier entreé, add ⅔ cup minced ham to the filling.

Vegetable Filling (recipe follows)
⅓ cup butter or margarine, at room temperature
5 large eggs, separated
½ cup sour cream
¼ cup all-purpose flour
¼ teaspoon *each* salt, pepper, and ground nutmeg
½ cup grated Parmesan cheese

Prepare Vegetable Filling and set aside.

In a medium-size bowl, beat butter until creamy; beat in egg yolks, sour cream, flour, salt, pepper, nutmeg, and 2 tablespoons of the cheese.

In a large bowl, beat egg whites with an electric mixer on high speed just until they hold stiff, moist peaks; fold in yolk mixture.

Spread half the egg mixture in a buttered 7- by 11-inch baking dish; sprinkle with half the filling and 2 tablespoons of the cheese. Spread with remaining egg mixture. Spoon remaining filling in a strip down center; sprinkle with remaining ¼ cup cheese. Bake in a 350° oven until golden brown (30 to 35 minutes). Cut into squares to serve. Makes 6 servings.—*L. H., Sandy, UT*

VEGETABLE FILLING. Melt 2 tablespoons **butter** or margarine in a wide frying pan over medium-high heat. Add 8 ounces **mushrooms,** sliced; cook, stirring often, until all liquid has evaporated. Meanwhile, cook 2 packages (about 10 oz. *each*) **frozen mixed vegetables** according to package directions; drain. Stir vegetables into mushrooms; remove from heat.

Per serving: 358 calories, 20 g carbohydrates, 13 g protein, 26 g total fat (15 g saturated), 232 mg cholesterol, 478 mg sodium

SPINACH SOUFFLÉ

Canned cream of chicken soup gives this light spinach soufflé extra stability. It should be served at once, though—so seat your guests before you take it out of the oven.

1 can (about 10¾ oz.) condensed cream of chicken soup
½ cup *each* shredded Cheddar cheese and jack cheese
1 teaspoon dry mustard
¼ teaspoon ground nutmeg
6 large eggs, separated
1 package (about 10 oz.) frozen chopped spinach, thawed and squeezed dry
¼ cup thinly sliced green onions
2 teaspoons lemon juice

In a 3- to 4-quart pan, stir together soup, Cheddar and jack cheeses, mustard, and nutmeg. Cook over low heat, stirring often, until cheese is melted. Remove from heat. Add egg yolks, 2 at a time, beating well after each addition. Add spinach, onions, and lemon juice; stir to blend.

In a large bowl, beat egg whites with an electric mixer on high speed just until they hold stiff, moist peaks. Pour soup mixture over egg whites; fold gently together. Pour mixture into a well-buttered 2-quart soufflé dish or straight-sided deep baking dish. Bake in a 375° oven until center of soufflé feels set when lightly pressed and jiggles only slightly when dish is gently shaken (30 to 35 minutes). Serve at once. Makes 6 servings.—*O. F., Castro Valley, CA*

Per serving: 221 calories, 7 g carbohydrates, 14 g protein, 16 g total fat (7 g saturated), 240 mg cholesterol, 621 mg sodium

WALNUT CHARD CRÊPES

Serve these creamy chard crêpes as a main dish or as an accompaniment for meat or fish.

10 to 12 Blender Crêpes (recipe follows)
2 pounds Swiss chard
3 tablespoons butter or margarine
1 large onion, chopped
1 cup coarsely chopped walnuts
2 small packages (about 3 oz. *each*) cream cheese, diced
½ cup shredded Parmesan cheese

Prepare Blender Crêpes.

Discard tough stem ends from chard; then rinse chard and drain well. Coarsely chop chard stems; thinly slice chard leaves. Melt butter in a 5- to 6-quart pan over medium-high heat. Add onion and chard stems; cook, stirring often, until onion is soft (about 7 minutes). Add chard leaves; cover and cook, stirring often, until leaves are wilted (about 5 minutes). Add walnuts and cream cheese; stir until cheese is melted.

Spoon filling down center of crêpes; roll to enclose. Arrange crêpes, seam side down, in a 9- by 13-inch baking dish. (At this point, you may cover and refrigerate until next day.)

Bake crêpes, covered, in a 375° oven until heated through (about 20 minutes; about 35 minutes if refrigerated). Sprinkle with Parmesan cheese and bake for 5 more minutes. Makes 4 to 6 servings.—*N. L., Moose, WY*

BLENDER CRÊPES. In a blender or food processor, combine 3 large **eggs,** ⅔ cup **all-purpose flour,** and 1 cup **milk;** whirl until smoothly blended. Heat a 6- to 7-inch crêpe pan or other flat-bottomed frying pan over medium heat. Add ¼ teaspoon **butter** or margarine and swirl to coat pan surface. Stir batter and pour 2 to 2½ tablespoons into pan, quickly tilting pan so batter coats pan bottom.

Cook until surface of crêpe feels dry and edge is lightly browned. Turn with a spatula and cook until browned on other side. Turn out onto a plate. Repeat with remaining batter, stacking crêpes as made. Makes 12 to 14 crêpes.

Per serving: 486 calories, 26 g carbohydrates, 17 g protein, 37 g total fat (15 g saturated), 170 mg cholesterol, 665 mg sodium

EGGPLANT CRÊPES

For a meatless entrée, fill baked eggplant slices with ricotta and Parmesan cheeses, then top with marinara sauce and bake.

- 2 medium-size eggplants (about 2 lbs. *total*)
- ⅓ cup olive oil or salad oil
- 2 cups ricotta cheese
- 4 large egg yolks
- 1 cup (about 4 oz.) grated Parmesan cheese
- 2 cloves garlic, minced or pressed
- 1 cup (about 4 oz.) shredded mozzarella cheese
- 2 cups homemade or purchased marinara sauce, heated

Cut unpeeled eggplants lengthwise into ⅓-inch slices. Arrange slices in 2 shallow 10- by 15-inch baking pans; brush cut sides with oil. Bake in a 425° oven until browned (about 20 minutes). Remove from oven; reduce oven temperature to 350°.

In a bowl, beat ricotta cheese, egg yolks, Parmesan cheese, and garlic until blended. Place 2 to 3 tablespoons of the ricotta filling along one long side of each eggplant slice; roll up. (Reserve small end slices for another use.) Place crêpes, seam side down, in a shallow 3-quart casserole. (At this point, you may cover and refrigerate until next day.)

Bake, uncovered, in a 350° oven until heated through (about 20 minutes; about 35 minutes if refrigerated). Immediately sprinkle crêpes with mozzarella cheese. Offer hot marinara sauce to pour over crêpes to taste. Makes 4 to 6 servings.
—*Connie Linden, Corona del Mar, CA*

Per serving: 629 calories, 26 g carbohydrates, 31 g protein, 46 g total fat (19 g saturated), 256 mg cholesterol, 1,232 mg sodium

BAKED CHILE PUFF

Blanket cheese-stuffed green chiles with a fluffy egg batter to make this easy oven version of chiles rellenos.

- 8 ounces jack cheese
- 2 large cans (about 7 oz. *each*) whole green chiles
  Egg Batter (recipe follows)
- 1 cup (about 4 oz.) shredded Cheddar cheese
- 1 cup homemade or purchased guacamole
- 1 small firm-ripe tomato (about 4 oz.), diced

Cut jack cheese into as many equal-size sticks as you have chiles; insert a cheese stick into each chile. Arrange stuffed chiles in a single layer in a buttered 1½- to 2-quart baking dish (about 2 inches deep).

Prepare Egg Batter and spread evenly over chiles. Sprinkle batter with Cheddar cheese. Bake in a 350° oven until casserole is puffy and appears set in center when dish is gently shaken (18 to 20 minutes). To serve, spoon out of dish; top each serving with guacamole and tomato. Makes 6 servings.—*Ruth Hagerman, Colorado Springs, CO*

EGG BATTER. Separate 3 large **eggs**. In a large bowl, beat whites with an electric mixer on high speed just until they hold stiff, moist peaks. In another bowl, beat yolks with 2 table-spoons **milk** and 3 tablespoons **all-purpose flour** until blended. Fold yolk mixture into whites; use at once.

Per serving: 402 calories, 15 g carbohydrates, 19 g protein, 30 g total fat (14 g saturated), 170 mg cholesterol, 689 mg sodium

LEEK & HAM QUICHE

Cut this rich quiche into generous wedges for a luncheon entrée.

    Pastry for a single-crust 9-inch pie
- 1 package (about 2.4 oz.) leek soup mix
- 1½ cups milk
- ½ cup half-and-half
- 1½ cups (about 6 oz.) shredded Swiss cheese
- 3 large eggs, lightly beaten
- 1 teaspoon dry mustard
    Dash of pepper
- 1 large can (about 4¼ oz.) deviled ham
- 2 tablespoons fine dry bread crumbs

On a lightly floured board, roll pastry into an 11½-inch round. Fit into a 9-inch pie pan; trim and flute edge. Bake in a 450° oven until golden (7 to 10 minutes). Let cool. Reduce oven temperature to 325°.

In a 2-quart pan, stir together soup mix and milk. Cook over medium heat, stirring, until mixture boils and thickens. Stir in half-and-half, cheese, eggs, mustard, and pepper. Remove from heat.

In a small bowl, mix deviled ham and bread crumbs; spread ham mixture over bottom of pastry shell. Pour egg mixture over ham mixture; bake on lowest rack of a 325° oven until center of pie jiggles only slightly when pan is gently shaken (50 to 60 minutes). Let stand for about 10 minutes before serving. Makes 6 servings.
—*L. S., Pueblo, CO*

Per serving: 481 calories, 27 g carbohydrates, 20 g protein, 32 g total fat (12 g saturated), 150 mg cholesterol, 1,102 mg sodium

Buy to Save. *Food saving starts with marketing. Figure needs before you buy*

Serve to Save. *She saves the best who serves only as much as family will eat*

Store to Save. *Find out how each food keeps best; store each kind accordingly*

RUTH TAYLOR

Save Cooking Fats. *Use drippings you need in cooking; sell the rest to butcher*

1942 to 1945

Save in every way you can—and then save some more!" In February 1943, Sunset's editors suggested this motto as the guiding principle for a "victory kitchen." It was good advice for the World War II years, when many foods were rationed and shortages of others were not uncommon. Each family member received a book of ration coupons: blue for canned goods, red for meat, fish, and dairy products. Grocers marked products with both prices and ration points.

Such restrictions had a definite influence on home cooking. Westerners became more appreciative of the bounty of fresh (and unrationed) produce around them: Kitchen Cabinet contributors often wrote of using victory garden vegetables. Choice cuts of beef required more red stamps than chicken, so reliable poult recipes like Chicken Sauté were treasured. And main dishes made with a minimum of meat, such as Kidney Bean Casserole, were popular for family meals.

In 1942, sugar was the first food to be rationed nationwide. Butter, too, was scarce—in 1943, it commanded three times as many precious ration points per pound as oil or vegetable shortening. Our editors acknowledged the situation when describing Cheese-frosted Biscuits: "At first glance, these biscuits may seem a bit extravagant as to ration points, but you won't need to serve any butt or margarine with them. The 'frosting' is absorbed during baking, and the result a rich and delectable hot bread." Treats like these aside, coping with wartime lim tations usually meant making substitutions in baked goods; the use of molasses and shortening rather than sugar and butter in Victory Spice Cake was typical of the times.

CHICKEN SAUTÉ

1 chicken (3 to 4 lbs.)
Flour
1 clove garlic, quartered
Salad oil (preferably olive oil)
½ pound fresh mushrooms, thinly sliced, or 1 can (6 or 8 oz.) sliced mushrooms, drained
2 tablespoons chopped parsley
1 cup white table wine (Sauterne, Hock, Riesling, or Chablis)
Salt, pepper, and herbs to taste

Cut chicken into serving-size pieces (quarters or eighths); rinse and pat dry. Roll chicken pieces in flour. In a frying pan, sauté garlic in salad oil until golden; then remove and discard garlic. Add chicken and brown nicely on all sides. Remove chicken to a roasting pan, leaving drippings in frying pan. Sauté mushrooms in these drippings for a few minutes; add chopped parsley and wine. Season this mushroom mixture to taste with salt, pep per, and herbs; pour over the chicken. Bake, uncovered, in a moderate oven (350 for 45 minutes to 1 hour, basting frequent Serve with rice. Serves 6.—*Mrs. N. F., Burlingame, CA (August 1942)*

Chicken Sauté can be prepared ahead of time, more convenient. Fry it, place it in the roasti pan, pour the mushroom-wine mixture over and then finish the cooking later.

KIDNEY BEAN CASSEROLE

With meat at a premium, a good dried bean recipe is a thing to treasure. Here's one of the best we've tasted.

1⅓ cups (about ½ pound) dried kidney beans
1½ cups sliced apples
2 large onions, thinly sliced
6 to 8 thin slices salt pork, cut in small pieces
¼ cup tomato juice or tomato sauce
½ cup brown sugar
½ teaspoon salt
¼ teaspoon pepper

Pick over and wash beans carefully; soak overnight in cold water. In the morning, cover and simmer slowly in the soaking water for 1 hour. (Add more water during cooking if necessary.) Drain cooked beans, reserving ½ cup of the liquid. Put half of the beans in a 2- to 2½-quart casserole; add half of the apples, then half of the onions and half of the salt pork. Repeat layers, using remaining beans, apples, onions, and salt pork. Mix together the ½ cup bean liquid, tomato juice, sugar, salt, and pepper; pour over all. Cover and bake in a moderate oven (350°) for 2 to 2½ hours, or until onions and apples are very tender, flavors are well blended, and casserole is lightly browned on top. Serves 6 to 8.—*E. B., Oakland, CA (January 1943)*

CHEESE-FROSTED BISCUITS

2 cups sifted all-purpose flour
3 teaspoons baking powder
½ teaspoon salt
¼ cup shortening
⅔ to ¾ cup milk
¼ pound cold-pack sharp Cheddar cheese food
½ cup butter or margarine

Mix and sift dry ingredients; cut in shortening until well mixed. With a fork, quickstir in enough milk to make a soft but not sticky dough. Turn dough out onto a lightly floured board and knead 16 to 18 strokes. Roll dough about ⅓ inch thick and cut into rounds with a floured 1½-inch biscuit cutter. Place the rounds close together in a greased 7- by 11-inch baking pan.

Combine cheese food and butter in the top of a double boiler and melt slowly over hot water; stir to blend smoothly. Pour cheese mixture evenly over biscuits. Bake in a hot oven (450°) about 15 minutes, or until biscuits are well browned. Serve hot. Makes about 24 small biscuits.—*J. R. J., Los Angeles (June 1945)*

VICTORY SPICE CAKE

2⅓ cups sifted all-purpose flour
2 teaspoons ground cinnamon
1½ teaspoons ground ginger
1 teaspoon ground allspice
½ teaspoon ground cloves
1¼ teaspoons baking soda
1 cup buttermilk or sour milk
1 cup molasses
⅓ cup melted shortening
1 cup seedless raisins
Grated rind of 1 orange

Mix and sift flour and spices. Dissolve baking soda in buttermilk; add molasses. Combine flour and buttermilk mixtures. Add shortening, raisins, and orange rind; mix well. Spread batter in a greased 8-inch-square pan, and bake in a moderate oven (350°) 45 to 50 minutes, or until a wooden pick inserted in center of cake comes out clean. This is delicious served warm with cream or hard sauce as a pudding, and it is equally good served cold as a cake.—*Miss H. D., San Francisco (August 1942)*

Save Vegetable Juices. *Use juices from cooked vegetables in soups and sauces*

Save Fruit Juices. *Use them in cooking fruits; in cold drinks and fruit gelatins*

Save Bread and Cracker Crumbs. *Use to stuff poultry and top baked dishes*

Save Empty Tin Cans. *Wash; remove top, bottom, label; step on can to flatten*

M·E·A·T·S

First of all, select a good piece of meat," counseled Mrs. J. L. B. of Coeur d'Alene, Idaho as she shared a pot roast recipe in a 1939 Kitchen Cabinet. "Let a reliable butcher be your guide." In that time before precut roasts in computer-coded wrapping, the meatman shown waiting on our heroine in the accompanying illustrations was likely to be a bold, mustachioed fellow with a dashing air. Today's meat dealers probably wouldn't be depicted quite so rakishly, but they're just as helpful when you're choosing beef for Cranberry-Port Pot Roast or Wine-braised Chuck Roast (both on page 74). • Cooking meat in wine has been popular with our contributors for decades. In 1942, Mrs. T. G. K. of Boise offered tips for simmering round steak in claret, burgundy, or zinfandel. You'll find contemporary variations on this theme in Hunter's Beef (page 74) and Pork Chops with Walnuts & Wine (page 80). • Make-ahead entrées won points even in 1935. "This dish may be prepared the day before serving," E. P. of San Francisco confided about a casserole not unlike Enchiladas Carnitas (page 84). "It is a treasure for the business woman giving a company dinner."

Soy-Honey Barbecued Flank Steak

"The teriyaki treatment for barbecuing steaks is popular all over the West, and good cooks keep devising new variations," we remarked about a July, 1960 *Kitchen Cabinet* contribution. The comment still holds true today, as this 1993 recipe proves. Here, some novel ingredients—red wine vinegar, honey, and a generous measure of fresh ginger—add up to satisfying teriyaki taste.

- ½ cup red wine vinegar
- ¼ cup soy sauce
- 3 tablespoons honey
- ¼ cup minced fresh ginger
- 1 tablespoon olive oil or salad oil
- 4 large cloves garlic, minced or pressed
- 1 teaspoon pepper
- 1 flank steak (about 2 lbs.), trimmed of fat
- Lime wedges (optional)
- Soy sauce and pepper

In a large, shallow dish, stir together vinegar, the ¼ cup soy sauce, honey, ginger, oil, garlic, and the 1 teaspoon pepper. Add steak and turn to coat with marinade. Cover and refrigerate for at least 30 minutes or until next day, turning steak over 3 or 4 times.

Lift steak from marinade and drain briefly (discard marinade). Place steak on a grill 4 to 6 inches above a solid bed of hot coals. Cook, turning once, until meat is browned on both sides and done to your liking; cut to test (10 to 12 minutes for medium-rare).

Transfer steak to a serving board; garnish with lime wedges, if desired. To serve, cut steak across the grain into thin slanting slices. Season to taste with soy sauce and pepper.

Makes 6 servings.—*Beth Ann Hite, Peoria, AZ*

Per serving: 226 calories, 6 g carbohydrates, 25 g protein, 10 g total fat (4 g saturated), 62 mg cholesterol, 434 mg sodium

Sesame Flank Steak

Toasted sesame seeds and aromatic sesame oil give this steak its rich flavor.

- ¼ cup sesame seeds
- ¼ cup thinly sliced green onions
- 3 tablespoons soy sauce
- 2 tablespoons Oriental sesame oil or salad oil
- 1 tablespoon *each* vinegar, firmly packed brown sugar, minced fresh ginger, and minced garlic
- 1 teaspoon *each* dry mustard and Worcestershire
- 1 flank steak (about 1½ lbs.), trimmed of fat

Toast sesame seeds in a wide frying pan over medium-high heat, stirring often, until golden (2 to 4 minutes). Crush seeds, using a mortar and pestle; pour into a bowl. Stir in onions, soy sauce, oil, vinegar, sugar, ginger, garlic, mustard, and Worcestershire.

Place steak in a large, shallow dish. Pour soy mixture over steak; turn to coat. Cover and refrigerate for at least 4 hours or until next day, turning steak over 3 or 4 times.

Lift steak from marinade and drain briefly (discard marinade). Place steak on a grill 4 to 6 inches above a solid bed of hot coals. Cook, turning once, until browned on both sides and done to your liking; cut to test (10 to 12 minutes for medium-rare). To serve, cut steak across the grain into thin slanting slices. Makes 4 servings.—*Mrs. Scott Kemper, Sacramento*

Per serving: 263 calories, 4 g carbohydrates, 26 g protein, 15 g total fat (5 g saturated), 62 mg cholesterol, 471 mg sodium

Barbecue Steak Western

Delightful for a special occasion, this thick steak is marinated in a tangy blend of lemon, Worcestershire, and horseradish.

- 1 beef top round steak (about 3½ lbs.), about 2 inches thick, trimmed of fat
- Meat tenderizer (optional)
- ½ cup *each* salad oil and finely chopped onion
- ⅓ cup lemon juice
- 2 tablespoons catsup
- 1 tablespoon *each* Worcestershire and prepared horseradish
- 1 teaspoon paprika
- 1 clove garlic, minced or pressed
- 2 dry bay leaves

If desired, sprinkle steak with meat tenderizer according to package directions.

In a large, shallow dish, stir together oil, onion, lemon juice, catsup, Worcestershire, horseradish, paprika, garlic, and bay leaves. Place steak in dish and turn to coat with marinade. Cover and refrigerate until next day, turning steak over 3 or 4 times.

Lift steak from marinade and drain briefly (reserve marinade). Set steak aside. Pour marinade into a small pan; bring to a boil. Place steak on a grill 4 to 6 inches above a solid bed of low coals. (Or place on a rack in a broiler pan and broil 4 to 6 inches below heat.)

Cook, turning about every 10 minutes and basting with marinade, until meat is done to your liking; cut to test (35 to 40 minutes for rare). To serve, cut steak across the grain into thin slanting slices. Makes 6 to 8 servings.—*H. E. C., Salem, OR*

Per serving: 346 calories, 3 g carbohydrates, 41 g protein, 18 g total fat (4 g saturated), 107 mg cholesterol, 137 mg sodium

Korean Beef Strips

Thinly sliced and marinated in soy and sesame, beef chuck cooks quickly on the grill. (For easier slicing, partially freeze the meat before you cut it.)

½ cup *each* soy sauce, salad oil, and thinly sliced green onions

2 cloves garlic, minced or pressed

4 teaspoons sesame seeds

2 teaspoons sugar

1 teaspoon Oriental sesame oil

1 teaspoon finely minced fresh ginger or ½ teaspoon ground ginger

About 3 pounds boneless beef chuck, trimmed of fat and cut into ¼-inch-thick slices

In a large bowl, stir together soy sauce, salad oil, onions, garlic, sesame seeds, sugar, sesame oil, and ginger. Add beef and mix gently to coat with marinade. Cover and refrigerate for 3 to 6 hours.

Lift meat from marinade and drain briefly (discard marinade). Arrange meat, a portion at a time, on a grill 3 to 4 inches above a solid bed of low coals. Cook, turning once, until browned on outside but still pink in center; cut to test (about 2 minutes). Makes 6 to 8 servings.
—*I. M., San Diego, CA*

Per serving: 373 calories, 2 g carbohydrates, 36 g protein, 23 g total fat (7 g saturated), 121 mg cholesterol, 670 mg sodium

Beef Satay with Peanut Sauce

Serve these skewered marinated beef cubes with a smooth, spicy peanut sauce for dipping.

2 teaspoons curry powder

⅓ cup soy sauce

2 tablespoons *each* lemon juice, firmly packed brown sugar, and salad oil

3 pounds boneless beef sirloin steak, trimmed of fat and cut into 1½-inch cubes

Spicy Peanut Sauce (recipe follows)

In a large (1-gallon) heavy-duty plastic bag, combine curry powder, soy sauce, lemon juice, sugar, and oil. Add beef; seal bag and rotate to mix well. Refrigerate for at least 12 hours or until next day, turning bag over 3 or 4 times.

Shortly before grilling meat, prepare Spicy Peanut Sauce.

Lift meat from marinade and drain briefly (discard marinade). Thread meat on metal skewers and arrange on a grill about 2 inches above a solid bed of hot coals. Cook, turning as needed, until meat is browned on all sides and done to your liking; cut to test (about 10 minutes for medium-rare).

Serve satay with peanut sauce for dipping. Makes 6 to 8 servings.
—*A. M., Oakland, CA*

SPICY PEANUT SAUCE. In a food processor or blender, combine 1 large **onion** (cut into chunks), 2 cloves **garlic** (peeled), and 1 tablespoon **water**. Whirl until puréed; pour into a small pan and add 3 tablespoons **salad oil.** Cook over low heat, stirring often, until onion has lost any trace of raw flavor (about 10 minutes).

Add ¼ teaspoon **ground red pepper** (cayenne); 1 teaspoon **ground coriander;** 2 tablespoons *each* firmly packed **brown sugar, lemon juice,** and **soy sauce;** and ¼ cup **peanut butter.** Stir until smoothly blended. Remove from heat and gradually stir in ¾ cup **milk.** Before serving, cook over low heat, stirring constantly, just until sauce is hot.

Per serving: 469 calories, 13 g carbohydrates, 49 g protein, 24 g total fat (6 g saturated), 134 mg cholesterol, 851 mg sodium

Thai Garlic Beef

Garnished with fresh tomato, lime wedges, and cilantro, this garlic-rubbed grilled steak makes a colorful summer entrée.

Thai Relish (recipe follows)

6 cloves garlic, minced or pressed

⅓ cup finely chopped cilantro

2 tablespoons lime juice

1 tablespoon coarsely ground pepper

1 boneless beef top sirloin steak (about 2 lbs.), about 1 inch thick, trimmed of fat

Tomato and lime wedges

Cilantro sprigs

Prepare Thai Relish; set aside.

Mix garlic, chopped cilantro, lime juice, and pepper. Rub mixture over steak; then place steak on a grill 4 to 6 inches above a solid bed of hot coals. Cook, turning once, until meat is browned on both sides and done to your liking; cut to test (12 to 15 minutes for medium-rare). Transfer to a platter. Garnish with tomato wedges, lime wedges, and cilantro sprigs.

To serve, cut steak across the grain into thin slices; serve with Thai Relish. Makes 6 servings.—*J. Hill, Sacramento*

THAI RELISH. In a bowl, mix 1 cup *each* finely diced **cucumber** and **papaya,** ¼ cup thinly sliced **green**

onions, 2 tablespoons **lime juice**, ¼ teaspoon **crushed red pepper flakes,** and 2 cloves **garlic,** minced or pressed.

Per serving: 198 calories, 6 g carbohydrates, 28 g protein, 7 g total fat (3 g saturated), 79 mg cholesterol, 64 mg sodium

FORGOTTEN SHORT RIBS

These short ribs have a delicious, slow-baked flavor. You might serve the rich sauce over hot cooked rice or noodles. Or try this: peel medium-size potatoes, roll them in salad oil, sprinkle with salt and coarsely ground pepper, and bake them alongside the meat in another covered casserole, for the same length of time.

3   **to 4 pounds beef short ribs, trimmed of fat**

Salt and pepper

1   **can (about 8 oz.) tomato sauce**

2   **tablespoons** *each* **molasses and cider vinegar**

1   **teaspoon liquid smoke flavoring**

1   **tablespoon dehydrated minced onion**

Sprinkle beef all over with salt and pepper, then place in a 3-quart casserole. In a small pan, stir together tomato sauce, molasses, vinegar, liquid smoke, and onion; bring to a boil, then reduce heat and simmer, uncovered, for 5 minutes.

Pour sauce over meat; cover and bake in a 275° oven until meat is very tender when pierced (3 to 4 hours). Before serving, spoon off and discard fat. If made ahead, cover and refrigerate until next day; lift off and discard solidified fat before reheating. Makes 4 to 6 servings.—*B. F., Carmichael, CA*

Per serving: 293 calories, 10 g carbohydrates, 27 g protein, 16 g total fat (7 g saturated), 80 mg cholesterol, 328 mg sodium

SHORT RIBS WITH NOODLES

This hearty casserole truly is an oven supper—you do all of the cooking in the oven, down to browning the meat and cooking the pasta. Serve with crusty rolls and a vinaigrette-dressed cabbage salad such as Spicy Red Coleslaw (page 41) or pungent Crisp Kraut Salad (page 47).

⅓   **cup all-purpose flour**

1   **teaspoon salt**

¼   **teaspoon pepper**

3   **pounds beef short ribs, trimmed of fat**

2   **cups hot water**

1   **package (about 1.4 oz.) onion soup mix**

6   **ounces dry medium-wide egg noodles or rotini**

Chopped parsley

Combine flour, salt, and pepper. Coat beef ribs with flour mixture; shake off excess. Arrange ribs in an ungreased roasting pan, broiler pan (at least 2 inches deep), or 9- by 13-inch baking pan, keeping pieces slightly apart. Bake in a 500° oven for 20 minutes. Remove from oven; reduce oven temperature to 325°.

Spoon off and discard fat from pan; add hot water and soup mix to pan. Cover pan tightly, return to oven, and bake until meat is tender when pierced (1½ to 2 hours).

Add noodles to pan liquid; stir until evenly moistened and covered with liquid. Cover and bake for 15 more minutes; stir, then cover again and continue to bake until noodles are tender to bite (about 5 more minutes), adding a little more water, if needed. Sprinkle with parsley before serving. Makes 4 to 6 servings. —*M. S., Spokane, WA*

Per serving: 424 calories, 35 g carbohydrates, 29 g protein, 18 g total fat (7 g saturated), 104 mg cholesterol, 1,201 mg sodium

SIMMERED CORNED BEEF

You simmer this corned beef ahead, then chill it in the cooking broth to serve cold for sandwiches or on a buffet platter.

Use the broth for soup, if you like: first lift off and discard the solidified fat, then strain the broth and discard the seasonings. Peel and dice 2 large potatoes and 3 large carrots; simmer them in the broth until tender. Garnish the soup with sour cream and sliced green onions.

About 5 pounds corned beef (bottom round or brisket)

1   **medium-size onion, chopped**

¼   **teaspoon** *each* **garlic powder and liquid hot pepper seasoning**

1   **teaspoon dry dill weed**

3   **dry bay leaves**

2   **cinnamon sticks (***each* **about 3 inches long)**

5   **whole cloves**

1   **orange (unpeeled), thinly sliced**

Place corned beef in a 6- to 8-quart pan; add 2 quarts water. Cover and bring to a boil over high heat; then reduce heat and simmer for 30 minutes. Taste water; if it's too salty, drain beef, discard water, and add 2 quarts more water to pan.

Add onion, garlic powder, hot pepper seasoning, dill weed, bay leaves, cinnamon sticks, cloves, and orange slices to pan. Cover and simmer until meat is tender when pierced (2½ to 3 hours). Remove from heat and let meat cool in broth; then cover and refrigerate until next day.

To serve, remove meat from broth (reserve broth for soup). Cut meat across the grain into thin slices. Makes 8 to 10 servings.—*J. T., North Hollywood, CA*

Per serving of meat: 447 calories, 0.8 g carbohydrates, 32 g protein, 34 g total fat (11 g saturated), 175 mg cholesterol, 2,019 mg sodium

WINE-BRAISED CHUCK ROAST

Chopped fresh mint garnishes this spicy baked pot roast. It's good with wide egg noodles and a green vegetable, such as steamed broccoli or Brussels sprouts.

- 1 boneless beef chuck roast (about 4 lbs.)
- 1 large onion, chopped
- 4 cloves garlic, slivered
- 1 cup *each* dry red wine and water
- 1 can (about 8 oz.) tomato sauce
- 2 tablespoons red wine vinegar
- 1 dry bay leaf
- 7 whole allspice
- 1 cinnamon stick (about 3 inches long)
- 1 teaspoon cumin seeds
- ½ teaspoon *each* salt and pepper
- 2 to 3 tablespoons chopped fresh mint

Trim excess fat from beef. Cook fat in a wide frying pan over medium heat until you have 2 tablespoons melted fat; discard unrendered pieces of fat.

Add onion and garlic to pan; cook, stirring often, until onion is soft. Then stir in wine, water, tomato sauce, vinegar, bay leaf, allspice, cinnamon stick, cumin seeds, salt, and pepper.

Set meat in a large baking pan; pour sauce around meat. Cover and bake in a 300° oven until meat is very tender when pierced (3 to 3½ hours). Transfer meat to a platter; slice and keep warm.

Pour sauce through a strainer into a 2- to 3-quart pan; skim and discard fat. Bring sauce to a boil; then boil, uncovered, until reduced to about 2 cups. Pour sauce over meat and sprinkle with mint. Makes 8 to 10 servings.—R. T., Elk Grove, CA

Per serving: 250 calories, 6 g carbohydrates, 33 g protein, 10 g total fat (4 g saturated), 95 mg cholesterol, 380 mg sodium

CRANBERRY-PORT POT ROAST

Perfect for a winter evening, this chunky beef roast bakes to tenderness in a savory port wine sauce. For color and sweet-tart flavor, cook tiny onions and bright cranberries along with the meat.

- 1 beef eye of round or rump roast (3½ to 4 lbs.), trimmed of fat
- 1 tablespoon salad oil
- 1 can (about 14½ oz.) beef broth
- 1¾ cups port
- ⅓ cup firmly packed brown sugar
- 2 packages (about 10 oz. *each*) frozen tiny onions
- 2 cups fresh or frozen cranberries
- 6 cups hot cooked egg noodles
- 2 tablespoons cornstarch blended with 3 tablespoons cold water
  Salt and pepper
  Parsley sprigs

Rub beef with oil and place in a large roasting pan. Bake in a 450° oven until meat is well browned (about 45 minutes), turning often. Add broth and port. Cover tightly; reduce oven temperature to 400° and bake for 1½ more hours.

Mix sugar and onions into pan juices; cover and bake for 1 more hour. Stir in cranberries; cover and bake until meat is tender when pierced (about 30 more minutes).

Arrange meat and noodles on a platter. With a slotted spoon, ladle onions and cranberries over noodles; keep warm.

Skim and discard fat from pan juices. Bring pan juices to a boil over high heat; stir in cornstarch mixture and cook, stirring, until sauce boils and thickens. Season sauce to taste with salt and pepper, then pour into a small bowl. Garnish meat and noodles with parsley sprigs; serve with sauce. Makes 10 to 12 servings.
—Dorothy B. Rosenthal, Pacific Palisades, CA

Per serving: 397 calories, 41 g carbohydrates, 36 g protein, 9 g total fat (3 g saturated), 107 mg cholesterol, 355 mg sodium

HUNTER'S BEEF

Soy, wine, and mushrooms give this round steak a woodsy, gamy flavor.

- 2 pounds beef round steak (about ¾ inch thick), trimmed of fat and cut into serving-size pieces
  Salt
- 2 to 3 tablespoons all-purpose flour
- 2 tablespoons solid vegetable shortening or salad oil
- 1 bunch green onions (ends trimmed), cut into 2-inch lengths
- 3 stalks celery, cut diagonally into 2-inch lengths
- 1 pound fresh mushrooms or 2 cans (about 6 oz. *each*) mushroom caps
- 3 tablespoons soy sauce
- ⅓ cup dry red wine
  Dash of ground red pepper (cayenne)
- ¼ to ½ teaspoon ground ginger or grated fresh ginger

Sprinkle beef with salt and dust with flour. Melt shortening in a wide, deep frying pan over medium-high heat. Add meat, a portion at a time (do not crowd pan); cook, turning as needed, until browned on both sides. As meat is browned, remove it from pan and set aside.

Return all meat (and any accumulated juices) to pan. Arrange onions, celery, and mushrooms over meat. Stir together soy sauce, wine, red pepper, and ginger; pour over meat. Reduce heat, cover, and simmer until meat is tender when pierced (1½ to 2 hours). Makes 6 to 8 servings. —W. A., Los Angeles

Per serving: 229 calories, 8 g carbohydrates, 27 g protein, 10 g total fat (3 g saturated), 66 mg cholesterol, 526 mg sodium

PEPPER BEEF STIR-FRY

For a quick dinner, stir-fry thin-sliced steak with cracked black pepper and slivers of red and green bell pepper.

1 **pound boneless beef sirloin steak, trimmed of fat and cut across the grain into thin 1- by 3-inch strips**

2 **teaspoons cracked black pepper**

1 **clove garlic, minced or pressed**

2 **tablespoons Worcestershire**

3 **to 4 tablespoons salad oil**

1 **large onion, thinly sliced**

1 *each* **large red and green bell pepper (about 1 lb. *total*), seeded and cut into thin slivers**

   Salt

   Romaine lettuce leaves, rinsed and crisped (optional)

In a shallow dish, mix beef, pepper, garlic, and Worcestershire. Let stand for 15 minutes.

Heat 2 tablespoons of the oil in a wide frying pan or wok over high heat. Add meat, about half at a time (do not crowd pan); cook, stirring, until lightly browned (1 to 2 minutes). As meat is cooked, remove it from pan and set aside. Add more oil to pan as needed.

Add 1 tablespoon more oil, onion, and bell peppers to pan; cook, stirring, just until vegetables are tender-crisp to bite (2 to 3 minutes). Return meat (and any accumulated juices) to

pan. Season to taste with salt and pour onto a platter; garnish with lettuce, if desired. Makes 4 servings. —*Marie Carroll, Mountainair, NM*

Per serving: 311 calories, 13 g carbohydrates, 26 g protein, 17 g total fat (3 g saturated), 69 mg cholesterol, 152 mg sodium

GARLIC BEEF

In Provence, garlic is a favorite ingredient—and this Provençal-style stew calls for the legendary 30 cloves. To speed up the task of peeling the garlic, place the cloves, a few at a time, on a hard surface; then press them firmly with the flat side of a knife blade or cleaver.

3½ **pounds boneless beef chuck, trimmed of fat and cut into 1½-inch chunks**

1 **tablespoon soy sauce**

1⅓ **cups beef broth**

30 **cloves garlic (about 6 oz. *total*), peeled**

1⅓ **cups dry red wine or beef broth**

   Salt

   Chopped parsley

In a 5- to 6-quart pan, combine beef and soy sauce. Cover and cook over medium heat for 30 minutes. Uncover and bring to a boil over high heat; boil until juices have evaporated. When meat starts to sizzle, turn it often until well browned on all sides. Add broth and stir well; then add garlic and wine. Bring to a boil; then reduce heat, cover, and simmer until meat is very tender when pierced (about 1½ hours). Garlic may disintegrate and thicken sauce slightly.

Skim and discard fat from sauce. Season stew to taste with salt; then transfer to serving dish and sprinkle with parsley. Makes 6 servings.—*Peg Roberts, Santa Barbara, CA*

Per serving: 308 calories, 9 g carbohydrates, 45 g protein, 9 g total fat (3 g saturated), 121 mg cholesterol, 677 mg sodium

HOT & SOUR BEEF WITH CUCUMBER

Season broiled steak strips with cucumber, lime, soy, and spicy red pepper, then chill to make a refreshing, Thai-inspired main-dish salad.

1 **boneless beef sirloin steak (about 1 lb.), about 1¼ inches thick**

1 **medium-size cucumber (about 8 oz.)**

¼ **cup *each* lime juice and thinly sliced red onion**

2 **tablespoons soy sauce or fish sauce (*nuoc mam* or *nam pla*)**

½ **teaspoon Oriental sesame oil (optional)**

¼ **to ½ teaspoon ground red pepper (cayenne)**

   Butter lettuce leaves, rinsed and crisped

1 **teaspoon sesame seeds**

   Mint or cilantro sprigs

Slash rim of fat on steak at 2-inch intervals. Place steak on a rack in a broiler pan and broil about 3 inches below heat, turning once, until well browned on both sides and rare to medium-rare; cut to test (about 12 minutes).

Meanwhile, peel cucumber and cut in half lengthwise; scrape out and discard seeds. Thinly slice cucumber crosswise.

Cut cooked steak across the grain into thin slices. In a large bowl, mix cucumber, steak, lime juice, onion, soy sauce, sesame oil (if used), and red pepper. Cover and refrigerate until cold (at least 1 hour) or for up to 6 hours. Arrange lettuce leaves on a platter. Pile steak mixture onto lettuce; garnish with sesame seeds and mint sprigs. Serve as a salad; or roll steak mixture in lettuce to eat. Makes 4 servings.—*Yupa Holzner, Lake Arrowhead, CA*

Per serving: 220 calories, 4 g carbohydrates, 22 g protein, 12 g total fat (5 g saturated), 68 mg cholesterol, 569 mg sodium

Apple Cider Stew

Chopped apples break down as they simmer, thickening the cooking juices to make a rich sauce for this beef-and-sweet potato stew.

- 3 to 4 pounds lean boneless beef stew meat, trimmed of fat and cut into 2-inch chunks

  About 3 cups apple cider

- 2 medium-size tart apples (about 12 oz. *total*), peeled, cored, and chopped

- 1 cinnamon stick (about 3 inches long)

- 2 tablespoons cider vinegar

- 12 to 16 small onions (*each* about 1½ inches in diameter), peeled

- 2 pounds sweet potatoes, peeled and cut into 2-inch chunks

  Parsley sprigs

In a 5- to 6-quart pan, combine beef and ½ cup of the cider. Cover and cook over medium heat for about 30 minutes. Uncover and bring to a boil over high heat; boil until juices have evaporated. When meat starts to sizzle, turn it often until well browned on all sides (about 1 hour).

Lift meat from pan; pour off and discard fat from pan. To pan, add 1½ cups more cider, apples, cinnamon stick, and vinegar. Stir to scrape browned bits free from pan.

Return meat to pan; add onions and sweet potatoes. Cover and simmer until meat pulls apart easily (about 1½ hours), adding more cider as needed to keep pan from cooking dry. Lift meat and vegetables from pan; arrange on platter. Remove and discard cinnamon stick; then skim and discard fat from pan juices. Pour juices over meat. Garnish with parsley sprigs. Makes 6 to 8 servings. —*Barbara Keenan, Fort Morgan, CO*

Per serving: 409 calories, 44 g carbohydrates, 39 g protein, 8 g total fat (3 g saturated), 104 mg cholesterol, 132 mg sodium

Baked Beef Stew with Carrots

This oven stew takes time to cook, but it doesn't demand much attention.

- 2½ pounds boneless beef chuck, trimmed of fat and cut into 1-inch cubes

- 2 medium-size onions, chopped

- 1 tablespoon all-purpose flour

- 2 cups beef broth

- ¼ cup red wine vinegar

- 2 teaspoons dry thyme

- 1 teaspoon pepper

- 4 cups ¼-inch-thick carrot slices

  Salt and pepper

  About 6 cups hot mashed potatoes

In a shallow 3- to 3½-quart casserole, mix beef and onions. Bake in a 450° oven, stirring occasionally, until meat is well browned (40 to 45 minutes). Remove from oven. Sprinkle meat mixture with flour; stir gently to coat. Reduce oven temperature to 350°.

In a 1½-quart pan, bring broth, vinegar, thyme, and the 1 teaspoon pepper to a boil. Add to meat and onions, stirring to scrape browned bits free. Stir in carrots. Cover tightly and bake until meat is very tender when pierced (1½ to 2 more hours). If stew is soupy, uncover and continue to bake to reduce liquid. Season to taste with salt and pepper; serve with potatoes. Makes 6 servings.—*Natalie Haney, Roseville, CA*

Per serving: 490 calories, 52 g carbohydrates, 37 g protein, 16 g total fat (5 g saturated), 90 mg cholesterol, 1,304 mg sodium

Cabbage-Paprika Stroganoff

For extra-tangy flavor, the creamy paprika sauce for this stew is made with half plain yogurt, half sour cream. For a lower-fat entrée, use reduced-fat sour cream, low-fat yogurt, and eggless noodles.

- 6 slices bacon

- 1½ pounds beef top round steak, trimmed of fat and cut across the grain into ¼-inch-thick slices

- 1 large onion, thinly sliced

- 1 medium-size head green cabbage (about 1½ lbs.), coarsely shredded

- 1 tablespoon paprika

- 1 cup *each* sour cream and plain yogurt

- 6 cups hot cooked egg noodles

- 2 tablespoons minced parsley

Cook bacon in a wide frying pan over medium heat until crisp. Lift out, drain, crumble, and set aside; reserve drippings in pan.

Heat drippings over medium-high heat. Add beef, a portion at a time (do not crowd pan); cook, stirring, just until meat is no longer pink. As meat is cooked, remove it from pan with a slotted spoon and set aside. Pour off and discard all but 1½ tablespoons fat from pan.

To pan, add onion, cabbage, and paprika. Cook, stirring often, until liquid has evaporated and vegetables are soft and sweet-tasting (about 30 minutes).

Stir sour cream and yogurt into cabbage mixture. Return meat (and any accumulated juices) to pan; stir until heated through, but do not boil. Spoon meat mixture onto a platter; mound noodles alongside. Sprinkle with bacon and parsley. Makes 4 servings.—*Ann U. Cress, Golden, CO*

Per serving: 914 calories, 80 g carbohydrates, 53 g protein, 42 g total fat (18 g saturated), 216 mg cholesterol, 414 mg sodium

Rocky Mountain Chili

Colorful carrot slices give a mellow sweetness to this noteworthy chili.

- 2 slices bacon
- 2 pounds lean boneless beef stew meat, trimmed of fat and cut into 1-inch cubes
- 2 large onions, chopped
- 2 cloves garlic, minced or pressed
- 2 tablespoons chili powder
- 1 teaspoon *each* dry oregano and ground cumin
- 4 cups water
- 4 beef bouillon cubes
- 1 cup (about 6 oz.) dried red beans
- 4 cups thinly sliced carrots
  Salt and pepper

Cook bacon in a 5-quart pan over medium heat until crisp. Lift out, drain, crumble, and set aside; reserve drippings in pan.

Increase heat to medium-high. Add beef, a portion at a time (do not crowd pan); cook, turning as needed, until well browned on all sides. As meat is browned, remove it from pan and set aside. Add onions and garlic to pan; cook, stirring often, until onions are soft. Stir in chili powder, oregano, cumin, water, and bouillon cubes. Return meat (and any accumulated juices) to pan.

Sort through beans; discard any debris. Rinse beans, drain, and add to pan. Bring to a boil; reduce heat, cover, and simmer until meat and beans are tender (about 2 hours).

Skim and discard fat from chili. Bring to a boil; add carrots, reduce heat, cover, and simmer until carrots are tender to bite (about 30 minutes). Stir in bacon and season to taste with salt and pepper. Makes 6 servings. —*M. L., Canon City, CO*

Per serving: 387 calories, 34 g carbohydrates, 32 g protein, 14 g total fat (5 g saturated), 81 mg cholesterol, 775 mg sodium

Fiesta Tamale Pie

On a chilly evening, tamale pie is sure to please. This version of a long-time Western favorite combines beef and sausage in the filling; the cornmeal topping is crusted with melted Cheddar cheese.

- 2 tablespoons salad oil
- 1 medium-size onion, chopped
- 1 clove garlic, minced or pressed
- 1 pound lean ground beef
- 8 ounces bulk pork sausage
- 1 large can (about 28 oz.) tomatoes
- 1 can (about 17 oz.) whole-kernel corn, drained
- 1 tablespoon chili powder
- ½ teaspoon *each* dry oregano and ground cumin
- 1 cup pitted ripe olives, drained
  Cornmeal Topping (recipe follows)
- 1½ cups (about 6 oz.) shredded Cheddar cheese

Heat oil in a wide frying pan over medium heat; add onion and garlic and cook, stirring often, until onion is soft. Crumble in beef and sausage and cook, stirring often, until browned; spoon off and discard fat from pan. Cut up tomatoes; then add tomatoes and their liquid, corn, chili powder, oregano, and cumin to pan. Bring to a boil; then reduce heat, cover, and simmer for 10 minutes. Stir in olives.

Spread meat mixture in a shallow 3-quart casserole. Prepare Cornmeal Topping and spoon evenly over meat mixture, then sprinkle with cheese. Bake in a 350° oven until topping feels set when lightly touched (about 45 minutes). Makes 6 servings. —*Mrs. D. DeM., Los Angeles*

Cornmeal Topping. In a bowl, beat 2 large **eggs** to blend; then beat in 1 cup *each* **milk** and **cornmeal.**

Per serving: 636 calories, 47 g carbohydrates, 33 g protein, 37 g total fat (14 g saturated), 167 mg cholesterol, 1,133 mg sodium

Ground Beef & Cheese Pie

Serve wedges of this main-dish pie for brunch or supper, accompanied with fresh asparagus or a green salad. The pastry is quickly made with packaged biscuit mix.

- Quick Pastry (recipe follows)
- 1½ pounds lean ground beef
- 1 medium-size onion, chopped
- ½ teaspoon salt
- ¼ teaspoon pepper
- 1 large egg
- 1 large egg white
- 2 cups large-curd cottage cheese
- ⅓ cup shredded Parmesan cheese
  Chopped parsley (optional)

Prepare Quick Pastry. On a lightly floured board, roll pastry into an 11½-inch round. Fit pastry into a 9-inch pie pan; trim and flute edge.

Crumble beef into a wide nonstick frying pan and cook over medium heat, stirring often, until juices begin to form. Then add onion, salt, and pepper; cook, stirring, until meat is no longer pink and liquid has evaporated. Turn filling into prepared crust.

In a bowl, stir together egg, egg white, and cottage cheese until well blended; spoon over meat filling in pie. Sprinkle with Parmesan cheese. Bake in a 375° oven until topping feels set when lightly pressed (about 25 minutes). Sprinkle with parsley, if desired; serve hot. Makes 6 servings. —*A. M., San Diego, CA*

Quick Pastry. In a bowl, combine 1 cup **biscuit mix** (baking mix), 1 large **egg yolk,** and 2½ tablespoons **milk.** Mix with a fork until evenly blended, then press into a ball with your hands.

Per serving: 517 calories, 18 g carbohydrates, 35 g protein, 33 g total fat (14 g saturated), 171 mg cholesterol, 906 mg sodium

ISLAND MEATBALLS

Hot cooked rice or cracked wheat goes well with these glazed meatballs.

- 2 pounds lean ground beef
- 1 medium-size onion, finely chopped
- 2 large eggs
- 1 teaspoon salt
- ½ teaspoon *each* pepper and dry basil
- 1½ tablespoons salad oil
- ⅔ cup slivered almonds
- 2 tablespoons soy sauce
- 1 tablespoon cornstarch
- ⅓ cup firmly packed brown sugar
- ¼ cup red wine vinegar
- 1 can (about 15¼ oz.) pineapple chunks

In a large bowl, combine beef, onion, eggs, salt, pepper, and basil. Mix until well blended; then shape into 32 equal balls.

Heat oil in a wide frying pan over medium heat; add almonds and cook, stirring often, until lightly browned (about 3 minutes). Lift from pan and place in a 2½-quart casserole. Dip meatballs in soy sauce; add to pan, a portion at a time (do not crowd pan), and cook, turning as needed, until browned on all sides. Transfer to casserole; discard drippings from pan.

In a small bowl, stir together cornstarch, sugar, and vinegar. Stir in any soy sauce left from coating meatballs. Drain liquid from pineapple into sugar mixture; add pineapple chunks to casserole. Pour sugar mixture into frying pan and cook over medium heat, stirring, until thickened; pour into casserole. Cover and bake in a 350° oven until meatballs are no longer pink in center; cut to test (25 to 30 minutes). Skim and discard fat from sauce. Makes 6 to 8 servings.—*R. G., Kaneohe, HI*

Per serving: 474 calories, 27 g carbohydrates, 28 g protein, 29 g total fat (8 g saturated), 139 mg cholesterol, 705 mg sodium

HAMBURGER STEAK, SOUBISE

Cook this giant hamburger patty for a few minutes on top of your range, then slip it under the broiler to brown the top.

- ¼ cup butter or margarine
- 3 medium-size onions, thinly sliced
- 1½ cups boiling water
- 2 pounds lean ground beef
- ¾ teaspoon salt
   Dash of pepper
- ⅛ teaspoon garlic salt
- ¼ teaspoon smoke-flavored salt
- 1 cup sour cream
   Paprika
   Parsley sprigs (optional)

Melt 3 tablespoons of the butter in a wide frying pan over medium heat. Add onions and cook, stirring, for 5 minutes. Add boiling water and simmer, uncovered, until almost all liquid has evaporated (about 20 minutes).

Meanwhile, in a large bowl, combine beef, salt, pepper, garlic salt, and smoke-flavored salt; mix until well blended. Shape into an 8-inch patty.

Melt remaining 1 tablespoon butter in an 8-inch-round baking pan over medium heat. Fit patty into pan. Cook on top of the range until nicely browned on bottom (about 5 minutes). Then broil about 3 inches below heat until done to your liking; cut to test (about 6 minutes for rare). Using 2 spatulas, carefully lift meat from pan and place on a platter; keep warm. Discard pan drippings.

Stir sour cream into onion mixture; stir just until heated through, but do not boil. Pour sauce over meat; sprinkle with paprika and garnish with parsley sprigs, if desired. Makes 6 servings.—*B. P., Davis, CA*

Per serving: 473 calories, 9 g carbohydrates, 29 g protein, 36 g total fat (17 g saturated), 127 mg cholesterol, 570 mg sodium

CHILES RELLENOS MEATBALLS

Chiles in the meatballs, cumin and more chiles in the sauce—this lively dish delivers potent Mexican flavor.

- 1 large egg
- ⅓ cup fine dry bread crumbs
- ¼ cup milk
- 1 tablespoon chopped parsley
- 1 pound lean ground beef
- 1 can (about 4 oz.) whole green chiles
- 5 to 6 ounces jack cheese
   Tomato Sauce (recipe follows)

In a large bowl, beat egg to blend. Add bread crumbs, milk, parsley, and beef; mix until well blended, then divide into 10 equal portions. Cut chiles lengthwise into 10 strips, each about 1 inch wide; reserve any extra chiles for sauce. Cut cheese into 10 about ¾-inch cubes. Wrap each cheese cube in a chile strip, then mold a portion of meat around each cube. Set meatballs in a shallow 10- by 15-inch baking pan. Bake in a 450° oven until browned (about 20 minutes). Meanwhile, prepare Tomato Sauce.

Transfer meatballs to a shallow 2-quart casserole; top with sauce. Reduce oven temperature to 350°; return meatballs to oven and continue to bake until sauce is bubbly (about 20 minutes). Makes 4 servings.—*Lyn Hagaman Ortega, Corrales, NM*

TOMATO SAUCE. In a 2- to 3-quart pan, combine ½ cup chopped **onion,** 1 clove **garlic** (minced or pressed), 1 can (about 14½ oz.) **ready-cut tomatoes,** ¾ teaspoon **dry oregano,** ⅛ teaspoon **ground cumin,** and any extra **green chiles** (chopped). Bring to a boil over high heat; then reduce heat and simmer, uncovered, stirring often, until reduced to 2 cups.

Per serving: 471 calories, 16 g carbohydrates, 34 g protein, 30 g total fat (14 g saturated), 162 mg cholesterol, 698 mg sodium

Ground Beef Patties with Lemon Sauce

To make this inexpensive entrée, you brown thick beef patties in a skillet, then simmer them briefly in a sweet-tart lemon sauce. You might serve each patty on a toasted English muffin half.

1½ pounds lean ground beef
2 tablespoons finely chopped onion
½ teaspoon salt
1 teaspoon grated lemon peel
1 large egg
1 tablespoon salad oil
2 tablespoons white wine vinegar
½ teaspoon ground ginger
3 tablespoons firmly packed brown sugar
1 dry bay leaf
6 thin lemon slices
2 beef bouillon cubes

In a large bowl, combine beef, onion, salt, lemon peel, and egg. Mix until well blended; then shape into 6 thick patties.

Heat oil in a wide frying pan over medium-high heat. Add meat patties and cook, turning as needed, until well browned on both sides. Remove patties and set aside; pour off and discard any fat from pan.

To pan, add vinegar, ginger, sugar, bay leaf, lemon slices, and bouillon cubes. Bring to a boil, stirring until bouillon cubes and sugar are dissolved.

Return beef patties to pan. Reduce heat, cover, and simmer, turning once or twice, until meat is done to your liking; cut to test (about 8 minutes for medium-well). Remove and discard bay leaf from sauce; offer sauce to spoon over patties. Makes 6 servings. —J. P., Lynnwood, WA

Per serving: 290 calories, 9 g carbohydrates, 21 g protein, 19 g total fat (7 g saturated), 104 mg cholesterol, 547 mg sodium

Beef & Mushroom Bake

Joe's Special is a San Francisco favorite known throughout the West. Here, it's transformed into a savory casserole with a bubbly cheese topping. Serve it with a crisp green salad.

1 pound lean ground beef
1 large onion, finely chopped
8 ounces mushrooms, sliced
2 packages (about 10 oz. *each*) frozen chopped spinach, thawed and squeezed dry
1 cup sour cream
1½ teaspoons Italian herb seasoning (or a scant ½ teaspoon *each* dry basil, marjoram, oregano, and thyme)
1 teaspoon salt
⅛ teaspoon ground nutmeg
1 cup (about 4 oz.) shredded Cheddar cheese
1 cup (about 4 oz.) grated Parmesan cheese

Crumble beef into a wide nonstick frying pan and cook over medium-high heat, stirring often, for 2 to 3 minutes. Add onion and mushrooms; cook, stirring often, until almost all liquid has evaporated (about 5 minutes). Remove from heat and stir in spinach, sour cream, herb seasoning, salt, nutmeg, and ½ cup each of the Cheddar and Parmesan cheeses. Spoon mixture into a shallow 2-quart casserole; sprinkle with remaining ½ cup each Cheddar and Parmesan cheeses. (At this point, you may cover and refrigerate for up to 4 hours.)

Bake, uncovered, in a 350° oven until heated through (about 20 minutes; 30 to 35 minutes if refrigerated). Makes 4 to 6 servings. —B. C., Oak Harbor, WA

Per serving: 591 calories, 14 g carbohydrates, 37 g protein, 43 g total fat (23 g saturated), 130 mg cholesterol, 1,182 mg sodium

Hungarian Cabbage Rolls

Green cabbage leaves stuffed with a spicy beef-barley filling bake in a tomato-sauerkraut sauce.

1 large head cabbage (about 2¼ lbs.)
¼ cup butter or margarine
2 large onions, chopped
1½ teaspoons ground allspice
1 pound lean ground beef
1 cup cooked barley or rice
1 large egg
2 tablespoons all-purpose flour
   Salt and pepper
1 can (about 14½ oz.) sauerkraut, drained
2 cans (about 8 oz. *each*) tomato sauce
¼ cup firmly packed brown sugar

Fill a 6- to 8-quart pan half-full with water; bring to a boil. Core cabbage and immerse in boiling water; boil until leaves are flexible enough to pull from head. Drain and let cool. Remove 12 large leaves from cabbage; then shred remaining cabbage.

Melt 2 tablespoons of the butter in pan over medium-high heat. Add onions and allspice; cook, stirring often, until onions are soft. Mix in beef, barley, egg, and flour. Season to taste with salt and pepper. Put about ¼ cup of the meat mixture on each large cabbage leaf; roll to enclose.

Melt remaining 2 tablespoons butter in pan over medium-high heat. Add shredded cabbage; stir until lightly browned. Stir in sauerkraut, tomato sauce, and sugar; then pour mixture into a 9- by 13-inch baking pan. Top with cabbage rolls. Cover and bake in a 350° oven until meat is no longer pink in center; cut to test (about 1½ hours). Makes 6 servings. —Toni Young, Borrego Springs, CA

Per serving: 449 calories, 40 g carbohydrates, 19 g protein, 25 g total fat (11 g saturated), 113 mg cholesterol, 801 mg sodium

LIVER IN LEMON BUTTER

Even those who normally don't care for liver enjoy it prepared this way. Sautéed liver slices, coated in crisp cracker crumbs, are topped with a simple lemon butter sauce sweetened with just a touch of sugar.

¼ cup all-purpose flour
½ teaspoon salt
⅛ teaspoon pepper
1 large egg
1 pound beef liver, thinly sliced
½ cup salted soda cracker crumbs
6 tablespoons butter or margarine
3 tablespoons lemon juice
1 teaspoon sugar

Combine flour, salt, and pepper. In a shallow bowl, beat egg to blend. Coat liver slices lightly with flour mixture; dip each slice in beaten egg, then dip in cracker crumbs to coat evenly on both sides. Melt ¼ cup of the butter in a wide frying pan over medium-high heat. Add liver slices and cook, turning once, until nicely browned on both sides but still pink and juicy in center; cut to test (3 to 4 minutes).

Transfer liver to a platter and keep warm. Melt remaining 2 tablespoons butter in pan, add lemon juice and sugar, and stir until sugar is dissolved. Pour sauce over liver. Serve at once. Makes 4 servings.—*A. A., Berkeley, CA*

Per serving: 406 calories, 21 g carbohydrates, 26 g protein, 24 g total fat (15 g saturated), 501 mg cholesterol, 664 mg sodium

PORK CHOPS WITH WALNUTS & WINE

Toasted walnuts add a nice crunch to juicy pork chops baked with onions and red wine. Serve with steamed carrots tossed with melted butter and a dusting of nutmeg.

2 tablespoons butter or margarine
4 pork rib chops (about 2 lbs. *total*)
¾ cup walnut halves or pieces
1 large onion, sliced
1 large clove garlic, minced or pressed
⅓ cup dry red wine or beef broth
½ cup minced parsley
Salt and pepper

Melt 1 tablespoon of the butter in a wide frying pan over medium-high heat. Add pork chops and cook, turning as needed, until well browned on both sides. Transfer chops to a 9- by 13-inch baking dish.

Add walnuts and remaining 1 tablespoon butter to pan. Stir until nuts are golden (2 to 3 minutes). Lift out nuts; set aside. Add onion and garlic to pan; cook, stirring often, until onion is soft. Stir in wine. Spoon onion mixture over chops (set frying pan aside). Cover and bake in a 350° oven until meat near bone is faintly pink to white but still moist; cut to test (about 35 minutes).

Transfer chops to a platter; keep warm. Pour onion and juices from baking pan into frying pan; add parsley. Bring to a boil over high heat; boil, uncovered, until almost all liquid has evaporated (about 4 minutes). Stir in walnuts; season to taste with salt and pepper. Spoon sauce over chops. Makes 4 servings. —*Deborah Morgan, Albuquerque*

Per serving: 494 calories, 9 g carbohydrates, 33 g protein, 36 g total fat (11 g saturated), 100 mg cholesterol, 114 mg sodium

BAKED PORK CHOPS WITH HERB STUFFING

This easy variation of stuffed pork chops saves you the step of cutting a pocket in each chop. Instead, you simply brown the chops, alternate them with spoonfuls of vegetable-rich bread dressing in a casserole, and bake. If you like, start acorn squash halves baking—they'll need about 1 hour in all—then put the meat and dressing in the oven about half an hour later.

2 tablespoons butter or margarine
6 pork rib or loin chops (2 to 2½ lbs. *total*), about ¾ inch thick
1 cup *each* chopped celery and chopped onion
3 tablespoons chopped parsley
¾ teaspoon salt
½ teaspoon *each* pepper, dry sage, and dry thyme
4 cups soft bread crumbs
2 large eggs, beaten

Melt butter in a wide frying pan over medium-high heat. Add chops and cook, turning as needed, just until browned on both sides. Remove from pan and set aside. Add celery and onion; cook, stirring often, until soft. Remove pan from heat. Add parsley, salt, pepper, sage, thyme, bread crumbs, and eggs.

Place one pork chop at one end of a greased 7- by 11-inch baking dish. Spoon a sixth of the stuffing mixture over chop; place another chop on top, overlapping slightly. Continue alternating stuffing with chops to use remaining stuffing and chops.

Bake in a 350° oven until meat near bone is faintly pink to white but still moist; cut to test (30 to 35 minutes). Makes 6 servings.—*J. M., Petaluma, CA*

Per serving: 413 calories, 19 g carbohydrates, 24 g protein, 26 g total fat (10 g saturated), 152 mg cholesterol, 548 mg sodium

Pork Chops with Rhubarb Dressing

Rhubarb, brown sugar, and fragrant spices go into the dressing for these tender chops. In the oven, the fruit cooks down to make a sweet-sour sauce.

- ½ teaspoon dry rosemary
- ¾ teaspoon salt
- ⅛ teaspoon pepper
- 6 pork loin or shoulder chops (2 to 2½ lbs. *total*), about ¾ inch thick
- 2 tablespoons salad oil
- 4 slices firm-textured white bread, cut into ½-inch cubes
- ¾ cup firmly packed brown sugar
- ½ teaspoon ground cinnamon
- ¼ teaspoon ground allspice
- 2 to 2¼ pounds rhubarb, cut into ½-inch pieces
- 3 tablespoons all-purpose flour

Mix rosemary, salt, and pepper; sprinkle evenly over chops. Heat oil in a wide frying pan over medium-high heat; add chops and cook, turning as needed, until browned on both sides. Set chops aside (reserve pan drippings).

In a large bowl, combine bread cubes, sugar, cinnamon, allspice, rhubarb, and flour. Spread half the mixture in a greased 9- by 13-inch baking dish. Arrange chops on top; then spoon 3 tablespoons of the drippings over chops (if needed, add water to drippings to make this amount). Top with remaining rhubarb mixture. (At this point, you may cover and refrigerate until next day.) Bake, covered, in a 350° oven for 45 minutes. Then uncover and continue to bake until meat in thickest part is faintly pink to white but still moist; cut to test (about 15 more minutes). Makes 6 servings.
—*L. G., Bremerton, WA*

Per serving: 508 calories, 46 g carbohydrates, 29 g protein, 23 g total fat (7 g saturated), 84 mg cholesterol, 448 mg sodium

Black Currant Pork Chops

Fruit preserves, mustard, and tart raspberry vinegar make a tangy-sweet glaze for these succulent chops. Serve them on a bed of egg noodles. Complement the dish with a blush wine such as white Zinfandel or Anjou rosé from France's Loire valley.

- 6 center-cut pork loin chops (about 2½ lbs. *total*), trimmed of fat
  Pepper
- 1 tablespoon butter or margarine
- 3 tablespoons black currant preserves or currant jelly
- 1½ tablespoons Dijon mustard
- ¼ cup raspberry vinegar or white wine vinegar

Sprinkle pork chops generously with pepper. Melt butter in a wide frying pan over medium-high heat. Add chops and cook, turning as needed, until well browned on both sides.

Stir together preserves and mustard; spoon evenly over chops. Reduce heat to medium-low. Cover and cook until meat in thickest part is faintly pink to white but still moist; cut to test (about 10 minutes). With a slotted spoon, transfer chops to a platter; keep warm.

Add vinegar to pan and bring to a boil over high heat, stirring to scrape browned bits free. Then boil, uncovered, until sauce is reduced to about ¼ cup (2 to 3 minutes). Spoon sauce

over chops. Makes 6 servings.
—*Carmela Meely, Walnut Creek, CA*

Per serving: 219 calories, 7 g carbohydrates, 27 g protein, 8 g total fat (3 g saturated), 83 mg cholesterol, 195 mg sodium

Pork Chops with Orange Slices

Subtly seasoned with soy and ginger and served with juicy fried orange slices, these pork chops have an Oriental flavor.

- 6 center-cut pork loin chops (about 3 lbs. *total*), about 1 inch thick
- 2 tablespoons soy sauce
- ½ teaspoon dry mustard
- 1 teaspoon ground ginger
- 1 tablespoon firmly packed brown sugar
- 3 large oranges (1½ to 1¾ lbs. *total*)
- ½ cup powdered sugar

Trim excess fat from pork chops; place fat in a wide frying pan over medium heat. While fat is melting, mix soy sauce, mustard, ginger, and brown sugar; rub mixture into chops.

When pan is glazed with melted fat, lift out and discard any unmelted fat. Add chops to pan and cook, turning as needed, until well browned on both sides. Reduce heat to medium-low. Cover and cook until meat in thickest part is faintly pink to white but still moist; cut to test (12 to 15 minutes). Transfer to a platter and keep warm.

Cut unpeeled oranges into about ¼-inch-thick slices. Dust slices heavily with powdered sugar; then add to pan drippings and cook, turning once, until lightly browned on both sides. Arrange orange slices alongside chops. Makes 6 servings.
—*L. W., Albany, CA*

Per serving: 327 calories, 32 g carbohydrates, 34 g protein, 10 g total fat (3 g saturated), 95 mg cholesterol, 444 mg sodium

SAUTÉED PORK WITH RED PEPPERS

Fresh lemon juice and a light, garlicky sauce give tender pork slices a zesty flavor. Add a side dish of butter-steamed zucchini for appealing contrast to the meat and sweet, bright sautéed red pepper strips.

2 pounds boneless center-cut pork loin, trimmed of fat and cut into ½-inch-thick slices

4 cloves garlic, minced or pressed

Pepper

2 tablespoons butter or margarine

3 large red bell peppers (about 1½ lbs. *total*), seeded and cut into ½-inch-wide strips

About 2 tablespoons salad oil

¾ cup *each* dry white wine and chicken broth

Lemon wedges

Sprinkle pork with garlic and pepper. Set aside.

Melt butter in a wide frying pan over medium-high heat. Add bell peppers and cook, stirring often, until soft (about 10 minutes); transfer to a platter and keep warm.

Add 1 tablespoon of the oil to pan; increase heat to high. Add pork, a portion at a time (do not crowd pan), and cook, turning as needed, until browned on both sides. Add more oil to pan as needed. As meat is cooked, transfer it to platter with peppers, being sure spoon up all browned bits of garlic from pan.

Add wine and broth to pan. Bring to a boil; then boil, uncovered, until sauce is reduced to ½ cup (about 8 minutes).

Pour sauce evenly over meat and peppers. Garnish with lemon wedges. Makes 4 servings.—*Nadine Vickrey, Denver*

Per serving: 388 calories, 10 g carbohydrates, 36 g protein, 22 g total fat (8 g saturated), 109 mg cholesterol, 334 mg sodium

SHERRIED PORK LOIN WITH ONION BLOSSOMS

Small onions, scored to make many-petaled "blossoms," roast alongside a pork loin, sharing a sprightly sherry and marmalade baste with the meat.

⅓ cup dry sherry

2 tablespoons orange marmalade

2 teaspoons grated orange peel

½ teaspoon ground white pepper

2 cloves garlic, minced or pressed

1 pork loin roast (about 3½ lbs.), trimmed of fat, bones cracked

6 small onions (about 6 oz. *each*)

Orange wedges

In a small bowl, mix sherry, marmalade, orange peel, white pepper, and garlic. Rub half the mixture all over pork. Peel onions, leaving root ends attached. Starting at stem end, cut each onion into eighths to within 1 inch of root end. Set meat, bones down, and onions, cut side up, in a large roasting pan. Spoon remaining sherry mixture into cuts in onions.

Roast in a 375° oven until a meat thermometer inserted in thickest part of pork registers 155°F (1 to 1¼ hours). Transfer to a platter. Serve with orange wedges. Makes 6 servings. —*Mickey Strang, McKinleyville, CA*

Per serving: 349 calories, 20 g carbohydrates, 42 g protein, 11 g total fat (4 g saturated), 109 mg cholesterol, 106 mg sodium

ROAST PORK WITH SOY-GARLIC BASTE

A simple blend of soy, garlic, and seasonings doubles as baste and sauce for this rolled and tied pork roast. You might accompany the meat with nutty-tasting brown rice and crisp stir-fried sugar snap peas or Chinese pea pods.

1 lean boneless pork leg or loin roast (3½ to 4 lbs.), rolled and tied

Pepper

2 tablespoons salad oil

2 green onions, thinly sliced

2 cloves garlic, minced or pressed

¼ cup soy sauce

½ cup water

4 teaspoons sugar

1 tablespoon dry sherry (optional)

1½ teaspoons minced fresh ginger or ½ teaspoon ground ginger

1 teaspoon vinegar

Sprinkle pork lightly with pepper; then place, fat side up, on a rack in a large roasting pan. Roast in a 325° oven until a meat thermometer inserted in thickest part of meat registers 155°F (1¾ to 2 hours). Meanwhile, heat oil in a small pan over high heat. Stir in onions and garlic; remove from heat. Stir in soy sauce, water, sugar, sherry (if used), ginger, and vinegar.

During last 30 minutes of roasting, brush meat with soy-garlic mixture several times.

To serve, remove meat to a platter and keep warm. Combine remaining baste with pan drippings; bring to a boil. If sauce is too salty, stir in a little water. Skim and discard fat from sauce; offer sauce to spoon over meat. Makes 6 to 8 servings.—*Y. W., Los Angeles*

Per serving: 383 calories, 4 g carbohydrates, 50 g protein, 17 g total fat (5 g saturated), 165 mg cholesterol, 722 mg sodium

Pork & Apple Sauté

A mustard-accented cream sauce provides a smooth, rich-tasting finish for sliced pork tenderloin sautéed with Golden Delicious apples and a generous quantity of onion. Fluffy couscous is a good accompaniment for the dish.

1 pork tenderloin (about 1 lb.), trimmed of fat and silvery membranes

½ teaspoon *each* salt and dry oregano

⅛ teaspoon pepper

3 tablespoons all-purpose flour

¼ cup butter or margarine

2 medium-size onions, chopped

1 large Golden Delicious apple (about 8 oz.), cored and thinly sliced

2 tablespoons Dijon mustard

1 cup milk

2 tablespoons sweet pickle relish

Chopped parsley

Cut pork across the grain into ⅛-inch-thick slanting slices. Combine salt, oregano, pepper, and flour. Coat meat with flour mixture; shake off excess. Set remaining flour mixture aside.

Melt butter in a wide frying pan over medium-high heat. Add meat and cook, turning as needed, until browned on both sides; lift out and set aside. Add onions to pan and cook, stirring often, until golden. Add apple and remaining flour mixture. Cook, stirring, until bubbly. Remove from heat and gradually stir in mustard and milk. Then return to heat and cook, stirring, until sauce boils and thickens.

Return meat (and any accumulated juices) to pan; cook, stirring, until heated through (3 to 5 more minutes). Stir in relish; then spoon mixture into a serving dish and sprinkle with parsley. Makes 4 servings.—*E. R., Huntington Beach, CA*

Per serving: 347 calories, 18 g carbohydrates, 27 g protein, 18 g total fat (10 g saturated), 113 mg cholesterol, 712 mg sodium

Stir-fried Pork & Asparagus

For a simple dinner, marinate strips of pork loin briefly, then stir-fry them with fresh asparagus and serve over rice or tender Chinese noodles.

1 pound boneless pork loin, trimmed of fat and cut into thin strips

¼ cup reduced-sodium soy sauce

1 tablespoon sake

2 teaspoons ground ginger

1½ pounds slender asparagus (tough ends snapped off), cut into 3- to 4-inch lengths

½ cup plus 2 tablespoons water

2 teaspoons salad oil

1 tablespoon sliced green onion

In a bowl, mix pork, soy sauce, sake, and ginger; let stand for at least 5 or up to 30 minutes.

Place asparagus and ½ cup of the water in a wide frying pan or wok. Cover and cook over high heat, stirring occasionally, until asparagus is tender-crisp to bite (2 to 4 minutes). Drain asparagus, transfer to a platter, and keep warm.

Add oil to pan. With a slotted spoon, lift meat from marinade (reserve marinade); add meat to pan. Cook, stirring, until meat is no longer pink in center; cut to test (2 to 3 minutes). Add marinade and remaining 2 tablespoons water; stir gently until sauce is boiling. Pour meat mixture over asparagus; sprinkle with onion. Makes 4 servings.—*Kimiko Bigelow, San Jose, CA*

Per serving: 235 calories, 8 g carbohydrates, 30 g protein, 9 g total fat (3 g saturated), 67 mg cholesterol, 663 mg sodium

Oven-barbecued Spareribs

These saucy, richly flavored ribs are casual, pick-up-and-eat food at its most delicious. Of course, they're messy to eat, too—so be sure to have plenty of napkins handy! Serve them for a leisurely weekend supper, with such traditional side dishes as Confetti Coleslaw (page 41) and Red Potato Salad with Yogurt (page 48).

About 4 pounds spareribs, cut into serving-size pieces

¼ cup lemon juice

⅓ cup tomato-based chili sauce or catsup

1 teaspoon prepared horseradish

1 tablespoon Worcestershire

½ teaspoon *each* salt and paprika

½ cup orange juice

2 teaspoons dry mustard

¼ cup firmly packed brown sugar

1 clove garlic, minced or pressed

2 lemons, sliced

Arrange spareribs in a large roasting pan or broiler pan. Bake in a 450° oven for 45 minutes to render excess fat. Meanwhile, in a medium-size bowl, stir together lemon juice, chili sauce, horseradish, Worcestershire, salt, paprika, orange juice, mustard, sugar, and garlic.

Remove ribs from oven; spoon off and discard fat from pan. Reduce oven temperature to 350°. Pour about half the chili sauce mixture evenly over ribs; then top ribs evenly with lemon slices. Return to oven and continue to bake until meat is tender when pierced (about 1 more hour); baste generously about every 15 minutes with remaining sauce. Cut ribs apart before serving, if you wish. Makes 4 servings.—*L. F., Portland*

Per serving: 817 calories, 30 g carbohydrates, 53 g protein, 54 g total fat (20 g saturated), 214 mg cholesterol, 793 mg sodium

ENCHILADAS CARNITAS

Braised with vegetables and piquant seasonings until meltingly tender, juicy pork shoulder makes a delicious filling for enchiladas.

- 2 pounds boneless pork shoulder or butt, trimmed of fat and cut into 1½-inch chunks
- 4¼ cups water
- 1 large onion, chopped
- 1 large carrot, chopped
- 1 teaspoon chili powder
- ½ teaspoon dry oregano
- 3 cloves garlic, minced or pressed
- 1 jar (about 1 lb.) tomatillo salsa
- 12 corn tortillas (each about 6 inches in diameter)
- 4 cups (about 1 lb.) shredded jack cheese

In a 5- to 6-quart pan, combine pork and ¼ cup of the water. Cover and cook over medium heat for 10 minutes. Uncover and increase heat to high; cook, stirring often, until drippings are well browned (about 10 minutes). Add remaining 4 cups water, onion, carrot, chili powder, oregano, and garlic; stir to scrape browned bits free from pan. Bring to a boil; then reduce heat, cover, and simmer until meat is very tender when pierced (about 1 hour).

Uncover; cook over high heat, stirring often, until almost all liquid has evaporated (15 to 20 minutes). Remove from heat and let cool; then shred meat.

Pour salsa into a wide frying pan and warm over medium heat. Dip tortillas, one at a time, into salsa. Spoon a twelfth of the meat mixture and 1 tablespoon of the cheese down center of each tortilla; roll to enclose. Lay filled tortillas, seam side down, in a 9- by 13-inch baking dish. Top enchiladas with remaining salsa and remaining 3¼ cups cheese. (At this point, you may cover and refrigerate until next day.) Bake, uncovered, in a 400° oven until filling is heated through (about 20 minutes; about 40 minutes if refrigerated). Makes 6 servings.—*Jane King, Davis, CA*

Per serving: 581 calories, 34 g carbohydrates, 39 g protein, 31 g total fat (16 g saturated), 140 mg cholesterol, 1,346 mg sodium

PORK CHILI VERDE

Serve this succulent Mexican-style stew with warm tortillas or hot rice.

- 2½ pounds pork kebabs; or 2½ pounds boneless pork shoulder, trimmed of fat and cut into 1-inch cubes
- 1 cup chicken broth
- 6 cloves garlic, minced or pressed
- 2 cans (about 14½ oz. *each*) Mexican-style stewed tomatoes
- 2 large cans (about 7 oz. *each*) diced green chiles
- 1 medium-size onion, chopped
- 2 teaspoons minced fresh oregano or 1 teaspoon dry oregano
- Warm flour tortillas or hot cooked rice (optional)
- Lime wedges

In a 5- to 6-quart pan, combine pork, ½ cup of the broth, and garlic. Cover and cook over medium heat for 30 minutes. Uncover and continue to cook, stirring often, until drippings are well browned (about 20 more minutes). Add remaining ½ cup broth; stir to scrape browned bits free from pan.

Add tomatoes, chiles, onion, and oregano. Bring to a boil; then reduce heat, cover, and simmer, stirring occasionally, until meat pulls apart easily (about 1½ hours). If desired, serve with tortillas or over rice; offer lime wedges to squeeze over meat mixture. Makes 6 to 8 servings. —*Susan S. Bouchard, Scottsdale, AZ*

Per serving: 269 calories, 98 g carbohydrates, 27 g protein, 10 g total fat (3 g saturated), 86 g cholesterol, 999 mg sodium

OVEN SWEET & SOUR PORK

Richly browned pork chunks combine with dried fruits and a sweet-tart sauce of honey and fruit juices in this sturdy entrée. Serve it over wide egg noodles or short-grain rice.

- Vegetable oil cooking spray
- 3 to 3½ pounds boneless pork butt, trimmed of fat and cut into 1-inch cubes
- 1 cup chicken broth
- ½ cup apple juice
- 3 tablespoons lemon juice
- 1 tablespoon honey
- 2 tablespoons soy sauce
- ½ teaspoon garlic powder
- ¼ teaspoon *each* ground ginger and pepper
- 1 package (about 8 oz.) mixed dried fruit
- 1 tablespoon cornstarch blended with 1 tablespoon cold water

Coat a large roasting pan (at least 10 by 14 inches) with cooking spray. Arrange pork in pan, spacing pieces slightly apart. Bake in a 500° oven until meat is browned (about 25 minutes). Remove pan from oven and let stand for about 5 minutes to cool slightly. Meanwhile, reduce oven temperature to 350°.

Spoon off and discard any fat from pan. Gradually add broth and apple juice to pan, stirring to scrape browned bits free. In a small bowl, stir together lemon juice, honey, soy sauce, garlic powder, ginger, and pepper; pour over meat and mix lightly. Stir in dried fruit. Cover and continue to bake until meat is tender when pierced (about 45 more minutes).

Transfer meat and fruit to a serving dish; keep warm. Pour pan juices into a 1½-quart pan; skim and discard fat from juices. Stir in cornstarch mixture and cook over high heat, stirring, until sauce boils and thickens. Pour sauce over meat and fruit. Makes 6 servings.—*S. S., Mercer Island, WA*

Per serving: 393 calories, 32 g carbohydrates, 35 g protein, 14 g total fat (5 g saturated), 116 mg cholesterol, 638 mg sodium

PORK & SAUERKRAUT STEW

The tender little Swiss or German dumplings called *spaetzle* are often paired with sauerkraut, as in this satisfying stew. Many well-stocked markets sell spaetzle in convenient packaged form, but if you can't find them, just substitute fettuccine.

1½ pounds boneless pork shoulder or butt, trimmed of fat and cut into 1-inch cubes

3¼ cups water

1 can (about 14½ oz.) sauerkraut, drained

¼ cup tomato paste

2 tablespoons sugar

3 tablespoons paprika

1 pound carrots, peeled and cut diagonally into ⅓-inch-thick slices

1 package (about 10½ oz.) dry spaetzle; or 10 ounces dry fettuccine

Chopped parsley

Combine pork and ¼ cup of the water in a 5- to 6-quart pan. Cover and cook over medium-high heat for 10 minutes. Uncover and increase heat to high; cook, stirring often, until drippings are well browned (about 10 minutes).

Add remaining 3 cups water, sauerkraut, tomato paste, sugar, and paprika. Bring to a boil; then reduce heat, cover, and simmer for 1 hour. Add carrots; cover and continue to cook until meat is tender when pierced (about 30 more minutes).

When meat is almost done, cook spaetzle in a 5- to 6-quart pan in

about 3 quarts boiling water until just tender to bite (about 10 minutes); or cook according to package directions. Drain well; spoon onto individual plates, top with stew, and sprinkle with parsley. Makes 4 to 6 servings.—*Ann Bartos Rushton, Denver*

Per serving: 477 calories, 62 g carbohydrates, 31 g protein, 12 g total fat (4 g saturated), 128 mg cholesterol, 412 mg sodium

STRAW & HAY PASTA

White and green pastas—to the fanciful eye, straw and hay—are classic partners in this dish, known as *paglia e fieno* in Italy.

4 ounces *each* dry green and white vermicelli or other thin dry pasta strands (or use 8 ounces dry green or white pasta)

1¼ cups half-and-half or 1½ cups whipping cream

⅓ to ½ cup thinly slivered cooked ham

⅓ cup frozen tiny peas

⅓ to ¾ cup grated Parmesan cheese

In a 4- to 5-quart pan, cook pasta in about 2 quarts boiling water until just tender to bite (8 to 10 minutes); or cook according to package directions.

Meanwhile, in another 4- to 5-quart pan, combine half-and-half, ham, and peas. Cook over medium-high heat, stirring often, until steaming. (Or pour whipping cream into pan, bring to a boil over high heat, and boil, uncovered, until reduced to 1¼ cups. Stir in ham and peas; simmer for 1 to 2 minutes to thaw peas.) Remove from heat.

Drain pasta and pour into cream mixture. With 2 forks, lift pasta to mix with cream. Do this for 3 to 4 minutes; pasta will absorb much of the liquid. Then add ⅓ cup of the cheese and mix well. At the table, offer more

cheese to add to taste. Makes 4 servings.—*Gladys Kent, Port Angeles, WA*

Per serving: 389 calories, 48 g carbohydrates, 18 g protein, 14 g total fat (8 g saturated), 44 mg cholesterol, 444 mg sodium

ITALIAN-STYLE LAMB CHOPS

A robust, herb-seasoned red wine marinade permeates these broiled rib chops. You might serve Risotto with Mushrooms (page 161) alongside.

8 lamb rib chops (about 2 lbs. *total*), about 1 inch thick

1 cup dry red wine

¼ cup chopped onion

3 tablespoons soy sauce

2 tablespoons lemon juice

1 tablespoon sugar

2 teaspoons *each* dry oregano and dry thyme

3 tablespoons chopped parsley

Trim and discard fat from chops; then place chops in a large (1-gallon) heavy-duty plastic bag. Add wine, onion, soy sauce, lemon juice, sugar, oregano, and thyme. Seal bag and rotate to mix ingredients well. Refrigerate for at least 30 minutes or up to 6 hours, turning bag over 3 or 4 times.

Lift chops from marinade and drain briefly (reserve marinade). Set chops aside. Pour marinade into a small pan and bring to a boil.

Place chops on a lightly oiled rack in a broiler pan. Broil about 6 inches below heat, turning once and basting several times with marinade, until browned on both sides and done to your liking; cut to test (8 to 10 minutes for medium-rare). Transfer chops to a platter and sprinkle with parsley. Makes 4 servings.—*Carole Van Brocklin, Port Angeles, WA*

Per serving: 196 calories, 6 g carbohydrates, 21 g protein, 10 g total fat (3 g saturated), 66 mg cholesterol, 645 mg sodium

Roast Lamb with Chile Rice

While this festive leg of lamb is roasting, cook a colorful, jalapeño-spiced rice-vegetable pilaf to enjoy alongside. Just before serving, stir the juices from the roasting pan into the cumin-scented pilaf.

- 1 **leg of lamb (5 to 5½ lbs.), trimmed of fat**
- 3 **tablespoons olive oil**
- 1½ **teaspoons cumin seeds**
- 1½ **cups thinly sliced green onions**
- 1 **cup long-grain white rice**
- 2 **large carrots, diced**
- 2 **large thin-skinned potatoes (about 1 lb. *total*), peeled and diced**
- 1 **or 2 fresh jalapeño chiles, seeded and minced**
- 3 **cups chicken broth**

Rub lamb all over with 1 tablespoon of the oil and 1 teaspoon of the cumin seeds. Then set meat on a rack in a large roasting pan. Roast in a 350° oven until a meat thermometer inserted in thickest part of meat at bone registers 140° to 145°F for medium-rare (about 1½ hours).

About 30 minutes before meat is done, combine remaining 2 tablespoons oil, onions, and rice in a 5- to 6-quart pan. Cook over medium-high heat, stirring often, until onions are soft. Stir in remaining ½ teaspoon cumin seeds, carrots, potatoes, chiles, and broth.

Bring rice mixture to a boil; then reduce heat, cover, and simmer until potatoes are tender when pierced (25 to 30 minutes).

Transfer meat to a platter. Skim and discard fat from pan juices; stir juices into rice mixture. Serve rice mixture with meat. Makes 8 to 10 servings.—*Monia Ibarra, Eugene, OR*

Per serving: 395 calories, 28 g carbohydrates, 39 g protein, 13 g total fat (3 g saturated), 108 mg cholesterol, 453 mg sodium

Crusted Lamb & Potatoes

A savory crust of garlic, lemon, and stuffing mix makes this half-leg of lamb special. Roasted atop a bed of sliced potatoes, it's perfect for a small dinner party.

- 3 **pounds russet potatoes, peeled and cut into ¾-inch-thick slices**
- 1½ **cups chicken broth**
  Upper thigh half (3 to 3½ lbs.) of 1 leg of lamb, trimmed of fat
  Seasoning Paste (recipe follows)
  Salt and pepper

Arrange potatoes over bottom of a large roasting pan; pour broth into pan, then set lamb on potatoes. Roast in a 400° oven for 45 minutes. Meanwhile, prepare Seasoning Paste.

Spread paste evenly over meat and potatoes. Continue to roast until crust on meat is well browned and a meat thermometer inserted in thickest part of meat at bone registers 140° to 145°F for medium-rare (about 25 more minutes). Transfer meat and potatoes to a platter; pour any pan juices over all. Season meat and potatoes to taste with salt and pepper. Makes 6 servings.—*Mrs. W. Shultz, Blaine, WA*

Seasoning Paste. In a small bowl, mash together 3 cloves **garlic,** minced or pressed; 1 small **onion,** minced; 3 tablespoons minced **parsley;** 1 cup

seasoned **stuffing mix;** 3 tablespoons **butter** or margarine, at room temperature; 1 tablespoon **grated lemon peel;** and 2 tablespoons **lemon juice.**

Per serving: 525 calories, 48 g carbohydrates, 44 g protein, 16 g total fat (7 g saturated), 136 mg cholesterol, 612 mg sodium

Lemon-Mustard Roast Lamb

When boned and butterflied, leg of lamb lies flat—and roasts quickly.

- ½ **cup lemon juice**
- ¼ **cup firmly packed brown sugar**
- ⅓ **cup Dijon mustard**
- 3 **tablespoons Worcestershire**
- 2 **cloves garlic, minced or pressed**
- 2 **tablespoons olive oil or salad oil**
- 1 **leg of lamb (5 to 6 lbs.), boned and butterflied**

In a small bowl, stir together lemon juice, sugar, mustard, Worcestershire, garlic, and oil. Trim and discard excess fat from lamb; then set lamb in a large (1-gallon) heavy-duty plastic bag and pour mustard mixture over it. Seal bag and rotate to coat meat with marinade. Refrigerate for at least 4 hours or until next day, turning bag over 3 or 4 times.

Lift meat from marinade and drain briefly (reserve marinade). Spread meat out flat on a rack in a foil-lined large roasting or broiler pan; pour marinade into a small pan and bring to a boil.

Roast meat in a 500° oven, basting every 10 minutes with marinade, until a meat thermometer inserted in thickest part of meat registers 140° to 145°F for medium-rare (35 to 45 minutes). Transfer to meat to a platter. Makes 8 to 10 servings.—*Cathy Olsten, Ketchum, ID*

Per serving: 321 calories, 8 g carbohydrates, 38 g protein, 13 g total fat (4 g saturated), 119 mg cholesterol, 362 mg sodium

LAMB STEW WITH RAVIOLI

The tasty little dumplings in this stew are none other than canned ravioli! Choose meat- or cheese-filled pasta, as you prefer.

- ⅓ cup all-purpose flour
- 1 teaspoon salt
- ⅛ teaspoon pepper
- ½ teaspoon ground ginger
- 2 pounds boneless lamb stew meat, trimmed of fat and cut into 1½-inch cubes
- 3 tablespoons salad oil
- 1 medium-size onion, chopped
- 1 clove garlic, minced or pressed
- 2 cups boiling water
- ½ cup dry white wine or water
- 6 to 8 medium-size carrots, cut into ½-inch-thick slices
- ½ cup minced parsley
- 1 package (about 10 oz.) frozen peas
- 1 can (about 15 oz.) ravioli

Mix flour, salt, pepper, and ginger. Coat lamb with flour mixture; shake off excess. Reserve 2 tablespoons of the remaining flour mixture.

Heat oil in a 4- to 5-quart pan over medium-high heat. Add meat, a portion at a time (do not crowd pan); cook, turning as needed, until browned on all sides. As meat is browned, remove it from pan and set aside.

Add onion and garlic to pan; cook, stirring often, for 5 minutes. Stir in boiling water, wine, and carrots; then return meat (and any accumulated juices) to pan. Reduce heat, cover, and simmer until meat is tender when pierced (about 1½ hours).

Mix the reserved 2 tablespoons flour mixture with enough water to make a paste; stir into stew and cook, stirring, until gravy is thickened. Add parsley, peas, and ravioli; cover and simmer until peas and ravioli are heated through (8 to 10 more minutes). Serve in wide soup plates or deep dinner plates. Makes 6 servings. —H. N., San Francisco

Per serving: 405 calories, 34 g carbohydrates, 33 g protein, 15 g total fat (5 g saturated), 88 mg cholesterol, 871 mg sodium

OVEN LAMB SHANK STEW

Surrounded with celery, carrots, and onion halves, lamb shanks bake to fork-tender succulence. Serve with a country-style loaf and a crisp salad.

- 4 lamb shanks (about 3½ lbs. *total*), cracked
- 4 small onions, cut into halves
- 3 stalks celery, cut crosswise into thirds
- 1 cup dry red wine
- ⅔ cup catsup
- 3 tablespoons lemon juice
- 4 cloves garlic, minced or pressed
- 1 teaspoon dry oregano
- 4 slender carrots, cut crosswise into halves

Place lamb shanks side by side or slightly overlapping in a deep 5-quart casserole. Tuck onions and celery around meat. In a small bowl, stir together wine, catsup, lemon juice, garlic, and oregano; pour evenly over meat and vegetables. Cover tightly and bake in a 400° oven, basting once or twice, for 1 hour.

Add carrots to casserole, cover, and continue to bake until carrots are tender when pierced and meat pulls easily from bones (about 1 more hour); baste once or twice. Skim and discard fat from cooking juices (tilt the casserole to do this). Serve stew in wide, shallow bowls. Makes 4 servings.—A. H., Long Beach, CA

Per serving: 399 calories, 31 g carbohydrates, 48 g protein, 10 g total fat (3 g saturated), 139 mg cholesterol, 665 mg sodium

LAMB & BROWN RICE PILAF

Hot cooked artichoke hearts and small onions go well with this dish.

- ¼ cup lemon juice
- 3 tablespoons salad oil
- 2 tablespoons firmly packed brown sugar
- 1 clove garlic, minced or pressed
- 1 tablespoon tomato-based chili sauce
- ½ teaspoon dry oregano
- 1 to 1½ pounds boneless lamb leg or loin, trimmed of fat and cut into ¾-inch cubes
- 4 ounces mushrooms, sliced
- 1 cup brown rice
- 2 to 2¼ cups chicken broth
- ¼ cup dried currants

In a large, shallow dish, stir together lemon juice, 2 tablespoons of the oil, sugar, garlic, chili sauce, and oregano. Add lamb and stir to coat; then cover and refrigerate for 2 to 4 hours, stirring 3 or 4 times.

Heat remaining 1 tablespoon oil in a wide frying pan over medium heat. Lift meat from marinade and drain briefly (reserve marinade). Add meat to pan, a portion at a time (do not crowd pan); cook, turning as needed, until browned on all sides. As meat is browned, remove it from pan and set aside.

Add mushrooms to pan and cook, stirring often, until golden. Return meat (and any accumulated juices) to pan; add rice. Mix marinade with enough broth to make 2½ cups liquid; add liquid to pan. Bring to a boil; then reduce heat, cover, and simmer until rice and meat are tender to bite and liquid has been absorbed (about 1¼ hours). Stir in currants. Makes 4 servings.—L. F., San Francisco

Per serving: 485 calories, 53 g carbohydrates, 28 g protein, 18 g total fat (3 g saturated), 70 mg cholesterol, 668 mg sodium

LEMON-MINT LAMB MEATBALLS

Poaching makes these minted lamb meatballs moist and tender. Present them on a bed of hot cooked brown or white rice.

    2   pounds lean ground lamb
    2   large eggs
    ¼   cup all-purpose flour
    1   tablespoon dry mint
    1   teaspoon *each* salt and pepper
    2   tablespoons salad oil
    ⅓   cup finely chopped parsley
    1½ cups thinly sliced green onions
    1   can (about 14½ oz.) chicken broth
    ⅓   cup lemon juice
    1   tablespoon cornstarch blended
        with 1 tablespoon cold water
        Chopped parsley and shredded
        lemon peel

In a large bowl, combine lamb, eggs, flour, mint, salt, and pepper. Mix until well blended; then form meat mixture into about 1-inch balls. Set meatballs aside.

Heat oil in a wide frying pan or 5-quart pan over medium heat. Add the ⅓ cup parsley and onions; cook, stirring often, until limp. Stir in broth and lemon juice; bring to a simmer.

Drop meatballs into simmering broth mixture. Continue to simmer, uncovered, stirring occasionally, until meatballs are no longer pink in center; cut to test (about 15 minutes).

With a slotted spoon, transfer meatballs to a serving dish. Skim and discard fat from sauce. Stir in cornstarch mixture; cook, stirring, until sauce is thickened. Pour sauce over meatballs. Sprinkle with chopped parsley and lemon peel. Makes 6 servings.—*P. L., La Mesa, CA*

Per serving: 381 calories, 9 g carbohydrates, 31 g protein, 24 g total fat (8 g saturated), 172 mg cholesterol, 780 mg sodium

SPICED LAMB-STUFFED PEPPERS

Choose red, yellow, or green bell peppers—or two of each color—as containers for this fragrantly spiced lamb-and-rice stuffing. Toasted pine nuts make a nice garnish.

    6   medium-size bell peppers
        (about 2¼ lbs. *total*), any color
    1½ pounds lean ground lamb
    1   large onion, chopped
    2   cups cooked rice
    ½   cup *each* catsup and raisins
    1   teaspoon ground allspice
    ½   teaspoon *each* ground cumin,
        ground cinnamon, and black
        pepper
    2   large eggs
        Salt and ground red pepper
        (cayenne)

Trim tops of bell peppers down just far enough to remove stems; pull out and discard seeds. Trim pepper flesh away from stems and finely chop; discard stems. Rinse pepper shells and stand them, open ends up, in a shallow 1½- to 2-quart casserole.

Crumble lamb into a wide frying pan. Cook over medium heat, stirring often, until well browned. Add onion and chopped bell pepper; cook, stirring often, until onion is soft. Remove pan from heat; spoon off and discard fat. Stir in rice, catsup, raisins, allspice, cumin, cinnamon, black pepper, and eggs; blend well. Season to taste with salt and red pepper.

Fill peppers equally with rice mixture, packing lightly. Bake in a 375° oven until peppers are soft when pierced (30 to 40 minutes). Makes 6 servings.—*Cathleen Ohanesian, Hollywood, CA*

Per serving: 492 calories, 47 g carbohydrates, 26 g protein, 23 g total fat (9 g saturated), 151 mg cholesterol, 337 mg sodium

POLENTA WITH SAUSAGE SAUCE

For a warming cold-weather dinner, offer bowls of soft, creamy polenta topped with an herbed tomato-sausage sauce.

    1   pound mild Italian sausages,
        casings removed
    1   large onion, chopped
    1   cup dry white or red wine
    5½ cups water
    1   can (about 6 oz.) tomato paste
    1   teaspoon dry oregano
    ¾   teaspoon dry thyme
        Salt and pepper
    1½ cups polenta or yellow cornmeal
    1   cup milk
        Grated Parmesan cheese

Crumble sausage into a wide frying pan. Cook over high heat, stirring often, until browned (5 to 7 minutes). Spoon off and discard fat from pan. Add onion; cook, stirring, until lightly browned (about 5 minutes). Add wine, 1 cup of the water, tomato paste, oregano, and thyme. Bring to a boil; then reduce heat and simmer, uncovered, stirring occasionally, until sauce is reduced to 3 cups (about 10 minutes). Season to taste with salt and pepper.

While sauce is simmering, smoothly mix polenta, remaining 4½ cups water, and milk in a 3- to 4-quart pan. Bring to a boil over high heat, stirring. Reduce heat to low; continue to cook, stirring often, until polenta is thick and creamy (8 to 10 more minutes).

To serve, spoon polenta into shallow bowls; top with sausage sauce. Offer cheese to add to taste. Makes 4 servings.—*Nancy Gils Carbó, Foster City, CA*

Per serving: 594 calories, 58 g carbohydrates, 25 g protein, 25 g total fat (9 g saturated), 73 mg cholesterol, 1,137 mg sodium

Sausage, Basil & Port Fettuccine

Italian sausage, fresh tomatoes, and both red and green onions combine in a rich, savory sauce for fettuccine.

- 1¼ pounds mild or hot Italian sausages, casings removed
- 2 cloves garlic, minced or pressed
- 1½ cups sliced green onions
- 3 cups thinly sliced red onions
- 1½ cups port
- 12 ounces dry fettuccine
- 3 cups chopped ripe tomatoes
- 2 tablespoons balsamic vinegar
- ¾ cup chopped fresh basil
- Salt and pepper
- Basil sprigs

Break sausages into 1-inch chunks and place in a wide frying pan. Cook over medium-high heat, stirring often, until browned (8 to 10 minutes). Lift from pan with a slotted spoon and set aside. Pour off and discard all but 2 tablespoons fat from pan.

Add garlic, green onions, and red onions to pan. Cook, stirring often, until onions are very soft (12 to 15 minutes). Add port and bring to a boil over high heat; then boil, uncovered, until reduced by half (about 5 minutes).

Meanwhile, in a 5- to 6-quart pan, cook fettuccine in about 3 quarts boiling water until just tender to bite (8 to 10 minutes); or cook according to package directions.

Add tomatoes, sausage, and vinegar to port mixture; cook, stirring often, until bubbly (about 2 minutes). Stir in chopped basil; season to taste with salt and pepper.

Drain pasta and pour onto a warm platter; spoon sausage mixture over pasta. Garnish with basil sprigs.

Makes 6 servings.—*Thomas Shook, Tempe, AZ*

Per serving: 629 calories, 64 g carbohydrates, 25 g protein, 24 g total fat (8 g saturated), 111 mg cholesterol, 698 mg sodium

Lentil-Sausage Stew

For long-simmered flavor in under an hour, try this combination of lentils and sausage in a tangy tomato sauce.

- 1½ cups (about 12 oz.) lentils
- About 5 cups water
- 1 teaspoon salt
- 1 clove garlic, minced or pressed
- 1 pound mild or hot Italian sausages, casings removed
- 1 large onion, chopped
- 2 carrots, sliced
- 1 can (about 8 oz.) tomato sauce
- 3 tablespoons red wine vinegar

Sort through lentils, discarding any debris. Rinse lentils, drain, and place in a heavy 4- to 5-quart pan. Add 5 cups of the water, salt, and garlic. Bring to a boil; then reduce heat so liquid simmers. Cover pan.

Cut sausages into ½-inch-thick slices and place in a wide frying pan. Cook over medium-high heat, stirring often, until browned (8 to 10 minutes). Lift from pan with a slotted spoon and add to lentils. Pour off and discard all but 1 tablespoon fat from frying pan. Add onion to pan and cook, stirring often, until soft. Then add onion and carrots to lentils. Cover and simmer until lentils are almost tender to bite (about 20 minutes).

Stir in tomato sauce and vinegar and continue to cook until lentils are tender to bite and almost all liquid has been absorbed (about 15 more minutes). Makes 6 servings.—*R. J., Torrance, CA*

Per serving: 423 calories, 42 g carbohydrates, 28 g protein, 17 g total fat (6 g saturated), 45 mg cholesterol, 1,131 mg sodium

Zucchini-Sausage Bake

Start by making a hearty sauce of vegetables and browned Italian sausage; then stir in white rice, pour the mixture into a casserole, and bake until the rice is tender. Sprinkle with grated Parmesan cheese just before serving.

- 1 pound hot or mild Italian sausages, casings removed
- 1 large onion, chopped
- 1 large red bell pepper (about 8 oz.), seeded and chopped
- 1 can (about 14½ oz.) tomatoes
- About 12 ounces zucchini, thinly sliced
- ½ teaspoon dry oregano
- 1 cup beef broth
- ½ cup long-grain white rice
- ½ cup grated Parmesan cheese

Crumble sausage into a wide frying pan. Cook over medium-high heat, stirring often, until browned (8 to 10 minutes). Lift from pan with a slotted spoon and set aside. Pour off and discard all but 2 tablespoons fat from pan.

Add onion and bell pepper to pan; cook, stirring often, until vegetables begin to brown (8 to 10 minutes). Cut up tomatoes; add tomatoes and their liquid. Add zucchini, oregano, and broth. Bring to a boil; then reduce heat and simmer, uncovered, for 5 to 10 minutes to blend flavors. Stir in rice.

Pour rice mixture into a shallow 2-quart baking dish and sprinkle evenly with sausage. Cover tightly and bake in a 350° oven until rice is tender to bite (50 to 55 minutes). Sprinkle with cheese before serving. Makes 4 to 6 servings.—*Neva Rawling, Salt Lake City*

Per serving: 413 calories, 28 g carbohydrates, 21 g protein, 24 g total fat (9 g saturated), 62 mg cholesterol, 1,254 mg sodium

Pigs in a Quilt

Pork sausage links and sweet sliced apples and plums are concealed beneath this puffy, cornmeal-sprinkled oven pancake. Serve it for a weekend supper or brunch, along with flaky biscuits and cold cider or hot spiced tea, depending on the season.

8 ounces pork sausage links
1 large Golden Delicious apple (about 8 oz.), peeled, cored, and cut into ½-inch-thick slices
2 large firm-ripe Santa Rosa-type plums (about 8 oz. *total*), pitted and cut into ½-inch-thick slices
⅓ cup butter or margarine
3 large eggs
¾ cup *each* all-purpose flour and milk
1 teaspoon yellow cornmeal
Warm maple syrup

In a wide frying pan with an oven-proof handle, cook sausages over medium heat until browned. Remove from pan and set aside. Add apple; cook, stirring, for 3 minutes. Add plums; cook plum and apple slices, turning gently, until soft (about 3 more minutes).

Spoon off and discard fat from pan; then add butter. When butter is melted, remove pan from heat and arrange sausages in a spoke pattern between fruit slices.

In a blender or food processor, combine eggs, flour, and milk; whirl until smooth.

Pour batter over sausages and fruit. Bake in a 425° oven for 10 minutes. Sprinkle evenly with cornmeal and continue to bake until puffy and golden (about 10 more minutes). Cut into wedges and serve at once with syrup. Makes 4 servings.—*Barbara Keenan, Fort Morgan, CO*

Per serving: 599 calories, 36 g carbohydrates, 16 g protein, 44 g total fat (20 g saturated), 245 mg cholesterol, 603 mg sodium

Gdansk Sausage Skillet

Kielbasa sautéed with potatoes, caraway seeds, onions, and apple wedges makes an uncommon sort of hash for a quick family supper.

2 tablespoons butter or margarine
2 medium-size onions, thinly sliced
1 large apple (about 8 oz.), cored and cut into thin wedges
1 teaspoon caraway seeds
1 pound kielbasa (Polish sausage), cut diagonally into ½-inch-thick slices
1 tablespoon salad oil
About 1 pound russet potatoes, scrubbed and cut into ⅛-inch-thick slices
3 tablespoons chopped parsley
Salt and pepper

Melt butter in a wide frying pan over medium heat. Add onions, apple, and caraway seeds; cook, stirring often, until onions are very soft (about 15 minutes). Remove onion mixture from pan; set aside.

Add sausage slices to pan and cook, stirring often, until lightly browned (about 10 minutes). Remove sausage slices from pan with a slotted spoon and set aside with onions.

Add oil and potato slices to pan. Cook, turning potatoes carefully with a wide spatula, until most potato slices are lightly browned and tender when pierced (about 15 minutes).

Return onion mixture and sausage to pan; cover and cook, turning mixture once or twice with spatula, until all ingredients are heated through (about 10 minutes). Stir in parsley; season to taste with salt and pepper. Makes 4 to 6 servings. —*Susan Weissman, Aurora, CO*

Per serving: 472 calories, 31 g carbohydrates, 15 g protein, 32 g total fat (12 g saturated), 73 mg cholesterol, 1,034 mg sodium

Cumin Cabbage & Sausages

Make this dish with fully cooked sausages, such as smoked sausage links, garlic frankfurters, or kielbasa. You might round out the meal with dark rye or pumpernickel bread or boiled potatoes with parsley butter.

If you enjoy beer with meals, keep this combination in mind—it's a good example of "beer cuisine." Pour a foamy lager or full-bodied ale to complement the smoky and spicy flavors.

2 tablespoons butter or margarine
1 large head cabbage (about 2 lbs.), finely shredded
2 teaspoons ground cumin
½ teaspoon salt
⅛ teaspoon pepper
1 can (about 8 oz.) tomato sauce
1 teaspoon Dijon mustard
2 medium-size apples, about 12 oz. *total* (unpeeled), cored and finely diced
1½ pounds fully cooked sausages (see suggestions in recipe introduction above)

Melt butter in a 3½- to 5-quart pan over medium heat. Add cabbage and cook, stirring, until limp. Stir in cumin, salt, pepper, tomato sauce, mustard, and apples. Cover and cook until cabbage and apples are tender to bite (about 15 minutes). Arrange sausages atop cabbage mixture, cover, and cook until sausages are heated through (about 10 more minutes).

To serve, spoon cabbage mixture in center of a wide rimmed platter; then arrange sausages around cabbage. Makes 6 servings.—*J. T., North Hollywood, CA*

Per serving: 468 calories, 22 g carbohydrates, 18 g protein, 35 g total fat (14 g saturated), 86 mg cholesterol, 1,720 mg sodium

COMPANY VEAL SAUTÉ

A piquant sauce flavored with capers and dill distinguishes this entrée. Serve it with tiny red potatoes.

1½ pounds boneless veal round steak, cut into ½-inch-thick slices

1 large egg

1 tablespoon water

About 3 tablespoons all-purpose flour

2 tablespoons butter or margarine

2 tablespoons salad oil

¾ cup chicken broth

2 tablespoons *each* lemon juice and drained capers

2 large egg yolks

¼ cup whipping cream

½ teaspoon dry dill weed

Salt and pepper

Trim fat and membrane from veal. In a shallow bowl, beat egg with water to blend. Dip each veal slice into beaten egg, then coat on both sides with flour. Melt butter in oil in a wide frying pan over medium heat. Add veal slices, a few at a time (do not crowd pan). Cook, turning as needed, until browned on both sides and no longer pink in center; cut to test (about 10 minutes). As meat is cooked, transfer it to a serving dish and keep warm.

When all meat has been cooked, add broth, lemon juice, and capers to pan. Simmer for 5 minutes, then remove from heat. In a small bowl, beat egg yolks, cream, and dill weed to blend. Stirring rapidly, add a small amount of hot broth mixture to yolk mixture; then return mixture to pan. Cook over low heat, stirring, just until hot. Season to taste with salt and pepper; pour over meat. Makes 4 to 6 servings.—*M. M., Oakland, CA*

Per serving: 307 calories, 5 g carbohydrates, 28 g protein, 19 g total fat (7 g saturated), 242 mg cholesterol, 378 mg sodium

VEAL & ARTICHOKE STEW

If you'd like to make this stew ahead, cook it until the veal is tender; let cool, then cover and refrigerate for up to a day. Reheat before serving, adding the artichokes for the last 10 minutes or so.

3 tablespoons all-purpose flour

1 teaspoon paprika

½ teaspoon *each* salt, dry basil, and dry rosemary

¼ teaspoon pepper

2 pounds boneless veal stew meat, trimmed of fat and cut into 1½-inch cubes

About ¼ cup salad oil

1 clove garlic, minced or pressed

8 ounces mushrooms, sliced

1 cup chicken broth

1 package (about 9 oz.) frozen artichoke hearts, thawed

Combine flour, paprika, salt, basil, rosemary, and pepper. Coat veal with flour mixture and shake off excess; reserve remaining flour mixture. Heat 2 tablespoons of the oil in a 4- to 5-quart pan over medium heat. Add meat, a portion at a time (do not crowd pan); cook, turning as needed, until browned on all sides. Add more oil to pan as necessary. As meat is browned, remove it from pan and set aside.

Add garlic and mushrooms to pan; cook, stirring often, until mushrooms are lightly browned. Blend in remaining flour mixture and cook, stirring, until bubbly. Stir in broth; bring to a boil. Return meat (and any accumulated juices) to pan; then reduce heat, cover, and simmer until meat is tender when pierced (about 1 hour). Add artichokes, cover, and simmer until tender to bite (8 to 10 more minutes). Makes 6 servings.—*F. N., San Francisco*

Per serving: 269 calories, 9 g carbohydrates, 28 g protein, 13 g total fat (2 g saturated), 105 mg cholesterol, 479 mg sodium

VEAL STROGANOFF

Hot cooked noodles or brown rice go well with this subtly seasoned dish.

2 tablespoons salad oil

1½ pounds boneless veal stew meat, trimmed of fat and cut into 1½-inch cubes

12 ounces mild Italian sausages, cut into 1-inch-thick slices

1 medium-size onion, chopped

8 ounces mushrooms, quartered

1 cup beef broth

1 medium-size red bell pepper (about 6 oz.), seeded and chopped

½ cup dry sherry or beef broth

1 cup sour cream

2 tablespoons all-purpose flour

Ground nutmeg, salt, and pepper

Chopped parsley

Heat oil in a wide frying pan or 4- to 5-quart pan over medium-high heat. Add veal and sausage, a portion at a time (do not crowd pan); cook, turning as needed, until well browned on all sides. As meat is browned, remove it from pan and set aside.

Add onion and mushrooms to pan; cook, stirring often, until onion is soft. Return meat (and any accumulated juices) to pan; then add broth, bell pepper, and sherry. Bring to a boil; reduce heat, cover, and simmer until veal is tender when pierced (about 1 hour).

Increase heat to high and cook, uncovered, until liquid is reduced to about 1 cup. Skim and discard fat from stew, if necessary.

Stir together sour cream and flour until well blended, then stir into stew. Cook, stirring, until sauce is bubbly. Season to taste with nutmeg, salt, and pepper. Sprinkle with parsley. Makes 4 to 6 servings.—*M. W., San Francisco*

Per serving: 518 calories, 15 g carbohydrates, 36 g protein, 32 g total fat (12 g saturated), 153 mg cholesterol, 914 mg sodium

1946 to 1949

As if emerging from the shadow of wartime restrictions, the homemakers illustrated in our Kitchen Cabinet in the years just after World War II seem to bustle through their chores in a sunnier light. Shiny new housewares such as efficient electric mixers made meal preparation ever easier, but recipes for quick dishes to streamline busy-day cooking were always welcome. And one stop at the supermarket was all it took to find every ingredient for traditional specialties like Favorite Meatballs and Celery Victor, as well as for tempting, butter-rich muffins.

As new autos rolled into carports and gas rationing ended, ideas for portable picnic and barbecue dishes again flowed into Kitchen Cabinet. Cabin Cheese was designed to be prepared at home, then carried along for snacks at a distant vacation house. The Western eagerness for innovation in food continued unabated; a 1948 Dressing for Mixed Greens, for example, celebrated the "walloping" flavor of fresh garlic.

Favorite Meatballs. *Beat the eggs; add the beef, rice, onion, and seasonings*

Shape mixture into balls about 1 inch in diameter. Heat soup, water, mushrooms

Drop the balls into soup mixture; cover; simmer very gently for about 1½ hours

Or, put the balls in casserole, pour soup mixture over them, and bake 1½ hours

ANTONIO SOTOMAYOR

FAVORITE MEATBALLS

Few meatball recipes can match this one. It's an especially delicious version of the familiar "Yummy" or "Porcupine" meatballs.

- 2 **eggs**
- 1 **pound ground beef**
- ½ **cup raw rice**
- 1 **small onion, minced**
- 1 **teaspoon salt**
  Pepper to taste
  Dash of thyme and marjoram
- 1 **can (about 4 oz.) sliced mushrooms (optional)**
- 1 **can (about 10¾ oz.) condensed cream of mushroom soup, diluted with 2 cans water**

Beat eggs slightly; add beef, rice, onion, and seasonings. Mix well. Shape mixture into balls about 1 inch in diameter. If using canned mushrooms, drain them well, reserving the liquid. Put mushrooms (if used), mushroom soup, and water in a deep saucepan; bring to a boil. Drop balls into boiling soup mixture, cover pan tightly, and simmer very, very gently for about 1½ hours. Add reserved mushroom liquid or more hot water as necessary during cooking. Or, put balls in a 2½- to 3-quart casserole, pour boiling soup mixture over them, and bake, covered, in a moderately hot oven (375°) for 1½ hours. Serves 6. —J. L. B., Berkeley, CA (April 1946)

DRESSING FOR MIXED GREENS

When a walloping garlic taste is desired in this dressing, sprinkle the garlic buds with the sugar, then crush lightly with a fork before adding the oil.

To make dressing, combine ¼ cup **olive oil** or salad oil and 2 cloves **garlic,** cut lengthwise, in a pint jar. Let stand for at least 1 hour or up to 24 hours; remove and discard garlic. To oil, add ¼ cup *each* **white wine vinegar** and chopped **parsley;** ¼ cup **whipping cream** or sour cream; 1 teaspoon **sugar;** ½ teaspoon **salt;** ¼ teaspoon **dry mustard;** and coarsely ground **pepper** to taste. Shake until well blended. Makes about ¾ cup.—V. D. S., San Diego, CA (January 1948)

CELERY VICTOR

When you want a first course for a special dinner, serve this favorite Western salad.

- 2 medium-sized bunches celery
- 2 or 3 bouillon cubes
  About 1 cup French dressing (made with 1 part vinegar to 3 parts oil, plus seasonings, including minced garlic, to taste)
- 1 bunch watercress, cleaned and chilled
- 1 can (about 2 oz.) anchovy fillets, drained
  Mayonnaise
  Paprika

Trim root ends of celery, remove a few of the tougher outside stalks, and cut enough off leafy ends of stalks so that each bunch is just the right length for a salad plate. Cut each bunch lengthwise in halves; wash thoroughly. Tie each bunch with string so that stalks will not separate during cooking. Cook until tender (12 to 15 minutes) in boiling water to which bouillon cubes have been added; drain well. Marinate in French dressing in the refrigerator for several hours, or overnight. Just before serving, arrange beds of watercress on 4 individual salad plates. Drain celery and lay a bunch, cut-side up, on each plate. Crisscross 4 anchovy fillets over each serving of celery; garnish salad with mayonnaise and dust with paprika. Serves 4.—R. G., Pasadena, CA (July 1946)

Celery Victor. Trim the celery to fit salad plate; cut lengthwise in halves; wash well

Tie each bunch with string. Cook in boiling water flavored with bouillon cubes

Marinate in French dressing in refrigerator several hours. Take off the strings

Arrange cut side up on watercress; garnish with anchovies and mayonnaise

CABIN CHEESE

This nippy cheese appetizer can be served in a dozen different ways.

- ¼ cup butter (½ cube)
- ¼ pound blue or Roquefort cheese, crumbled
- ¼ pound sharp Cheddar cheese, diced
- 1 tablespoon Worcestershire sauce
  Dash of Tabasco
- 1 tablespoon minced chives or green onion tops
- ½ teaspoon lemon juice
  Pinch of salt
  Dash of curry powder

Paprika or cayenne

Blend butter with cheeses by creaming with a fork, frequently dipped in very hot water, or by using an electric mixer on low speed. Add Worcestershire sauce, Tabasco, chives, lemon juice, salt, and curry powder. Blend well. Press into bowl and sprinkle with paprika or cayenne. Chill several hours before serving. Makes about 1¾ cups.—J. A. H., Santa Ana, CA (April 1949)

(Spread cheese on tiny crackers and broil; use to stuff celery; form into balls and roll in chopped nuts for a salad accompaniment.)

FRENCH TEA PUFFS

Delicate and light as the proverbial feather are these sweet little muffins.

- ⅓ cup shortening
- ¼ cup sugar
- 1 large egg, separated
- 1½ cups sifted cake flour
- 2¼ teaspoons baking powder
- ¼ teaspoon salt
- ½ teaspoon ground nutmeg
- ½ cup milk

Cream shortening and sugar until light. Beat in egg yolk. Sift together flour, baking powder, salt, and nutmeg. Add to creamed mixture alternately with milk. (Do not overmix.) Beat egg white until stiff, then fold into batter. Fill well-greased 1¾-inch muffin cups half full with batter. Bake in a moderately hot oven (375°) 18 to 20 minutes or until golden. Remove from pans while hot. Brush on all sides with **melted butter** (you will need a total of about 1½ tablespoons), then roll in a mixture of 3 tablespoons **sugar** and 1 teaspoon **ground cinnamon.** Makes 24 small puffs.—M. S., La Crescenta, CA (January 1947)

P·O·U·L·T·R·Y

Chicken and turkey are comparatively new on the list of foods that are not only popular, but also economical and easy to use. In the past, price and preparation could be daunting: a 1940 Kitchen Cabinet suggested braising chicken when "your family calls for fried chicken but your budget can only stand fricasseeing hens." And a 1936 recipe began, "Have the dealer draw and quarter the chicken." • Not until the late 1950s did we begin to propose using chicken breasts instead of a cut-up whole bird—and even then, they were usually frozen. Turkey parts, ground turkey, and turkey sausage weren't widely available until the 1980s. It's only fairly recently that we've been able to offer such quick, appetizing choices as Salsa Chicken with Cheese (1979; page 100) and Chili con Pavo (1991; page 108). • Way back in 1938, we presented hot biscuits filled with chicken and gravy as a "grand idea for a Fourth of July supper on the terrace." Today, we suspect you'd prefer colorful Chicken Ratatouille (page 104) or spicy Tandoori Chicken (page 107) to that rather fussy combination.

FIVE-SPICE ROAST CHICKEN

Chinese spices blended with soy and sherry season this crisp, almost lacquered-looking roast chicken and the fragrant sauce that goes with it. To complete the meal, choose simple accompaniments, such as steamed broccoli flowerets and brown rice.

- 1 teaspoon salad oil
- 1½ teaspoons Chinese five-spice (or ½ teaspoon *each* crushed anise seeds and ground ginger and ¼ teaspoon *each* ground cinnamon and ground cloves)
- 3 tablespoons soy sauce
- 1 tablespoon *each* sugar and dry sherry
- 1 clove garlic, minced or pressed
- 1 large chicken (4½ to 5 lbs.)
- 3 tablespoons thinly sliced green onions

In a small pan, stir oil with five-spice over medium heat until hot. Stir in soy sauce, sugar, sherry, and garlic.

Reserve chicken neck and giblets for other uses; pull off and discard lumps of fat from chicken. Rinse chicken inside and out, pat dry, and place, breast up, on a rack in a 9- by 13-inch baking pan. Rub chicken generously with five-spice mixture. Pour remaining mixture into cavity of chicken.

Roast in a 400° oven until meat near thighbone is no longer pink; cut to test (1¼ to 1½ hours). Tilt chicken to drain juices from cavity into pan, then carefully transfer bird to a platter. Stir pan juices to scrape browned bits free.

Pour juices into a small pitcher; skim and discard fat from juices, then stir in onions. Offer sauce to spoon over chicken. Makes 4 servings.—*Doreen Holton, Maui, HI*

Per serving: 657 calories, 6 g carbohydrates, 68 g protein, 38 g total fat (11 g saturated), 211 mg cholesterol, 976 mg sodium

PLUM-GLAZED CHICKEN

Plum jam mixed with vinegar and spices makes a shiny glaze for chicken pieces.

- ¾ cup plum jam
- ¼ cup cider vinegar
- 2 tablespoons Worcestershire or soy sauce
- 1 tablespoon catsup
- 2 teaspoons finely chopped fresh ginger or 1 teaspoon ground ginger
- ½ teaspoon ground cinnamon
- ¼ teaspoon dry mustard
- ⅛ teaspoon *each* ground cloves and liquid hot pepper seasoning
- 1 chicken (3½ to 4 lbs.), cut up and trimmed of fat

In a small pan, stir together jam, vinegar, Worcestershire, catsup, ginger, cinnamon, mustard, cloves, and hot pepper seasoning. Cook over medium-low heat, stirring, until heated through. Remove from heat.

Rinse chicken and pat dry. Then arrange, skin side down, in a greased 9- by 13-inch baking pan. Brush some of the sauce over chicken. Bake in a 375° oven for 30 minutes, basting occasionally. Turn chicken pieces over, brush with remaining sauce, and continue to bake, basting occasionally, until meat near thighbone is no longer pink; cut to test (20 to 25 more minutes). Makes 4 servings.—*J. B., Santa Rosa, CA*

Per serving: 609 calories, 42 g carbohydrates, 52 g protein, 26 g total fat (7 g saturated), 165 mg cholesterol, 309 mg sodium

CHICKEN ADOBO

Pickling spices provide a short-cut seasoning for this quickly prepared braised chicken. Serve with rice and a colorful garnish of tomato and parsley.

- 1 chicken (about 3½ lbs.), cut up and trimmed of fat
- 1 medium-size onion, quartered
- ½ cup *each* water and distilled white vinegar
- 1 tablespoon whole mixed pickling spices
- 2 tablespoons soy sauce
- 1 clove garlic, minced or pressed
- 2 tablespoons salad oil
- 1 medium-size firm-ripe tomato (about 6 oz.), cut into wedges
  Parsley sprigs

Rinse chicken, pat dry, and place in a 4- to 5-quart pan. Add onion, water, vinegar, pickling spices, soy sauce, and garlic. Bring to a boil over high heat. Then reduce heat, cover, and simmer until meat near thighbone is no longer pink; cut to test (30 to 35 minutes).

With a slotted spoon, lift chicken and onion from broth. Pat chicken dry, then set chicken and onion aside. Skim and discard fat from broth. Bring broth to a boil over high heat; boil, uncovered, until reduced to ¾ cup (about 5 minutes). Return onion to broth; keep warm.

Heat oil in a wide frying pan over medium-high heat. Add chicken, a portion at a time (do not crowd pan); cook, turning as needed, until browned on all sides. As chicken is browned, transfer it to a shallow bowl; keep warm.

To serve, pour onion-broth mixture over chicken. Garnish with tomato and parsley sprigs. Makes 4 servings.—*Mary Lou Sanelli, Sequim, WA*

Per serving: 513 calories, 8 g carbohydrates, 49 g protein, 31 g total fat (8 g saturated), 154 mg cholesterol, 663 mg sodium

Jayne's Chinese Chicken

Baked to succulence in a sauce flavored with Asian-style seasonings, cut-up chicken (or duck, if you prefer) is good with fresh pineapple spears and hot, fluffy rice.

⅔ cup hoisin sauce

½ cup dry white wine or chicken broth

⅓ cup maple syrup

1½ tablespoons soy sauce

3 star anise (or 1 teaspoon anise seeds and ¼ teaspoon ground cinnamon)

2 large cloves garlic, minced or pressed

1 teaspoon ground coriander

1 teaspoon whole Szechwan or black peppercorns

½ teaspoon dry mustard

1 chicken (3½ to 4½ lbs.), cut up and trimmed of fat

In a large, shallow dish, stir together hoisin sauce, wine, syrup, soy sauce, star anise, garlic, coriander, peppercorns, and mustard. Rinse chicken and pat dry; add to hoisin marinade and turn to coat. Cover and refrigerate for 1 to 2 days, turning chicken over 3 or 4 times.

Place chicken and its marinade in a 9- by 13-inch baking dish. Bake, uncovered, in a 350° oven for 1 to 1¼ hours; baste every 15 minutes during the first 45 minutes of cooking, then more often for the remainder of cooking time. When chicken is done, skin should be well browned and meat near thighbone no longer pink; cut to test.

To serve, skim and discard fat from pan juices; serve juices with chicken. Makes 4 servings.—*Jayne Reber, Mendocino, CA*

Per serving: 723 calories, 44 g carbohydrates, 57 g protein, 32 g total fat (9 g saturated), 178 mg cholesterol, 1,405 mg sodium

Jayne's Chinese Duck

Follow directions for **Jayne's Chinese Chicken,** but substitute 1 **duck** (4 to 5 lbs.), cut up and trimmed of fat, for chicken. After marinating, place duck pieces and their marinade in a 9- by 13-inch baking dish. Cover and bake in a 350° oven for 2 hours. Spoon off and discard fat from dish. Uncover and continue to bake, basting often, until skin is well browned and thigh meat is tender enough to shred easily with a fork (20 to 30 more minutes).

To serve, skim and discard fat from pan juices; serve juices with duck. Makes 4 servings.

Per serving: 947 calories, 44 g carbohydrates, 43 g protein, 63 g total fat (21 g saturated), 186 mg cholesterol, 1,365 mg sodium

Chicken, Artichoke & Mushroom Casserole

When *Sunset* celebrated its fiftieth anniversary with a special issue in 1979, this casserole was featured as an example of a classic *Kitchen Cabinet* recipe from the 1950s. Try it with crusty bread and Salad Italiano with Basil Dressing (page 39).

1 chicken (3 to 3½ lbs.), cut up and trimmed of fat

Salt, pepper, and paprika

¼ cup butter or margarine

1 can (about 14 oz.) water-packed artichoke hearts, drained

4 ounces mushrooms, sliced

2 tablespoons all-purpose flour

⅔ cup chicken broth

3 tablespoons dry sherry

¼ teaspoon dry rosemary

Rinse chicken and pat dry. Then sprinkle lightly with salt, pepper, and paprika. Set aside.

Melt butter in a wide frying pan over medium heat. Add chicken, a few pieces at a time (do not crowd pan); cook, turning as needed, until browned on all sides. As chicken is browned, arrange it in a shallow 3-quart casserole, keeping pieces slightly apart.

Cut artichokes lengthwise into halves. Then arrange artichokes between chicken pieces; set aside.

Discard all but 3 tablespoons drippings from frying pan. Add mushrooms and cook over medium heat, stirring often, until golden. Blend in flour and cook, stirring, until bubbly. Remove from heat and gradually stir in broth, sherry, and rosemary; return to heat and cook, stirring constantly, until sauce boils and thickens. Pour sauce evenly over chicken and artichokes. Cover and bake in a 375° oven until meat near thighbone is no longer pink; cut to test (about 40 minutes). Makes 4 servings.—*R. McL., Vacaville, CA*

Per serving: 551 calories, 10 g carbohydrates, 47 g protein, 35 g total fat (12 g saturated), 164 mg cholesterol, 361 mg sodium

Baked Chicken with Garlic Spaghetti

Thin strands of spaghetti, bold with sautéed garlic and marinara sauce, make a savory bed for baked chicken.

1 chicken (about 3½ lbs.), cut up and trimmed of fat

Salt and pepper

½ teaspoon *each* dry rosemary and dry thyme

1 can or jar (about 15 oz.) marinara sauce

12 ounces dry spaghetti

⅓ cup butter or margarine

3 cloves garlic, minced or pressed

½ teaspoon *each* dry oregano and onion powder

Chopped parsley

Rinse chicken, pat dry, and sprinkle with salt, pepper, rosemary, and thyme. Arrange chicken pieces, skin side down, in a greased shallow baking pan. Bake in a 375° oven for 20 minutes. Baste with ½ cup of the marinara sauce; bake for 10 more minutes.

Turn chicken skin side up, baste with ½ cup more marinara sauce, and continue to bake until meat near thighbone is no longer pink; cut to test (about 20 more minutes).

When chicken is almost done baking, cook spaghetti in a 5- to 6-quart pan in about 3 quarts boiling water until just tender to bite (8 to 10 minutes); or cook according to package directions. Drain spaghetti well and set aside.

Melt butter in a wide frying pan over medium heat. Add garlic; cook, stirring often, until soft (about 5 minutes). Add oregano, onion powder, and spaghetti; toss until well mixed and heated through.

Heat remaining marinara sauce and pour into a small serving dish. To serve, pour spaghetti mixture onto a warm rimmed platter and top with chicken. Sprinkle with parsley. Offer sauce to spoon over individual servings. Makes 4 to 6 servings.—*R. C., Tucson*

Per serving: 887 calories, 60 g carbohydrates, 51 g protein, 49 g total fat (17 g saturated), 195 mg cholesterol, 815 mg sodium

CHICKEN-RICE-TOMATILLO BAKE

Chicken pieces bake on a rice pilaf with a difference: it's treated to tangy tomatillos, ground cumin, and minced cilantro. To accompany this hearty casserole, offer fresh corn on the cob coated with melted butter and sprinkled with cracked black pepper.

- 1 **chicken (about 3½ lbs.), cut up and trimmed of fat**
- 2 **tablespoons salad oil**
- 1 **medium-size onion, chopped**
- 1 **clove garlic, minced or pressed**
- 1 **cup long-grain white rice**
- 1 **can (about 13 oz.) tomatillos**
  About 1 cup chicken broth
- 1 **can (about 4 oz.) whole green chiles, thinly sliced crosswise**
- 1 **teaspoon ground cumin**
- 2 **tablespoons minced cilantro**
  Cilantro sprigs

Rinse chicken and pat dry. Heat oil in a wide frying pan over medium-high heat. Add chicken, a portion at a time (do not crowd pan); cook, turning as needed, until browned on all sides. As chicken is browned, remove it from pan and set aside. Pour off and discard all but 2 tablespoons fat from pan.

Add onion, garlic, and rice to pan; cook, stirring often, until rice is golden (about 5 minutes). Set aside.

Drain liquid from tomatillos and add enough of the broth to make 2 cups. Cut each tomatillo in half. In a 9- by 13-inch baking dish, mix broth mixture, tomatillos, chiles, cumin, minced cilantro, and rice mixture.

Arrange chicken pieces, skin side up, atop rice. Bake, uncovered, in a 350° oven until rice is tender to bite and meat near thighbone is no longer pink; cut to test (40 to 45 minutes). Garnish with cilantro sprigs. Makes 4 servings.—*Robin Warren, Fort Bragg, CA*

Per serving: 699 calories, 47 g carbohydrates, 53 g protein, 32 g total fat (8 g saturated), 157 mg cholesterol, 661 mg sodium

DEVILISHLY SPICY CHICKEN

Simmered in beer and chili sauce and seasoned with plenty of dry mustard, this chicken tastes decidedly piquant. To balance the heat, stir sweet green peas into the cooking pan at the last minute.

- 1 **chicken (about 4 lbs.), cut up, skinned, and trimmed of fat**
- 2 **tablespoons butter or margarine**
- 2 **medium-size onions, chopped**
- 1 **tablespoon dry mustard**
- 1 **can or bottle (about 12 oz.) beer**
- ⅓ **cup tomato-based chili sauce**
- 3 **tablespoons Worcestershire**
- 4 **cups hot cooked egg noodles**
- 1 **package (about 10 oz.) frozen tiny peas, thawed**

Rinse chicken, pat dry, and set aside.

Melt butter in a wide frying pan over medium-high heat. Add onions and cook, stirring often, until golden brown (12 to 15 minutes). Stir in mustard; then add beer, chili sauce, and Worcestershire. Add all chicken pieces except breasts; turn to coat. Reduce heat, cover, and simmer for 20 minutes.

Turn chicken over; add breast pieces to pan. Cover and continue to simmer until meat near thighbone is no longer pink; cut to test (about 20 more minutes).

Spoon noodles onto a warm deep platter. Lift chicken from pan and arrange over noodles; keep warm. Bring cooking liquid to a boil over high heat; then boil, uncovered, stirring often, until reduced to 2 cups (6 to 8 minutes). Add peas and stir until heated through. Spoon sauce over chicken. Makes 4 to 6 servings. —*Barbara Keenan, Fort Morgan, CO*

Per serving: 526 calories, 53 g carbohydrates, 48 g protein, 13 g total fat (5 g saturated), 177 mg cholesterol, 612 mg sodium

RAVIOLI CHICKEN

This one-pan meal is substantial, eye-catching, and quick to prepare.

- 1 chicken (about 3 lbs.), cut up and trimmed of fat
  Salt and pepper
- 3 to 4 tablespoons all-purpose flour
- 2 tablespoons butter or margarine
- 2 tablespoons salad oil
- 1 medium-size onion, sliced
- ¼ cup water
- 1 clove garlic, minced or pressed
- 1 can (about 15 oz.) ravioli
- ½ cup *each* dry white wine and hot water
- 12 pitted ripe olives
  Chopped parsley

Rinse chicken and pat dry. Sprinkle with salt and pepper; dust with flour. Melt butter in oil in a wide, deep frying pan over medium-high heat. Add chicken, a portion at a time (do not crowd pan); cook, turning as needed, until browned on all sides. As chicken is browned, remove it from pan and set aside. Add onion to pan and cook, stirring often, until soft. Spoon off and discard almost all fat from pan.

Return chicken (and any accumulated juices) to pan; add the ¼ cup water and garlic. Then reduce heat, cover, and cook until meat near thighbone is no longer pink; cut to test (35 to 40 minutes). Remove chicken from pan and keep warm. Skim and discard fat from pan juices.

To pan juices, add ravioli, wine, hot water, and olives. Bring to a boil; then reduce heat and simmer just until heated through. To serve, arrange a portion of ravioli beside chicken on each plate; top with sauce and sprinkle with parsley. Makes 4 servings.—*H. N., San Francisco*

Per serving: 703 calories, 26 g carbohydrates, 46 g protein, 43 g total fat (13 g saturated), 162 mg cholesterol, 785 mg sodium

CHICKEN SALSA

Steam or sauté tender little summer squash to accompany this easy baked chicken.

- 1 chicken (3½ to 4 lbs.), cut up and trimmed of fat
- 1 large can (about 15 oz.) tomato sauce
- 1 cup medium-hot or mild purchased salsa
- 1 clove garlic, minced or pressed
- 1 small onion, thinly sliced
- 2 teaspoons ground cumin
- 1 teaspoon dry oregano
- 8 flour tortillas (*each* 7 to 9 inches in diameter)
  Salt

Rinse chicken, pat dry, and arrange on a rack in a 12- by 15-inch broiler pan. Broil 3 to 4 inches below heat, turning as needed, until browned on all sides (15 to 20 minutes).

Arrange chicken, skin side up, in a shallow 3-quart casserole. In a large bowl, stir together tomato sauce, salsa, garlic, onion, cumin, and oregano. Pour sauce over chicken. Cover tightly and bake in a 350° oven for 25 minutes.

Brush tortillas lightly with hot water; then stack and wrap in foil. Uncover chicken; place wrapped tortillas in oven.

Continue to bake until tortillas are hot (about 15 minutes) and meat near chicken thighbone is no longer pink; cut to test (15 to 20 more minutes). Season chicken to taste with salt. Offer tortillas to eat with chicken and sauce. Makes 4 servings.—*Lyn McNeel, Tularosa, NM*

Per serving: 744 calories, 54 g carbohydrates, 59 g protein, 31 g total fat (8 g saturated), 165 mg cholesterol, 1,774 mg sodium

HAWAIIAN HONEY CHICKEN

Tangy mustard punctuates the sprightly honey-citrus glaze for these chicken pieces.

- 1 teaspoon grated lemon peel
- 2 teaspoons grated orange peel
- ¼ cup lemon juice
- ½ cup orange juice
- ¼ cup honey
- 2 tablespoons soy sauce
- 1 tablespoon salad oil
- 1 teaspoon dry mustard
- 1 chicken (3 to 3½ lbs.), cut up, skinned (if desired), and trimmed of fat

In a large bowl, stir together lemon peel, orange peel, lemon juice, orange juice, honey, soy sauce, oil, and mustard. Rinse chicken and pat dry; then add to marinade and turn to coat. Cover and refrigerate for 2 to 4 hours, turning occasionally.

Lift chicken from marinade and drain briefly (reserve marinade). Place chicken, skin side up, on a greased rack in a foil-lined 12- by 15-inch broiler pan. Bake in a 350° oven for 25 minutes. Meanwhile, pour reserved marinade into a 1- to 2-quart pan. Bring to a boil over high heat; then boil, uncovered, until reduced to about ⅓ cup.

Brush chicken with reduced marinade. Then continue to bake until meat near thighbone is no longer pink; cut to test (about 20 more minutes). Makes 4 servings.—*L.O., Seattle*

Per serving: 508 calories, 23 g carbohydrates, 45 g protein, 26 g total fat (7 g saturated), 143 mg cholesterol, 652 mg sodium

OVEN-BARBECUED CHICKEN

There's no need to light the grill to make this super-saucy chicken—you cook it right in your oven. Chili-sparked pineapple juice glazes and flavors the pieces as they bake.

- 3   tablespoons firmly packed brown sugar
- 1   tablespoon cornstarch
- ¾   cup pineapple juice
- 3   tablespoons catsup
- ¼   cup cider vinegar
- 1   tablespoon chili powder
- 1   teaspoon ground ginger
- ⅛   teaspoon ground allspice
- 1   tablespoon soy sauce
- 2   cloves garlic, minced or pressed
- 1   chicken (about 3½ lbs.), cut up and trimmed of fat

In a 1- to 1½-quart pan, mix sugar and cornstarch. Stir in pineapple juice, catsup, vinegar, chili powder, ginger, allspice, soy sauce, and garlic. Bring to a boil over high heat, stirring. Remove from heat.

Rinse chicken and pat dry. Then arrange chicken, skin side down, in a foil-lined shallow 10- by 15-inch baking pan. Brush some of the sauce over chicken. Bake in a 400° oven for 20 minutes. Turn chicken pieces over and brush with remaining sauce. Continue to bake until skin is well browned and meat near thighbone is no longer pink; cut to test (about 25 more minutes). Makes 4 servings. —*Betty Jane Morrison, Lakewood, CO*

Per serving: 515 calories, 24 g carbohydrates, 49 g protein, 24 g total fat (7 g saturated), 154 mg cholesterol, 558 mg sodium

ORANGE-ALMOND CHICKEN

Here's an elegant main dish for a birthday or other special occasion. It's delicious with tender-crisp spring asparagus spears.

- 1   chicken (about 3½ lbs.), cut up and trimmed of fat
- 1   teaspoon *each* salt and paprika
- ¼   teaspoon pepper
- ¼   cup butter or margarine
- ⅔   cup slivered almonds or chopped hazelnuts
- 1   cup orange juice

Rinse chicken and pat dry. Combine salt, paprika, and pepper; rub mixture into all sides of chicken. Melt butter in a wide frying pan over medium-high heat. Add chicken, a portion at a time (do not crowd pan); cook, turning as needed, until browned on all sides. As chicken is browned, remove it from pan and set aside.

Return all chicken pieces (and any accumulated juices) to pan. Then reduce heat to low, cover, and cook until meat near thighbone is no longer pink; cut to test (35 to 40 minutes).

Meanwhile, toast almonds in another wide frying pan over medium heat, stirring often, until golden (about 5 minutes). Pour out of pan and set aside.

Transfer chicken to a platter and keep warm. Skim and discard fat from pan juices. Pour orange juice into chicken cooking pan and stir to scrape browned bits free. Then bring to a boil over high heat and boil, uncovered, until reduced by half. Pour sauce over chicken; sprinkle with almonds. Makes 4 servings. —*E. D., Burlingame, CA*

Per serving: 712 calories, 12 g carbohydrates, 53 g protein, 50 g total fat (16 g saturated), 188 mg cholesterol, 814 mg sodium

CRISPY OVEN-FRIED CHICKEN FOR A DOZEN

This convenient, crisp-crusted chicken definitely belongs on your list of entrées to serve a crowd at a picnic or potluck. The chicken doesn't require much tending as it bakes; lining the baking pans with foil makes cleanup easier.

- 3   chickens (about 3½ lbs. *each*), cut up and trimmed of fat
- 1¾ cups all-purpose flour
- ⅔   cup yellow cornmeal
- 1   tablespoon chili powder
- 2   teaspoons seasoned salt
- 1¼ teaspoons *each* dry thyme and dry oregano
- ½   cup grated Parmesan cheese
- 1½ cups buttermilk
- ¾   cup (¼ lb. plus ¼ cup) butter or margarine

Rinse chicken and pat dry. In a large, shallow pan, combine flour, cornmeal, chili powder, seasoned salt, thyme, oregano, and cheese. Pour buttermilk into a shallow bowl.

Dip chicken, a few pieces at a time, in buttermilk and drain briefly; then coat evenly with flour mixture and shake off excess. Set chicken pieces aside.

Divide butter equally between 2 foil-lined shallow 10- by 15-inch baking pans. Set pans in a 400° oven until butter is melted. Turn chicken in butter to coat; then arrange pieces, skin side down, in baking pans. Bake on the 2 middle oven racks for 25 minutes. Turn chicken pieces over and continue to bake until coating is well browned and meat near thighbone is no longer pink; cut to test (25 to 30 more minutes). Serve hot or cold. Makes 12 servings.—*C. W., Pearl City, HI*

Per serving: 683 calories, 22 g carbohydrates, 54 g protein, 41 g total fat (15 g saturated), 200 mg cholesterol, 403 mg sodium

Asparagus Chicken Stir-fry

Ever since woks became widely available in the early 1970s, stir-frying has been popular with *Sunset* readers. This simple dish—easily made in a wok or a wide frying pan—combines fresh asparagus with sliced mushrooms and lean, tender strips of skinless chicken breast.

- 1 pound asparagus
- 1 tablespoon *each* cornstarch, dry sherry, and soy sauce
- ½ cup chicken broth
- 2 tablespoons salad oil
- 1 tablespoon Oriental sesame oil
- 1 tablespoon minced fresh ginger
- 2 cloves garlic, minced or pressed
- 1½ pounds chicken breasts, boned, skinned, and cut into ½- by 1-inch strips
- 8 ounces mushrooms, thinly sliced
- 6 to 8 green onions, cut diagonally into 1-inch pieces

Snap off and discard tough ends of asparagus; then cut asparagus diagonally into 1-inch pieces. Set aside. In a small bowl, stir together cornstarch, sherry, soy sauce, and broth; set aside.

Heat salad oil and sesame oil in a wide frying pan or wok over high heat. Add ginger, garlic, and chicken. Cook, stirring, until chicken is no longer pink in center; cut to test (about 2 minutes). Remove mixture from pan with a slotted spoon and set aside.

Add mushrooms, onions, and asparagus to pan and cook, stirring, for 1 minute. Return chicken (and any accumulated juices) to pan; stir broth mixture and pour into pan. Bring to a boil, stirring; then boil, stirring, until sauce is clear and thickened. Makes 4 servings.—*Arlene Ulmer, Sebastopol, CA*

Per serving: 271 calories, 10 g carbohydrates, 30 g protein, 12 g total fat (2 g saturated), 65 mg cholesterol, 463 mg sodium

Salsa Chicken with Cheese

Boneless chicken breasts are pounded thin and quickly sautéed, topped with zesty tomato sauce and cheese, and finished under the broiler.

- 6 boneless, skinless chicken breast halves (about 2¼ lbs. *total*)
- 1½ tablespoons butter or margarine
- 1½ tablespoons salad oil
- 1 medium-size onion, chopped
- 1 clove garlic, minced or pressed
- 2 stalks celery, thinly sliced
- 1 can (about 4 oz.) diced green chiles
- 1 can (about 14½ oz.) stewed tomatoes
- ½ cup chicken broth
- ¼ teaspoon ground cumin
- ½ teaspoon *each* dry oregano and sugar
- Salt and pepper
- 1½ cups (about 6 oz.) shredded Cheddar cheese

Rinse chicken and pat dry. Place each breast half between 2 sheets of plastic wrap and pound with a flat-surfaced mallet to a thickness of about ¼ inch.

Melt butter in oil in a wide frying pan over medium-high heat. Add chicken, half at a time; cook, turning once, until browned on both sides (about 4 minutes). As chicken is browned, transfer it to a heatproof platter and keep warm in a 250° oven.

To frying pan, add onion, garlic, and celery; stir often until onion is soft. Add chiles, tomatoes, broth, cumin, oregano, and sugar. Stir often until sauce is thickened (about 10 minutes). Season sauce to taste with salt and pepper; pour over chicken. Sprinkle with cheese and broil 3 inches below heat until cheese is melted (3 to 5 minutes). Makes 6 servings.—*J. F., El Granada, CA*

Per serving: 398 calories, 9 g carbohydrates, 48 g protein, 18 g total fat (9 g saturated), 136 mg cholesterol, 701 mg sodium

Chinese Plum Chicken

To make the richly flavored glaze for these moist chicken breasts, start with a jar of Oriental plum sauce; then enhance it with minced onion, lemon peel, and spices.

- 4 chicken breast halves or 8 chicken thighs (2 to 2½ lbs. *total*), skinned
- 1 cup Oriental plum sauce (or 1 cup plum jam plus 1 tablespoon soy sauce)
- ¼ cup minced onion
- 1 teaspoon grated lemon peel
- 2 tablespoons lemon juice
- 1 tablespoon soy sauce
- ½ teaspoon *each* dry mustard and ground ginger
- ¼ teaspoon *each* pepper, liquid hot pepper seasoning, and crushed anise seeds

Rinse chicken and pat dry; then place, skinned side up, in a 9- by 13-inch baking pan. In a small bowl, stir together plum sauce, onion, lemon peel, lemon juice, soy sauce, mustard, ginger, pepper, hot pepper seasoning, and anise seeds. Pour sauce evenly over chicken. Bake in a 400° oven, basting halfway through baking, until meat near bone is no longer pink; cut to test (about 25 minutes for breasts, 35 minutes for thighs).

To serve, transfer chicken to a platter and spoon sauce on top. Makes 4 servings.—*Diane McPherson, Kihei, HI*

Per serving: 364 calories, 23 g carbohydrates, 43 g protein, 11 g total fat (3 g saturated), 116 mg cholesterol, 676 mg sodium

STUFFED CHICKEN BREASTS WITH CHUTNEY

This spinach filling is good enough to eat alone—but it's even better rolled inside chicken breasts and simmered in a simple sauce of balsamic vinegar and chutney.

3 tablespoons olive oil
2 cloves garlic, minced or pressed
1 large onion, chopped
2 cups chopped fresh spinach
8 small boneless, skinless chicken breast halves (about 2 lbs. *total*)
2 teaspoons balsamic vinegar
¼ cup *each* water and chopped chutney

Heat 1 tablespoon of the oil in a wide frying pan over medium-high heat. Add garlic and onion; cook, stirring occasionally, until onion is soft (about 5 minutes). Stir in spinach; remove from heat and let cool.

Rinse chicken and pat dry. Place each breast half between 2 sheets of plastic wrap and pound with a flat-surfaced mallet to a thickness of about ¼ inch. In center of each pounded chicken piece, mound an eighth of the spinach mixture. Roll chicken around filling to enclose; fasten with wooden picks.

Heat remaining 2 tablespoons oil in frying pan over medium-high heat. Add chicken rolls and cook, turning as needed, until browned on all sides. In a small bowl, stir together vinegar, water, and chutney. Pour over chicken. Reduce heat to medium, cover, and simmer until meat is no longer pink and filling is hot in center; cut to test (8 to 10 minutes). Remove chicken from pan; keep warm.

Increase heat to high and bring cooking liquid to a boil. Boil, uncovered, stirring occasionally, until reduced to ½ cup (about 5 minutes).

Pour sauce over chicken. Makes 8 servings.—*Constance Chaplin, Seal Beach, CA*

Per serving: 205 calories, 8 g carbohydrates, 27 g protein, 7 g total fat (1 g saturated), 66 mg cholesterol, 103 mg sodium

CHICKEN & APPLE SAUTÉ

From start to finish, this dish takes less then 30 minutes.

4 chicken breast halves (about 2 lbs. *total*)
¼ cup butter or margarine
2 large tart apples (about 1 lb. *total*), peeled, cored, and cut into ¼-inch-thick slices
1 large onion, chopped
⅔ cup dry sherry or apple juice
⅓ cup whipping cream

Rinse chicken and pat dry; set aside.

Melt 2 tablespoons of the butter in a wide frying pan over medium heat. Add apples; cook, turning often, until tender when pierced (2 to 3 minutes). Remove from pan; keep warm.

Melt remaining 2 tablespoons butter in pan. Add chicken, skin side down; cook until skin is well browned. Remove from pan and set aside with apples. Add onion to pan and cook, stirring often, until soft (about 5 minutes). Return chicken to pan, skin side up. Add sherry. Cover and simmer until meat in thickest part is no longer pink; cut to test (about 15 minutes).

Arrange chicken on a platter and top with apples; keep warm. Add cream to liquid in pan; bring to a boil. Then boil, uncovered, until sauce is reduced by about a third. Pour sauce over chicken. Makes 4 servings.—*M. S., China Lake, CA*

Per serving: 610 calories, 25 g carbohydrates, 39 g protein, 35 g total fat (16 g saturated), 169 mg cholesterol, 243 mg sodium

MARINATED CHICKEN BREASTS

Garnish each serving of this light warm-weather entrée with tomato wedges or marinated artichoke hearts.

12 chicken breast halves (about 6 lbs. *total*), skinned
2 cups water
½ teaspoon salt
⅔ cup salad oil (or ⅓ cup *each* salad oil and olive oil)
⅓ cup tarragon wine vinegar
1 teaspoon salt
½ teaspoon garlic salt
1 green onion, thinly sliced
¼ cup finely chopped parsley
Lettuce leaves, rinsed and crisped

Rinse chicken and pat dry. In a wide, deep frying pan or other large pan with a lid, combine water and the ½ teaspoon salt. Bring to a boil over high heat; add chicken. Then reduce heat, cover, and simmer until meat in thickest part is no longer pink; cut to test (20 to 25 minutes). Drain chicken; let stand until cool enough to handle. Then remove meat of each breast half from bones in one piece. Arrange chicken in a wide, shallow bowl.

In a medium-size bowl, stir together oil, vinegar, the 1 teaspoon salt, garlic salt, onion, and 2 tablespoons of the parsley. Pour marinade over chicken. Cover and refrigerate for at least 6 hours or until next day, turning chicken over 3 or 4 times.

To serve, lift chicken pieces from marinade and arrange on lettuce-lined individual plates. Spoon a little of the marinade over chicken; then sprinkle with remaining 2 tablespoons parsley. Makes 12 servings.
—*H. V., Auburn, CA*

Per serving: 272 calories, 0.6 g carbohydrates, 34 g protein, 14 g total fat (2 g saturated), 86 mg cholesterol, 431 mg sodium

Yogurt Chicken with Oranges

Yogurt and orange juice make a tangy low-calorie sauce for chicken breasts.

3 or 4 large oranges (1½ to 2½ lbs. *total*)

8 boneless, skinless chicken breast halves (about 3 lbs. *total*)

2 tablespoons butter or margarine

2 tablespoons salad oil

1 large onion, chopped

2 cloves garlic, minced or pressed

½ teaspoon *each* ground coriander and ground cumin

1 tablespoon sugar

1 tablespoon cornstarch

1 cup plain yogurt

Salt and pepper

Cut off and discard peel and all white membrane from 2 of the oranges, then thinly slice fruit crosswise and set aside. Grate enough peel (colored part only) from another orange to make 1 teaspoon peel; also squeeze juice from 1 or 2 oranges to make ¾ cup juice. Set aside.

Rinse chicken and pat dry. Melt butter in oil in a wide frying pan over medium heat. Add chicken to pan, a portion at a time (do not crowd pan); cook, turning as needed, until browned on both sides. As chicken is browned, remove it from pan and set aside.

Add onion and garlic to pan; cook, stirring often, until onion is soft. Return chicken (and any accumulated juices) to pan; then add orange juice, orange peel, coriander, cumin, and sugar. Bring to a boil. Reduce heat, cover, and simmer until meat in thickest part is no longer pink; cut to test (about 15 minutes). Lift chicken to a platter and keep warm.

Stir together cornstarch and yogurt; stir into pan juices and cook, stirring, just until thickened. Season sauce to taste with salt and pepper; pour over chicken. Garnish with orange slices. Makes 8 servings. —*K. J., Seattle*

Per serving: 293 calories, 9 g carbohydrates, 41 g protein, 9 g total fat (3 g saturated), 110 mg cholesterol, 155 mg sodium

Thai Basil Chicken

Fragrant fresh basil seasons the pungent, tart-sweet sauce that tops these pan-browned chicken breasts.

1 tablespoon salad oil

2 tablespoons minced garlic

4 boneless, skinless chicken breast halves (about 1½ lbs. *total*)

1 cup lightly packed fresh basil leaves, cut into thin slivers

3 tablespoons *each* lemon juice and water

1 tablespoon *each* soy sauce and sugar

½ teaspoon pepper

Heat oil in a wide frying pan over medium-high heat. Add garlic and cook, stirring often, until golden (3 to 4 minutes). Remove garlic from pan with a slotted spoon and place in a small bowl.

Rinse chicken, pat dry, and add to pan. Cook, turning as needed, until lightly browned on both sides. Add ½ cup of the basil to pan along with garlic, lemon juice, water, soy sauce, sugar, and pepper. Cover and simmer, spooning juices over chicken often, until meat in thickest part is no longer pink; cut to test (10 to 12 minutes). Transfer chicken to a platter; keep warm.

Bring pan juices to a boil over high heat; then boil, uncovered, until reduced to ¼ cup. Stir in remaining ½ cup basil; pour sauce over chicken. Makes 4 servings.—*J. Hill, Sacramento*

Per serving: 257 calories, 10 g carbohydrates, 41 g protein, 6 g total fat (1 g saturated), 99 mg cholesterol, 373 mg sodium

Slivered Chicken & Walnuts

Here's a quick dinner for two you can make in a wok or a frying pan. If you plan to serve rice alongside, start steaming it first; that way, it will be ready when the chicken is completed.

Cooking Sauce (recipe follows)

1 pound chicken breast, boned, skinned, and cut into thin strips

1 tablespoon soy sauce

1 teaspoon cornstarch

3 tablespoons salad oil

½ cup walnut halves

1 medium-size green bell pepper (about 6 oz.), seeded and cut into 1-inch squares

½ teaspoon minced fresh ginger

Prepare Cooking Sauce and set aside. In a large bowl, mix chicken, soy sauce, and cornstarch; set aside.

Heat oil in a wide frying pan or wok over medium-high heat. Add walnuts and cook, stirring often, until browned (2 to 3 minutes); remove from pan with a slotted spoon and set aside. Add chicken mixture to pan and cook, stirring, until meat is no longer pink in center; cut to test (1½ to 2 minutes). Remove chicken from pan with a slotted spoon.

Add bell pepper and ginger; cook, stirring, until pepper is bright green. Return chicken to pan; stir Cooking Sauce and add to pan. Cook, stirring, until sauce boils and thickens. Stir in walnuts. Makes 2 servings.—*T. B., Sunriver, OR*

Cooking Sauce. In a small bowl, stir together ½ teaspoon **cornstarch**, a dash of **liquid hot pepper seasoning**, ¾ teaspoon *each* **sugar** and **white wine vinegar**, 1 teaspoon **dry sherry**, and 1 tablespoon **soy sauce**.

Per serving: 550 calories, 14 g carbohydrates, 39 g protein, 38 g total fat (4 g saturated), 86 mg cholesterol, 1,133 mg sodium

Chicken Pasta Italiano

Chicken and ripe tomatoes make a fresh, simple sauce for pasta. Enhance the Italian mood with Garlic & Artichoke Bread (page 188).

½ cup (about 4 oz.) firmly packed chopped bacon

4 cloves garlic, minced or pressed

12 ounces boneless, skinless chicken breast, cut crosswise into ¼-inch-thick strips

4 medium-size ripe tomatoes (about 1½ lbs. *total*), seeded and chopped

½ cup dry sherry or chicken broth

1 tablespoon Italian herb seasoning (or ¾ teaspoon *each* dry basil, marjoram, oregano, and thyme)

⅛ teaspoon ground red pepper (cayenne)

6 ounces dry spaghetti

½ cup grated Parmesan cheese

Cook bacon in a wide frying pan over medium heat until crisp. Remove from pan with a slotted spoon and set aside. Pour off and discard all but 2 tablespoons drippings from pan.

Increase heat to high. Add garlic and chicken to pan; cook, stirring, until chicken is lightly browned (about 3 minutes). Remove chicken from pan and set aside. Add tomatoes, sherry, herb seasoning, and red pepper to pan. Bring to a boil over high heat; then boil, uncovered, stirring often, until almost all liquid has evaporated (about 10 minutes).

Meanwhile, in a 4- to 5-quart pan, cook spaghetti in about 2 quarts boiling water until just tender to bite (8 to 10 minutes); or cook according to package directions. Drain well, pour onto a warm deep platter, and keep hot.

Return chicken (and any accumulated juices) to tomato sauce; stir until heated through. Pour sauce over spaghetti, sprinkle with bacon, and mix gently, using 2 forks. Offer cheese to add to taste. Makes 3 servings.
—*J. G. Jacque, Sherman Oaks, CA*

Per serving: 635 calories, 60 g carbohydrates, 44 g protein, 19 g total fat (7 g saturated), 91 mg cholesterol, 578 mg sodium

Spiced Chicken with Capers

Brown rice or mild, fluffy couscous is a good partner for chicken simmered in orange juice with raisins, cinnamon, and cloves.

4 small boneless, skinless chicken breast halves (about 1 lb. *total*)

2 tablespoons salad oil

1 large onion, thinly sliced

2 cloves garlic, minced or pressed

¼ teaspoon *each* ground cinnamon and ground cloves

½ cup orange juice

2 tablespoons raisins

1 tablespoon drained capers
   Salt and pepper
   Parsley sprigs (optional)

Rinse chicken and pat dry. Heat oil in a wide frying pan over high heat; add chicken and cook, turning once, until lightly browned on both sides. Remove from pan and set aside. Reduce heat to medium-high. Add onion and garlic to pan and cook, stirring often, until onion is lightly browned (5 to 6 minutes). Stir in cinnamon, cloves, orange juice, raisins, and capers; bring to a boil.

Return chicken (and any accumulated juices) to pan. Reduce heat, cover, and simmer until meat in thickest part is no longer pink; cut to test (about 5 minutes). Season to taste with salt and pepper. Transfer chicken and pan juices to a serving dish; garnish with parsley sprigs, if desired. Makes 4 servings.—*Carmela Meely, Walnut Creek, CA*

Per serving: 237 calories, 13 g carbohydrates, 27 g protein, 8 g total fat (1 g saturated), 66 mg cholesterol, 132 mg sodium

Lemon Rosemary Chicken

Crusted with herb-seasoned whole wheat crumbs, these lemony baked chicken breasts are good with Couscous Provençal (page 163).

1¼ cups soft whole wheat bread crumbs

2 tablespoons minced fresh rosemary or 2 teaspoons dry rosemary

1 tablespoon minced parsley

1 teaspoon grated lemon peel

½ teaspoon pepper

6 boneless, skinless chicken breast halves (about 2¼ lbs. *total*)

1 tablespoon lemon juice
   Lemon wedges (optional)

In a bowl, mix bread crumbs, rosemary, parsley, lemon peel, and pepper. Rinse chicken and pat dry; then arrange, skinned side up, in an oiled shallow 10- by 15-inch baking pan. Moisten chicken with lemon juice; then press crumb mixture over each piece, covering evenly.

Bake chicken in a 400° oven until crumb topping is browned and meat in thickest part is no longer pink; cut to test (about 25 minutes). Serve with lemon wedges, if desired. Makes 6 servings.—*Diane Peacock, Crockett, CA*

Per serving: 216 calories, 5 g carbohydrates, 40 g protein, 3 g total fat (0.7 g saturated), 99 mg cholesterol, 167 mg sodium

Honey Chicken

A light and tangy honey-mustard glaze beautifully complements baked chicken breasts. Offer hot rice and Chinese pea pods alongside.

- 2 tablespoons sesame seeds
- 3 tablespoons honey
- ¼ cup *each* dry sherry and Dijon mustard
- 1 tablespoon lemon juice
- 6 boneless, skinless chicken breast halves (about 2¼ lbs. *total*)

Toast sesame seeds in a small frying pan over medium-high heat, stirring often, until golden (2 to 4 minutes). Pour into a small bowl and stir in honey, sherry, mustard, and lemon juice.

Rinse chicken and pat dry; then arrange, skinned side up, in a 9- by 13-inch baking pan. Drizzle with honey mixture. Bake in a 400° oven, basting several times with sauce, until meat in thickest part is no longer pink; cut to test (about 20 minutes).

To serve, transfer chicken to individual plates; stir any sauce left in pan until blended, then spoon over chicken. Makes 6 servings.—*Kathleen A. Vine, Tacoma, WA*

Per serving: 262 calories, 11 g carbohydrates, 40 g protein, 4 g total fat (0.8 g saturated), 99 mg cholesterol, 353 mg sodium

Chicken with Onion Marmalade

A honey-sweetened red onion "marmalade" makes a piquant, delicious topping for sherry-baked chicken breasts. Accompany the dish with steamed, buttered tiny red potatoes and fresh green beans.

- 6 small boneless, skinless chicken breast halves (1½ to 1¾ lbs. *total*)
- 3 tablespoons cream sherry
- 2 medium-size red onions, thinly sliced
- ½ cup dry red wine
- 1 tablespoon *each* red wine vinegar and honey
  Salt and pepper
  Parsley sprigs

Rinse chicken, pat dry, and place in a large heavy-duty plastic bag. Add 2 tablespoons of the sherry. Seal bag and rotate to coat chicken with sherry. Refrigerate for at least 30 minutes or up to 6 hours, turning bag over 3 or 4 times.

Meanwhile, in a wide frying pan, combine onions, red wine, vinegar, and honey. Cook over medium-high heat, stirring often, until liquid has evaporated. (At this point, you may cover and set aside for up to 6 hours; reheat over medium-high heat, stirring often, before continuing.) Remove onion mixture from heat, stir in remaining 1 tablespoon sherry, and season to taste with salt and pepper.

Lift chicken from bag and arrange, skinned side up, in a 9- by 13-inch baking pan; add any sherry from bag. Bake in a 450° oven just until meat in thickest part is no longer pink; cut to test (about 15 minutes). With a slotted spoon, transfer chicken to a platter. Spoon onion mixture over chicken. Garnish with parsley sprigs. Makes 6 servings.—*Mrs. L. K. Ross, Elk Grove, CA*

Per serving: 195 calories, 9 g carbohydrates, 29 g protein, 2 g total fat (0.4 g saturated), 72 mg cholesterol, 88 mg sodium

Chicken Ratatouille

Bake mild chicken breasts and an herbed vegetable medley in separate pans in the same oven, then serve them together. The combination is good hot or cold; either way, serve with crusty sourdough bread.

- 1 large onion
- 1 medium-size green bell pepper (about 6 oz.), seeded
- 1 small eggplant (about 12 oz.)
- 8 to 12 ounces zucchini, cut into 1-inch-thick slices
- 2 large cloves garlic, minced or pressed
- 2 teaspoons dry basil
- 1 tablespoon olive oil or salad oil
- 3 medium-size tomatoes (1 to 1¼ lbs. *total*), cut into wedges
- 4 boneless, skinless chicken breast halves (about 1½ lbs. *total*)
  Salt and pepper

Cut onion, bell pepper, and unpeeled eggplant into 1-inch chunks. Place in a shallow 12- by 15-inch baking pan; mix in zucchini. Then mix in garlic, basil, and oil. Cover tightly and bake in a 450° oven for 45 minutes.

Uncover pan; stir in three-fourths of the tomatoes. Rinse chicken, pat dry, and arrange, skinned side up, in a 9- by 13-inch baking pan; place in oven alongside vegetables. Continue to bake vegetables and chicken, uncovered, until eggplant is very tender to bite and meat in thickest part of chicken is no longer pink; cut to test (15 to 20 more minutes). During baking, stir vegetables occasionally and baste chicken with pan juices once or twice. Season vegetables and chicken to taste with salt and pepper.

Spoon vegetables onto a platter, top with chicken, and garnish with remaining tomatoes. Makes 4 servings.—*Karla Larkson, Clarkston, WA*

Per serving: 312 calories, 22 g carbohydrates, 43 g protein, 6 g total fat (1 g saturated), 99 mg cholesterol, 131 mg sodium

CHICKEN WINGS ORIENTAL

Two-step baking turns out glazed chicken wings that are crisp and saucy at the same time.

    2 pounds chicken wings
    1 large egg
    ⅓ cup cornstarch
    1 tablespoon salad oil
    ½ cup *each* sugar and chicken broth
    ½ cup white wine vinegar
    ¼ cup catsup
    1 teaspoon soy sauce
    2 cloves garlic, minced or pressed
    2 teaspoons cornstarch blended with 2 teaspoons cold water

Cut off and discard chicken wingtips; then rinse chicken and pat dry. In a shallow bowl, beat egg until blended. Spread the ⅓ cup cornstarch in another shallow bowl. Dip chicken in egg to coat, then dip in cornstarch to coat lightly on all sides.

Pour oil into a shallow 10- by 15-inch baking pan; set pan in a 450° oven until oil is hot. Arrange chicken in a single layer in pan. Bake until lightly browned on bottom (about 20 minutes). Then turn chicken over and continue to bake until lightly browned on other side (about 20 more minutes). Remove pan from oven; spoon off and discard fat.

When chicken is almost done, in a 2-quart pan, mix sugar, broth, vinegar, catsup, soy sauce, and garlic. Bring to a boil over high heat; boil, stirring, until reduced to ¾ cup. Stir cornstarch mixture; add to broth mixture. Bring to a rolling boil, stirring.

Brush all the sauce over chicken. Continue to bake until sauce is bubbly (about 5 minutes). Makes 4 servings.—*Mrs. Ann Andersen, Sitka, AK*

Per serving: 444 calories, 37 g carbohydrates, 25 g protein, 21 g total fat (5 g saturated), 112 mg cholesterol, 472 mg sodium

CHICKEN WITH BARLEY & PECANS

Toasted pecans and minced parsley top a comforting blend of barley, chicken, and sliced fresh mushrooms simmered in broth.

    8 chicken thighs (about 2 lbs. *total*), skinned and trimmed of fat
    3 tablespoons olive oil or salad oil
    ½ cup pecan halves
    1 large onion, chopped
    1 pound mushrooms, thinly sliced
    1 cup pearl barley
    2 cloves garlic, minced or pressed
    3 cups chicken broth
    2 tablespoons minced parsley

Rinse chicken, pat dry, and set aside. Heat 1 tablespoon of the oil in a wide frying pan over medium-low heat. Add pecans and cook, stirring, until nuts taste toasted and are golden inside; break a nut to test (about 7 minutes). Remove from pan with a slotted spoon and set aside.

Increase heat to medium-high; heat 1 tablespoon more oil in pan. Add chicken, a portion at a time (do not crowd pan); cook, turning as needed, until browned on all sides. As chicken is browned, remove it from pan and set aside.

Heat remaining 1 tablespoon oil in pan. Add onion and mushrooms; cook, stirring often, until onion is soft and mushrooms are lightly browned (12 to 15 minutes). Add barley and garlic; cook, stirring, until barley starts to turn golden (about 2 minutes). Add broth; bring to a boil. Then reduce heat, cover, and simmer for 20 minutes.

Return chicken (and any accumulated juices) to pan. Cover and continue to simmer until barley is tender to bite and chicken meat near bone is no longer pink; cut to test (about 30 more minutes). Sprinkle with pecans and parsley. Makes 4 servings.—*Ann K. Shapleigh, Concord, CA*

Per serving: 585 calories, 52 g carbohydrates, 36 g protein, 27 g total fat (4 g saturated), 107 mg cholesterol, 873 mg sodium

OVEN-FRIED CHICKEN & SPARERIBS

Cornmeal in the coating gives oven-fried chicken and ribs a crisp crust.

    About 1½ pounds country-style spareribs, trimmed of fat
    ½ cup biscuit mix (baking mix)
    3 tablespoons yellow cornmeal
    ¼ teaspoon garlic powder
    1 teaspoon salt
    ½ teaspoon *each* dry rosemary, pepper, and paprika
    ¼ cup butter or margarine, melted
    About 1½ pounds whole chicken legs, trimmed of fat

Cut between spareribs to separate into serving-size portions. Combine biscuit mix, cornmeal, garlic powder, salt, rosemary, pepper, and paprika. Dip ribs, a few pieces at a time, in butter and drain briefly; then coat evenly with cornmeal mixture and shake off excess. Arrange ribs on a rack in a 12- by 15-inch broiler pan. Bake in a 400° oven for 15 minutes.

Meanwhile, cut chicken drumsticks and thighs apart, if desired. Rinse chicken and pat dry. Dip chicken in butter and drain briefly; then coat evenly with cornmeal mixture and shake off excess.

Arrange chicken next to ribs on rack. Continue to bake until meat near chicken thighbone is no longer pink; cut to test (50 to 55 more minutes). Both pork and chicken should be browned and crisp. Makes 4 servings.—*N. H., Tacoma, WA*

Per serving: 663 calories, 15 g carbohydrates, 42 g protein, 47 g total fat (19 g saturated), 183 mg cholesterol, 983 mg sodium

Yorkshire Chicken with Caramelized Shallots

Puffy, golden Yorkshire pudding is a traditional partner for roast beef—but as this recipe shows, it's just as good as an egg-rich topping baked over browned chunks of chicken thigh.

- 1 pound boneless chicken thighs, skinned and trimmed of fat
- 1½ cups all-purpose flour
  About 2 tablespoons olive oil
- 12 ounces small shallots, peeled
- 1 cup milk
- 2 large eggs
- 2 tablespoons butter or margarine, melted and cooled
- ¼ teaspoon pepper
- 1 teaspoon dry rosemary

Rinse chicken, pat dry, and cut into 1-inch pieces. Coat chicken with ½ cup of the flour; shake off excess. Heat 2 tablespoons of the oil in a wide non-stick frying pan over medium-high heat. Add chicken, half at a time (do not crowd pan); cook, turning as needed, until browned on all sides (5 to 7 minutes), adding more oil as needed. As chicken is browned, use a slotted spoon to transfer it to a shallow 2½- to 3-quart oval or round baking dish. Add shallots to pan; reduce heat, cover, and cook, stirring often, until golden brown (10 to 15 minutes). Scatter shallots over chicken.

In a blender or food processor, combine remaining 1 cup flour, milk, eggs, butter, and pepper; whirl until smooth. Stir rosemary into batter; then pour batter evenly over chicken. Bake in a 375° oven until puffy and well browned (45 to 50 minutes). Serve at once. Makes 4 servings.
—*Mrs. August Vaz, Castro Valley, CA*

Per serving: 488 calories, 52 g carbohydrates, 25 g protein, 20 g total fat (7 g saturated), 184 mg cholesterol, 186 mg sodium

Garlic Chicken & Grapes

Red or green grapes add a refreshing touch to sesame-baked chicken.

- 2 cloves garlic, minced or pressed
- 2 tablespoons salad oil
- 3 pounds chicken thighs or breast halves, trimmed of fat
- 3 tablespoons *each* Dijon mustard and soy sauce
- 2 tablespoons *each* honey and white wine vinegar
- 1 tablespoon sesame seeds
- 2 cups seedless red or green grapes

In a 9- by 13-inch baking pan, mix garlic and oil. Rinse chicken, pat dry, and arrange in pan, skin side down. If using thighs, cover and bake in a 400° oven for 25 minutes; then uncover. If using breasts, bake, uncovered, in a 400° oven for 10 minutes. Meanwhile, in a small bowl, stir together mustard, soy sauce, honey, and vinegar; set aside.

Turn chicken over; top evenly with mustard mixture and sprinkle with sesame seeds. Continue to bake until meat near bone is no longer pink; cut to test (about 15 more minutes). Sprinkle grapes over chicken; bake for 5 more minutes. Transfer chicken and grapes to a platter. Skim and discard fat from pan juices; offer juices with chicken. Makes 6 servings.
—*Carmela Meely, Walnut Creek, CA*

Per serving: 394 calories, 13 g carbohydrates, 30 g protein, 24 g total fat (6 g saturated), 109 mg cholesterol, 794 mg sodium

Apple Country Chicken

Pungent curry powder accents the sweetness of Golden Delicious apples in this cider-simmered chicken. Top the dish with tart yogurt, if you like; serve with fluffy white rice or a brown rice pilaf.

- 1 teaspoon curry powder
- 1 large Golden Delicious apple (about 8 oz.), cored and chopped
- 1 large yellow onion, finely chopped
- 1 tablespoon lemon juice
- 4 ounces mushrooms, sliced
- 1 teaspoon chicken-flavored instant bouillon
- 2 cups apple juice or cider
- 3¼ to 3½ pounds chicken thighs, skinned and trimmed of fat
- 1 tablespoon all-purpose flour
- 2 tablespoons sliced green onion
- 1 cup plain yogurt (optional)

Place curry powder in a wide frying pan and stir over medium heat until slightly darker in color (3 to 4 minutes). Add apple, yellow onion, lemon juice, mushrooms, bouillon, and 1½ cups of the apple juice; bring to a boil.

Rinse chicken and add to pan. Then reduce heat, cover, and simmer until meat near bone is no longer pink; cut to test (about 30 minutes). With a slotted spoon, transfer chicken to a platter; keep warm.

In a small bowl, smoothly blend flour and remaining ½ cup apple juice. Gradually add to sauce in pan, stirring constantly; increase heat to high and cook, stirring, until sauce is thickened. Pour over chicken. Garnish with green onion; offer yogurt to add to taste, if desired. Makes 4 to 6 servings.—*Carolyn E. Gilbaugh, Wenatchee, WA*

Per serving: 313 calories, 25 g carbohydrates, 36 g protein, 7 g total fat (2 g saturated), 145 mg cholesterol, 366 mg sodium

CHICKEN WITH CRUNCHY RICE

This colorful one-dish meal features spicy chicken legs served with rice and crisp fresh vegetables—bell pepper, green onions, and carrot slices.

- 4 *each* chicken drumsticks and thighs (about 2 lbs. *total*), trimmed of fat
- 2 tablespoons salad oil
- 1 teaspoon *each* curry powder and ground coriander
- ½ teaspoon ground ginger
- 1 cup long-grain rice
- 1 can (about 10¾ oz.) condensed chicken broth
- 1 cup boiling water
- Sautéed Vegetable Medley (recipe follows)
- Salt and pepper
- ½ cup dry-roasted cashews or peanuts

Rinse chicken and pat dry. Heat oil in a 3½- to 5-quart pan over medium heat. Add chicken, sprinkle with curry powder and coriander, and cook, turning as needed, until well browned on all sides.

Lift chicken from pan and set aside. Add ginger, rice, broth, and water to pan; top with chicken. Bring to a boil. Then reduce heat, cover, and simmer until rice is tender to bite and meat near thighbone is no longer pink; cut to test (35 to 40 minutes). Meanwhile, prepare Sautéed Vegetable Medley.

Transfer chicken to a platter and keep warm. Stir Sautéed Vegetable Medley into rice; season to taste with salt and pepper.

Spoon rice alongside chicken; sprinkle with cashews. Makes 4 servings.—*M. W., Burton, WA*

Per serving: 645 calories, 45 g carbohydrates, 38 g protein, 34 g total fat (10 g saturated), 154 mg cholesterol, 1,194 mg sodium

SAUTÉED VEGETABLE MEDLEY. Melt 2 tablespoons **butter** or margarine in a wide frying pan over medium heat. Add 6 **green onions,** thinly sliced; 1 medium-size **green, red, or yellow bell pepper** (about 6 oz.), seeded and cut into slivers; and 1 medium-size **carrot,** thinly sliced.

Cook, stirring often, until carrot is tender-crisp to bite (about 5 minutes). Stir in 2 tablespoons **regular or reduced-sodium soy sauce.**

TANDOORI CHICKEN

To give these juicy chicken legs their zesty flavor, slip a gingery seasoning paste beneath the skin of each piece before grilling. On the side, you might serve crunchy Ginger–Sweet Potato Salad (page 49).

- 6 whole chicken legs (about 3 lbs. *total*), trimmed of fat
- 1 teaspoon *each* grated fresh ginger and ground allspice
- ¼ to ½ teaspoon crushed red pepper flakes
- 2 cloves garlic, minced or pressed
- 1 tablespoon lemon juice
- Plain yogurt

Rinse chicken and pat dry. In a small bowl, mash together ginger, allspice, red pepper flakes, garlic, and lemon juice to make a paste. Loosen skin of each chicken leg and spread 1 teaspoon of the paste between meat and skin. Brush any remaining paste over chicken skin.

Arrange chicken on an oiled grill 6 inches above a solid bed of medium-hot coals. Cook, turning often, until meat near thighbone is no longer pink; cut to test (about 45 minutes). Offer cold yogurt to spoon over chicken. Makes 6 servings.—*J. B., Berkeley, CA*

Per serving: 263 calories, 0.8 g carbohydrates, 29 g protein, 15 g total fat (4 g saturated), 103 mg cholesterol, 98 mg sodium

CURRIED CHICKEN WITH LIME

The flavor of fresh lime permeates these chicken pieces as they simmer.

- ½ cup all-purpose flour
- 1 teaspoon salt
- Dash of pepper
- 1 chicken (about 3 lbs.), cut up and trimmed of fat; or 4 *each* drumsticks and thighs, trimmed of fat
- 2 tablespoons butter or margarine
- 2 tablespoons salad oil
- 1 large onion, thinly sliced
- 2 teaspoons curry powder
- 1 clove garlic, minced or pressed
- ½ teaspoon *each* ground ginger and ground cinnamon
- 1 tablespoon firmly packed brown sugar
- 1 cup dry white wine or chicken broth
- 1 lime, very thinly sliced

Combine flour, salt, and pepper. Rinse chicken and pat dry; then coat with flour mixture and shake off excess.

Melt butter in oil in a wide frying pan over medium heat. Add chicken, a portion at a time (do not crowd pan); cook, turning as needed, until browned on all sides. As chicken is browned, remove it from pan and set aside. Spoon off and discard all but 1½ tablespoons fat from pan.

To pan, add onion and curry powder; stir for 3 minutes. Add garlic, ginger, cinnamon, sugar, and wine. Return chicken (and any accumulated juices) to pan; bring to a boil. Set aside 3 lime slices for garnish; scatter remaining slices over chicken. Reduce heat, cover, and simmer until meat in thickest part is no longer pink; cut to test (35 to 40 minutes). Garnish with reserved lime slices. Makes 4 servings.—*H. N., San Francisco*

Per serving: 693 calories, 19 g carbohydrates, 45 g protein, 48 g total fat (14 g saturated), 189 mg cholesterol, 640 mg sodium

TURKEY & LIMA STEW

Repeated deglazing gives this stew its rich color and flavor. Serve over noodles or another favorite pasta.

- 1 large onion, chopped
- 2 cups sliced mushrooms
- 1 cup thinly sliced carrots
- 1 teaspoon dry thyme
   About 3 cups chicken broth
- 2 tablespoons lemon juice
- 2 pounds boneless, skinless turkey thighs, trimmed of fat and cut into 1-inch chunks
- 1 tablespoon cornstarch
- 1 package (about 10 oz.) frozen baby lima beans, thawed

In a 5- to 6-quart pan, combine onion, mushrooms, carrots, thyme, and 1 cup of the broth. Bring to a boil over high heat; then boil, stirring occasionally, until liquid evaporates and vegetables begin to brown (about 10 minutes). To deglaze, add ¼ cup more broth and stir to scrape browned bits free. Then continue to cook, stirring occasionally, until vegetables begin to brown again. Repeat deglazing and browning steps about 2 more times, using ¼ cup more broth each time, until mixture is richly browned. Deglaze one last time with lemon juice.

Stir turkey and ½ cup more broth into vegetable mixture. Bring to a boil over high heat. Then reduce heat to low, cover, and simmer until turkey chunks are no longer pink in center; cut to test (about 40 minutes). Skim and discard fat from sauce.

Smoothly blend cornstarch with ¾ cup of the broth. Add cornstarch mixture and beans to pan; bring to a boil over medium-high heat, stirring. Continue to boil, stirring, until beans are tender to bite. Makes 6 servings. —*Lita J. Vertz, Corvallis, OR*

Per serving: 298 calories, 20 g carbohydrates, 36 g protein, 8 g total fat (2 g saturated), 114 mg cholesterol, 655 mg sodium

OVEN-BAKED TURKEY LEGS

For small families—and for those who prefer dark meat—turkey drumsticks are an economical buy. These are baked in a spicy soy marinade. Serve them with mashed potatoes, cranberry sauce, and steamed sliced carrots.

- 4 to 6 turkey drumsticks (about 1¼ lbs. *each*)
- 1 cup water
- ¼ cup soy sauce
- ½ cup thinly sliced green onions
- 1 clove garlic, minced or pressed
- 1½ teaspoons Chinese five-spice (or ½ teaspoon *each* crushed anise seeds and ground ginger and ¼ teaspoon *each* ground cinnamon and ground cloves)
- ¼ cup cornstarch blended with ¼ cup cold water

Rinse turkey, pat dry, and place in a large roasting pan. Stir together water, soy sauce, onions, garlic, and five-spice. Pour marinade over turkey, cover, and refrigerate for at least 4 hours or until next day, turning turkey over 3 or 4 times.

Bake, covered, in a 350° oven for 1½ hours, turning turkey over after about 45 minutes. After turkey has baked for 1½ hours, uncover and continue to bake, turning several times, until meat is very tender when pierced (about 45 more minutes). Lift turkey from pan and arrange in a serving dish; keep warm.

Skim and discard fat from pan juices; pour juices into a 1½- to 2-quart pan. Stir cornstarch mixture, then add to pan juices; cook over medium-high heat, stirring, until sauce boils and thickens. Offer sauce to spoon over meat. Makes 4 to 6 servings.—*K. S., Fresno, CA*

Per serving: 630 calories, 9 g carbohydrates, 80 g protein, 28 g total fat (9 g saturated), 242 mg cholesterol, 1,045 mg sodium

CHILI CON PAVO

Enliven bowlfuls of this quick chili with toppings such as corn chips, cheese, chopped cilantro, lime, and creamy yogurt.

- ½ cup pimento-stuffed green olives or calamata olives
- 1 tablespoon salad oil
- 1 pound ground turkey or ground turkey sausage
- 1 large onion, chopped
- 1 fresh jalapeño chile, seeded and minced
- 3 tablespoons chili powder
- 1 large can (about 7 oz.) diced green chiles
- 1 large can (about 28 oz.) tomatoes
- 2 cans (about 15 oz. *each*) red kidney beans
- ⅛ teaspoon ground cloves
   Toppings (choices follow)

Slice pimento-stuffed olives (or cut flesh from calamata olives and discard pits). Set olives aside. Heat oil in a 4- to 5-quart pan over high heat. Crumble in turkey; add onion and jalapeño chile. Cook, stirring often, until meat is browned.

Stir chili powder and green chiles into turkey mixture. Cut up tomatoes; add tomatoes and their liquid, beans and their liquid, cloves, and olives. Bring to a boil; then reduce heat and simmer, uncovered, until flavors are blended (about 15 minutes). Ladle into bowls; offer toppings to add to taste. Makes 4 to 6 servings.—*Sheryl Roberts, Las Vegas*

TOPPINGS. In separate bowls, arrange **corn chips,** shredded **Cheddar cheese,** chopped **cilantro, lime wedges,** and **plain yogurt.**

Per serving: 381 calories, 41 g carbohydrates, 28 g protein, 13 g total fat (2 g saturated), 66 mg cholesterol, 1,550 mg sodium

OREGONIAN CHILI

Turkey is the surprise ingredient in this thick, rich, well-seasoned chili.

- 2 large onions, chopped
- 3 tablespoons salad oil
- 1 cup chopped green bell pepper
- 2 cloves garlic, minced or pressed
- 2 pounds ground turkey
- 1 can (about 14½ oz.) tomatoes
- 3 cans (about 15 oz. *each*) red kidney beans, drained and rinsed
- 2 large cans (about 15 oz. *each*) tomato sauce
- ¼ cup soy sauce
- 3 tablespoons chili powder
- 1 teaspoon *each* ground cumin, dry sage, and dry thyme
- 2 limes, cut into wedges

Set aside ¾ cup of the onions. Heat oil in a 6- to 8-quart pan over medium-high heat. Add remaining onions, bell pepper, and garlic; cook, stirring often, until onions are soft.

Crumble turkey into pan. Increase heat to high and cook, stirring gently, until drippings begin to brown. Cut up tomatoes; add tomatoes and their liquid, beans, tomato sauce, soy sauce, chili powder, cumin, sage, and thyme. Stir to scrape browned bits free. Bring to a boil; then reduce heat, cover, and simmer for 30 minutes. Pour into a tureen or large serving bowl; mound reserved onions on top and garnish with lime wedges. Makes 8 servings.—*Marilyn Malsom, Newport, OR*

Per serving: 407 calories, 38 g carbohydrates, 32 g protein, 15 g total fat (3 g saturated), 83 mg cholesterol, 1,577 mg sodium

PASTA & BEANS WITH SAUSAGE

Lean but flavorful turkey Italian sausage has become a popular ingredient in all sorts of robust dishes, from soups to spaghetti sauces. Here, it combines with macaroni and white kidney beans in a hearty stew.

- 1 pound turkey Italian sausages, casings removed
- 1 large onion, chopped
- 4 cloves garlic, minced or pressed
- 1 can (about 14½ oz.) chicken or beef broth
- 2 cans (about 15 oz. *each*) cannellini (white kidney beans), drained and rinsed
- 2 cups cooked macaroni or rigatoni
- 1 can (about 8 oz.) tomato sauce
- ¼ cup dry red wine
- 3 tablespoons minced fresh basil or 2 teaspoons dry basil
- 1 tablespoon minced fresh oregano or 1 teaspoon dry oregano
  About ½ cup grated Parmesan cheese

Break sausage into small chunks and place in a 5- to 6-quart pan; add onion, garlic, and ¼ cup of the broth. Cook over high heat, stirring often, until liquid evaporates and vegetables begin to brown (about 15 minutes). To deglaze, add ¼ cup more broth and stir to scrape browned bits free. Continue to cook, stirring occasionally, until vegetables begin to brown again.

Add remaining broth, beans, macaroni, tomato sauce, wine, basil, and oregano. Cook, stirring often, until mixture is heated through (about 5 minutes); mix in ½ cup of the cheese. Ladle into bowls; offer more cheese to add to taste. Makes 4 to 6 servings.—*Nancy Gonzalez, Millbrae, CA*

Per serving: 443 calories, 46 g carbohydrates, 32 g protein, 14 g total fat (4 g saturated), 55 mg cholesterol, 1,582 mg sodium

WESTERN TURKEY CASSEROLE

Shredded jack cheese forms a golden crust over strips of zesty sautéed turkey breast and mild green chiles in this creamy casserole. It's good with tender-crisp green beans and a pan of freshly baked Cornmeal Bread (page 179).

- 2 tablespoons salad oil
- 1 pound boneless, skinless turkey breast, cut across the grain into ¼-inch-thick strips
- 1 small onion, chopped
- 1 cup purchased taco sauce
- 2 cups (about 8 oz.) shredded jack cheese
- ¼ cup all-purpose flour
- 4 large eggs
- ¾ cup milk
- 2 large cans (about 7 oz. *each*) whole green chiles

Heat oil in a wide frying pan over medium heat; add turkey and onion. Cook, stirring often, until turkey strips are white on outside and just barely pink in center; cut to test (about 5 minutes). Stir in taco sauce and remove from heat.

In a large bowl, mix cheese and flour; then beat in eggs and milk until mixture is well blended. Split chiles; discard any seeds.

Arrange half the chiles over bottom of a greased shallow 1¾- to 2½-quart casserole. Top with half the turkey mixture, then with half the cheese mixture. Repeat layers, using remaining chiles, turkey mixture, and cheese mixture.

Bake in a 350° oven until cheese topping is golden brown (about 40 minutes). Let casserole stand for about 5 minutes before serving. Makes 6 servings.—*Jean Slaughter, Las Vegas*

Per serving: 414 calories, 17 g carbohydrates, 34 g protein, 22 g total fat (9 g saturated), 233 mg cholesterol, 661 mg sodium

GAME HEN DINNER FOR TWO

A single little bird, simmered with carrots, onions, and fresh spinach, makes a satisfying dinner for two. To complete the meal, just pour a fruity red wine and warm a slender French bread baguette.

- 1 Cornish game hen (about 1½ lbs.), thawed if frozen
- 2 tablespoons butter or margarine
- 6 small onions (*each* about 1½ inches in diameter), peeled
- 1 cup beef broth
- ½ cup dry red wine
- 1 tablespoon Dijon mustard
- ½ teaspoon dry basil
- 3 slender carrots, cut crosswise into halves
- 8 ounces fresh spinach

Reserve game hen neck and giblets for other uses. With poultry or kitchen shears or a heavy knife, cut hen in half through breastbone and along one side of backbone; rinse hen halves and pat dry.

Melt butter in a wide frying pan over medium heat. Add hen halves and onions; cook, turning as needed, until hens and onions are well browned on all sides (about 15 minutes). Lift out hen halves and onions; set aside.

Pour broth into pan and bring to a boil over high heat; then boil, uncovered, until reduced to ⅓ cup.

Stir in wine, mustard, and basil. Return hen halves and onions to pan; add carrots.

Cover and simmer until carrots are tender when pierced and meat near thighbone is is no longer pink; cut to test (about 15 minutes).

Meanwhile, discard stems and any yellow or wilted leaves from spinach; then rinse spinach and drain well.

Push hens and vegetables to one side of pan; push spinach into broth and stir until wilted. Serve meat and vegetables with broth. Makes 2 servings.—*Mary Lange, Fresno, CA*

Per serving: 749 calories, 21 g carbohydrates, 48 g protein, 47 g total fat (17 g saturated), 205 mg cholesterol, 1,386 mg sodium

CORNISH HENS WITH WILD RICE STUFFING

Golden roasted hens filled with a rosemary-scented wild rice stuffing are a delightful choice for a special meal. If your guests are hearty eaters, serve one bird per person; for lighter appetites, allow just half a hen per person (you can snip the roasted birds in half with poultry shears).

- Wild Rice Stuffing (recipe follows)
- 5 Cornish game hens (about 1½ lbs. *each*), thawed if frozen
- 5 tablespoons butter or margarine, melted

Prepare Wild Rice Stuffing.

Reserve game hen necks and giblets for other uses; rinse hens inside and out and pat dry. Stuff hens equally with Wild Rice Stuffing, packing it in lightly; close cavities with skewers.

Arrange hens, breast up, on a rack in a roasting pan. Bake in a 375° oven, basting often with butter, until meat near thighbone is no longer pink; cut to test (about 1 hour).

To serve, transfer hens to a platter and remove skewers. If desired, skim and discard fat from pan juices; then offer juices to pour over meat. Makes 5 servings.—*E. F., San Jose, CA*

WILD RICE STUFFING. Melt ½ cup (¼ lb.) **butter** or margarine in a wide frying pan over medium heat. Add ½ cup *each* chopped **celery**, chopped **onion**, and chopped **parsley;** cook, stirring often, until onion is soft (7 to 10 minutes).

Thoroughly rinse ½ cup **wild rice** with hot water; drain. Add to pan along with ½ cup **long-grain white rice,** 2 cups **chicken broth,** 2 table-spoons **lemon juice,** and ½ teaspoon **dry rosemary**. Bring to a boil over high heat; then reduce heat, cover, and simmer until liquid has been absorbed (about 30 minutes). Use warm.

Per serving: 1,078 calories, 29 g carbohydrates, 87 g protein, 66 g total fat (26 g saturated), 329 mg cholesterol, 908 mg sodium

GRILLED GAME HENS WITH CILANTRO MARINADE

Mild-flavored game hens take well to highly seasoned sauces and marinades; here, they soak in a distinctive blend of cilantro, garlic, honey, and marsala.

- ⅔ cup minced cilantro
- 1 teaspoon dry mustard
- 4 cloves garlic, minced or pressed
- 2 tablespoons soy sauce
- 3 tablespoons honey
- ¼ cup marsala or apple juice
- 4 Cornish game hens (about 1½ lbs. *each*), thawed if frozen

In a 1- to 1½-quart pan, combine ½ cup of the cilantro, mustard, garlic, soy sauce, honey, and marsala. Bring to a boil over high heat; remove from heat and let cool.

Reserve game hen necks and giblets for other uses. With poultry or kitchen shears or a heavy knife, split hens lengthwise through breastbone. Pull hens open. Then place, skin side up, on a flat surface and press firmly, cracking bones slightly, so birds lie reasonably flat. Rinse hens, pat dry, and place in a large (1-gallon) heavy-duty plastic bag. Pour in cilantro mixture. Seal bag and rotate to coat hens with marinade; then refrigerate for at least 1 hour or until next day.

Lift hens from marinade and drain briefly (reserve marinade). Place hens, skin side up, on a grill 4 to 6 inches above a solid bed of medium coals. Cook, turning often, for 20 minutes. Meanwhile, pour marinade into a small pan and bring to a boil.

Baste hens with marinade and continue to cook, turning often, until meat near thighbone is no longer pink; cut to test (15 to 20 more minutes). Sprinkle with remaining cilantro. Makes 4 servings.—*Karen Bennett, Seaside, CA*

Per serving: 799 calories, 17 g carbohydrates, 83 g protein, 41 g total fat (11 g saturated), 264 mg cholesterol, 763 mg sodium

Braised Cornish Game Hens

Stuffed with rice and simmered in wine in a Dutch oven, two Cornish hens make a generous meal for two.

- 2 **Cornish game hens (about 1½ lbs. each), thawed if frozen**
- 6 **tablespoons butter or margarine**
- 2 **green onions, sliced**
- ½ **cup thinly sliced celery**
- 1 **cup cooked rice**
- 1 **tablespoon minced parsley**
- ¼ **teaspoon dry rosemary**

- ¼ **cup all-purpose flour**
- ½ **teaspoon *each* salt and paprika**
- ½ **cup dry white wine or chicken broth**
- 1 **can (6 or 8 oz.) sliced mushrooms**

Reserve game hen necks and giblets for other uses. Rinse hens inside and out; pat dry.

Melt 2 tablespoons of the butter in a wide frying pan over medium-high heat; add onions and celery. Cook, stirring often, until soft (about 5 minutes). Remove from heat and stir in rice, parsley, and rosemary. Stuff hens equally with rice mixture; close cavities with skewers.

Combine flour, salt, and paprika. Coat hens lightly with flour mixture; reserve remaining flour mixture. Melt remaining ¼ cup butter in a 4- to 5-quart pan over medium heat; add hens and cook, turning as needed, until browned on all sides. Pour wine over hens; reduce heat, cover, and simmer for 30 minutes.

Drain mushrooms and reserve ½ cup of the liquid. Add mushrooms to pan. Cover and continue to simmer until meat near thighbone is no longer pink; cut to test (about 15 more minutes). Lift hens to a platter, remove skewers, and keep warm. Blend remaining flour mixture with the reserved ½ cup mushroom liquid; stir into pan juices. Increase heat to medium-high and cook, stirring, until sauce boils and thickens. Serve sauce with hens. Makes 2 servings.—*H. W., San Carlos, CA*

Per serving: 1,521 calories, 46 g carbohydrates, 93 g protein, 105 g total fat (42 g saturated), 440 mg cholesterol, 1,654 mg sodium

Cornish Game Hens with Mustard Crust

For an elegant dinner, try butterflied hens brushed with a garlicky mustard coating. Alongside, you might serve steamed or boiled small red potatoes and crisp sugar snap peas or Chinese pea pods.

- ¼ **cup butter or margarine**
- ¼ **cup Dijon mustard**
- 1 **tablespoon minced fresh rosemary or 1 teaspoon dry rosemary**
- 2 **cloves garlic, minced or pressed**
- 4 **Cornish game hens (about 1½ lbs. each), thawed if frozen**
  Rosemary sprigs (optional)
  Salt and pepper

Melt butter in a small pan over medium heat. Remove from heat and stir in mustard, minced rosemary, and garlic. Set mustard-butter mixture aside.

Reserve game hen necks and giblets for other uses. With poultry or kitchen shears or a heavy knife, split hens lengthwise along one side of backbone. Pull hens open. Then place, skin side up, on a flat surface and press firmly, cracking bones slightly, so birds lie reasonably flat.

Rinse butterflied hens, pat dry, and coat on both sides with mustard-butter mixture. Then set hens slightly apart in 2 shallow 10- by 15-inch baking pans.

Bake in a 450° oven until meat near thighbone is no longer pink; cut to test (25 to 30 minutes). Transfer to a platter or individual plates; garnish with rosemary sprigs, if desired. Season to taste with salt and pepper. Makes 4 servings.—*Kathy Donahue, Occidental, CA*

Per serving: 779 calories, 0.5 g carbohydrates, 82 g protein, 47 g total fat (15 g saturated), 280 mg cholesterol, 494 mg sodium

Baked Chiles Rellenos. *Arrange chile peppers and cheese strips in casserole*

Beat the eggs slightly; then beat in the milk, flour, and salt thoroughly

Pour the egg mixture over the cheese strips and the green chile peppers

Bake in a moderate oven for 45 minutes or until the custard is just firm

FRANK STAUFFACHER

In their innovative approach to everyday foods, many Kitchen Cabinet recipes from the early 1950s still seem timely nearly half a century later. One contribute found a way to simplify her favorite Chiles Rellenos by transforming it into a casserole; another disregarded almost every rule of cake-baking by stirring up Crazy Chocolate Cake right in the baking pan. Of the latter, our editors commented, "Surprisingly enough, the texture is excellent."

Hawaiian readers provided bright-flavored recipes such as Pork Chops Hawaiian and Orange Rice, reflecting the diverse tastes of the soon-to-be-fiftieth state. And of course, there was plenty of room for traditional family favorites like Italian-accented Braciole, a meat roll stuffed with eggs and cheese that's still a wonderful choice for an ample spaghetti dinner.

BAKED CHILES RELLENOS

Chiles rellenos made by this method will save you time and fuss and you don't forfeit flavor.

- 1 can (about 4 oz.) whole green chiles
- ½ pound sharp Cheddar cheese
- 2 eggs
- 2 cups milk
- ½ cup flour
- 1 teaspoon salt

Cut the chiles into pieces about 2 inches square; then arrange them over the bottom of a buttered 2-quart casserole (no deeper than 2½ inches).

Cut the cheese into long fingers and arrange in an even layer over chiles. Beat eggs slightly, then beat in milk, flour, and salt. Pour egg mixture over cheese. Bake in a moderate oven (350°) for 45 to 50 minutes, or until custard is just set. Serves 6. —*J. A. J., Oroville, CA (January 1951)*

Fresh green chiles may be roasted, skinned, seeded, and used in place of the canned.

PORK CHOPS HAWAIIAN

Surprisingly large amounts of brown sugar, vinegar, garlic, and ginger are called for in the marinade, but they blend so well that, after baking, these chops have no one dominant flavor.

- 6 pork chops, cut 1 inch thick
- 1 cup vinegar
- ½ cup soy sauce
- 1 cup brown sugar, firmly packed
- 2 tablespoons dry mustard
- 6 cloves garlic, minced, or 1½ teaspoons garlic purée
- 2 tablespoons grated ginger root

Place pork chops in glass dish and pour over mixture of vinegar, soy sauce, brown sugar, mustard, garlic, and ginger. Marinate for 24 hours, turning once. Remove chops from marinade and place in a single layer in a baking pan. Bake in a moderately hot oven (375°) for 45 minutes. Serves 6.—*W. C. M., Lanikai, Oahu, HI (January 1954)*

Candied ginger may be substituted for the ginger root; use approximately 4 pieces, minced.

CRAZY CHOCOLATE CAKE

If you are looking for a cake you can mix together in a jiffy, here it is.

- 1½ cups cake flour
- 1 cup sugar
- 3 tablespoons unsweetened cocoa
- 1 teaspoon baking soda
- ½ teaspoon salt
- 6 tablespoons melted shortening or salad oil
- 1 tablespoon distilled white vinegar
- 1 teaspoon vanilla
- 1 cup cold water

Sift flour, measure, then sift again with sugar, cocoa, baking soda, and salt into an ungreased 9-inch-square baking pan. Make three depressions. Into one, pour the melted shortening; into the second, the vinegar; and into the third, the vanilla. Pour the cold water over all and mix with a fork, but do not beat.

Bake in a moderate oven (350°) for 30 minutes or until done. Cool in the pan on a rack, as this is a soft cake. Serves 6 to 8. —R. J. H., Wenatchee, WA (June 1951)

Frost with chocolate or mocha powdered sugar icing when cool. Serve right from the pan.

Crazy Chocolate Cake. *Sift all the dry ingredients into an ungreased baking pan*

Make three depressions. Pour oil in one, vinegar in another, vanilla in the third

Pour cold water over all and mix together with fork. Batter is very thin and soupy

Bake in moderate oven. Cool right in the pan on a wire rack. Frost cake when cool

BRACIOLE

When this stuffed steak roll is sliced, each piece reveals the colorful filling.

- 3 pounds round steak, 1 to 1½ inches thick
- 4 tablespoons (½ cube) butter or margarine, softened
- 1 clove garlic, mashed
- 4 hard-cooked eggs, sliced
- ½ cup chopped parsley
- ⅓ cup grated Parmesan cheese
- 1 teaspoon salt
- ½ teaspoon *each* pepper and dried oregano leaves
- 2 tablespoons shortening
- 1 jar (about 30 oz.) marinara sauce
- 1 pound dry spaghetti, cooked and drained

Have the butcher "butterfly" the round steak (cut it almost in half crosswise so that when spread out it will lie flat). Blend butter with garlic and rub all over one side of meat. Over this arrange sliced eggs, then sprinkle with parsley, cheese, salt, pepper, and oregano. Roll carefully so that filling stays in place. Tie securely with string.

Melt shortening in a heavy pan; add meat roll and brown on all sides. Pour marinara sauce over meat, then cover and simmer on top of the range or in a moderately slow (325°) oven for 2 hours, or until tender. Slice meat roll and arrange around platter of cooked spaghetti. Serve with the tomato sauce. Serves 8 to 10.—R. J. S., San Diego, CA (May 1953)

ORANGE RICE

As something different to serve with baked ham, we think you'll like rice flavored with orange juice and peel, celery, and onion.

- 3 tablespoons butter or margarine
- ⅔ cup sliced celery
- 2 tablespoons chopped onion
- 1 cup water
- 2 tablespoons grated orange peel
- 1 cup orange juice
- 1 teaspoon salt
- 1 cup uncooked rice

Melt butter in a heavy saucepan with a cover, add celery and onion, and cook, stirring occasionally, until tender and light brown.

Stir in water, orange peel, orange juice, and salt; then bring to a boil. Add rice, cover, and steam over low heat for about 20 minutes, or until rice is tender. Serves 6. —L. A. B., Hilo, HI (April 1954)

You'll find this rice dish is also a good accompaniment for frankfurters or roast pork.

S·E·A·F·O·O·D

The West's abundant fish and shellfish have long inspired Sunset contributors. No fewer than 14 recipes for salmon—fresh, kippered, and canned—were included in a Kitchen Cabinet collection published in 1938. In this chapter, you'll find choice salmon specialties of more recent origin, among them Grilled Salmon & Pineapple (page 116) and Curried Tomato Salmon (page 117). • Early Kitchen Cabinet seafood recipes often featured stirring accounts of catching salmon, trout, surf fish, and crab, as well as diving for abalone. Today, however, much of the seafood our readers use is the result of aquaculture (breeding fish in captivity). Still, despite the lack of adventure involved in landing the fish, dishes like Oven-crisp Trout and Baked Trout with Sourdough Stuffing (recipes on facing page) are well worth trying. • Entrées starring shellfish—especially crab—have been winners for years. In 1941, we hailed a Dungeness crab stew as "a salute to our famous Pacific Coast crab." Today, we can celebrate that favorite shellfish with classic recipes such as Cracked Crab in Spicy Tomato Sauce and Butter-basted Crab (both on page 129).

Bacon-stuffed Trout

Coated in Parmesan cheese and crushed croutons, these plump trout are filled with a mixture of sautéed onion and crisp bacon. For fragrance and flavor, tuck bay leaves into the fish before fastening them closed.

- 6 slices bacon
- 1 large onion, chopped
- 6 whole trout (about 8 oz. *each*), cleaned
- 3 dry bay leaves, split lengthwise
- 1 large egg
- 1 teaspoon water
- ½ cup crushed seasoned croutons
- ¼ cup grated Parmesan cheese
- ⅛ teaspoon *each* garlic powder and pepper
- 6 tablespoons butter or margarine
  Lemon wedges

Cook bacon in a wide frying pan over medium heat until crisp; lift out, drain, crumble, and set aside. Pour off and discard all but 2 tablespoons drippings from pan. Add onion to pan and cook, stirring often, until soft. Stir in bacon.

Rinse trout inside and out; pat dry. Place a sixth (about 2 tablespoons) of the bacon-onion mixture in cavity of each fish; top with half a bay leaf. Fasten fish closed with wooden picks or skewers.

In a shallow bowl, beat egg with water to blend. In another shallow bowl, combine crushed croutons, cheese, garlic powder, and pepper. Dip each fish in egg mixture, then dip in crumb mixture to coat well on all sides.

Place butter in a large, shallow baking pan; set in a 500° oven to melt. When butter is melted, add fish to pan; turn in butter to coat. Bake until fish is just opaque but still moist in thickest part; cut to test (12 to

15 minutes). Remove wooden picks. Serve with lemon. Makes 6 servings.
—*H. H., Port Angeles, WA*

Per serving: 393 calories, 6 g carbohydrates, 28 g protein, 28 g total fat (12 g saturated), 142 mg cholesterol, 412 mg sodium

Oven-crisp Trout

Whole trout from the market or a fisherman friend are delicious prepared this way. Fill the fish with parsley butter and roll them in bread crumbs and Swiss cheese, then bake to golden crispness.

- 6 whole trout (about 8 oz. *each*), cleaned
  Salt and pepper
- ¼ cup butter or margarine, at room temperature
- ½ cup finely chopped parsley
- 1 large egg
- ¼ cup milk
- ½ teaspoon salt
- ¾ cup fine dry bread crumbs
- ½ cup shredded Swiss cheese

Rinse trout inside and out; pat dry. Sprinkle cavity of each fish lightly with salt and pepper. In a small bowl, mix 2 tablespoons of the butter with parsley; spread mixture inside cavity of each fish. In a shallow bowl, beat egg with milk and the ½ teaspoon salt to blend. In another shallow bowl, combine bread crumbs and cheese. Dip each fish in egg mixture, then dip in crumb mixture to coat well on all sides. Arrange fish in a well-greased shallow baking pan; sprinkle with any remaining crumb mixture. Dot with remaining 2 tablespoons butter. Bake in a 500° oven until fish is just opaque but still moist in thickest part; cut to test (12 to 15 minutes). Makes 6 servings.—*A. J., Scottsdale, AZ*

Per serving: 351 calories, 11 g carbohydrates, 29 g protein, 21 g total fat (8 g saturated), 131 mg cholesterol, 476 mg sodium

Baked Trout with Sourdough Stuffing

Sourdough French bread crumbs, mixed with green onions and moistened with melted butter and white wine, make a tempting stuffing for baked trout. You'll have some extra stuffing; spread it in the baking pan before adding the fish.

- 3 cups soft sourdough French bread crumbs
- 2 tablespoons finely chopped parsley
- 5 green onions, thinly sliced
  About ½ teaspoon salt
  About ⅛ teaspoon pepper
- 3 tablespoons dry white wine
- ¼ cup butter or margarine, melted
- 6 to 8 large whole trout (8 to 12 oz. *each*), cleaned

In a medium-size bowl, combine bread crumbs, parsley, onions, ½ teaspoon of the salt, and ⅛ teaspoon of the pepper. Drizzle wine and 2 tablespoons of the butter over crumb mixture; mix lightly until evenly moistened.

Rinse trout inside and out; pat dry. Brush cavity of each fish with some of the remaining 2 tablespoons butter and sprinkle lightly with salt and pepper. Stuff cavities lightly, using about ¼ cup stuffing for each fish. Fasten fish closed with wooden picks or skewers.

Spread remaining stuffing in a greased large, shallow baking pan; top with fish and drizzle with any remaining butter. Bake in a 350° oven until fish is just opaque but still moist in thickest part; cut to test (15 to 20 minutes). Remove wooden picks. Makes 6 to 8 servings.—*M. S., China Lake, CA*

Per serving: 330 calories, 11 g carbohydrates, 31 g protein, 17 g total fat (6 g saturated), 98 mg cholesterol, 415 mg sodium

SICILIAN TROUT WITH BALSAMIC SAUCE

Sweet currants and salty capers come together with garlic and herbs to stuff trout in style.

½ cup *each* chopped green bell pepper and sliced green onions

2 tablespoons *each* dried currants, minced parsley, and drained capers

1 clove garlic, minced or pressed

4 boned trout (6 to 8 oz. *each*)

3 tablespoons balsamic vinegar

3 tablespoons minced fresh basil or parsley

1 tablespoon extra-virgin olive oil
Lemon wedges

In a medium-size bowl, mix bell pepper, onions, currants, parsley, capers, and garlic. Rinse trout and pat dry; then open each fish and place skin side down. Spoon a fourth of the vegetable mixture onto one side of each fish; fold other side over to enclose.

Arrange fish in a lightly oiled large, shallow baking pan and bake in a 400° oven until just opaque but still moist in thickest part; cut to test (about 20 minutes). Meanwhile, in a small bowl, stir together vinegar, basil, and oil until well blended.

Transfer fish to a platter or individual plates; serve with vinegar mixture and lemon wedges. Makes 4 servings. —*Roxanne Chan, Albany, CA*

Per serving: 359 calories, 6 g carbohydrates, 42 g protein, 18 g total fat (3 g saturated), 115 mg cholesterol, 217 mg sodium

GRILLED SALMON & PINEAPPLE

Subtle Asian-style seasonings flavor a marinated salmon fillet and the juicy fresh pineapple rings that accompany it.

3 tablespoons *each* lime juice and Oriental sesame oil

1 tablespoon *each* minced fresh ginger, firmly packed brown sugar, and soy sauce

1 salmon fillet (about 2 lbs.), about 1 inch thick in thickest part

1 medium-size pineapple (3 to 3¼ lbs.), peeled, cut crosswise into 6 slices, and cored

1 teaspoon sesame seeds

1 tablespoon sliced green onion
Lime wedges

In a large, shallow dish, stir together lime juice, oil, ginger, sugar, and soy sauce. Rinse salmon and pat dry; add salmon and pineapple to marinade and turn to coat. Cover and refrigerate for 30 to 45 minutes, turning fish and fruit over occasionally.

Meanwhile, toast sesame seeds in a small frying pan over medium-high heat, stirring often, until golden (2 to 4 minutes). Pour out of pan and set aside.

Lift fish and pineapple from marinade and drain briefly (discard marinade). Set fish, skin side down, on a piece of heavy-duty foil cut to same size as fish.

In a barbecue with a lid, place pineapple and fish (foil side down) on a grill 4 to 6 inches above a solid bed of low coals. Cover barbecue and open vents. Cook fish until just opaque but still moist in thickest part; cut to test (10 to 12 minutes). Cook pineapple slices, turning occasionally, until browned on both sides (about 10 minutes).

Transfer fish and fruit to a platter; sprinkle with sesame seeds and onion. Serve with lime wedges. Makes 6 servings.—*J. Hill, Sacramento*

Per serving: 315 calories, 17 g carbohydrates, 31 g protein, 14 g total fat (2 g saturated), 83 mg cholesterol, 155 mg sodium

BARBECUED SALMON FILLETS

You can use this method to barbecue one large salmon fillet or two smaller ones. If you like, substitute orange juice for the wine in the basting sauce and increase the lemon juice to 5 tablespoons.

1 or 2 large salmon fillets (3 to 4 lbs. *total*)

¼ cup butter or margarine, melted; or ¼ cup salad oil

½ cup rosé or dry white wine

¼ cup *each* lemon juice and soy sauce
Parsley sprigs and lemon wedges (optional)

Rinse salmon and pat dry. Cut heavy-duty foil to the same size as fish; place fish on foil, skin side down.

In a small bowl, stir together butter, wine, lemon juice, and soy sauce. In a barbecue with a lid, place fish, foil side down, on a grill 4 to 6 inches above a solid bed of low coals. Brush fish generously with butter mixture. Cover barbecue and open vents. Cook, basting with butter mixture about every 5 minutes, until fish is just opaque but still moist in thickest part; cut to test (15 to 20 minutes).

To serve, slide fish, still on foil, onto a board. Garnish with parsley sprigs and lemon wedges, if desired. Slice fish down to skin and lift each serving away from skin. Heat butter mixture until bubbly and offer to spoon over fish. Makes 8 to 10 servings.—*J. B., Lake Oswego, OR*

Per serving: 296 calories, 1 g carbohydrates, 35 g protein, 15 g total fat (4 g saturated), 108 mg cholesterol, 466 mg sodium

WALLA WALLA SALMON

In the Pacific Northwest, imaginative cooks embellish local salmon with a variety of toppings. Here, the finishing touches are provided by sweet onions simmered in teriyaki sauce and a sprinkling of golden toasted almonds and coconut.

    Teriyaki Sauce (recipe follows)
¼   cup sliced almonds
¼   cup sweetened shredded coconut
1   tablespoon salad oil
2   large mild onions, thinly sliced
4   pieces salmon fillet (about 6 oz. each)
    Lemon wedges

Prepare Teriyaki Sauce; set aside.

Toast almonds in a wide frying pan over medium-low heat, stirring often, until light golden (about 6 minutes). Add coconut; stir until toasted (2 to 3 minutes). Pour almonds and coconut out of pan and set aside.

Heat oil in pan over medium heat. Add onions and 3 tablespoons of the Teriyaki Sauce; cook, stirring often, until onions are very soft (15 to 20 minutes). Remove from heat.

Rinse salmon and pat dry; then arrange, skin side up, on a greased rack in a 12- by 15-inch broiler pan. Broil 3 to 4 inches below heat, turning once and brushing with remaining Teriyaki Sauce, until fish is just opaque but still moist in thickest part; cut to test (6 to 8 minutes). Transfer to a serving dish and top with onions, coconut, and almonds. Serve with lemon wedges. Makes 4 servings. —*Sheryl Kindle Fullner, Everson, WA*

TERIYAKI SAUCE. In a small bowl, stir together 3 tablespoons **soy sauce,** 2 tablespoons **dry sherry** or water, and 1 tablespoon *each* **Oriental sesame oil** and minced **fresh ginger.**

Per serving: 422 calories, 16 g carbohydrates, 38 g protein, 22 g total fat (4 g saturated), 94 mg cholesterol, 872 mg sodium

CURRIED TOMATO SALMON

Salmon steaks poached in a curry-seasoned tomato sauce make a quick dinner for two.

1   tablespoon olive oil
1   small onion, chopped
2   cloves garlic, minced or pressed
1   tablespoon curry powder
2   teaspoons chopped fresh thyme or 1 teaspoon dry thyme
2   large firm-ripe tomatoes (about 1 lb. *total*), seeded and chopped
2   salmon steaks (4 to 6 oz. *each*), ¾ to 1 inch thick
    Salt and pepper
    Thyme sprigs (optional)

Heat oil in a wide frying pan over medium-high heat. Add onion and garlic; cook, stirring often, until onion is tinged with brown.

Reduce heat to low. Stir in curry powder and chopped thyme; cook, stirring, for about 1 minute. Add tomatoes and cook, stirring occasionally, until tomatoes begin to fall apart and almost all liquid has evaporated (about 5 minutes).

Rinse salmon, pat dry, and place in pan; spoon sauce over fish. Reduce heat, cover, and simmer until fish is just opaque but still moist in thickest part; cut to test (about 10 minutes).

Transfer fish to individual plates. Season sauce to taste with salt and pepper; spoon sauce over fish. Garnish with thyme sprigs, if desired. Makes 2 servings.—*Vicky Hay, Phoenix*

Per serving: 318 calories, 18 g carbohydrates, 28 g protein, 16 g total fat (2 g saturated), 69 mg cholesterol, 78 mg sodium

SALMON GRILL DIABLE

It takes just 10 minutes to grill these salmon steaks over hot coals. Season the fish with a piquant, red pepper–spiked lemon-mustard butter.

⅓   cup butter or margarine, at room temperature
2   tablespoons lemon juice
2   teaspoons Dijon mustard
⅛   teaspoon ground red pepper (cayenne)
1   tablespoon finely chopped parsley
6   large salmon steaks (6 to 8 oz. *each*), about 1 inch thick
    Olive oil
    Salt and black pepper

In a small bowl, beat butter until creamy; gradually add lemon juice, beating until mixture is fluffy. Beat in mustard, red pepper, and parsley. If made ahead, cover and refrigerate for up to 24 hours; bring to room temperature before using.

Rinse salmon and pat dry; coat lightly with oil, then sprinkle with salt and black pepper. Arrange fish on a grill about 6 inches above a solid bed of hot coals. Cook, turning once, until just opaque but still moist in thickest part; cut to test (about 10 minutes).

Transfer fish to a platter; top each steak with a sixth of the butter mixture. Makes 6 servings.—*M. E., Carmel, CA*

Per serving: 360 calories, 0.4 g carbohydrates, 35 g protein, 23 g total fat (8 g saturated), 123 mg cholesterol, 221 mg sodium

SALMON FLORENTINE

Gently poached salmon fillets and fresh spinach bake briefly in a smooth lemon-mustard sauce to make this company entrée.

- 1½ to 2 pounds fresh spinach
- ¼ cup butter or margarine
- 1 large onion, chopped
- 1½ cups water
- 1 tablespoon lemon juice
  Salt and pepper
- 2 pounds skinless salmon fillets
- 2 tablespoons all-purpose flour
- 1 teaspoon Dijon mustard
- 2 tablespoons grated Parmesan cheese

Discard stems and any yellow or wilted leaves from spinach. Rinse spinach, drain well, and cut into shreds; set aside.

Melt 2 tablespoons of the butter in a wide frying pan over medium heat; add onion and cook, stirring often, until soft. Add spinach, cover, and cook just until wilted. Transfer spinach mixture to a shallow 2-quart baking dish.

In frying pan, combine water, lemon juice, and a dash each of salt and pepper. Bring to a boil over high heat. Rinse salmon and add to pan. Then reduce heat, cover, and simmer until fish is just opaque but still moist in thickest part; cut to test (about 10 minutes). Lift fish from pan and arrange on spinach. Reserve 1 cup of the poaching liquid; discard remainder.

Melt remaining 2 tablespoons butter in pan; blend in flour and cook, stirring, until bubbly. Remove from heat and gradually stir in the reserved 1 cup poaching liquid. Return to heat and cook, stirring, until sauce boils and thickens. Stir in mustard and cheese; season to taste with salt and pepper. Pour sauce over fish. Bake in a 350° oven until fish

and spinach are heated through (15 to 20 minutes). Makes 6 servings. —*R. M., Lake Oswego, OR*

Per serving: 336 calories, 9 g carbohydrates, 34 g protein, 18 g total fat (7 g saturated), 105 mg cholesterol, 272 mg sodium

FINNISH FISH STEW

The reader who contributed this 1963 dish saved it for times when she could prepare the recipe with fresh local salmon, but it's just as good with fillets of halibut or rockfish.

- 6 tablespoons butter or margarine
- 4 medium-size potatoes (about 1½ lbs. *total*), peeled and thinly sliced
- 2 medium-size onions, thinly sliced
- 1 teaspoon salt
- ¼ teaspoon pepper
- 2 dry bay leaves, finely crushed
- ¼ teaspoon ground allspice
  About 1½ pounds salmon, halibut, or rockfish fillets

Melt 2 tablespoons of the butter in a wide, deep frying pan (or in an electric frying pan); remove from heat. Arrange half the potatoes over bottom of pan. Cover with half the onions. Combine salt, pepper, bay leaves, and allspice; sprinkle about a third of the mixture over onions.

Rinse fish and pat dry; then cut into 4 to 6 equal pieces. Arrange fish evenly over onions; sprinkle with half the remaining salt mixture. Top evenly with remaining potatoes, then with remaining onions; sprinkle with remaining salt mixture and dot with remaining ¼ cup butter. Cover and cook over lowest heat (or in electric frying pan set at 175°) until potatoes are tender when pierced (1½ to 2 hours). Makes 4 to 6 servings.—*B. H., Aberdeen, WA*

Per serving: 424 calories, 25 g carbohydrates, 30 g protein, 23 g total fat (10 g saturated), 112 mg cholesterol, 649 mg sodium

CURRY-BROILED FISH FILLETS

Coat fish fillets with curry-flavored mayonnaise, then cloak them in toasted crumbs before slipping them under the broiler. To serve, drizzle with a quick sauce of fresh lime juice, chutney, and butter.

- 1½ cups soft bread crumbs
- ⅓ cup mayonnaise
- 2 teaspoons curry powder
- 1¼ pounds halibut, flounder, lingcod, or rockfish fillets (¾ to 1 inch thick)
  Salt
- 2 tablespoons butter or margarine
- 2 tablespoons finely chopped chutney or ginger marmalade
- 2 tablespoons lime or lemon juice

Spread bread crumbs in a shallow baking pan and broil 4 to 6 inches below heat until toasted (2 to 3 minutes); set aside. In a small bowl, mix mayonnaise and curry powder.

Rinse fish and pat dry; cut into 4 equal pieces, if necessary. Sprinkle fillets lightly with salt; then spread one side of each fillet with mayonnaise mixture, using half of it. Set fillets, mayonnaise side down, in crumbs; then spread tops of fillets with remaining mayonnaise mixture and turn to coat with remaining crumbs. Transfer fillets to a well-greased shallow baking pan. Broil about 5 inches below heat, turning once, until fish is just opaque but still moist in thickest part; cut to test (8 to 10 minutes).

Meanwhile, melt butter in a small pan. Add chutney and lime juice; stir until well blended. Remove from heat. Transfer fish to a platter; serve with chutney butter. Makes 4 servings. —*H. N., San Francisco*

Per serving: 424 calories, 15 g carbohydrates, 32 g protein, 26 g total fat (7 g saturated), 72 mg cholesterol, 341 mg sodium

Vegetable-topped Fish Fillets

Baking firm, lean fish at a high temperature is a quick, easy method that yields delicious results. Here, baked fillets of rockfish (often sold in the West as red snapper or rock cod) or lingcod are topped with mushrooms, onion, and diced tomato simmered briefly in chili sauce and wine.

 2 **pounds rockfish or lingcod fillets (about 1 inch thick)**
    Salt, pepper, and dry tarragon
 1 **tablespoon salad oil**
 3 **tablespoons butter or margarine**
 1 **medium-size onion, chopped**
 4 **ounces mushrooms, sliced**
 1 **medium-size tomato (about 6 oz.), seeded and chopped**
 ¼ **cup *each* dry white wine and tomato-based chili sauce**
 ⅓ **cup grated Parmesan cheese**

Rinse fish and pat dry; cut into 6 equal pieces, if necessary. Sprinkle fish lightly with salt, pepper, and tarragon; then place in a greased baking pan just large enough to hold fillets in a single layer. Drizzle each piece with ½ teaspoon of the oil. Bake in a 500° oven until fish is just opaque but still moist in thickest part; cut to test (about 10 minutes).

Meanwhile, melt butter in a wide frying pan over medium-high heat. Add onion and mushrooms; cook, stirring often, until onion is soft. Remove from heat and stir in tomato, wine, and chili sauce.

Spoon off and discard pan juices from fish. Spoon tomato mixture evenly over fish, then sprinkle with cheese. Broil about 4 inches below heat just until cheese begins to melt (2 to 3 minutes). Makes 6 servings.
—*J. F., Lake Oswego, OR*

Per serving: 279 calories, 8 g carbohydrates, 31 g protein, 13 g total fat (5 g saturated), 72 mg cholesterol, 388 mg sodium

Red Snapper Florentine

To streamline the preparation of this entrée, start with frozen spinach.

 2 **packages (about 10 oz. *each*) frozen chopped spinach, thawed and squeezed dry**
 ¼ **cup *each* mayonnaise and sour cream**
 ¼ **cup grated Parmesan cheese**
 1¼ **pounds Pacific red snapper or rockfish fillets**
 2 **tablespoons lemon juice**
 ½ **teaspoon pepper**
    Lemon wedges

In a 9- by 13-inch baking dish, mix spinach, mayonnaise, sour cream, and 2 tablespoons of the cheese. Spread mixture evenly in dish.

Rinse fish and pat dry; cut into 4 equal pieces, if necessary. Arrange fish in a single layer on top of spinach, overlapping thinner edges of fillets if necessary so all will fit in dish. (At this point, you may cover and refrigerate for up to 6 hours.)

Drizzle lemon juice over fish; sprinkle with pepper and remaining 2 tablespoons cheese. Bake, uncovered, in a 350° oven until fish is just opaque but still moist in thickest part; cut to test (about 15 minutes). Serve with lemon wedges. Makes 4 servings.—*Susan Swart, Pasadena, CA*

Per serving: 330 calories, 7 g carbohydrates, 36 g protein, 18 g total fat (5 g saturated), 71 mg cholesterol, 376 mg sodium

Fish Fillets with Sherry-Mushroom Sauce

Almost any mild, white-fleshed fish works well in this dish. Start by sautéing the fillets; then sauce them with sherry, soy, fresh ginger, mushrooms, and green onions.

 2 **tablespoons olive oil, butter, or margarine**
 4 **ounces mushrooms, thinly sliced**
 1½ **pounds sea bass, rockfish, or other mild-flavored white-fleshed fish fillets (about ¾ inch thick)**
 1 **teaspoon cornstarch**
 ⅓ **cup water**
 ¼ **cup dry sherry**
 1 **tablespoon soy sauce**
 2 **cloves garlic, minced or pressed**
 2 **teaspoons minced fresh ginger**
 ½ **cup sliced green onions**

Heat 1½ tablespoons of the oil in a wide frying pan over medium heat. Add mushrooms and cook, stirring often, until lightly browned (about 8 minutes). Remove mushrooms from pan and set aside.

Rinse fish and pat dry. Heat remaining 1½ teaspoons oil in pan over medium-high heat. Add fish, arranging it in a single layer. Cover and cook until fish is just opaque but still moist in thickest part; cut to test (about 8 minutes). Transfer fish to a platter and keep warm.

In a small bowl, stir together cornstarch, water, sherry, soy sauce, garlic, and ginger. Pour sherry mixture into pan; add mushrooms and stir to scrape browned bits free. Increase heat to high and bring sauce to a boil, stirring. Stir in onions; then pour sauce over fish. Makes 4 to 6 servings.
—*Edith Beccaria, San Francisco*

Per serving: 210 calories, 4 g carbohydrates, 26 g protein, 8 g total fat (1 g saturated), 56 mg cholesterol, 302 mg sodium

CHILE CHEESE FISH STACKS

Crisply coated with chili-seasoned crumbs, these savory "sandwiches" are filled with cream cheese and mild green chiles. You might serve them with sliced ripe tomatoes and wedges of hot cornbread.

1½ pounds rockfish, sole, or cod fillets (¼ to ½ inch thick)

1 can (about 4 oz.) whole green chiles

1 small package (about 3 oz.) cream cheese with chives

½ cup fine dry bread crumbs

½ teaspoon chili powder

¼ teaspoon garlic salt

1 large egg

2 tablespoons salad oil

2 tablespoons butter or margarine

Lemon wedges

Rinse fish, pat dry, and cut into 8 equal pieces. Split chiles; discard seeds. Cover 4 pieces of fish with a layer of chiles (cut to fit). Thinly slice cream cheese; top chiles equally with cheese, then with remaining 4 pieces of fish. In a shallow bowl, combine bread crumbs, chili powder, and garlic salt. In another shallow bowl, beat egg to blend. Dip each fish stack in egg, then turn in crumb mixture to coat well on all sides.

Place oil and butter in a 7- by 11-inch baking pan and set in a 500° oven to melt butter. When butter is melted, swirl pan to combine butter and oil. Set fish stacks in pan and turn to coat with butter mixture.

Return pan to oven and bake until fish is just opaque but still moist in thickest part; cut to test (8 to 10 minutes). Serve with lemon wedges. Makes 4 servings.—*J. H., Santa Barbara, CA*

Per serving: 382 calories, 8 g carbohydrates, 35 g protein, 23 g total fat (9 g saturated), 124 mg cholesterol, 541 mg sodium

SNAPPY SNAPPER

A caper-accented tomato sauce tops baked fillets of rockfish (which often masquerades as red snapper in Western fish markets).

About 1 pound rockfish fillets (½ to ¾ inch thick)

1 lime

1 teaspoon olive oil

1 medium-size green bell pepper (about 6 oz.), seeded and sliced

1 small onion, thinly sliced

1 clove garlic, minced or pressed

1 can (about 14½ oz.) Italian-style stewed tomatoes

1 tablespoon drained capers

Chopped parsley

Rinse fish and pat dry; cut into 4 equal pieces, if necessary. Arrange fish in a single layer in a shallow 2- to 2½-quart casserole. Cut lime in half and squeeze juice over fish. Bake in a 350° oven until fish is just opaque but still moist in thickest part; cut to test (about 15 minutes).

Meanwhile, heat oil in a wide frying pan over high heat. Add bell pepper, onion, and garlic; cook, stirring often, until onion is lightly browned (about 5 minutes). Add tomatoes and capers. Bring to a boil; then reduce heat to medium and simmer, uncovered, until liquid has evaporated (about 10 minutes).

Spoon pan juices from fish into tomato sauce. Bring to a boil; then boil, uncovered, until liquid has evaporated (about 1½ minutes). Spoon sauce over fish. Sprinkle with parsley. Makes 4 servings.—*JoAnne Wiltz, Santee, CA*

Per serving: 175 calories, 14 g carbohydrates, 23 g protein, 3 g total fat (0.6 g saturated), 40 mg cholesterol, 485 mg sodium

CRUSTY PACIFIC FISH

West Coast favorites such as fresh rockfish, halibut, and lingcod taste wonderful when coated in cornmeal, then sautéed and served with a lively sour cream sauce.

Tangy Fish Sauce (recipe follows)

About 2 pounds rockfish, halibut, or lingcod fillets (½ to ¾ inch thick)

Salt and pepper

½ cup *each* yellow cornmeal and all-purpose flour

½ cup buttermilk

¼ cup butter or margarine

¼ cup salad oil or solid vegetable shortening

Prepare Tangy Fish Sauce.

Rinse fish and pat dry; cut into 6 equal pieces, if necessary. Sprinkle fish with salt and pepper. In a shallow bowl, combine cornmeal and flour. Pour buttermilk into another shallow bowl. Dip each piece of fish in buttermilk and drain briefly; then dip in cornmeal mixture to coat lightly on both sides. Set aside.

Melt butter in oil in a wide frying pan over medium heat. Add fish, arranging it in a single layer. Cook, turning once, until browned on both sides and just opaque but still moist in thickest part; cut to test (about 5 minutes). Serve immediately, with Tangy Fish Sauce. Makes 6 servings. —*I. R., North Sacramento, CA*

TANGY FISH SAUCE. In a small bowl, stir together 1 cup **sour cream,**

2 tablespoons **buttermilk**, 3 tablespoons chopped **pimento-stuffed green olives**, 2 tablespoons chopped **parsley**, ¼ teaspoon **salt**, and ⅛ teaspoon **paprika.** Cover and refrigerate for at least 30 minutes to blend flavors. Makes about 1¼ cups.

Per serving of fish: 334 calories, 9 g carbohydrates, 30 g protein, 19 g total fat (7 g saturated), 74 mg cholesterol, 180 mg sodium

Per tablespoon of Tangy Fish Sauce: 27 calories, 0.6 g carbohydrates, 0.5 g protein, 3 g total fat (2 g saturated), 5 mg cholesterol, 65 mg sodium

BROILED FISH DIJON

This quick-to-cook entrée is good with a variety of fish—so take advantage of specials at your market, choosing sea bass or any similar firm, white-fleshed type.

> **About 1½ pounds sea bass or rockfish fillets (¾ to 1 inch thick)**
> 4 **teaspoons lemon juice**
> 3 **tablespoons Dijon mustard**
> 1 **clove garlic, minced or pressed**
> **Paprika**
> 2 **tablespoons drained capers**

Rinse fish and pat dry; cut into 4 equal pieces, if necessary. Arrange fish in a single layer in a shallow 10-by 15-inch baking pan or in a broiler pan. Drizzle with lemon juice. In a small bowl, stir together mustard and garlic. Spread fillets evenly with mustard mixture, covering completely.

Broil 6 to 8 inches below heat until fish is just opaque but still moist in thickest part; cut to test (10 to 12 minutes). Sprinkle fish lightly with paprika, then sprinkle with capers. Transfer fish to a platter and serve hot. Or, to serve cold, let cool; then cover and refrigerate for at least 30 minutes or up to 2 hours. Makes 4 servings. —*Suzanne Isken, Tarzana, CA*

Per serving: 179 calories, 0.6 g carbohydrates, 31 g protein, 3 g total fat (0.9 g saturated), 70 mg cholesterol, 497 mg sodium

SAUTÉED SESAME FISH

For this pan-fried fish, choose thick fillets of lingcod or rockfish; or use halibut steaks. Top the hot, sesame-crusted fish with a relish of lemon juice, parsley, and green onions.

> **Lemon Relish (recipe follows)**
> 2 **pounds rockfish or lingcod fillets or halibut steaks (about 1 inch thick)**
> **Salt and pepper**
> **About ¼ cup all-purpose flour**
> ½ **cup fine dry bread crumbs**
> ¼ **cup sesame seeds**
> 1 **large egg**
> 2 **tablespoons milk**
> **About 2 tablespoons butter or margarine**
> **About 2 tablespoons salad oil**

Prepare Lemon Relish and set aside.

Rinse fish and pat dry; cut into 6 equal pieces, if necessary. Sprinkle fish with salt and pepper and dust lightly with flour. In a shallow bowl, combine bread crumbs and sesame seeds. In another shallow bowl, beat egg with milk to blend. Dip fish pieces into egg-milk mixture, then dip in crumb mixture to coat evenly on all sides.

Melt butter in oil in a wide frying pan over medium heat. Add fish, arranging it in a single layer. Cook, turning once, until fish is browned on both sides and just opaque but still moist in thickest part; cut to test (8 to 10 minutes). Serve with Lemon Relish. Makes 6 servings.—*M. D., Morro Bay, CA*

LEMON RELISH. In a small bowl, stir together ¼ cup *each* chopped **parsley** and **fresh lemon juice** and ½ cup thinly sliced **green onions.**

Per serving: 276 calories, 8 g carbohydrates, 31 g protein, 13 g total fat (4 g saturated), 81 mg cholesterol, 178 mg sodium

BAKED FISH FILLETS

A zesty, caper-dotted tomato sauce laced with pimento-stuffed green olives makes a colorful foil for fillets of firm white fish, such as rockfish or sea bass. Accompany the dish with Crisp Spinach Salad (page 39).

> 2 **tablespoons olive oil**
> ¼ **cup chopped onion**
> 1 **can (about 14½ oz.) stewed tomatoes**
> 2 **teaspoons sugar**
> ⅛ **teaspoon ground cloves**
> 2 **pounds fillets or boneless chunks of rockfish, sea bass, sturgeon, or turbot (at least 1 inch thick)**
> **About 3 tablespoons butter or margarine, melted**
> ½ **cup pimento-stuffed green olives, sliced**
> 1 **tablespoon drained capers**
> 1 **tablespoon minced parsley**

Heat oil in a heavy 2-quart pan or wide frying pan over medium-high heat. Add onion and cook, stirring often, until soft. Add tomatoes, sugar, and cloves. Bring to a boil; then reduce heat and simmer, uncovered, stirring often, until sauce is thickened (about 15 minutes).

Meanwhile, rinse fish and pat dry; cut into 6 equal pieces, if necessary. Brush fish all over with butter and arrange in a shallow baking pan. Bake in a 400° oven until fish is just opaque but still moist in thickest part; cut to test (10 to 12 minutes).

Transfer fish to a platter. Pour any pan juices from fish into tomato sauce and stir to blend well. Remove sauce from heat, stir in olives and capers, and spoon over fish. Sprinkle with parsley. Makes 6 servings. —*L. W., Albany, CA*

Per serving: 221 calories, 7 g carbohydrates, 29 g protein, 8 g total fat (1 g saturated), 53 mg cholesterol, 574 mg sodium

HALIBUT WITH TOMATOES & DILL

Roasted cherry tomatoes, seasoned with garlic and fresh dill, make a light and colorful sauce for thick halibut fillets or steaks that bake separately in the same oven. If you can't find halibut, choose another firm, white-fleshed fish, such as rockfish, lingcod, Pacific snapper, mahi mahi, or orange roughy.

- 1 **pound cherry tomatoes, cut into halves**
- ½ **cup thinly sliced green onions**
- 2 **cloves garlic, minced or pressed**
- 2 **tablespoons chopped fresh dill or ½ teaspoon dry dill weed**
- 2 **tablespoons olive oil**
- 1½ **to 2 pounds halibut fillets or steaks (or rockfish or lingcod fillets), about 1 inch thick**
- 2 **tablespoons lemon juice**
- **Dill sprigs (optional)**

Arrange tomatoes, cut side up, in a 9- by 13-inch baking pan. In a small bowl, mix onions, garlic, chopped dill, and oil. Distribute onion mixture over tomatoes. Bake on top rack of a 425° oven for 25 minutes.

Rinse fish and pat dry; cut into 4 to 6 equal pieces, if necessary. Place fish in a baking pan just large enough to hold pieces in a single layer. Drizzle with lemon juice, cover, and set on bottom oven rack. Continue to bake until tomatoes are lightly browned and fish is just opaque but still moist in thickest part; cut to test (10 to 12 minutes).

With a slotted spoon, transfer fish to a platter. Add pan juices from fish to tomato mixture and stir well; spoon over fish. Garnish with dill sprigs, if desired. Makes 4 to 6 servings.—*Heide Gohlert, Cheney, WA*

Per serving: 248 calories, 6 g carbohydrates, 34 g protein, 9 g total fat (1 g saturated), 51 mg cholesterol, 97 mg sodium

HALIBUT WITH VEGETABLE CREST

Baked halibut steaks or fillets are topped with a luscious, fluffy mixture of cream cheese and chopped fresh vegetables in this elegant main dish. To round out the menu, offer poppy seed rolls and steamed sugar snap peas.

- 2 **halibut or salmon steaks (or 2 pieces halibut or salmon fillet), about 8 oz. *each***
- 3 **tablespoons lemon juice**
- 2 **tablespoons cream cheese, at room temperature**
- ½ **cup *each* finely grated carrot and chopped seeded tomato**
- 3 **tablespoons *each* sliced green onions and mayonnaise**
- 1 **tablespoon minced parsley**
- ¼ **teaspoon pepper**
- **Salt**
- **Lime wedges (optional)**

Rinse fish and pat dry; then arrange in a shallow 1½- to 2-quart baking dish. Drizzle fish evenly with lemon juice.

In a small bowl, mix cream cheese, carrot, tomato, onions, mayonnaise, parsley, and pepper; season to taste with salt. Mound vegetable mixture evenly atop fish. (At this point, you may cover and refrigerate for up to 6 hours.)

Bake, uncovered, in a 400° oven until fish is just opaque but still moist in thickest part; cut to test (about 15 minutes). Transfer fish to individual plates; serve with lime wedges, if desired. Makes 2 servings. —*Micky Kolar, Fountain Hills, AZ*

Per serving: 429 calories, 8 g carbohydrates, 40 g protein, 26 g total fat (6 g saturated), 87 mg cholesterol, 279 mg sodium

GRILLED SOY-LEMON HALIBUT

A tart teriyaki marinade perfectly complements mild-tasting halibut. Vegetables cooked on the grill make good accompaniments; try red bell pepper quarters, slender Japanese eggplant, and whole green onions.

- 3 **pounds halibut, shark, or sea bass steaks or fillets (¾ to 1 inch thick)**
- 2 **tablespoons butter or margarine, melted**
- 3 **tablespoons soy sauce**
- 2 **tablespoons lemon juice**
- 1 **tablespoon *each* sugar and Worcestershire**
- 1 **tablespoon minced fresh ginger**
- 1 **clove garlic, minced or pressed**
- ⅛ **teaspoon pepper**
- **Lemon wedges**

Rinse fish and pat dry; cut into 6 equal pieces, if necessary. In a large, shallow dish, stir together butter, soy sauce, lemon juice, sugar, Worcestershire, ginger, garlic, and pepper. Add fish and turn to coat; cover and refrigerate for 1 to 2 hours, turning occasionally.

Lift fish from marinade and drain briefly (discard marinade). Place fish on a grill 4 to 6 inches above a solid bed of hot coals. Cover barbecue, open vents, and cook, turning once, until fish is just opaque but still moist in thickest part; cut to test (8 to 10 minutes). Serve with lemon wedges. Makes 6 servings.—*Debbie Stevens, Manhattan Beach, CA*

Per serving: 228 calories, 2 g carbohydrates, 39 g protein, 6 g total fat (2 g saturated), 64 mg cholesterol, 390 mg sodium

Skewered Fish, Northwest Style

Baste these skewers of big scallops, halibut chunks, and vegetables with a spicy blend of soy, wine, and Worcestershire as they sizzle under the broiler.

- ¼ cup *each* Worcestershire, soy sauce, and dry white wine
- 2 tablespoons olive oil or salad oil
- 8 ounces boneless, skinless halibut or other firm-textured white-fleshed fish fillets
- 8 ounces sea scallops
- 12 small mushrooms (*each* about 1 inch in diameter)
- 1 medium-size green bell pepper (about 6 oz.), seeded and cut into 1-inch pieces

In a large bowl, stir together Worcestershire, soy sauce, wine, and oil. Rinse fish and scallops and pat dry. Cut fish into about 1-inch cubes; cut scallops in half. Add fish and scallops to marinade and stir to coat well. Cover and refrigerate for at least 10 minutes or up to 4 hours, stirring occasionally.

Lift fish and scallops from marinade and drain briefly (reserve marinade). Thread fish, scallops, mushrooms, and bell pepper pieces equally on 4 thin metal skewers, alternating ingredients. Arrange skewers slightly apart on a rack in a broiler pan; set aside.

Pour marinade into a small pan and bring to a boil over high heat; remove from heat.

Broil skewers about 3 inches below heat, turning once and brushing with marinade, until fish is just opaque but still moist in thickest part; cut to test (about 8 minutes). Makes 4 servings.—*Micki Kent, Bainbridge Island, WA*

Per serving: 226 calories, 10 g carbohydrates, 24 g protein, 9 g total fat (1 g saturated), 37 mg cholesterol, 1,319 mg sodium

Macadamia Parmesan Sole

Buttery macadamia nuts, a Western treat, combine with Parmesan cheese to enhance oven-fried sole fillets.

- ¾ cup grated Parmesan cheese
- 2 tablespoons all-purpose flour
- 2 large eggs
- 4 sole fillets (4 to 6 oz. *each*)
- 2 tablespoons salad oil
- 2 tablespoons butter or margarine
- ½ cup finely chopped salted roasted macadamia nuts
  Watercress or parsley sprigs
  Lemon wedges

Place a shallow 10- by 15-inch baking pan in oven as it heats to 425°.

In a shallow bowl, mix cheese and flour. In another shallow bowl, beat eggs to blend. Rinse fish and pat dry; dip each fillet in eggs, then dip in cheese mixture to coat well on both sides. Set fish aside.

Remove pan from oven and add oil and butter. Swirl until butter is melted. Place fish in pan and turn to coat with butter mixture; then sprinkle evenly with nuts. Bake until fish is just opaque but still moist in thickest part; cut to test (7 to 10 minutes). Transfer fish to a platter; garnish with watercress sprigs and lemon wedges. Makes 4 servings. —*Moiree van Westen, Bellingham, WA*

Per serving: 418 calories, 4 g carbohydrates, 33 g protein, 30 g total fat (8 g saturated), 143 mg cholesterol, 403 mg sodium

Grilled Fish Picante

Despite its fearsome reputation, shark has become a popular food fish. It has a firm, meaty texture, few bones, and—quite often—a pleasingly modest price. Here, it's grilled and topped with a zesty lime-cilantro butter.

- 4 shark or salmon steaks (6 to 8 oz. *each*), about 1 inch thick
- 2 tablespoons lime juice
- ½ cup purchased mild salsa
  Lime Butter (recipe follows)
- 2 tablespoons butter or margarine, melted
  Lime wedges and cilantro sprigs

Rinse fish, pat dry, and place in a large, shallow dish. Drizzle evenly with lime juice and salsa. Cover and refrigerate for at least 30 minutes or up to 2 hours, turning fish over once. Meanwhile, prepare Lime Butter.

Lift fish from dish; drizzle with melted butter. Arrange on a grill 4 to 6 inches above a solid bed of medium coals. Cook, turning once, until just opaque but still moist in thickest part; cut to test (10 to 12 minutes). Transfer to a platter. Spoon 2 teaspoons Lime Butter onto each steak; garnish with lime wedges and cilantro sprigs. Serve with remaining Lime Butter. Makes 4 servings.—*J. Hill, Sacramento*

LIME BUTTER. In a small bowl, combine ⅓ cup **butter** or margarine, at room temperature; ½ teaspoon **grated lime peel;** 2 tablespoons **lime juice;** 1 tablespoon minced **cilantro;** and ¼ teaspoon **crushed red pepper flakes.** Beat until fluffy. Makes about 6 tablespoons.

Per serving of fish: 289 calories, 3 g carbohydrates, 37 g protein, 14 g total fat (5 g saturated), 105 mg cholesterol, 518 mg sodium

Per tablespoon of Lime Butter: 91 calories, 0.4 g carbohydrates, 0.1 g protein, 10 g total fat (6 g saturated), 27 mg cholesterol, 104 mg sodium

Sole Fillets & Oysters Thermidor

Dating from the 1950s, this creamy combination of fish and shellfish is well suited to special occasions. When serving the dish for company, the contributor liked to bake it in individual gratin dishes, then garnish each serving with a ring of hot cooked peas.

- 4 large sole fillets (6 to 8 oz. *each*)
- 1 jar (about 10 oz.) small Pacific or other small oysters, drained
- ¼ cup butter or margarine
- 4 ounces mushrooms, sliced
- 2 tablespoons thinly sliced green onion (white part only)
- 2 tablespoons chopped green bell pepper
- 3 tablespoons all-purpose flour
- 1 cup milk
- ¼ cup dry sherry
- ¼ cup grated Parmesan cheese
- ½ teaspoon dry mustard
  Salt and pepper
  Parsley sprigs or snipped chives

Rinse fish, pat dry, and arrange in a greased shallow 2½- to 3-quart baking dish; place 2 or 3 oysters on each fillet.

Melt butter in a wide frying pan over medium heat. Add mushrooms, onion, and bell pepper; cook, stirring often, until vegetables are soft. Blend in flour and cook, stirring, until bubbly. Remove from heat and gradually stir in milk; return to heat and cook, stirring, until sauce boils and thickens. Stir in sherry, cheese, and mustard; season to taste with salt and pepper.

Spoon sauce over fish and oysters. Bake in a 350° oven until fish is just opaque but still moist in thickest part; cut to test (about 20 minutes). If desired, broil about 4 inches below heat until lightly browned. Garnish with parsley sprigs. Makes 4 servings.—*H. N., San Francisco*

Per serving: 451 calories, 13 g carbohydrates, 48 g protein, 20 g total fat (11 g saturated), 178 mg cholesterol, 483 mg sodium

Parsee Fish

This distinctive dish from Pakistan has its origins in the cooking of people who came to that country from Persia (now Iran). Be sure you prepare the recipe with unsweetened coconut milk, not the canned coconut cream sold as a drink mixer.

- 4 sole fillets (about 6 oz. *each*)
- 1 tablespoon sweetened flaked coconut
- 1 clove garlic, peeled
- 2 canned whole green chiles, seeded
- ½ teaspoon sugar
- 1 teaspoon salt
- ⅓ cup coconut milk or milk
- 2 large eggs
- ½ medium-size cucumber, peeled, seeded, and finely chopped
- 1 tablespoon butter or margarine
  Paprika

Rinse fish, pat dry, and arrange in a single layer in a greased baking pan. In a blender or food processor, combine coconut, garlic, chiles, sugar, salt, and 1 tablespoon of the coconut milk. Whirl until smooth. Spread coconut mixture evenly over fish. In a small bowl, beat eggs and remaining coconut milk to blend; stir in cucumber, then pour mixture evenly over fish. Dot with butter.

Bake in a 325° oven until fish is just opaque but still moist in thickest part; cut to test (20 to 25 minutes). Transfer fish to a platter, leaving cooking liquid in pan; sprinkle with paprika. Makes 4 servings.—*E. B., Los Angeles*

Per serving: 284 calories, 4 g carbohydrates, 36 g protein, 13 g total fat (7 g saturated), 196 mg cholesterol, 771 mg sodium

Quick Sole & Shrimp Casserole

This casserole couldn't be simpler. Just alternate layers of sole fillets, shrimp, and fresh mushrooms; then top with a creamy tartar sauce mixture and bake.

- 1 pound sole fillets
- 4 ounces small cooked shrimp
- 3 tablespoons fine dry bread crumbs
  About ¼ teaspoon pepper
- 2 tablespoons lemon juice
- 4 ounces mushrooms, thinly sliced
- 2 tablespoons purchased tartar sauce or mayonnaise
- 2 tablespoons thinly sliced green onion
- 1 clove garlic, minced or pressed
- 1½ tablespoons butter or margarine, at room temperature
- ¼ cup dry vermouth (optional)

Rinse fish and pat dry. Arrange half the fish evenly over bottom of a greased shallow 1½-quart baking dish. Sprinkle evenly with half each of the shrimp, bread crumbs, pepper, lemon juice, and mushrooms. Repeat layers.

In a small bowl, stir together tartar sauce, onion, garlic, and butter; dot butter mixture over top of casserole. If using vermouth, drizzle it over casserole. (At this point, you may cover and refrigerate for up to 8 hours.)

Bake, covered, in a 350° oven until fish is just opaque but still moist in thickest part; cut to test (about 30 minutes; about 40 minutes if refrigerated). To serve, lift portions of fish from cooking liquid with a slotted spatula and transfer to individual plates. Makes 4 servings.—*C. J., San Anselmo, CA*

Per serving: 249 calories, 6 g carbohydrates, 29 g protein, 12 g total fat (4 g saturated), 125 mg cholesterol, 297 mg sodium

Swordfish Steaks with Mushrooms

Firm swordfish steaks are especially juicy when flavored in a lemony marinade and topped with a wine-laced mushroom sauce. If you like, use shark in place of the swordfish.

2 pounds swordfish or shark steaks (about ¾ inch thick)

3 tablespoons lemon juice

¼ cup dry white wine or water

1 clove garlic, minced or pressed

½ teaspoon *each* dry oregano, salt, and pepper

¼ teaspoon fennel seeds, crushed

2 tablespoons olive oil or salad oil

8 ounces mushrooms, sliced

2 or 3 green onions, thinly sliced

Rinse fish and pat dry; cut into 6 equal pieces, if necessary. In a large, shallow dish, stir together lemon juice, wine, garlic, oregano, salt, pepper, and fennel seeds. Add fish and turn to coat; then cover and refrigerate for 30 minutes, turning occasionally.

Lift fish from marinade and drain briefly (reserve marinade). Then place fish on a rack in a broiler pan and broil about 4 inches below heat, turning once, until just opaque but still moist in thickest part; cut to test (8 to 10 minutes).

Meanwhile, heat oil in a wide frying pan over medium-high heat. Add mushrooms to pan and cook, stirring often, until soft (about 5 minutes). Stir in marinade, bring to a boil, and boil gently, uncovered, for 2 minutes. Stir in onions; then remove pan from heat.

Transfer fish to a platter; top with mushroom sauce. Makes 6 servings. —C. S., San Pedro, CA

Per serving: 224 calories, 3 g carbohydrates, 28 g protein, 10 g total fat (2 g saturated), 53 mg cholesterol, 308 mg sodium

Grilled Tuna Steaks

Tuna steaks (known as *ahi* in Hawaii) take well to grilling after a quick soak in an Asian-style marinade of lime, soy, ginger, and garlic. A selection of tropical fruits, such as pineapple spears, papaya slices, and melon wedges, goes nicely with this dish.

3 tablespoons lime juice

2 tablespoons reduced-sodium soy sauce

1 tablespoon *each* minced fresh ginger and minced garlic

4 tuna (ahi) steaks (about 7 oz. *each*), about 1 inch thick

Lime wedges

Oriental sesame oil (optional)

In a large, shallow dish, stir together lime juice, soy sauce, ginger, and garlic. Rinse fish, pat dry, and add to marinade; turn to coat. Cover and refrigerate for at least 1 hour or until next day, turning occasionally.

Lift fish from marinade and drain briefly (discard marinade). Place fish on a lightly oiled grill 4 to 6 inches above a solid bed of hot coals. Cook, turning once, until fish is browned on outside but still pale pink in thickest part; cut to test (6 to 7 minutes). Serve with lime wedges and, if desired, sesame oil. Makes 4 servings.—*Jane Ingraham, Durango, CO*

NOTE: *If you want to enjoy your tuna rare, but the fish has not been frozen,* freeze it at 0°F for at least 7 days to destroy any potentially harmful organisms. Then thaw the fish in the refrigerator before cooking.

Per serving: 197 calories, 1 g carbohydrates, 42 g protein, 2 g total fat (0.4 g saturated), 79 mg cholesterol, 217 mg sodium

Tuna Carbonara

This pasta dish is a good choice for a spur-of-the-moment supper.

8 ounces dry vermicelli

4 large eggs

2 tablespoons butter or margarine

2 tablespoons olive oil

1 large red bell pepper (about 8 oz.), seeded and cut into thin strips

3 cloves garlic, minced or pressed

1 can (about 9¼ oz.) water-packed chunk-style tuna, drained

1 cup (about 4 oz.) grated Parmesan cheese

¼ cup chopped parsley

Salt and pepper

In a 4- to 5-quart pan, cook vermicelli in about 2 quarts boiling water until just tender to bite (8 to 10 minutes); or cook pasta according to package directions.

Meanwhile, in a bowl, beat eggs to blend; set aside. Also melt butter in oil in a wide frying pan over medium-high heat. Add bell pepper and garlic; cook, stirring often, until pepper is soft.

Drain pasta well; add hot pasta to pan along with tuna. Cook, stirring constantly, until tuna is heated through. Reduce heat to low and immediately add eggs, cheese, and parsley to pan; quickly mix sauce with pasta by lifting pasta with 2 forks. Season to taste with salt and pepper. Makes 4 servings.—*D. S., Fairbanks, AK*

Per serving: 618 calories, 48 g carbohydrates, 43 g protein, 27 g total fat (12 g saturated), 275 mg cholesterol, 864 mg sodium

SHRIMP & PEA POD STIR-FRY

Plump pink shrimp and crisp green Chinese pea pods make a colorful stir-fry to serve over steamed short-grain rice.

- 2 tablespoons soy sauce
- 1 tablespoon minced fresh ginger
- ¼ cup dry sherry or water
- ¼ cup unseasoned rice vinegar
- 1½ teaspoons cornstarch
- 2 tablespoons salad oil
- 1 cup sliced mushrooms
- 1 clove garlic, minced or pressed
- 1 pound medium-size raw shrimp (about 36 per lb.), shelled and deveined
- 4 ounces Chinese pea pods (also called snow or sugar peas), ends and strings removed

  About 3 cups hot cooked short-grain rice
- ¼ cup thinly sliced green onions

In a small bowl, stir together soy sauce, ginger, sherry, vinegar, and cornstarch. Set aside.

Heat 1 tablespoon of the oil in a wide frying pan or wok over high heat. Add mushrooms and garlic; cook, stirring often, until mushrooms are lightly browned. Remove from pan and set aside. Heat remaining 1 tablespoon oil in pan. Add shrimp and cook, stirring, until just opaque in center; cut to test (about 3 minutes). Return mushroom mixture to pan along with pea pods; stir soy mixture and pour into pan. Cook, stirring, until sauce boils and thickens and pea pods turn a brighter green.

Spoon rice onto a platter; top with shrimp mixture and sprinkle with onions. Makes 4 servings.—*Mike Humason, Thousand Oaks, CA*

Per serving: 406 calories, 50 g carbohydrates, 25 g protein, 9 g total fat (1 g saturated), 140 mg cholesterol, 661 mg sodium

SHRIMP WITH SAUCE VERDE

These hot, succulent steeped shrimp are topped with a pesto-like blend of toasted almonds, parsley, and fresh jalapeño chile.

- ¼ cup whole unblanched almonds
- 2 cups lightly packed parsley sprigs
- ⅓ cup olive oil
- 3 tablespoons white wine vinegar
- 1 clove garlic, peeled
- 1 tablespoon drained capers
- 1 fresh jalapeño chile, seeded
  Salt
- 1 pound large raw shrimp (31 to 35 per lb.), shelled and deveined

Toast almonds in a wide frying pan over medium heat, stirring often, until golden beneath skins (about 5 minutes). Pour almonds into a food processor or blender and let cool. To processor, add parsley, oil, vinegar, garlic, capers, and chile. Whirl until smoothly puréed. Season to taste with salt.

In a 4- to 5-quart pan, bring 2 quarts water to a boil over high heat. Add shrimp to pan, cover, and immediately remove from heat. Let stand until shrimp are just opaque in center; cut to test (2 to 3 minutes). Drain shrimp and mound on a platter; spoon sauce over shrimp. Makes 4 servings.—*L. K. Ross, Elk Grove, CA*

Per serving: 319 calories, 6 g carbohydrates, 21 g protein, 24 g total fat (3 g saturated), 140 mg cholesterol, 207 mg sodium

SHRIMP STROGANOFF

Shrimp in a rich sour-cream sauce are superb served over rice or fresh pasta such as fettuccine.

- 6 tablespoons butter or margarine
- 1½ to 2 pounds large raw shrimp (31 to 35 per lb.), shelled and deveined
- 1½ cups sliced mushrooms
- 2 tablespoons minced onion
- 1 clove garlic, minced or pressed
- 3 tablespoons all-purpose flour
- 1 cup chicken broth (or ½ cup *each* dry white wine and chicken broth)
- 1 teaspoon catsup
- ½ teaspoon Worcestershire
- 1 cup sour cream
- 1 tablespoon chopped fresh dill or parsley (or 1 teaspoon dry dill weed)
  Salt
  Dill sprigs

Melt 3 tablespoons of the butter in a wide frying pan over medium-high heat. Add shrimp and cook, stirring often, until just opaque in center; cut to test (4 to 5 minutes). Remove shrimp from pan and keep warm.

Melt remaining 3 tablespoons butter in pan; add mushrooms and cook, stirring often, for 2 minutes. Add onion and garlic; cook, stirring often, until onion is soft but not browned (about 3 minutes). Blend in flour and cook, stirring, until bubbly. Remove from heat and gradually stir in broth. Return to heat and cook, stirring, until sauce boils and thickens. Stir in catsup and Worcestershire. Blend in sour cream, chopped dill, and shrimp; stir just until heated through (do not boil). Remove from heat and season to taste with salt. Garnish with dill sprigs. Makes 6 servings.—*M. R., Davis, CA*

Per serving: 325 calories, 7 g carbohydrates, 24 g protein, 22 g total fat (13 g saturated), 211 mg cholesterol, 479 mg sodium

SHRIMP & CAPERS

For an unusual cool entrée, top beer-simmered shrimp with a spicy honey-mustard dressing.

- 1 bottle or can (about 12 oz.) beer
- ½ cup minced onion
- ¾ teaspoon celery seeds
- 1 dry bay leaf
- 1 pound large raw shrimp (31 to 35 per lb.), shelled and deveined
- ½ cup tomato-based chili sauce
- 1 tablespoon honey-flavored mustard
  Spinach leaves, rinsed and crisped
- 2 tablespoons drained capers

In a wide frying pan, bring beer, onion, celery seeds, and bay leaf to a boil over high heat; boil for 2 minutes. Add shrimp. Reduce heat, cover, and simmer, stirring occasionally, until shrimp are just opaque in center; cut to test (about 3 minutes). Remove shrimp from pan with a slotted spoon; place in a bowl.

Bring beer mixture to a boil; then boil, uncovered, until reduced to ⅓ cup. Discard bay leaf. Add chili sauce and mustard to beer mixture; blend well. Cover shrimp and beer dressing separately and refrigerate until cool (at least 1 hour) or until next day.

To serve, arrange spinach on 4 plates; top equally with shrimp, then with beer dressing. Sprinkle with capers. Makes 4 servings.—*Audrey Thibodeau, Fountain Hills, AZ*

Per serving: 165 calories, 16 g carbohydrates, 20 g protein, 2 g total fat (0.3 g saturated), 140 mg cholesterol, 708 mg sodium

SCALLOPS LA JOLLA

Large scallop shells make perfect individual baking dishes for poached scallops in a creamy cheese sauce.

- 3 pounds sea scallops
- 1½ cups dry white wine
- 2 tablespoons lemon juice
- 12 ounces mushrooms, sliced
- 1 medium-size green bell pepper (about 6 oz.), seeded and diced
- 1 cup whipping cream
- ¼ cup butter or margarine
- ¼ cup all-purpose flour
- 1 cup (about 4 oz.) diced Swiss cheese
- ½ cup grated Romano or Parmesan cheese
  Salt and pepper
- 2 tablespoons butter or margarine
  Paprika

Rinse scallops and pat dry. In a 3-quart pan, bring wine and lemon juice almost to a boil; add scallops, mushrooms, and bell pepper. Reduce heat, cover, and simmer until scallops are just opaque in center; cut to test (6 to 8 minutes). Drain, reserving 2 cups of the cooking liquid; discard remaining cooking liquid. Set scallops and vegetables aside.

In a medium-size bowl, whip cream until stiff; set aside.

Melt the ¼ cup butter in scallop cooking pan; blend in flour and cook, stirring, until bubbly. Remove from heat and gradually stir in scallop cooking liquid; return to heat and cook, stirring, until sauce boils and thickens. Add Swiss cheese and ¼ cup of the Romano cheese; reduce heat and stir until cheese is melted and sauce is smooth. Remove from heat and fold in whipped cream. Season to taste with salt and pepper. Stir in scallops and vegetables.

Divide scallop mixture among 6 to 8 individual 1½- to 2-cup baking dishes. Sprinkle with remaining ¼ cup Romano cheese, dot with the 2 tablespoons butter, and sprinkle with paprika. Broil about 4 inches below heat until browned (about 3 minutes). Makes 6 to 8 servings. —*A. J., La Jolla, CA*

Per serving: 510 calories, 14 g carbohydrates, 42 g protein, 28 g total fat (16 g saturated), 150 mg cholesterol, 542 mg sodium

SAUTÉED SCALLOPS & SHRIMP IN BÉARNAISE CREAM

Reduced vinegar, minced shallots, and tarragon give this sauce for sea scallops and shrimp the flavor of a classic béarnaise. Serve the elegant dish with steamed fresh broccoli or asparagus spears.

- 1 pound sea scallops
- 2 tablespoons butter or margarine
- 8 ounces large raw shrimp (31 to 35 per lb.), shelled, deveined, and split lengthwise
- ⅓ cup minced shallots
- ¾ cup tarragon wine vinegar or white wine vinegar
- ½ cup chicken broth
- ¼ teaspoon dry tarragon
- 1 tablespoon Dijon mustard
- ½ cup whipping cream
  Salt and ground white pepper

Rinse scallops, pat dry, and cut in half horizontally.

Melt butter in a wide frying pan over medium-high heat. Add scallops and shrimp. Cook, stirring, until scallops and shrimp are just opaque in center; cut to test (3 to 4 minutes). Remove shellfish from pan and keep warm.

Add shallots, vinegar, broth, and tarragon to pan. Bring to a boil over high heat; then boil, uncovered, until reduced to ½ cup. Pour any accumulated liquid from shellfish into pan; stir in mustard and cream. Return to a boil; then boil, uncovered, stirring often, until sauce is reduced to about ¾ cup.

Stir scallops and shrimp into sauce; season to taste with salt and white pepper. Makes 4 servings. —*Moiree van Westen, Bellingham, WA*

Per serving: 313 calories, 9 g carbohydrates, 30 g protein, 17 g total fat (10 g saturated), 156 mg cholesterol, 537 mg sodium

CHAFING DISH CRAB

This rich-tasting entrée, flecked with pimento and parsley, is a festive choice for a buffet dinner. You might accompany the crab with hot cooked white or brown rice or spoon it into puff pastry shells. A mixed green salad tossed with crisp croutons and a light vinaigrette is delicious alongside.

- 3 tablespoons butter or margarine
- 8 ounces mushrooms, sliced
- 3 tablespoons all-purpose flour
- 1 cup half-and-half
- ½ cup dry white wine or half-and-half
- 2 tablespoons lemon juice
- ½ teaspoon dry dill weed or 1 tablespoon chopped fresh dill
- 1 pound flaked cooked crabmeat
- 1 jar (about 2 oz.) sliced pimentos, drained
- ⅓ cup grated Parmesan cheese
  Salt and pepper
  Chopped parsley

Melt butter in a chafing dish or wide frying pan over medium-high heat. Add mushrooms; cook, stirring often, until mushrooms are browned and almost all liquid has evaporated (about 7 minutes).

Blend in flour and cook, stirring, until mixture is bubbly. Remove from heat and gradually stir in half-and-half and wine. Return to heat and cook, stirring, until sauce boils and thickens.

Stir in lemon juice, dill weed, crab, pimentos, and cheese. Stir until heated through, but do not boil. Season to taste with salt and pepper; sprinkle with parsley. Keep warm over hot water or on a warming tray. Makes 4 servings. —A. M., Portland

Per serving: 361 calories, 11 g carbohydrates, 30 g protein, 20 g total fat (11 g saturated), 164 mg cholesterol, 560 mg sodium

DILLED CRAB & SHRIMP CAKES

Crab cakes, a turn-of-the-century favorite, have made a comeback nearly 100 years later—as this 1990s variation of the dish attests.

- 1 large egg plus 1 large egg white
- 1 tablespoon chopped fresh dill or 1 teaspoon dry dill weed
- 2 teaspoons Worcestershire
- ½ teaspoon dry mustard
- 6 ounces *each* flaked cooked crabmeat and chopped small cooked shrimp
- 1 cup *each* fine dry bread crumbs and diced red bell pepper
- ¼ cup reduced-calorie or regular mayonnaise
- 2 tablespoons sliced green onion
- 1½ tablespoons butter or margarine
  Dill sprigs (optional)
  Lemon or lime wedges

In a large bowl, beat egg and egg white to blend. Add chopped dill, Worcestershire, mustard, crab, shrimp, bread crumbs, bell pepper, mayonnaise, and onion; mix until well blended. Shape mixture into 12 patties, each about ½ inch thick.

Melt 1½ teaspoons of the butter in a wide nonstick frying pan over medium heat. Place 4 crab cakes in pan; cook, turning once, until golden on both sides (6 to 10 minutes). Remove from pan and keep warm.

Repeat to cook remaining crab cakes, using remaining 1 tablespoon butter. Garnish with dill sprigs, if desired; serve with lemon wedges. Makes 4 servings.—*Joyce Albert, Seattle*

Per serving: 305 calories, 23 g carbohydrates, 24 g protein, 12 g total fat (5 g saturated), 195 mg cholesterol, 630 mg sodium

BROILED CRAB SANDWICHES

For an informal supper, serve these hot crab sandwiches with steaming Tomato-Potato Soup (page 24).

- 1 bunch green onions
- 1 pound flaked cooked crabmeat
- ¼ cup tomato-based chili sauce or catsup
- 3 tablespoons lemon juice
- 5 tablespoons mayonnaise
- 8 slices French bread, toasted; or 4 English muffins, split and toasted
- 2 large eggs, separated
- ⅓ cup shredded mild Cheddar or Swiss cheese

Trim and discard ends of onions; then thinly slice onions and place in a medium-size bowl. Add crab, chili sauce, 2 tablespoons of the lemon juice, and 1 tablespoon of the mayonnaise. Mix until well blended. Spread crab mixture evenly over toast or muffin halves.

In bowl, blend remaining ¼ cup mayonnaise and 1 tablespoon lemon juice; blend in egg yolks and cheese. In a small bowl, beat egg whites with an electric mixer on high speed until they hold stiff peaks; fold into mayonnaise mixture. Spread mixture over sandwiches, covering crab filling. Arrange sandwiches on a rack in a broiler pan. Broil 5 inches below heat until browned (3 to 4 minutes). Makes 4 servings.—*J. D., Ojai, CA*

Per serving: 481 calories, 34 g carbohydrates, 34 g protein, 23 g total fat (5 g saturated), 240 mg cholesterol, 1,044 mg sodium

BUTTER-BASTED CRAB

This hot cracked crab can be pre-pared in the microwave or in a con-ventional oven. Try it with a loaf of crusty sourdough bread and whole cooked artichokes to dip in the abun-dant lemon butter that coats the crab.

- ¼ **cup butter or margarine**
- ¼ **teaspoon grated lemon peel**
- 3 **tablespoons lemon juice**
- 1 **tablespoon thinly sliced green onion**
- 1 **teaspoon** *each* **minced parsley and soy sauce**
  Liquid hot pepper seasoning
- 1 **large Dungeness crab (about 2 lbs.), cooked, cleaned, and cracked**
  Lemon or lime wedges

To prepare in a microwave oven, place butter in microwave-safe glass measure; microwave on HIGH (100%) for 30 seconds or until melted. Stir in lemon peel, lemon juice, onion, parsley, and soy sauce; season to taste with hot pepper seasoning. Micro-wave on HIGH (100%) for 30 seconds or until bubbly. Cover and set aside. (Or combine the preceding ingredi-ents in a small pan and stir over medium heat until bubbly, 3 to 5 minutes.)

Rinse crab and drain well. Arrange crab pieces in an even layer in a 7- by 11-inch microwave-safe baking dish. Brush butter mixture over crab, cover, and microwave on HIGH (100%) for 3 to 4 minutes or until heated through. (Or cover and bake in a 300° oven until heated through, about 20 minutes.) As crab heats, brush it several times with but-ter mixture in dish. Serve with lemon wedges. Makes 2 servings.—*J. V., Palo Alto, CA*

Per serving: 322 calories, 2 g carbohydrates, 22 g protein, 25 g total fat (15 g saturated), 171 mg cho-lesterol, 715 mg sodium

SOFT CRAB TACOS WITH LIME-PINEAPPLE SALSA

Sweet fresh crab, heated briefly in a chile-tomato sauce, and spoonfuls of lime-pineapple salsa make a mar-velous filling for warm corn tortillas.

- **Lime-Pineapple Salsa (recipe follows)**
- 2 **tablespoons olive oil**
- 1 **small red onion, finely chopped**
- 1 **clove garlic, minced or pressed**
- 1 **large firm-ripe tomato (about 8 oz.), chopped**
- 1 **can (about 4 oz.) diced green chiles**
- 12 **corn tortillas (each about 6 inches in diameter)**
- 1 **pound flaked cooked crabmeat**
  Salt

Prepare Lime-Pineapple Salsa and set aside.

Heat oil in a wide frying pan over medium-high heat. Add onion and garlic; cook, stirring often, until onion begins to brown. Add tomato and chiles; cook, stirring occasion-ally, until tomato is soft (8 to 10 minutes).

Meanwhile, brush tortillas lightly with hot water; then stack, wrap in foil, and heat in a 350° oven until warm (10 to 15 minutes).

Remove tomato mixture from heat, blend in crab, and season to taste with salt. To eat, spoon about ⅓ cup of the crab filling onto a tortilla; add salsa to taste. Fold tortilla to enclose filling and eat out of hand. Makes 6 servings.—*Heather Sager, Carlsbad, CA*

LIME-PINEAPPLE SALSA. In a medium-size bowl, mix ½ cup chopped **cucumber;** 1 fresh **jalapeño chile,** seeded and minced; 1 cup diced **fresh or canned pineapple;** 1 teaspoon **grated lime peel;** 3 table-spoons **lime juice;** and 2 tablespoons minced **cilantro.**

Per serving: 266 calories, 32 g carbohydrates, 19 g protein, 7 g total fat (0.9 g saturated), 76 mg cho-lesterol, 414 mg sodium

CRACKED CRAB IN SPICY TOMATO SAUCE

Accompany this saucy cracked crab with a mixed green salad and hot sourdough French bread.

- 2 **cups catsup**
- 1 **cup water**
- 3 **whole cloves**
- 1 **teaspoon seasoned salt**
- ½ **teaspoon** *each* **dry thyme and sugar**
- 1 **tablespoon Worcestershire**
- 1 **teaspoon prepared horseradish**
- 1 **dry bay leaf**
- 2 **large Dungeness crabs (about 2 lbs. each), cooked, cleaned, and cracked**

In a 5-quart or larger pan, combine catsup, water, cloves, seasoned salt, thyme, sugar, Worcestershire, horse-radish, and bay leaf. Bring to a simmer over medium heat, stirring occasionally.

Rinse crabs and drain well. Add crab pieces to simmering sauce; cook just until heated through. Serve crab with sauce that clings to shells; offer extra sauce on the side. Makes 4 servings.—*J. M., Grants Pass, OR*

Per serving: 244 calories, 35 g carbohydrates, 24 g protein, 2 g total fat (0.3 g saturated), 109 mg cho-lesterol, 1,837 mg sodium

HANGTOWN FRY

This classic egg-and-oyster dish takes its name from California's Mother Lode town of Placerville, called Hangtown in its brawling youth. Traditional versions include crisp bacon, which is still delicious on the side. (For another interpretation of the dish, see Gold Country Special, page 64.)

- 5 large eggs
- 2 tablespoons whipping cream
- 4 ounces shucked oysters (if large, cut into bite-size pieces)
   All-purpose flour
- 3 tablespoons cracker crumbs
- 3 tablespoons butter or margarine
   Salt and pepper

In a medium-size bowl, beat eggs with cream to blend; set aside.

Coat oysters with flour; shake off excess. Dip oysters in egg mixture, then roll in cracker crumbs to coat well; set slightly apart on a rack and let stand until surface is slightly dried (about 30 minutes). Cover and refrigerate remaining egg mixture while oysters are standing.

Melt 2 tablespoons of the butter in a wide frying pan over medium-high heat. Place oysters slightly apart in pan. Cook, turning once, until golden on both sides (about 2 minutes). Lift oysters from pan, drain on paper towels, and keep warm.

Melt remaining 1 tablespoon butter in pan; add egg mixture. Cook, lifting cooked portion with a wide spatula to let uncooked eggs flow underneath, until eggs are set but still moist. Slide eggs out of pan onto a warm platter; top with oysters. Season to taste with salt and pepper. Makes 2 servings.—*Mrs. Ester Brightman, Central Valley, CA*

Per serving: 478 calories, 15 g carbohydrates, 22 g protein, 37 g total fat (19 g saturated), 626 mg cholesterol, 487 mg sodium

STEAMED CLAMS WITH GARLIC

Plenty of fresh garlic—up to ½ cup, if you like—gives these succulent steamed clams an assertive flavor and a wonderful perfume.

- 1 teaspoon butter or margarine
- 2 medium-size onions, thinly sliced
- ¼ to ½ cup chopped garlic
- ¼ cup water
- 2 medium-size tomatoes (about 12 oz. *total*), chopped
- 1 teaspoon *each* paprika, dry thyme, and black pepper
- ⅛ teaspoon ground red pepper (cayenne)
- 1 cup dry white wine
- 36 small hard-shell clams in shell, scrubbed

Melt butter in a 5- to 6-quart pan over medium heat. Add onions, garlic, and water. Cook, stirring often, until liquid has evaporated and onions are soft (about 10 minutes).

Stir in tomatoes, paprika, thyme, black pepper, and red pepper; cook, uncovered, for 5 minutes. Add wine and bring to a boil over high heat. Add clams; reduce heat, cover, and boil gently until shells pop open (about 10 minutes).

To serve, ladle clams and tomato sauce into wide individual bowls;

discard any unopened clams. Makes 4 servings.—*Susie Wyshak, San Francisco*

Per serving: 184 calories, 19 g carbohydrates, 13 g protein, 2 g total fat (0.7 g saturated) 30 mg cholesterol, 71 mg sodium

PUGET SOUND STEAMED CLAMS

Serve clams and rice in wide soup bowls, with plenty of crusty bread.

- ¼ cup olive oil or salad oil
- 1 large onion, chopped
- 2 cloves garlic, minced or pressed
- 1 teaspoon *each* dry basil and dry oregano
- ¼ teaspoon fennel seeds, crushed (optional)
- 3 tablespoons chopped parsley
- 1 cup dry white wine or chicken broth
- 1 bottle (about 8 oz.) clam juice
- 20 to 30 small hard-shell clams in shell, scrubbed
- 2 medium-size tomatoes (about 12 oz. *total*), seeded and chopped
- 2 cups cooked rice

Heat oil in a 5- to 6-quart pan over medium heat. Add onion and garlic; cook, stirring often, until onion is soft. Stir in basil, oregano, fennel seeds (if used), and parsley. Add wine and clam juice. Bring to a boil; then reduce heat, cover, and simmer gently for about 5 minutes.

Add clams, cover, and simmer until shells pop open (10 to 12 minutes); stir often, pushing unopened clams down into broth. Stir in tomatoes and rice, cover, and continue to simmer until heated through. To serve, ladle clams and rice into shallow individual bowls; discard any unopened clams. Makes 4 servings. —*B. W., Mercer Island, WA*

Per serving: 378 calories, 40 g carbohydrates, 12 g protein, 15 g total fat (2 g saturated), 19 mg cholesterol, 176 mg sodium

PASTA WITH SAKE CLAM SAUCE

Here's an interesting variation on a traditional Italian dish; robust flavor and time-saving preparation make it a standout. Vermicelli or other tender pasta is sauced with sake and chopped clams, then tossed with Parmesan cheese, hot red pepper, and fresh parsley.

10 ounces dry vermicelli or thin spaghetti

2 cans (about 6½ oz. *each*) chopped clams

¾ cup finely chopped onion

2 cloves garlic, minced or pressed

1 cup sake or dry vermouth

2 tablespoons drained capers

¼ cup *each* finely chopped parsley and grated Parmesan cheese

About ⅛ teaspoon crushed red pepper flakes

In a 5- to 6-quart pan, cook vermicelli in about 3 quarts boiling water until just tender to bite (8 to 10 minutes); or cook according to package directions.

Meanwhile, drain clams, reserving ½ cup of the juice. In a wide frying pan, combine the reserved ½ cup clam juice, onion, garlic, and ¼ cup of the sake. Cook over high heat, stirring, until mixture is reduced by about three-fourths. Add remaining ¾ cup sake, clams, and capers; reduce heat and simmer for about 3 minutes.

Drain pasta well and transfer to a warm wide bowl. Add clam sauce and mix gently until almost all liquid has been absorbed. Sprinkle with parsley, cheese, and red pepper flakes; mix again. Makes 4 servings.
—Laura Wyckoff, Portland

Per serving: 433 calories, 60 g carbohydrates, 24 g protein, 4 g total fat (1 g saturated), 36 mg cholesterol, 331 mg sodium

SESAME-GINGER STEAMED MUSSELS

Mussels steamed in a light wine broth are infused with Asian flavors.

2 tablespoons Oriental sesame oil

1½ tablespoons minced fresh ginger

3 cloves garlic, minced or pressed

2 green onions, thinly sliced

2 tablespoons soy sauce

1 cup dry white wine or water

1 cup chicken broth

2 pounds mussels in shell, scrubbed

1 tablespoon cornstarch blended with 1 tablespoon cold water

¼ cup chopped cilantro

In a 4- to 5-quart pan, combine oil, ginger, and garlic; stir over medium-high heat for 1 minute. Remove from heat; stir in onions, soy sauce, wine, and broth. Pull beard from each mussel with a swift tug. Add mussels to broth, cover, and bring to a boil. Then reduce heat and simmer until mussels pop open (6 to 8 minutes). With a slotted spoon, transfer mussels to a serving bowl; keep warm. Discard any unopened mussels.

Stir cornstarch mixture into cooking liquid. Bring to a boil over high heat, stirring; mix in cilantro. Pour sauce over mussels. Makes 3 servings.
—Janie Bogner, Vallejo, CA

Per serving: 246 calories, 10 g carbohydrates, 12 g protein, 12 g total fat (2 g saturated), 25 mg cholesterol, 1,277 mg sodium

MUSSELS & MILLET IN CURRY SAUCE

Don't be dismayed that millet is a major ingredient of most bird-seed mixtures. It's so rich in protein, B vitamins, and iron—and tastes so delicious—that it's a dietary mainstay in much of the world. Here, it cooks in a curry-spiced broth to make a fluffy setting for steamed mussels.

1 tablespoon salad oil

1 large onion, thinly sliced

1 tablespoon minced fresh ginger

1 teaspoon *each* mustard seeds and ground coriander

½ teaspoon *each* ground cumin and ground red pepper (cayenne)

¼ teaspoon ground turmeric

3 cups chicken broth

2 small tomatoes (about 8 oz. *total*), chopped

1 cup millet, rinsed and drained

1½ pounds mussels in shell, scrubbed

Salt and pepper

Plain yogurt

Heat oil in a 5- to 6-quart pan over medium-high heat. Add onion and ginger; cook, stirring often, until onion is soft (about 5 minutes). Stir in mustard seeds, coriander, cumin, red pepper, and turmeric. Add broth and tomatoes; bring to a boil.

Add millet to pan. Reduce heat, cover, and simmer for 15 minutes. Meanwhile, pull beard from each mussel with a swift tug.

Add mussels to pan; cover and simmer until millet is tender to bite and mussels pop open (6 to 8 minutes). Season to taste with salt and pepper. Ladle mussels and millet into bowls; discard any unopened mussels. Offer yogurt to add to taste. Makes 3 servings.—Emily Bader, Bothell, WA

Per serving: 435 calories, 64 g carbohydrates, 20 g protein, 11 g total fat (2 g saturated fat), 19 mg cholesterol, 257 mg sodium

SHRIMP CHINESE

Prepare onion and celery

Sauté mushrooms and other vegetables until tender-crisp

Mix cream sauce, vegetables, cashews, water chestnuts, shrimp

Put crisp noodles in dish; add shrimp mixture, top with noodles

Bake, uncovered, in moderate oven (350°) 35 to 40 minutes

JACK FAGAN

1955 to 1958

As any student of history—even culinary history—can attest, progress doesn't always mean continuous improvement. So it is that many recipes from the mid to late 1950s appear, if not unappealing, at least rather quaint by modern standards. In retrospect, it seems we were a bit too eager to embrace the multitude of canned, frozen, and packaged foods that filled our ever-expanding supermarket shelves. Perhaps this trend reflected the shift of Westerners to suburbia (even Sunset moved its editorial offices from downtown San Francisco to quieter Menlo Park at the beginning of the 1950s). Or maybe we were watching too much television!

In any event—canned chow mein noodles notwithstanding—there's almost nothing authentically Asian about cream-sauced Shrimp Chinese from 1957. Tomato Paste Salad and Cheddar Chicken Casserole (which originally called for "1 package frozen chicken breasts") still taste delicious, though we've updated the casserole to start with fresh chicken. (You may want to make further adjustments and use lower-fat versions of both recipes' prepared ingredients.)

Some of the dishes from this period do show the fresh simplicity and sophistication which helped define the future of Western food. One satisfying example is Vegetable Casserole, a vegetarian entrée from 1956.

CHEDDAR CHICKEN CASSEROLE

Chunks of chicken and crunchy cashews turn this macaroni and cheese casserole into company fare. It's a good choice for a potluck supper.

- 3 green onions, cut up
- 3 celery tops
- 2 chicken breast halves (about 1 lb. total), rinsed
- 1 cup dry elbow macaroni, cooked and drained
- 1 cup (about 4 oz.) shredded Cheddar cheese
- ½ cup dry-roasted cashews
- 2 cans (about 10¾ oz. each) condensed cream of chicken soup
- ¾ cup crushed Cheddar cheese crackers

In a 2½- to 3-quart pan, combine about 6 cups water, onions, and celery. Bring to a boil over high heat. Add chicken and return to a boil. Cover tightly, remove from heat, and let stand until meat in thickest part is no longer pink; cut to test (about 20 minutes). If chicken is not done, return it to water, cover, and let stand longer, checking at 2- to 3-minute intervals. Remove chicken from water and let cool; then break meat into chunks and discard skin and bones. Strain cooking water; reserve ⅔ cup and discard remainder.

Spread macaroni in a greased 2-quart casserole. Sprinkle with cheese, then cover with chicken. Sprinkle with cashews. Stir together soup and the reserved ⅔ cup cooking water; pour over cashews. Sprinkle with crackers. Bake in a moderate oven (350°) until casserole is bubbly in center and browned on top (40 to 45 minutes). Makes 4 to 6 servings.—V. M., Berkeley, CA (August 1958)

VEGETABLE CASSEROLE

Sliced tomatoes keep this dish moist.

- 2 cups cooked spaghetti (1 cup uncooked)
- 1 package (about 10 oz.) frozen peas, partially thawed
- 1 medium-sized onion, chopped
- 1 green pepper, seeded and chopped
- 3 tomatoes, peeled and cut in ½-inch-thick slices
- 1 cup soft bread crumbs
- ½ teaspoon salt
- Pepper
- 1 cup (about 4 oz.) shredded Cheddar cheese

Place half of the spaghetti in a greased 1½- to 2-quart casserole. Mix the peas, onion, and green pepper; sprinkle half the mixture over spaghetti. Cover with half the tomato slices, then sprinkle with half the crumbs, ¼ teaspoon of the salt, and a dash of pepper. Repeat, using the remainder of the spaghetti, vegetable mixture, tomato, crumbs, salt, and another dash of pepper.

Cover and bake in a moderate oven (350°) for 30 minutes. Uncover and sprinkle with cheese. Return to oven for about 20 minutes, or until cheese melts and casserole is heated through. Serves 6 to 8.—*M. R., Sacramento, CA (August 1956)*

TOMATO PASTE SALAD

This red molded salad, flecked with green and white, has an appealing spicy flavor.

- 1 can (about 6 oz.) tomato paste
- 1½ cups water
- 1 package (about 3 oz.) lemon-flavored gelatin
- ½ pint (1 cup) cottage cheese
- ½ cup thinly sliced green onions
- ½ cup mayonnaise
- 1 tablespoon Worcestershire

In a 2-quart pan, stir together tomato paste and water; bring to a boil over medium-high heat. Remove from heat; add gelatin and stir until completely dissolved. Refrigerate until mixture begins to set. Using a rotary beater, beat in cottage cheese, onions, mayonnaise, and Worcestershire. Pour into a 1½-quart mold. Refrigerate until firm (at least 6 hours). To serve, unmold salad on a bed of **crisp greens.** Makes 8 servings. —*W. M., Covina, CA (September 1957)*

SHRIMP CHINESE

This colorful casserole is outstanding for its combination of crisp and soft textures.

- Triple recipe of White Sauce (page 61)
- 2 tablespoons butter or margarine
- 3 cups diagonally sliced celery
- 1 cup chopped onion
- 5 ounces mushrooms, sliced
- ¾ cup chopped green pepper
- 1 can (about 8 oz.) water chestnuts, drained and sliced or diced
- 6 ounces dry-roasted cashews, chopped
- 1 jar (about 4 oz.) sliced pimentos, drained
- ¾ pound cooked small shrimp
- 2 cans (about 3 oz. *each*) chow mein noodles

Prepare a triple recipe of White Sauce, using a 2-quart pan.

Melt butter in a wide frying pan over medium-high heat. Add celery, onion, mushrooms, and green pepper; cook, stirring often, until onion is tender-crisp. Stir in water chestnuts, cashews, pimentos, and shrimp. Add White Sauce and stir gently to mix well.

Spread half the noodles in a buttered 3½-quart casserole; cover with shrimp mixture, then top with remaining noodles. Bake in a moderate oven (350°) until bubbly and heated through (35 to 40 minutes). Makes 6 to 8 servings.—*W. M. J., Seattle (April 1957)*

VEGETABLE CASSEROLE

Sprinkle half of vegetable mixture over the layer of spaghetti

Top with tomato slices, crumbs, and seasonings; repeat layers

After casserole bakes for 30 minutes, uncover, top with cheese

Spoon down in casserole so each person gets some of each layer

V·E·G·E·T·A·R·I·A·N
E·N·T·R·E·E·S

No matter what their reasons for choosing meatless main dishes, the cooks who share ideas for vegetarian cooking in Kitchen Cabinet have always been imaginative. "As we live some distance from the stores, and my husband drives home every day for lunch, I am occasionally rather put to it to provide an interesting meal out of supplies on hand," explained the creator of Carrot Ingenuity in 1936. Today's equivalent of that innovative dish is Zucchini-Carrot Pizza Crust with Mushrooms (page 140). • During the Great Depression, thrifty rice, nut, and bean entrées such as a 1931 Kidney Bean Loaf were popular—though sometimes challenging. "Too much baking or too hot an oven will cause it to melt," warned the contributor. You'll have no such problems with Lentil-Nut Shepherd's Pie (facing page). • Pasta has always been popular for meatless meals. "Try Better Macaroni and Cheese," urged a 1935 reader, "and see if you do not agree with me that the addition of dry mustard is a real improvement to macaroni and cheese." Now it's Dijon mustard that makes the difference, as in Artichoke Pesto Pasta (page 137).

LENTIL-NUT SHEPHERD'S PIE

Like the traditional shepherd's pie, this savory dish is topped with spoonfuls of mashed potato. The filling, though, is made without the usual beef or lamb; it's a combination of herb-seasoned lentils, bread crumbs, and crunchy walnuts.

1½ cups (about 12 oz.) lentils
2 cloves garlic, minced or pressed
1½ teaspoons *each* dry thyme and dry savory
½ teaspoon rubbed sage
5½ cups canned vegetable broth
1 cup chopped walnuts
2 cups soft whole wheat bread crumbs
2 pounds thin-skinned potatoes, peeled and cut into 2-inch chunks
1 cup (about 4 oz.) shredded sharp Cheddar cheese

Sort through lentils, discarding any debris. Rinse and drain lentils; place in a 3- to 4-quart pan and add garlic, thyme, savory, sage, and 3½ cups of the broth. Bring to a boil over high heat; then reduce heat, cover, and simmer until lentils are tender to bite (25 to 30 minutes). Remove from heat and stir in walnuts and bread crumbs.

While lentils are simmering, combine potato chunks and remaining 2 cups broth in a 2- to 3-quart pan. Bring to a boil over high heat; then reduce heat, cover, and simmer until potatoes mash easily (15 to 20 minutes). Drain, reserving liquid. Leaving potatoes in pan, beat or mash them until smooth; then mix in ½ cup of the reserved liquid. Stir in cheese.

Stir remaining potato-cooking liquid into lentil mixture; spoon into an oiled shallow 2- to 2½-quart baking dish. Drop potatoes in spoonfuls onto lentil mixture. Bake in a 375° oven until potatoes are deep golden (35 to 40 minutes). Makes 6 servings. — *Patricia Stearns, Fresno, CA*

Per serving: 570 calories, 72 g carbohydrates, 28 g protein, 21 g total fat (5 g saturated), 20 mg cholesterol, 1,138 mg sodium

CURRIED GARBANZOS

Serve this spicy bean stew over rice, perhaps with toppings of raisins, chutney, and peanuts on the side.

3 tablespoons salad oil
1 large onion, finely chopped
3 cloves garlic, minced or pressed
1 tablespoon minced fresh ginger
1 large tomato (about 8 oz.), chopped
1½ teaspoons ground cumin
1 teaspoon ground coriander
½ teaspoon *each* ground red pepper (cayenne) and ground turmeric
2 cans (about 15 oz. *each*) garbanzo beans, drained and rinsed
¾ cup water
2 tablespoons lime juice
¼ cup chopped cilantro (optional)
Lime wedges

Heat oil in a wide frying pan over medium heat. Add onion, garlic, and ginger; cook, stirring often, until onion is lightly browned. Add tomato; cook, stirring, until almost all liquid has evaporated. Add cumin, coriander, red pepper, and turmeric; reduce heat to low and stir until spices are aromatic (3 to 5 minutes). Add garbanzos and water. Bring to a boil; then reduce heat, cover, and simmer, stirring occasionally, until mixture is thick (about 20 minutes).

Stir lime juice into garbanzo mixture; pour mixture into a serving bowl and sprinkle with cilantro, if desired. Serve with lime wedges. Makes 4 to 6 servings.—*Leila Advani, Santa Clara, CA*

Per serving: 223 calories, 25 g carbohydrates, 7 g protein, 11 g total fat (1 g saturated), 0 mg cholesterol, 196 mg sodium

TORTELLINI WITH MUSHROOM-CHEESE SAUCE

Ready-made tortellini—fresh, frozen, or dried—offer a shortcut to elegant entrées like this one. The plump pasta rings are topped with a garlic- and basil-accented mushroom sauce that's mellowed with cream cheese. Serve with sesame breadsticks.

1 package (about 12 oz.) frozen tortellini, 12 ounces fresh tortellini, or 1 package (7 to 8 oz.) dry tortellini
1 tablespoon butter or margarine
1 pound mushrooms, finely chopped
3 cloves garlic, minced or pressed
1 tablespoon minced fresh basil or 1 teaspoon dry basil
2 small packages (about 3 oz. *each*) cream cheese, cut into chunks
¾ cup milk
Parsley sprigs

In a 5- to 6-quart pan, cook tortellini in about 3 quarts boiling water until just tender to bite (15 to 20 minutes for frozen pasta, 4 to 6 minutes for fresh, 15 to 20 minutes for dry); or cook according to package directions.

Meanwhile, melt butter in a wide frying pan over medium-high heat. Add mushrooms, garlic, and basil; cook, stirring often, until all liquid has evaporated and mushrooms are beginning to brown (10 to 12 minutes). Add cream cheese and milk; cook, stirring, until cheese is melted and sauce just comes to a boil.

Drain tortellini well. Remove sauce from heat, add tortellini, and mix gently. Spoon pasta and sauce onto individual plates and garnish with parsley sprigs. Makes 4 servings.—*Linda Lum, Tacoma, WA*

Per serving: 488 calories, 49 g carbohydrates, 21 g protein, 24 g total fat (12 g saturated), 108 mg cholesterol, 563 mg sodium

LINGUINE WITH FRESH TOMATO SAUCE

Served hot or at room temperature, this simple pasta dish is fresh, pretty, and perfect for a summer supper. The sauce combines Roma tomatoes, sweet yellow peppers, and plenty of fragrant fresh basil.

- 3 pounds pear-shaped (Roma-type) tomatoes, coarsely chopped
- 2 large yellow bell peppers (about 1 lb. *total*), seeded and chopped
- 1 cup lightly packed slivered fresh basil; or ¼ cup dry basil
- 2 cloves garlic, minced or pressed
- 12 ounces fresh or dry linguine
  Salt and pepper
  Basil sprigs (optional)
  About ½ cup grated Parmesan cheese

In a 3- to 4-quart pan, combine two-thirds of the tomatoes, two-thirds of the bell peppers, half the slivered basil, and all the garlic. Cook over medium heat, stirring often, until tomatoes begin to fall apart (about 20 minutes). If serving hot, keep hot. If serving at room temperature, let cool; then cover and hold at room temperature for up to 6 hours.

In a 5- to 6-quart pan, cook linguine in about 3 quarts boiling water until just tender to bite (1 to 2 minutes for fresh pasta, 8 to 10 minutes for dry pasta); or cook according to package directions. Drain well. To serve hot, pour pasta into a warm wide bowl. To serve at room temperature, rinse pasta with cold water until cool, then drain well and pour into a wide bowl.

Stir remaining tomatoes, bell peppers, and slivered basil into sauce; season to taste with salt and pepper. Spoon hot sauce over hot pasta, cool sauce over cool pasta; mix gently. Garnish with basil sprigs, if desired. Offer cheese to add to taste. Makes 4 to 6 servings.—*Joanne Benvenist, Culver City, CA*

Per serving: 322 calories, 58 g carbohydrates, 15 g protein, 5 g total fat (2 g saturated), 56 mg cholesterol, 194 mg sodium

PASTA SALAD WITH ASPARAGUS & TOFU

When the weather is warm, try this refreshing green-and-golden salad for lunch or a light dinner. Start by marinating tofu in a basil dressing, then stir in mostaccioli and tender-crisp asparagus.

- Basil Dressing (recipe follows)
- 8 ounces regular tofu, rinsed, drained, and cut into ½-inch cubes
- 1 pound asparagus
- 6 ounces dry mostaccioli or penne

Prepare Basil Dressing. Add tofu and stir to coat, then let stand for at least 15 minutes or up to 1 hour.

Snap off and discard tough ends of asparagus; peel stalks, if desired. Then cut asparagus diagonally into 1½-inch pieces. In a 5- to 6-quart pan, cook asparagus, uncovered, in about 3 quarts boiling water until tender when pierced (about 4 minutes). Lift asparagus from pan with a slotted spoon; immerse in cold water until cool, then drain well.

Add pasta to boiling water and cook until just tender to bite (10 to 12 minutes; or time according to package directions). Drain, rinse with cold water until cool, and drain again. Add pasta and asparagus to tofu mixture; mix gently. Makes 6 servings.—*Linda Strader, Amado, AZ*

BASIL DRESSING. In a large bowl, stir together ½ cup **seasoned rice vinegar** (or ½ cup white wine vinegar plus 2 teaspoons sugar), ¼ cup grated **Parmesan cheese,** 3 tablespoons minced **fresh basil** or 1 tablespoon dry basil, 3 tablespoons **olive oil,** 1 tablespoon **Dijon mustard,** and 1 clove **garlic,** minced or pressed.

Per serving: 239 calories, 28 g carbohydrates, 9 g protein, 10 g total fat (2 g saturated), 3 mg cholesterol, 524 mg sodium

PASTA WITH BASIL-CILANTRO SAUCE

Cilantro adds pungent flavor to this rich, creamy pesto sauce for linguine. At the table, pass a chunk of Parmesan or Romano cheese to grate over each serving.

- 1½ cups firmly packed fresh basil leaves
- ½ cup firmly packed cilantro leaves
- 3 cloves garlic, peeled
- ¾ cup grated Parmesan cheese
- ½ cup olive oil
- ¼ cup *each* pine nuts and walnut pieces
- ½ cup half-and-half
- ¼ cup butter or margarine, melted
  Salt and pepper
- 1 pound dry linguine

In a food processor or blender, combine basil, cilantro, garlic, cheese, and oil; whirl until until smoothly puréed. Add pine nuts and walnuts; whirl until nuts are coarsely chopped. Add half-and-half and butter; whirl just until blended.

BAKED QUESADILLAS

These crisp half-moons are filled with jack or Cheddar cheese, a tangy chili sauce, fresh tomatoes, red onion, and cilantro. While the quesadillas are in the oven, prepare a mixed lettuce salad with sliced avocados to complete a quick lunch or supper.

    Chili Sauce (recipe follows)
 4 flour tortillas (*each* 7 to 9 inches in diameter)
1½ cups (about 6 oz.) shredded jack or Cheddar cheese
 2 small pear-shaped (Roma-type) tomatoes (about 4 oz. *total*), thinly sliced crosswise
 ½ cup chopped red onion
 ⅓ cup lightly packed cilantro leaves (optional)
    About ½ cup purchased green taco sauce

Prepare Chili Sauce.

Lightly brush both sides of each tortilla with water. Spread a fourth of the Chili Sauce over half of each tortilla; evenly distribute a fourth each of the cheese, tomatoes, onion, and cilantro (if used) over sauce on each tortilla. Fold plain half of tortilla over to cover filling.

Set quesadillas slightly apart on a large baking sheet.

Bake in a 500° oven until tortillas are crisp and golden (7 to 10 minutes). Transfer quesadillas to individual plates with a wide spatula; offer taco sauce to add to taste. Makes 4 servings.—*Ann Angulo, Provo, UT*

CHILI SAUCE. In a small bowl, stir together ¼ cup **reduced-calorie or regular mayonnaise,** 2 teaspoons **white wine vinegar,** and 1 teaspoon **chili powder.** Season to taste with **salt** and **pepper.**

Per serving: 341 calories, 27 g carbohydrates, 14 g protein, 20 g total fat (9 g saturated), 50 mg cholesterol, 707 mg sodium

AVOCADOWICHES

Stuffed with ripe avocado, vegetables, and Cheddar cheese, these pocket-bread sandwiches are a treat for lunch or a light supper. Adjust the amounts of garlic salt and hot pepper seasoning to make the filling as spicy as you like.

 1 large firm-ripe avocado, pitted, peeled, and diced
 1 tablespoon lemon juice
 ½ cup *each* thinly sliced green onions and diced celery
 1 can (about 2¼ oz.) sliced ripe olives, drained
 2 hard-cooked large eggs, chopped
 1 small tomato (about 4 oz.), peeled, seeded, and chopped
 ½ cup shredded Cheddar cheese
    Garlic salt and liquid hot pepper seasoning
 3 cups shredded iceberg lettuce
 4 warm pita breads (*each* about 6 inches in diameter), cut crosswise into halves

In a medium-size bowl, combine avocado and lemon juice; mash avocado with a fork, mixing in lemon juice thoroughly. Then stir in onions, celery, olives, eggs, tomato, and cheese. Season to taste with garlic salt and hot pepper seasoning. (At this point, you may cover and refrigerate for up to 2 hours.)

To serve, divide lettuce equally among pita bread halves; then spoon in avocado mixture. Makes 4 servings.—*K. H., Sunnyvale, CA*

Per serving: 380 calories, 43 g carbohydrates, 14 g protein, 18 g total fat (5 g saturated), 121 mg cholesterol, 607 mg sodium

JICAMA BURRITO BUNDLES

The wrapping is certainly familiar, but the filling is out of the ordinary. These crisp-baked tortillas hold a mixture of brown rice, Cheddar, red bell pepper, and crunchy jicama.

 4 large flour tortillas (*each* about 10 inches in diameter)
 2 tablespoons salad oil
 1 large onion, chopped
 1 small red bell pepper (about 5 oz.), seeded and chopped
 1 cup peeled, chopped jicama
 1 teaspoon cumin seeds
1½ cups cooked long-grain brown rice
 ⅓ cup chopped cilantro
1½ cups (about 6 oz.) shredded Cheddar cheese
    Salt
    Homemade or purchased salsa

Brush tortillas lightly with hot water; then stack, wrap in foil, and heat in a 350° oven until warm (10 to 15 minutes).

Meanwhile, heat oil in a wide frying pan over high heat. Add onion, bell pepper, jicama, and cumin seeds. Cook, stirring often, until vegetables begin to brown (8 to 10 minutes). Remove from heat. Stir rice, cilantro, and cheese into vegetable mixture. Season to taste with salt.

Remove tortillas from oven; increase oven temperature to 400°. Spoon a fourth of the rice mixture into center of each tortilla. Fold sides and ends of tortillas over filling to enclose; then place bundles, seam side down, in a shallow 10- by 15-inch baking pan. Brush lightly with water and bake until golden brown and crisp (about 30 minutes). Serve with salsa. Makes 4 servings. —*Christine Hanover, Lewiston, CA*

Per serving: 535 calories, 58 g carbohydrates, 19 g protein, 26 g total fat (11 g saturated), 45 mg cholesterol, 535 mg sodium

Homemade cookies were a popular
after-school treat in the 1960s

A SAMPLING FROM
—1959 to 1962—

As late as 1962, a certain formality still prevailed in the West. If Kitchen Cabinet's illustrator is to be trusted, one might don a pair of gloves to go out shopping for flank steak! When Tony Bennett first sang "I Left My Heart in San Francisco" that same year, the city's skyline was still gentle: the silhouette shown in the drawing alongside Asparagus Salad (facing page) does not yet include the jauntily pointed Transamerica building.

Chicken, once top choice for Sunday dinners and special occasions, had become more economical, and recipes such as Parmesan Chicken were mainstays for family suppers. Of course, hostesses might also serve this dish to company, perhaps preceding it with an antipasto such as Tuna-Olive Appetizer.

The dessert selections from these years show that today's obsession with chocolate is not entirely new—our editors remarked that Milk Chocolate Pie's contributor created her recipe from the memory of a dessert tasted 10 years earlier.

Our first course is an antipasto
(appetizer) served in the Italian style

TUNA-OLIVE APPETIZER

1 can (about 6⅛ oz.) tuna, drained
1 can (about 6 oz.) pitted ripe olives
1 small can (2 to 4 oz.) whole or sliced mushrooms
1 can (about 14 oz.) water-packed artichoke hearts
1 jar (about 3¼ oz.) cocktail onions
1 cup purchased giardiniera (Italian pickled vegetables)
1 can (about 8 oz.) tomato sauce
3 tablespoons olive oil or salad oil
¼ cup red wine vinegar

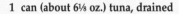

Turn tuna into a bowl, breaking it neatly into fairly large chunks. Drain olives, mushrooms, artichokes, onions, and giardiniera. Then add to tuna along with the tomato sauce, oil, and vinegar. Toss to blend together well, being careful not to mash the tuna. For best flavor, chill for several hours or overnight. Serve as you would a shrimp cocktail, with **saltine crackers.** Makes 8 servings.—K. J., San Jose, CA (October 1959)

FLANK STEAK STRIPS SAUTÉ

1 flank steak (about 1¾ lbs.)
1 teaspoon meat tenderizer
3 tablespoons flour
¼ cup olive oil or salad oil
1 large onion, thinly sliced
1 or 2 cloves garlic, minced or mashed
6 medium-sized carrots, thinly sliced
¼ teaspoon *each* thyme and marjoram
⅔ cup condensed beef broth
½ cup dry red wine

Sprinkle steak on both sides with meat tenderizer, pierce all over with a fork, and let

stand 30 minutes. Slice meat crosswise into strips about ¼ inch wide and mix with the flour until lightly coated. In a large frying pan, heat 2 tablespoons of the oil. Add onion and garlic; sauté until onion is soft. Remove onion and garlic from pan; reserve. Add remaining oil to pan and sauté the meat strips, turning frequently, until well browned. Return onion and garlic to pan along with carrots, thyme, marjoram, broth, and wine. Cover; simmer until carrots are tender to bite (about 15 minutes). Serves 4 to 6.—D. C., Sherman Oaks, CA (March 196

JACK FAGAN

A sale on flank steaks inspired the
experiments that led to this recipe

PARMESAN CHICKEN

2 cups fresh bread crumbs
¾ cup grated Parmesan cheese
¼ cup chopped parsley
1 clove garlic, mashed
½ teaspoon salt
⅛ teaspoon freshly ground pepper
2 chickens (2½ to 3 lbs. *each*)
   or 6 to 8 chicken breast halves
⅓ cup melted butter or margarine
2 tablespoons butter or margarine

Combine the crumbs with Parmesan cheese, parsley, garlic, salt, and pepper. Cut the chickens into serving-size pieces; rinse and pat dry. Dip each piece into the ⅓ cup melted butter, then dip into the crumb mixture to coat. Arrange chicken pieces in a large, shallow baking dish so they don't overlap. Dot with the 2 tablespoons butter. Bake in a moderate oven (350°) for about 1 hour. Makes 6 to 8 servings.—*E. M., San Mateo, CA (October 1960)*

Serve this easy baked chicken to warm up a winter evening

ASPARAGUS SALAD

½ pounds fresh asparagus, trimmed
1 can (about 10¾ oz.) condensed beef broth
2 slices onion
1 carrot, sliced
1 bay leaf
½ teaspoon *each* salt and black peppercorns
   Romaine lettuce leaves
1 can (about 2 oz.) anchovy fillets
   Ripe olives and hard-cooked egg quarters
   Tarragon-Anchovy Dressing (recipe follows)

...e asparagus into 6 bundles. Lay flat in a ...rge pan. Add broth, onion, carrot, bay leaf, salt, and peppercorns. Boil gently, uncovered, until tender, 8 to 10 minutes. Lift from stock; chill.

To serve, remove string and arrange each bundle of asparagus on a salad plate with lettuce; crisscross 2 anchovy fillets on top of each bundle. Garnish with olives and egg quarters. Sprinkle with dressing. Serves 6.—*H. N., San Francisco (April 1962)*

Tarragon-Anchovy Dressing. Blend well 6 tablespoons **salad oil**, 5 tablespoons **tarragon wine vinegar**, 1 tablespoon finely chopped **anchovies**, ½ teaspoon **dry mustard**, 1 teaspoon *each* **sugar**, minced **parsley**, and snipped **chives**, and **pepper** to taste.

Chilled poached asparagus spears with flavorful tarragon-anchovy dressing

MILK CHOCOLATE PIE

1 large bar (about 10 oz.) milk chocolate, at room temperature
¼ cups milk
2 tablespoons *each* cornstarch and flour
2 egg yolks, well beaten
1 teaspoon vanilla
1 tablespoon butter
   Baked 9-inch pie shell
   Sweetened whipped cream

...sing a vegetable peeler, pare down the ...ng side of the chocolate bar to make a few ...ng curls to use for garnish; set these aside. ...ald 2 cups of the milk in the top of a double boiler over gently boiling water. Chop remaining chocolate; stir into the scalded milk until melted.

Blend the remaining ¼ cup milk with the cornstarch and flour until smooth. Gradually add flour mixture to chocolate mixture; stir until thickened. Add some of the hot mixture to the egg yolks, then slowly blend this back into the hot mixture. Cook, stirring, until thickened; remove from heat, stir in vanilla and butter, and let cool slightly. Spread in pie shell; chill. Top with whipped cream and chocolate curls. —*G. H., Berkeley, CA (January 1960)*

This creamy, smooth pie melts in your mouth and tastes like candy

A·C·C·O·M·P·A·N·I·M·E·N·T·S

Potato Flitters, Spudzdelux, My Own Idea About Squash—is this the usually earnest Kitchen Cabinet, or some zany culinary situation comedy? These are all names of actual accompaniment recipes from the 1930s. Reading a 1929 recipe for Peanut Butter Macaroni, however, today's cook may well feel it would have been better to limit the whimsy to the title and keep it out of the ingredients! • Completing a dinner menu usually means adding vegetables to supplement the entrée. But pasta works well too: "These baked noodles can be served in place of potato—they're especially good with chicken or pot roast," our editors suggested in introducing Baked Noodles & Cottage Cheese. This 1943 recipe was an early version of the venerable Noodles Romanoff (page 151) from 1956. • Rounding out a meal without undue fuss has always been an important goal. A California reader recommended her 1931 Broiled Zucchini because "there are no stove dishes to wash afterwards." We can't quite make that claim for Posh Squash (page 157). It can, however, be prepared well in advance, another useful consideration for hassle-free cooking.

FROSTED ZUCCHINI OR POTATO ROUNDS

Thick zucchini or potato slices topped with an herb- and cheese-seasoned mayonnaise are nice for a side dish or a hot appetizer.

- 3 medium-size zucchini or thin-skinned potatoes (1 to 1¼ lbs. *total*)
- ½ cup mayonnaise
- ¼ cup thinly sliced green onions
- 3 tablespoons grated Parmesan cheese
- ½ teaspoon dry oregano
- ⅛ teaspoon garlic powder
   Dash of pepper
   About ¼ cup fine cracker crumbs

If using zucchini, cut crosswise into ¾-inch slices. If using potatoes, scrub and cut crosswise into ¾-inch slices.

Arrange zucchini or potato slices in a single layer on a steamer rack; cover and steam over about 1½ inches boiling water until barely tender when pierced (3 to 5 minutes for zucchini, about 15 minutes for potatoes). Drain vegetables and let cool; then gently pat dry.

In a small bowl, stir together mayonnaise, onions, cheese, oregano, garlic powder, and pepper. Frost one side of each vegetable slice with mayonnaise mixture, then dip frosted side in cracker crumbs.

Place frosted vegetable slices on a baking sheet, crumb side up. (At this point, you may cover and refrigerate for up to 8 hours; bring to room temperature before continuing.)

Broil vegetable slices about 4 inches below heat until topping is lightly browned (3 to 6 minutes). Makes 6 servings.—*A.Y., Castro Valley, CA*

Per serving of zucchini: 169 calories, 6 g carbohydrates, 3 g protein, 16 g total fat (3 g saturated), 13 mg cholesterol, 192 mg sodium

Per serving of potatoes: 227 calories, 18 g carbohydrates, 3 g protein, 16 g total fat (3 g saturated), 13 mg cholesterol, 196 mg sodium

ITALIAN OVEN-FRIED POTATOES

Fresh herbs, garlic, and Parmesan cheese enliven these richly browned potato chunks. They're good with lemon-drizzled chicken breasts.

- 2 pounds red thin-skinned potatoes, scrubbed and cut into 1-inch chunks
- 1 to 2 tablespoons olive oil
- 2 tablespoons *each* minced fresh oregano and minced fresh basil; or 2 teaspoons *each* dry oregano and dry basil
- 1 clove garlic, minced or pressed
- ⅓ cup grated Parmesan cheese
   Salt
   Oregano and basil sprigs (optional)

In a shallow 10- by 15-inch baking pan, mix potatoes and oil. Bake in a 475° oven until potatoes are richly browned (35 to 45 minutes). When potatoes begin to brown (but not before then), turn them over several times with a wide spatula.

Transfer potatoes to a serving bowl and sprinkle with minced oregano and basil, garlic, and 3 tablespoons of the cheese. Stir to mix; season to taste with salt. Sprinkle with remaining cheese; garnish with oregano and basil sprigs, if desired. Makes 4 servings.—*Mickey Strang, McKinleyville, CA*

Per serving: 264 calories, 42 g carbohydrates, 7 g protein, 8 g total fat (2 g saturated), 5 mg cholesterol, 141 mg sodium

CRUSTY POTATO CUPS

These savory potato-cheese cups are brown and crispy on the outside, soft and creamy within. To test for doneness, taste a few shreds of potato from the center of one cup; they should taste cooked, but should still be moist.

- 3 medium-size russet potatoes (about 1¼ lbs. *total*)
- 1 medium-size onion, minced
- 1¼ cups (about 5 oz.) shredded Swiss cheese
- ½ teaspoon salt
- ¼ teaspoon *each* pepper and ground nutmeg
   About 1½ tablespoons butter or margarine, at room temperature
   Paprika
- 12 thin tomato slices (from 2 or 3 medium-size tomatoes, peeled)
   Sour cream (optional)

Peel potatoes and coarsely shred into a bowl of water. When all have been shredded, lift from water and place on paper towels to blot up as much moisture as possible. Transfer potatoes to a large bowl; add onion, cheese, salt, pepper, and nutmeg. Mix well.

Generously butter twelve 2½-inch muffin cups; sprinkle butter lightly with paprika, then press potato mixture evenly into cups. Bake in a 450° oven until edges of cups are well browned and potato tastes done in center (about 45 minutes). Remove from oven and let cool for about 5 minutes.

Loosen edges of cups with a knife; then carefully lift out cups and invert each onto a tomato slice. Serve at once; offer sour cream to add to taste, if desired. Makes 12 potato cups. —*M. D., Morro Bay, CA*

Per potato cup: 102 thcalories, 10 g carbohydrates, 5 g protein, 5 g total fat (3 g saturated), 15 mg cholesterol, 142 mg sodium

TWO-WAY BAKED POTATOES

Bake potatoes in their jackets to make two irresistible dishes. The first night, serve fluffy mashed potatoes; a day or two later, offer crispy shells filled with crumbled bacon, green onions, and nippy Cheddar cheese. Accompanied with a substantial green salad, the second dish makes a perfect quick supper.

- 6 **medium-size russet potatoes (about 2¼ lbs. *total*), scrubbed**

    About ⅓ cup hot milk
- ¼ **cup butter or margarine, at room temperature**

    Salt and pepper
- ⅓ **cup butter or margarine, melted**
- 6 **slices bacon, crisply cooked, drained, and crumbled**
- ⅓ **cup thinly sliced green onions**
- ¾ **cup shredded Cheddar cheese**

Pierce each potato with a fork in several places. Bake in a 400° oven until poatoes feel soft when squeezed (45 minutes to 1 hour). Let stand until cool enough to handle; then cut each potato in half lengthwise and scoop out centers, leaving ⅛-inch-thick shells. Cover shells and refrigerate for up to 2 days.

To make mashed potatoes, place scooped-out potato centers in a large bowl and mash until smooth. Gradually add milk, beating until fluffy. Add the ¼ cup butter; beat until light and fluffy. Season to taste with salt and pepper.

To make baked potato skins, brush potato shells inside and out with the ⅓ cup butter. Place shells, cut side up, on a baking sheet. Bake in a 500° oven until browned and crisp (about 20 minutes). Sprinkle bacon, onions, and cheese evenly into potato shells. Then continue to bake just until cheese is melted (about 3 more minutes). Serve at once.

Makes 6 servings *each* of mashed potatoes and potato skins.—*M. M., Campbell, CA*

Per serving of mashed potatoes: 179 calories, 24 g carbohydrates, 3 g protein, 8 g total fat (5 g saturated), 23 mg cholesterol, 94 mg sodium

Per serving of potato skins: 209 calories, 6 g carbohydrates, 7 g protein, 18 g total fat (10 g saturated), 48 mg cholesterol, 297 mg sodium

FLUFFY POTATO CASSEROLE

A crisp onion topping provides a pleasing constrast to creamy mashed potatoes in this vegetable casserole. To double the recipe, use a 9- by 13-inch baking dish and increase the baking time to about 1 hour and 10 minutes. Cover the dish with foil if the onions begin to overbrown.

- 2 **cups mashed potatoes**
- 1 **large package (about 8 oz.) cream cheese, at room temperature**
- 1 **small onion, finely chopped**
- 2 **large eggs**
- 2 **tablespoons all-purpose flour**

    Salt and pepper
- 1 **can (about 2.8 oz.) French-fried onions**

In a large bowl, combine potatoes, cream cheese, chopped onion, eggs, and flour. Beat with an electric mixer on medium speed until ingredients are blended; then beat on high speed until light and fluffy. Season to taste with salt and pepper. Spoon into a greased 9-inch-square baking dish. (At this point, you may cover and refrigerate for up to 8 hours.)

Sprinkle French-fried onions evenly over potatoes. Bake, uncovered, in a 300° oven until heated through (about 35 minutes; about 45 minutes if refrigerated). Makes 6 to 8 servings.—*J.S., Sunnyvale, CA*

Per serving: 242 calories, 15 g carbohydrates, 6 g protein, 18 g total fat (8 g saturated), 98 mg cholesterol, 310 mg sodium

PAPRIKA POTATOES

Sweet Hungarian paprika and chopped onion season these simmered diced potatoes. Serve them topped with sour cream and shards of crisp bacon, as an accompaniment for roast chicken or pork loin.

- 4 **slices bacon, cut crosswise into ¼-inch-wide strips**
- 1 **medium-size onion, chopped**
- 1 **tablespoon sweet Hungarian or regular paprika**
- 1 **pound thin-skinned potatoes, scrubbed and cut into ½-inch cubes**

    About 1 cup water

    Salt and pepper

    Reduced-fat or regular sour cream

    Chopped parsley

Cook bacon in a wide frying pan over medium heat until crisp. Remove from pan with a slotted spoon and set aside. Pour off and discard all but 1 tablespoon drippings from pan. Add onion to pan and cook, stirring often, until soft.

Stir in paprika, potatoes, and 1 cup of the water. Bring to a boil; then reduce heat, cover, and simmer until potatoes are tender when pierced (about 15 minutes), stirring occasionally and adding more water as needed to prevent sticking. Season to taste with salt and pepper.

Top each serving of potatoes with a dollop of sour cream; sprinkle with parsley and bacon. Makes 4 servings.—*Ann Bartos Rushton, Denver*

Per serving: 172 calories, 25 g carbohydrates, 5 g protein, 6 g total fat (2 g saturated), 8 mg cholesterol, 128 mg sodium

ROCKY MOUNTAIN RACLETTE

Inspired by a classic Swiss Alpine dish, this Western *raclette* combines baked potatoes with bacon, onions, chiles, and cheese. Serve it with barbecued beef or chicken.

- 4 medium-size russet potatoes (about 1½ lbs. *total*), scrubbed
- 1 large mild white onion, thinly sliced and separated into rings
- ½ cup purchased Italian-style vinaigrette-type salad dressing
- ¼ cup butter or margarine, cut into small pieces
- 1 can (about 4 oz.) diced green chiles
- 10 slices bacon, crisply cooked, drained, and crumbled
- 1½ cups (about 6 oz.) shredded Swiss cheese

Pierce each potato with a fork in several places. Bake in a 400° oven until potatoes feel soft when squeezed (45 minutes to 1 hour). Meanwhile, place onion in a medium-size bowl. Pour salad dressing over onion and stir gently to mix; set aside.

Split each baked potato in half lengthwise. With a fork, lightly mash potato in each half; mix butter and chiles evenly into potatoes. Place potato halves in a large, shallow baking pan. Spoon onions and dressing evenly over potatoes; then sprinkle evenly with bacon and cheese. Broil 4 to 6 inches below heat until cheese is melted and bubbly (about 3 minutes). Makes 8 servings.—*S. H., Fort Collins, CO*

Per serving: 328 calories, 21 g carbohydrates, 11 g protein, 23 g total fat (10 g saturated), 42 mg cholesterol, 452 mg sodium

CHEESY CARAWAY POTATOES

Topped with Swiss cheese and buttery crumbs, this casserole of cubed potatoes in a creamy sauce is a good make-ahead choice.

- 1½ pounds thin-skinned potatoes, cooked, cooled, and cut into ½-inch cubes
- 5 tablespoons butter or margarine
- ⅓ cup thinly sliced green onions
- 3 tablespoons all-purpose flour
- 1½ cups chicken broth
- 1 teaspoon caraway seeds
- ½ teaspoon ground cumin
     Salt and ground white pepper
- 1 cup (about 4 oz.) shredded Swiss cheese
- ½ cup coarse soft bread crumbs
- ⅛ teaspoon paprika

Spread potatoes in a shallow 1-quart casserole; set aside. Melt butter in a 1½- to 2-quart pan over medium heat; measure 2 tablespoons of the melted butter and set aside. Then add onions to remaining melted butter in pan and cook, stirring often, until soft. Blend in flour and cook, stirring, until bubbly. Remove from heat and gradually stir in broth, caraway seeds, and cumin. Then return to heat and cook, stirring, until sauce boils and thickens. Season sauce to taste with salt and white pepper.

Pour sauce over potatoes and sprinkle with cheese. Combine bread crumbs with paprika and the reserved 2 tablespoons melted butter; sprinkle over cheese. (At this point, you may let cool, then cover and refrigerate for up to 8 hours.) Bake, uncovered, in a 400° oven until heated through (about 20 minutes; 30 to 35 minutes if refrigerated). Makes 4 to 6 servings.—*S. F., Irvine, CA*

Per serving: 340 calories, 32 g carbohydrates, 11 g protein, 19 g total fat (11 g saturated), 52 mg cholesterol, 510 mg sodium

SPICED SPINACH & POTATOES

Pan-fried potatoes don't have to be plain! These are combined with shredded spinach and spiced with coriander and ginger. You might serve the zesty dish with sautéed or broiled fish fillets or steaks; it's especially good with salmon.

- ¼ cup salad oil
- 1¼ pounds large russet potatoes, peeled and cut into ½-inch cubes
- 2 cloves garlic, minced or pressed
- 2 teaspoons ground coriander
- ½ teaspoon ground ginger
     About ½ cup water
- 12 ounces fresh spinach
     Salt and ground red pepper (cayenne)

Heat 3 tablespoons of the oil in a wide frying pan over medium-high heat. Add potatoes and cook, stirring occasionally, until well browned (10 to 15 minutes).

Reduce heat to low and add remaining 1 tablespoon oil, garlic, coriander, and ginger. Cook, stirring often, for 2 to 3 minutes. Add ½ cup of the water. Cover and simmer until potatoes are tender when pierced (5 to 10 minutes), adding more water as needed to prevent sticking.

Meanwhile, discard stems and any yellow or wilted leaves from spinach. Rinse spinach and drain well; then cut crosswise into ½-inch-wide strips.

Uncover pan and add spinach to potatoes. Increase heat to high and cook, stirring often, until spinach is wilted and almost all liquid has evaporated (about 2 minutes). Season to taste with salt and red pepper. Makes 4 servings.—*Betty Buckner, Port Angeles, WA*

Per serving: 241 calories, 26 g carbohydrates, 4 g protein, 14 g total fat (2 g saturated), 0 mg cholesterol, 59 mg sodium

FRUITED SWEET POTATO CASSEROLE

Accented with orange and pineapple, this sweet potato casserole is a good choice for a holiday dinner. You can prepare it a day ahead, then bake just before serving.

2½ to 3 pounds medium-size sweet potatoes or yams, scrubbed
1 can (about 15¼ oz.) pineapple tidbits, drained
1 tablespoon lemon juice
2 teaspoons grated orange peel
2 tablespoons firmly packed brown sugar
¼ cup butter or margarine

Place unpeeled sweet potatoes in a 5- to 6-quart pan and add enough water to cover. Bring to a boil over high heat; then reduce heat, partially cover, and boil gently until potatoes are tender when pierced (25 to 30 minutes). Drain, immerse in cold water until cool, and drain again. Then peel potatoes and cut into ½-inch-thick slices.

Spread a third of the potatoes in a greased 2-quart casserole; top with half the pineapple and sprinkle with half each of the lemon juice, orange peel, and sugar. Dot with 1 tablespoon of the butter. Top with half the remaining potatoes; then top with remaining pineapple, lemon juice, orange peel, and sugar. Dot with 1 more tablespoon butter. Cover with remaining potatoes and dot with remaining 2 tablespoons butter. (At this point, you may cover and refrigerate until next day.)

Bake, uncovered, in a 350° oven until casserole is heated through (35 to 40 minutes; about 45 minutes if refrigerated). Makes 8 to 10 servings. —K. S., Reno

Per serving: 200 calories, 35 g carbohydrates, 2 g protein, 6 g total fat (3 g saturated), 14 mg cholesterol, 67 mg sodium

SWEET POTATOES & APPLES CARAMEL

Serve this sweet, nutmeg-spiced vegetable-fruit casserole with a festive baked ham or alongside crisply browned roast pork or turkey.

About 4 medium-size sweet potatoes or yams (about 1¾ lbs. *total*), scrubbed
¼ cup granulated sugar
½ teaspoon salt
¼ teaspoon nutmeg
¼ cup butter or margarine, at room temperature
3 medium-size crisp, tart apples such as Granny Smith or Newtown Pippin (1 to 1¼ lbs. *total*), peeled, cored, and thinly sliced
⅔ cup firmly packed brown sugar

Cook, cool, peel, and slice sweet potatoes as directed for Fruited Sweet Potato Casserole (at left). Set aside.

In a small bowl, mix granulated sugar, salt, and nutmeg; thoroughly blend in butter with a fork.

Arrange a third of the sweet potatoes in a 2-quart casserole or 9-inch-square baking pan. Top evenly with a third of the apples, then a third of the sugar mixture.

Repeat layers 2 more times, using remaining sweet potatoes, apples, and sugar mixture. Cover and bake in a 350° oven until apples are tender when pierced (about 1 hour).

Remove from oven; uncover. Press brown sugar through a wire strainer over top of casserole to make an even layer. Then broil about 4 inches below heat until topping is melted and bubbly (2 to 3 minutes; watch closely to prevent scorching). Serve immediately. Makes 8 to 10 servings.—E. W., Northridge, CA

Per serving: 223 calories, 44 g carbohydrates, 1 g protein, 5 g total fat (3 g saturated), 14 mg cholesterol, 188 mg sodium

SWEET POTATO PUFF RAMEKINS

Spoon a spicy purée of yams and ripe banana into individual ramekins; then center each serving with a marshmallow and sprinkle with sliced almonds. During baking, the marshmallow hidden in each ramekin melts to form a sweet surprise.

1 large can (about 29 oz.) yams or sweet potatoes, drained
1 large ripe banana, mashed
3 tablespoons butter or margarine, at room temperature
2 large eggs, separated
¼ teaspoon *each* ground nutmeg and ground ginger
6 large marshmallows
3 tablespoons sliced almonds

Force yams, a portion at a time, through a potato ricer into a large bowl; or place in bowl and beat with an electric mixer until very smooth.

In a medium-size bowl, beat together banana, 2 tablespoons of the butter, egg yolks, nutmeg, and ginger until well blended; then stir banana mixture into yam mixture. In a small bowl, using clean beaters, beat egg whites with an electric mixer on high speed until they hold stiff peaks; then fold into yam mixture.

Use remaining 1 tablespoon butter to grease six ¾-cup ramekins. Divide yam mixture equally among ramekins; bury one marshmallow in each, then sprinkle with almonds. Set ramekins on a rimmed baking sheet. (Or spoon all the yam mixture into a well-buttered 8-inch-round baking pan; bury marshmallows in mixture and sprinkle with almonds.)

Bake in a 375° oven until heated through (about 20 minutes). Makes 6 servings.—S. R., Butte, MT

Per serving: 261 calories, 41 g carbohydrates, 5 g protein, 9 g total fat (4 g saturated), 86 mg cholesterol, 156 mg sodium

Toasted Cabbage with Noodles

Here's a fine example of an accompaniment that combines vegetable and pasta in a single tempting dish. You cook shredded green cabbage and chopped onion in butter until sweet-tasting and deep golden, then stir in cooked wide noodles. Try the combination with roast pork or grilled pork tenderloin.

½ cup (¼ lb.) butter or margarine

1 large onion, chopped

1 clove garlic, minced or pressed

1 medium-size head cabbage (about 1½ lbs.), finely shredded

2 tablespoons sugar

8 ounces dry wide egg noodles

Salt and pepper

Chopped fresh dill or parsley (optional)

Melt butter in a wide frying pan over medium heat. Add onion and garlic; cook, stirring often, until onion is soft. Add cabbage and cook, stirring often, until cabbage softens and turns a brighter green (about 5 minutes). Sprinkle with sugar. Continue to cook, stirring often, until cabbage turns amber in color and begins to brown lightly (20 to 25 more minutes).

Meanwhile, in a 4- to 5-quart pan, cook noodles in about 2 quarts boiling water until just tender to bite (8 to 10 minutes); or cook according to package directions. Drain well; pour into a warm shallow serving bowl or rimmed platter.

Add cabbage mixture to noodles and mix gently. Season to taste with salt and pepper. Sprinkle with dill, if desired. Makes 4 to 6 servings.
—Mrs. John Harmon, Boulder, CO

Per serving: 406 calories, 49 g carbohydrates, 9 g protein, 21 g total fat (12 g saturated), 93 mg cholesterol, 223 mg sodium

Noodles Romanoff

Plain egg noodles baked with cottage cheese and sour cream make a wonderfully rich-tasting partner for juicy grilled steaks or chops. The original recipe suggests, "If you like a very colorful casserole, add some chopped pimento or green pepper."

8 ounces dry egg noodles

1 cup low-fat cottage cheese

1 small clove garlic, minced or pressed

1 teaspoon Worcestershire

1 cup reduced-fat sour cream

¼ cup grated onion

¼ teaspoon liquid hot pepper seasoning

½ cup shredded Cheddar cheese

In a 4- to 5-quart pan, cook noodles in about 2 quarts boiling water until just tender to bite (8 to 10 minutes); or cook according to package directions. Drain well, pour into a large bowl, and stir in cottage cheese, garlic, Worcestershire, sour cream, onion, and hot pepper seasoning. Spoon into a greased 1½- to 2-quart casserole; sprinkle with Cheddar cheese. Bake in a 350° oven until heated through and golden brown on top (25 to 30 minutes). Makes 8 servings.—S. H., Bakersfield, CA

Per serving: 224 calories, 24 g carbohydrates, 12 g protein, 9 g total fat (4 g saturated), 47 mg cholesterol, 176 mg sodium

Asparagus & Pasta Stir-fry

Ginger and garlic flavor this simple combination of tender vermicelli and bright green fresh asparagus.

1 pound asparagus

6 ounces dry vermicelli or thin spaghetti

2 teaspoons salad oil

1 clove garlic, minced or pressed

1 teaspoon minced fresh ginger or ½ teaspoon ground ginger

½ cup diagonally sliced green onions

2 tablespoons soy sauce

⅛ teaspoon crushed red pepper flakes

Cilantro sprigs (optional)

Snap off and discard tough ends of asparagus; then cut asparagus stalks diagonally into 1½-inch pieces and set aside.

In a 4- to 5-quart pan, cook vermicelli in about 2 quarts boiling water until just tender to bite (8 to 10 minutes); or cook according to package directions.

Meanwhile, heat oil in a wide frying pan or wok over high heat. Add asparagus, garlic, ginger, and onions. Cook, stirring often, until asparagus is tender-crisp to bite (about 3 minutes). Add soy sauce and red pepper flakes; cook, stirring, for 1 more minute.

Drain pasta well; pour into pan with asparagus mixture and mix gently. Garnish with cilantro sprigs, if desired. Makes 4 to 6 servings.
—Diana K. Estey, Portland

Per serving: 161 calories, 29 g carbohydrates, 6 g protein, 2 g total fat (0.3 g saturated), 0 mg cholesterol, 417 mg sodium

Asparagus Spears with Egg Dressing

This creamy dressing was devised as a way to use leftover Easter eggs—but you can serve it any time of year, spooned over asparagus or another hot or cold cooked vegetable.

- 4 hard-cooked large eggs
- ¼ cup *each* chopped celery, chopped parsley, and mayonnaise
- 1 tablespoon *each* lemon juice and grated Parmesan cheese
- 1 teaspoon Dijon mustard
- ¼ teaspoon *each* celery salt and dry dill weed
- 2 pounds asparagus

Place eggs in a small bowl and chop finely, using a pastry blender or fork. Stir in celery, parsley, mayonnaise, lemon juice, cheese, mustard, celery salt, and dill weed. If made ahead, cover and refrigerate until next day.

Snap off and discard tough ends of asparagus; peel stalks, if desired. In a wide frying pan, cook asparagus, uncovered, in about 1 inch boiling water until just tender when pierced (4 to 5 minutes). Drain and serve hot. Or, to serve cold, immerse in cold water until cool, then drain again.

To serve, arrange asparagus spears on a platter and spoon egg dressing over them. Makes 6 servings.—*N. R., Bremerton, WA*

Per serving: 142 calories, 4 g carbohydrates, 7 g protein, 11 g total fat (2 g saturated), 148 mg cholesterol, 163 mg sodium

Hot Stuffed Tomatoes

Serve these warm, colorful spinach-stuffed tomatoes with cold sliced ham, turkey, or roast beef.

- 8 medium-size firm-ripe tomatoes (about 3 lbs. *total*)
- 12 ounces fresh spinach
- 1 tablespoon butter or margarine
- 1 tablespoon salad oil
- 1 medium-size onion, chopped
- 1¼ cups (about 5 oz.) shredded Parmesan cheese
- 2 tablespoons fine dry bread crumbs
- ⅛ teaspoon ground nutmeg

Cut off top quarter of each tomato. With a small spoon, scoop out tomato pulp to make hollow shells. Chop pulp and set aside. Discard stems and any yellow or wilted leaves from spinach; rinse spinach, drain well, and coarsely chop. Set aside.

Melt butter in oil in a wide frying pan over medium-high heat. Add onion and cook, stirring often, until soft (about 5 minutes). Stir in chopped tomatoes and spinach; cook, stirring, until spinach is wilted (3 to 4 minutes). Stir in 1 cup of the cheese, bread crumbs, and nutmeg.

Fill tomato shells equally with spinach mixture; then arrange in a 9-inch-square baking pan. Sprinkle evenly with remaining ¼ cup cheese and broil about 4 inches below heat just until heated through (3 to 4 minutes). Makes 8 servings.—*P. L., San Francisco*

Per serving: 149 calories, 11 g carbohydrates, 9 g protein, 8 g total fat (4 g saturated), 16 mg cholesterol, 351 mg sodium

Tomato Cheese Stacks

Crusty, cream cheese–filled tomato "sandwiches" go well with chicken or lean cuts of beef or lamb.

- 1 large package (about 8 oz.) cream cheese, at room temperature
- 1 clove garlic, minced or pressed
- ¼ cup chopped parsley
- ½ teaspoon dry savory

- Salt and pepper
- 3 or 4 large ripe tomatoes (1½ to 2 lbs. *total*)
- 3 tablespoons butter or margarine
- 3 tablespoons salad oil
- 1 large egg
- 1 tablespoon milk
- ⅔ cup seasoned fine dry bread crumbs
- ⅓ cup all-purpose flour

In a medium-size bowl, beat cream cheese, garlic, parsley, and savory until smoothly blended. Season to taste with salt and pepper.

Cut a thin slice off the top and bottom of each tomato (reserve these slices for other uses). Then cut tomatoes crosswise into ½-inch-thick slices; you need 12 slices total. Place slices on paper towels and let drain. Then spread cheese mixture evenly over 6 of the tomato slices; top with remaining 6 tomato slices.

Melt butter in oil in a wide frying pan over medium heat. Meanwhile, in a shallow bowl, beat egg with milk to blend. Place bread crumbs in another shallow bowl. Dust tomato "sandwiches" with flour; carefully dip in beaten egg, then dip in crumbs to coat. Add tomato sandwiches to pan and cook, turning once, until browned on both sides (4 to 6 minutes). Makes 6 servings. —*C. M., Truckee, CA*

Per serving: 331 calories, 17 g carbohydrates, 7 g protein, 27 g total fat (13 g saturated), 84 mg cholesterol, 454 mg sodium

Green Beans Supreme

For many families, holiday dinners just aren't complete without this familiar green bean casserole. It's creamy, crunchy, and easy to put together in a flash with a few twirls of the can opener.

SWEET & SOUR BAKED BEANS

For baked beans in a hurry, try this colorful crowd-size casserole. It appeared in *Kitchen Cabinet* in 1982—and ever since, it's been a popular contribution to potluck suppers and barbecues. Using canned beans cuts preparation and cooking time to a minimum.

    8   ounces sliced bacon
    4   large onions, thinly sliced
    1   cup firmly packed brown sugar
 1½   teaspoons dry mustard
    ½   cup cider vinegar
    2   cans (about 15 oz. *each*) butter beans, drained and rinsed
    1   can (about 15 oz.) green lima beans, drained and rinsed
    1   can (about 15 oz.) red kidney beans, drained and rinsed
    1   large can (about 28 oz.) baked beans

Cook bacon in a wide frying pan over medium heat until crisp. Lift out, drain, crumble, and set aside. Pour off and discard all but ¼ cup drippings from pan.

Add onions to drippings in pan and stir to separate onion slices into rings. Stir in sugar, mustard, and vinegar. Cook, uncovered, stirring occasionally, until liquid is reduced by about half (about 10 minutes).

In a 3- to 3½-quart casserole, combine butter beans, lima beans, kidney beans, and undrained baked beans. Add onion-vinegar mixture and bacon; stir gently to blend. (At this point, you may cover and refrigerate until next day.)

Bake, covered, in a 350° oven until bubbly and heated through (1¼ to 1½ hours). Makes 10 to 12 servings. —K. S., Puyallup, WA

Per serving: 350 calories, 60 g carbohydrates, 13 g protein, 8 g total fat (2 g saturated), 13 mg cholesterol, 678 mg sodium

RISOTTO WITH MUSHROOMS

A classic risotto—short-grain rice simmered in broth, then finished with white wine and Parmesan cheese—is dressed up with sliced fresh mushrooms to make this savory dish.

    2   teaspoons olive oil
    1   cup coarsely chopped onion
    1   clove garlic, minced or pressed
    1   cup short-grain white rice
 2¼   cups chicken broth
    8   ounces mushrooms, thinly sliced
    ¼   cup grated Parmesan cheese
    2   tablespoons dry white wine
        Parsley sprigs

Heat oil in a wide frying pan over medium heat. Add onion and garlic; cook, stirring often, until onion is soft (about 5 minutes). Add rice and cook, stirring, until opaque (2 to 3 minutes).

Stir broth and mushrooms into rice mixture. Increase heat to high and bring to a boil; then reduce heat and simmer, uncovered, until rice is tender to bite and almost all liquid has been absorbed (about 25 minutes). Stir occasionally at first, more often as mixture thickens.

Remove pan from heat; stir in cheese and wine. Spoon into a serving dish and garnish with parsley sprigs. Makes 4 to 6 servings. —Carmela Meely, Walnut Creek, CA

Per serving: 219 calories, 37 g carbohydrates, 6 g protein, 4 g total fat (1 g saturated), 3 mg cholesterol, 528 mg sodium

ALMOND PILAF WITH SHERRY

Flavored with sweet sherry, crisp almonds, and tarragon, this pilaf is an elegant companion for broiled lamb chops or grilled slices of turkey breast. The dish probably has its origins in the rice and vermicelli pilafs popular among descendants of the Armenians who settled around Fresno in California's Central Valley.

    ½   cup slivered almonds
    ½   cup 1-inch lengths of dry vermicelli
    ¼   cup butter or margarine
    1   cup long-grain white rice
 1¼   cups chicken broth
    ¾   cup cream sherry
 1½   teaspoons dry tarragon or 1 tablespoon finely chopped fresh tarragon
        Tarragon sprigs (optional)

Toast almonds in a wide frying pan over medium heat, stirring often, until golden (about 5 minutes). Pour out of pan and set aside.

Increase heat to medium-high; add vermicelli to pan and cook, stirring, until pasta is golden brown (about 2 minutes). Remove from pan and set aside.

Melt butter in pan; then add rice and cook, stirring, until rice is opaque and lightly toasted (2 to 3 minutes).

Add broth, sherry, vermicelli, and the 1½ teaspoons tarragon. Bring mixture to a boil; then reduce heat, cover, and simmer until rice is tender to bite (20 to 25 minutes).

Pour rice mixture into a serving bowl and sprinkle with almonds. Garnish with tarragon sprigs, if desired. Makes 6 servings.—*Kathy Lee, Arcadia, CA*

Per serving: 335 calories, 38 g carbohydrates, 6 g protein, 14 g total fat (5 g saturated), 21 mg cholesterol, 293 mg sodium

WILD RICE-MUSHROOM PILAF

The next time you serve salmon steaks or trout, complement the fish with this sophisticated dish—a combination of white and wild rices, generously laced with mushrooms and toasted pine nuts.

⅓ cup pine nuts or slivered almonds
1 tablespoon butter or margarine
8 ounces mushrooms, thinly sliced
1 cup dry sherry or chicken broth
2 cups chicken broth
½ cup wild rice, rinsed and drained
1 cup long-grain white rice
   Salt
   Chopped parsley

Toast pine nuts in a 2- to 3-quart pan over medium heat, stirring often, until golden (3 to 5 minutes). Pour out of pan and set aside.

Increase heat to high. Melt butter in pan; add mushrooms and cook, stirring often, until lightly browned (10 to 12 minutes). Stir in sherry, broth, and wild rice. Bring to a boil; then reduce heat, cover, and simmer for 25 minutes. Stir in white rice; cover and continue to simmer until both white and wild rices are tender to bite (about 20 more minutes). Stir in pine nuts and season to taste with salt; spoon into a serving dish and sprinkle with parsley. Makes 6 servings.—*Camille Thorson, Tucson*

Per serving: 257 calories, 42 g carbohydrates, 8 g protein, 7 g total fat (2 g saturated), 5 mg cholesterol, 361 mg sodium

TOMATO FRIED RICE

Here's a refreshing side dish for a quick summer supper of grilled turkey tenderloins or chicken breasts.

2 tablespoons butter or margarine
2 tablespoons salad oil
1 small onion, finely chopped
3 cups cold cooked rice
½ teaspoon sugar
   Dash of pepper
1 jar (about 2 oz.) sliced pimentos, drained
   About 1 tablespoon soy sauce
   About 2 tablespoons dry sherry, white wine, or water
2 medium-size tomatoes (about 12 oz. *total*), peeled, seeded, and diced
   Chopped parsley or sliced green onion tops

Melt butter in oil in a wide frying pan or wok over medium-high heat. Add chopped onion and cook, stirring often, until golden (about 2 minutes). Add rice; cook, stirring or turning with a wide spatula, until golden brown (about 7 minutes). Stir in sugar, pepper, pimentos, soy sauce, and sherry. Cook, turning with spatula, for about 1 more minute, adding a little more liquid if needed. Stir in tomatoes; cook, turning with spatula, until tomatoes are heated through (1 to 2 more minutes). Spoon into a serving dish and sprinkle with parsley. Makes 4 to 6 servings.—*M. R., Santa Barbara, CA*

Per serving: 238 calories, 31 g carbohydrates, 3 g protein, 11 g total fat (4 g saturated), 12 mg cholesterol, 263 mg sodium

GREEN-SPECKLED RICE

Parsley and chopped bell pepper add color to this stove-top dish; cream cheese gives it the luxurious texture of a risotto.

2 tablespoons butter or margarine
1 medium-size onion, chopped
½ cup chopped green bell pepper
2 cloves garlic, minced or pressed
¾ cup short-grain white rice
1½ cups chicken broth
1 small package (about 3 oz.) cream cheese, cut into ½-inch cubes
¾ cup chopped parsley
   Parsley sprigs

Melt butter in a 2- to 3-quart pan over medium-high heat. Add onion, bell pepper, and garlic; cook, stirring often, until onion is soft (about 5 minutes). Add rice and cook, stirring, until opaque (2 to 3 minutes).

Pour broth into pan and stir to scrape browned bits free. Increase heat to high and bring to a boil; then reduce heat, cover, and simmer until rice is tender to bite and all liquid has been absorbed (about 25 minutes).

Stir in cream cheese and chopped parsley; cover and let stand until cheese is melted (about 2 minutes). Stir gently to mix; spoon into a serving dish and garnish with parsley sprigs. Makes 4 servings.—*Mary Lou Sanelli, Sequim, WA*

Per serving: 296 calories, 36 g carbohydrates, 6 g protein, 14 g total fat (8 g saturated), 39 mg cholesterol, 503 mg sodium

BROWN RICE GRATIN

For a hearty, home-style dinner, serve meat loaf or oven-fried chicken with this creamy, crumb-topped brown rice and broccoli casserole.

2 cups fresh broccoli flowerets
3 cups cooked brown rice
2 cups (about 8 oz.) shredded Swiss or jarlsberg cheese
¾ cup chicken broth
½ cup sour cream
½ cup sliced green onions
¼ cup minced cilantro
2 tablespoons Dijon mustard
¼ teaspoon pepper
¼ cup fine dry bread crumbs
2 teaspoons butter or margarine, melted

Arrange broccoli on a steamer rack. Cover and steam over about 1 inch boiling water until barely tender when pierced (about 5 minutes).

Transfer broccoli to a large bowl and mix in rice, cheese, broth, sour cream, onions, cilantro, mustard, and pepper. Spread mixture evenly in a 9- by 13-inch baking dish. Combine bread crumbs and butter; sprinkle over rice mixture.

Bake in a 350° oven until rice mixture is heated through and crumbs are browned (15 to 20 minutes). Makes 6 to 8 servings.—*Sally Vog, Springfield, OR*

Per serving: 296 calories, 26 g carbohydrates, 14 g protein, 15 g total fat (9 g saturated), 40 mg cholesterol, 362 mg sodium

SPICED BULGUR WITH APPLE

A cinnamon-scented wheat pilaf, dotted with raisins and diced apple, goes well with lamb or pork chops.

- 2 tablespoons salad oil
- 1 medium-size onion, chopped
- 1 clove garlic, minced or pressed
- 2 teaspoons minced fresh ginger
- 1 cup bulgur
- ¼ teaspoon ground cinnamon
- 1½ cups chicken broth
- 1 small red-skinned apple (about 4 oz.)
- ¼ cup golden raisins
  Salt
- ¼ cup chopped salted roasted pistachio nuts

Heat oil in a 3- to 4-quart pan over medium heat. Add onion, garlic, and ginger; cook, stirring often, until onion is soft (about 5 minutes). Add bulgur; cook, stirring, until lightly toasted (about 3 minutes). Stir in cinnamon and broth; bring to a boil over high heat. Then reduce heat,

cover, and simmer until bulgur is tender to bite (about 10 minutes).

Meanwhile, core and finely dice apple. Lightly stir apple and raisins into bulgur mixture; season to taste with salt.

To serve, spoon bulgur mixture into a bowl and sprinkle with pistachios. Makes 4 to 6 servings.—*J. Hill, Sacramento*

Per serving: 239 calories , 35 g carbohydrates, 6 g protein, 10 g total fat (1 g saturated), 0 mg cholesterol, 335 mg sodium

COUSCOUS PROVENÇAL

Fluffy couscous mixed with artichokes, diced tomato, fresh basil, and capers makes a quick and colorful accompaniment for roasted or grilled chicken.

- 1 small onion, chopped
- 1 teaspoon olive oil
- 1½ cups chicken broth
- 1¼ cups couscous
- 1 can (about 14 oz.) water-packed artichoke hearts, drained and cut into ½-inch chunks
- 1 medium-size firm-ripe tomato (about 6 oz.), diced
- 2 tablespoons chopped fresh basil
- 1 tablespoon drained capers
- ¼ teaspoon pepper

Combine onion and oil in a 2½- to 3-quart pan. Cook over medium-high heat, stirring often, until onion is lightly browned. Add broth and bring to a boil over high heat. Stir in couscous; cover, remove from heat, and let stand until broth has been absorbed (about 5 minutes).

Add artichokes, tomato, basil, capers, and pepper to couscous; stir with a fork to mix well. Serve hot or warm. Makes 4 to 6 servings.—*Ellen Nishimura, Fair Oaks, CA*

Per serving: 225 calories, 43 g carbohydrates, 8 g protein, 2 g total fat (0.2 g saturated), 0 mg cholesterol, 352 mg sodium

BARLEY & PINE NUT CASSEROLE

Cooked in broth and flecked with fresh parsley and chives, this savory casserole is good with smoky meats, poultry, or plump sausages cooked on the barbecue. Or roast a chicken or a turkey half in the oven alongside the casserole to make a hearty family dinner.

- 6 tablespoons butter or margarine
- ¼ to ½ cup pine nuts or slivered almonds
- 1 medium-size onion, chopped
- 1 cup pearl barley
- ½ cup minced parsley
- ¼ cup snipped chives or thinly sliced green onions
- ¼ teaspoon *each* salt and pepper
- 2 cans (about 14½ oz. *each*) beef or chicken broth
  Parsley sprigs

Melt 2 tablespoons of the butter in a wide frying pan over medium heat. Add pine nuts and cook, stirring, until lightly toasted (3 to 5 minutes). Remove from pan with a slotted spoon and set aside.

Melt remaining ¼ cup butter in pan. Add chopped onion and barley; cook, stirring, until barley is lightly toasted. Remove from heat; stir in pine nuts, minced parsley, chives, salt, and pepper. Spoon barley mixture into a 1½-quart casserole. (At this point, you may cover and refrigerate until next day.)

In a 1½-quart pan, bring broth to a boil. Pour broth over barley mixture in casserole. Bake, uncovered, in a 375° oven until barley is tender to bite and almost all liquid has been absorbed (about 1 hour). Garnish with parsley sprigs. Makes 6 to 8 servings.—*J. S., Boise, ID*

Per serving: 249 calories, 26 g carbohydrates, 6 g protein, 14 g total fat (7 g saturated), 27 mg cholesterol, 1,003 mg sodium

1963 to 1966

The daily question of "what to have for dinner" was a challenge Kitchen Cabinet took on every month in the early 1960s—just as it does today. While flirting with appetizers such as Shrimp & Bacon Bits and baked treats like Tangerine Bread, contributors and editors alike realized that getting the evening's main course on the table was of primary importance.

Crabmeat Patties might have been party fare elsewhere, but fresh crab was still plentiful enough in the West of 30 years ago to serve often in season. Spit-roasting chicken on an electric barbecue, then an innovation in the kitchen or on the patio, was popular for spring and summer menus—and as the marinade for Spicy Barbecued Chicken shows, we were starting to forsake sour cream for tangy yogurt. Dishes for hiking trips or picnics remained in demand; we suggested a Breakfast Potato-Egg Scramble for a meal stirred up over the campfire.

What to serve at a 1960s party for teenagers? A hearty casserole, of course

SHRIMP & BACON BITS

1 pound (16 to 20) very large shrimp
  Boiling salted water
  About ½ pound thinly sliced bacon
1 clove garlic, minced or mashed
½ cup tomato-based chili sauce

Starting several hours before you plan to serve these, cook the shrimp in the boiling salted water until they turn pink, about 3 minutes. Drain and cool enough to shell and devein them. Also broil the bacon slices on one side only (they should not be crisp); drain bacon, then cut each slice in half crosswise. Blend the garlic with the chili sauce. Dip each shrimp into the sauce to coat all over, wrap in a half-slice of bacon, and secure with a toothpick. When all are prepared, cover and refrigerate until you are ready to broil and serve them.

Arrange the appetizers on a rack in a broiler pan and broil until they are heated through and the bacon is crisp, turning to brown and crisp both sides. Serve hot. Makes 16 to 20 appetizers.—*B. M., Sacramento (April 1964)*

Freshly cooked shrimp, seasoned and wrapped in bacon, for party tidbits

BREAKFAST POTATO-EGG SCRAMBLE

5 slices bacon, cut in pieces
1 small green pepper, seeded and diced
2 tablespoons finely chopped onion
3 large boiled potatoes, peeled and cubed
½ teaspoon salt
⅛ teaspoon pepper
½ cup shredded Cheddar cheese
6 eggs

In a large, heavy frying pan, sauté the bacon until slightly browned and crisp. Drain off all but about 3 tablespoons of the fat. To the pan add the green pepper, onion, potatoes, salt, and pepper. Cook over medium heat, stirring often, for 6 to 8 minutes, or until the potatoes are golden brown. Sprinkle cheese over top and stir in. Break eggs into the pan (without beating) and cook, stirring gently, just until eggs are set. Serves 4 to 6.—*L. R., North Bend, WA (September 1963)*

JACK FAGAN

Full of bacon, eggs, and potatoes to cook in one pan on a camping trip

CRABMEAT PATTIES

2 cups crabmeat, fresh or thawed frozen
1 cup salted soda cracker crumbs
4 teaspoons Worcestershire
⅛ teaspoon liquid hot pepper seasoning
3 tablespoons chopped parsley
1½ teaspoons prepared mustard
3 tablespoons mayonnaise
1 egg
3 tablespoons butter or margarine
    Chopped parsley and lemon wedges

Flake the crab into a large bowl. Add cracker crumbs, Worcestershire, hot pepper seasoning, the 3 tablespoons parsley, mustard, and mayonnaise. Stir until well blended. Add egg and stir until mixture is well blended.

Shape crab mixture with your hands into 8 patties. In a frying pan, melt 2 tablespoons of the butter. Put in the crab cakes and cook over medium heat (about 350° in an electric frying pan) until browned on both sides—takes about 3 minutes on each side. Add remaining 1 tablespoon butter when you turn cakes. Serve with additional chopped parsley on top and wedges of lemon. Makes 4 servings.—*M. R., Wilderville, OR (October 1966)*

The pure flavor of crab comes through deliciously in these little patties

TANGERINE (OR ORANGE) BREAD

2 cups flour
1 teaspoon baking powder
½ teaspoon *each* baking soda and salt
1 cup sugar
1 egg
3 tablespoons grated tangerine peel or orange peel
⅔ cup tangerine juice or orange juice
3 tablespoons melted butter or margarine
½ cup chopped dates or raisins
½ cup chopped walnuts or pecans

Sift flour, measure, and sift with baking powder, baking soda, salt, and sugar into a large bowl. Beat egg well and stir in tangerine peel, juice, and melted butter. Add egg mixture all at once to the flour mixture and stir until well blended. Add dates and walnuts; stir until blended. Turn into a well-buttered 5- by 9-inch loaf pan. Bake in a moderate oven (350°) until a cake tester inserted in the center comes out clean, about 50 minutes. Cool slightly before turning out of pan and slicing. Makes 1 loaf. —*M. K., La Jolla, CA (April 1963)*

If you have a tangerine tree, here's a delicious way to use the fruit

SPICY BARBECUED CHICKEN

2 chickens (2 to 3 lbs. *each*)
1 pint (2 cups) plain yogurt
1 clove garlic, crushed
1 teaspoon *each* ground ginger, chili powder, and ground cardamom
½ teaspoon *each* ground cloves and ground cinnamon
1½ teaspoons salt
4 bay leaves, ground or crushed

To grill the chickens, cut in quarters and twist wings enough so each wing tip is locked around the back side of its quarter. For spit-roasting, truss whole birds; tie wingtips over breasts, fasten neck skin to backs with a skewer, and tie drumsticks to tails.

Combine yogurt with all remaining ingredients. Put chickens in a baking dish; cover with yogurt mixture. Marinate chickens at least 4 hours, or overnight. Remove from marinade and place on greased grill, skin side up. Cook, turning as needed to brown evenly, for 40 to 45 minutes. Or put whole birds on spit and roast until meat is tender when pierced, 1¼ to 1½ hours. Makes 8 servings.—*J. F., Los Angeles (May 1966)*

Thick, spicy sauce gives this barbecued chicken a flavorful and crusty coating

S·A·U·C·E·S, S·A·L·S·A·S & P·R·E·S·E·R·V·E·S

There's hardly anything that grows in the West," a Sunset garden editor once observed, "that our readers can't make into jelly or pickles." This chapter pays tribute to the ways in which generations of Kitchen Cabinet cooks have preserved the bounty of Western orchards and gardens. • "Not all Westerners fully appreciate or know how to use the kumquat, which is truly a Western fruit, and a delicious one," lamented a reader from Pasadena, California in 1931, offering a recipe for Kumquat Marmalade. Yellow Tomato Preserves from 1937 featured "the small pear-shaped yellow tomatoes in an interesting sweet, which is so good with hot biscuits." You'll applaud Ripe Tomato Marmalade (page 173) in a similar role. • Sweet-Hot Mustard (page 168) is reminiscent of a 1936 sauce that was "especially good on ham, tongue, or cold meats of any kind"— and fairly sophisticated for its day, as it included tarragon vinegar. Chunky Salsa (facing page) recalls an uncooked Chili Relish from 1934, but bolsters the flavors with some sprightly additions.

SWEET-SOUR CHILE SAUCE

While tomatoes are plentiful, put up a batch of this tangy sauce. You'll enjoy it with meat loaf or spooned over frankfurters in toasted rolls.

- 6 cups peeled, coarsely chopped tomatoes (3 to 4 lbs. tomatoes)
- 1 large can (about 7 oz.) whole green chiles, seeded (if desired) and diced
- 1 small dried hot red chile, crumbled
- 4 large onions, chopped
- 1 tablespoon salt
- ½ teaspoon ground ginger
- 6 tablespoons firmly packed brown sugar
- 1 teaspoon ground cinnamon
- 1¾ cups white wine vinegar

In a heavy 5- to 6-quart pan, stir together tomatoes, canned chiles, dried chile, onions, salt, ginger, sugar, and cinnamon. Bring to a boil over high heat, stirring. Then reduce heat and boil gently, uncovered, stirring occasionally, until sauce is very thick (about 1 hour). As sauce thickens, reduce heat and stir more frequently to prevent sticking. Add vinegar; cook, uncovered, stirring often, for 15 to 20 more minutes.

Ladle hot sauce into hot, sterilized half-pint jars, leaving ¼-inch headspace. Wipe rims and threads clean; top with hot lids, then firmly screw on bands. Process in a boiling water canner for 15 minutes.

Or omit processing and ladle sauce into half-pint freezer containers, leaving ½-inch headspace; apply lids, let cool, and freeze for up to 6 months or refrigerate for up to 3 weeks. Makes about 6 half-pints. —*J. F., El Granada, CA*

Per tablespoon: 11 calories, 3 g carbohydrates, 0.2 g protein, 0.1 g total fat (0 g saturated), 0 mg cholesterol, 72 mg sodium

CHINESE PLUM SAUCE

This spicy homemade plum sauce is just right with crisp roast chicken or duck, or with grilled or broiled pork tenderloin.

- Spice Mixture (recipe follows)
- 2 cans (about 1 lb. *each*) purple plums in heavy syrup
- ¾ cup water
- 1 tablespoon salad oil
- ½ cup canned tomato sauce
- 1 medium-size onion, chopped
- 1 tablespoon *each* soy sauce and Worcestershire
- ¼ teaspoon liquid hot pepper seasoning
- 1 tablespon unseasoned rice vinegar or white wine vinegar

Prepare Spice Mixture and set aside.

Drain plums, reserving 1¼ cups of the syrup (discard remaining syrup). Pit plums; then place in a blender or food processor along with water and the 1¼ cups reserved syrup. Whirl until puréed; set aside.

Heat oil in a 3- to 4-quart pan over medium-high heat; stir in Spice Mixture. Stir in plum purée, tomato sauce, onion, soy sauce, Worcestershire, and hot pepper seasoning; bring to a boil, stirring. Then reduce heat and boil gently, uncovered, stirring often, until reduced to 3 cups (about 25 minutes). As sauce thickens, reduce heat and stir more frequently to prevent sticking. Stir in vinegar.

Serve sauce warm. Or, to store, let cool; then cover and refrigerate for up to 3 weeks. Reheat before serving, if desired. Makes 3 cups.—*Kathryn Williams, San Mateo, CA*

SPICE MIXTURE. In a small bowl, stir together 1 teaspoon **Chinese five-spice** (or ¼ teaspoon *each* anise seeds, ground cinnamon, ground ginger, and ground cloves); ½ teaspoon *each* **ground cinnamon, ground cumin,** and **dry mustard;** and ¼ teaspoon **pepper.**

Per tablespoon: 22 calories, 5 g carbohydrates, 0.2 g protein, 0.3 g total fat (0 g saturated), 0 mg cholesterol, 45 mg sodium

CHUNKY SALSA

This mild salsa is a versatile condiment. Serve it as a quick-to-make party dip for tortilla chips, celery sticks, or jicama or cucumber slices; or spoon it over hamburgers, frankfurters, burritos, or tacos. Or try it as a sauce for grilled or broiled chicken, fish, pork, or beef. If you prefer a spicier and more assertive salsa, increase the quantity of fresh or canned chiles.

- 1 can (about 14½ oz.) tomatoes
- 2 or 3 small fresh or pickled hot chiles, seeded (if desired) and finely minced
- 1 small green bell pepper (about 5 oz.), seeded and coarsely chopped
- ⅓ cup *each* coarsely chopped mild onion and coarsely chopped radishes
- 3 tablespoons thinly sliced green onions
- 1 can (about 4 oz.) diced green chiles
- 2 to 3 tablespoons chopped cilantro
- ½ cup shredded jack cheese

In a food processor or blender, whirl tomatoes and their liquid until coarsely puréed. Pour into a large bowl; stir in fresh or pickled chiles, bell pepper, mild onion, radishes, green onions, canned chiles, cilantro, and cheese. To store, cover and refrigerate for up to 5 days. Makes about 3½ cups.—*V. F., South Laguna, CA*

Per tablespoon: 7 calories, 0.8 g carbohydrates, 0.3 g protein, 0.3 g total fat (0.2 g saturated), 1 mg cholesterol, 30 mg sodium

CHEESE MIX FOR BAKED POTATOES

A rich blend of butter, sour cream, and Cheddar cheese makes a deluxe topping for hot baked potatoes. Another night, spoon it over broccoli spears, asparagus, or tender-crisp green beans.

- ½ cup (¼ lb.) butter or margarine, at room temperature
- 2 cups (about 8 oz.) finely shredded sharp Cheddar cheese
- 1 cup regular or reduced-fat sour cream
- 2 tablespoons sliced green onion tops or snipped chives

In a large bowl, beat butter, cheese, sour cream, and onion with an electric mixer on low speed until well blended.

To store, cover and refrigerate for up to 2 weeks. If desired, remove from refrigerator and let stand for 20 to 30 minutes at room temperature before using. Makes about 2½ cups. —W. H., Northridge, CA

Per tablespoon: 56 calories, 0.3 g carbohydrates, 2 g protein, 5 g total fat (3 g saturated), 15 mg cholesterol, 62 mg sodium

GINGER & LIME BUTTER

This tangy butter is superb with all sorts of broiled and barbecued foods; use it as a baste for chicken, turkey, lamb, or pork, or for seafood such as salmon, swordfish, halibut, trout, or shrimp. Or brush it over barbecued or baked papaya, cantaloupe, or pineapple. It's delicious, too, with hot cooked vegetables such as corn on the cob, zucchini, crookneck squash, green beans, and sugar snap peas.

- 1 cup (½ lb.) butter or margarine, at room temperature
- 2-inch-long piece fresh ginger, peeled and minced
- 1 teaspoon *each* coarsely ground pepper and grated lime peel
- ¼ cup lime juice

In a blender or food processor, combine butter, ginger, pepper, lime peel, and lime juice. Whirl until well blended, scraping down sides of container often. (Or combine ingredients in a bowl and beat with a wooden spoon until well blended.)

To store, cover and refrigerate for up to 1 week. Bring to room temperature before using. Makes about 1 cup.—I. R., Sacramento

Per tablespoon: 103 calories, 0.5 g carbohydrates, 0.1 g protein, 12 g total fat (7 g saturated), 31 mg cholesterol, 118 mg sodium

SWEET-HOT MUSTARD

Here's a tangy homemade mustard to enliven turkey or ham sandwiches.

- 3 tablespoons dry mustard
- 3 tablespoons distilled white vinegar or white wine vinegar
- 2 tablespoons water
- 1 tablespoon all-purpose flour
- 3 tablespoons sugar
- 3 tablespoons butter or margarine, cut into small chunks

In a 1- to 1½-quart pan, stir together mustard, vinegar, and water; let stand for 1 hour.

Mix flour and sugar; add to mustard mixture along with butter. Cook over medium-high heat, stirring, just until mixture comes to a boil. Remove from heat.

To store mustard, let it cool; then cover and refrigerate for up to 1 month. Serve mustard hot, warm, or cool. Makes about ¾ cup.—*Mrs. Bruce Farrington, Valier, MT*

Per tablespoon: 47 calories, 4 g carbohydrates, 0.5 g protein, 3 g total fat (2 g saturated), 8 mg cholesterol, 29 mg sodium

PICKLED GREEN BEANS

Crisp, tart, and refreshing, these spicy beans are a nice addition to the relish tray.

- 1 pound green beans, ends trimmed
- 2 dry bay leaves
- ½ teaspoon crushed red pepper flakes
- 2 teaspoons *each* fennel seeds and mustard seeds
- 1 cup *each* water and distilled white vinegar
- 1 tablespoon salt

In a 3½- to 5-quart pan, cook beans, uncovered, in about 2 quarts boiling water until bright green and barely tender-crisp to bite (about 3 minutes). Drain, immerse in cold water until cool, and drain again.

Lay 2 pint jars on their sides. Lay half the beans, parallel, in each jar; trim ends of beans so beans will fit jars. Then turn jars upright. To each jar, add 1 bay leaf and half each of the red pepper flakes, fennel seeds, and mustard seeds.

In a 1- to 2-quart pan, combine the 1 cup water, vinegar, and salt; bring to a boil over high heat.

PEACH & ORANGE MARMALADE

Juicy oranges complement plentiful summer peaches in this tangy marmalade. It's good on toasted egg bread or homemade corn muffins.

    6   medium-size Valencia oranges
        (about 2½ lbs. *total*)
    2   lemons
    12 medium-size ripe peaches (about
        4 lbs. *total*), peeled, halved, and
        pitted
        About 11 cups sugar

Rinse unpeeled oranges and lemons; cut into chunks. Discard ends and seeds. Whirl orange and lemon chunks, a portion at a time, in a food processor until coarsely chopped; set aside. Whirl peaches in processor until coarsely chopped. Measure all chopped fruit and juices; you should have a total of about 11 cups.

In a heavy 8-quart pan, combine fruit mixture and an equal quantity of sugar. Bring to a boil over high heat, stirring. Then reduce heat and boil gently, uncovered, stirring occasionally, until marmalade reaches the jell point (220°F), about 45 minutes. As marmalade thickens, reduce heat and stir more frequently to prevent sticking. Remove from heat and skim off any foam.

Ladle hot marmalade into hot, sterilized half-pint jars, leaving ¼-inch headspace. Wipe rims and threads clean; top with hot lids, then firmly screw on bands. Process in a boiling water canner for 5 minutes. Or omit processing and ladle marmalade into half-pint freezer containers, leaving ½-inch headspace; apply lids, let cool, and freeze for up to 1 year or refrigerate for up to 1 month. Makes about 12 half-pints.—*W. F., Mill Creek, CA*

Per tablespoon: 50 calories, 13 g carbohydrates, 0.1 g protein, 0 g total fat (0 g saturated), 0 mg cholesterol, 0.3 mg sodium

RIPE TOMATO MARMALADE

Thin, transparent slices of lemon and orange stud this sparkling red preserve. It's an out-of-the-ordinary topping for grilled or broiled meats—and a nice spread for breakfast toast, as well. Serve a glistening glass bowlful to distinguish toasted Oatmeal Yeast Bread (page 187).

        About 15 medium-size tomatoes
        (about 5½ lbs. *total*)
    2   small oranges (8 to 10 oz. *total*)
    2   small lemons
    7½ cups sugar
    1   teaspoon salt
    2   cinnamon sticks (*each* about 3
        inches long)

Peel and core tomatoes; then mash. You should have 10 cups of tomato pulp and juice.

Rinse unpeeled oranges and lemons and cut into thin slices; discard ends and seeds.

In a heavy 8- to 10-quart pan, combine tomatoes, oranges, lemons, sugar, salt, and cinnamon sticks. Bring to a boil over high heat, stirring. Then reduce heat and boil gently, uncovered, stirring occasionally, until thickened (about 1½ hours); fruit slices should be almost transparent. As marmalade thickens, reduce heat and stir more frequently to prevent sticking.

Remove from heat and skim off any foam; remove and discard cinnamon sticks.

Ladle hot marmalade into hot, sterilized half-pint jars, leaving ¼-inch headspace. Wipe rims and threads clean; top with hot lids, then firmly screw on bands. Process in a boiling water canner for 5 minutes. Or omit processing and ladle marmalade into half-pint freezer containers, leaving ½-inch headspace; apply lids, let cool, and freeze for up to 1 year or refrigerate for up to 1 month. Makes about 8 half-pints.—*E. B., Los Angeles*

Per tablespoon: 50 calories, 13 g carbohydrates, 0.2 g protein, 0.1 g total fat (0 g saturated), 0 mg cholesterol, 19 mg sodium

RHUBARB CONSERVE

Use the brightest red rhubarb you can find to make this colorful conserve. Serve it on toast for breakfast or brunch, or on biscuits or hot yeast rolls to accompany meats at dinner.

        About 2 pounds rhubarb, thinly
        sliced (about 7 cups)
    4   cups sugar
    ½   lemon (unpeeled), thinly sliced
    1   cup dried light (Calimyrna) figs,
        finely chopped
    2   tablespoons finely chopped
        crystallized ginger

In a heavy 6-quart pan, mix rhubarb and sugar. Stir in lemon, figs, and ginger. Bring to a boil over high heat, stirring. Then reduce heat and boil gently, uncovered, stirring occasionally, until thickened (about 30 minutes). As conserve thickens, reduce heat and stir more frequently to prevent sticking. Remove from heat and skim off any foam.

Ladle hot conserve into hot, sterilized half-pint jars, leaving ¼-inch headspace. Wipe rims and threads clean; top with hot lids, then firmly screw on bands. Process in a boiling water canner for 5 minutes. Or omit processing and ladle conserve into half-pint freezer containers, leaving ½-inch headspace; apply lids, let cool, and freeze for up to 1 year or refrigerate for up to 1 month. Makes about 5 half-pints.—*G. B., Puyallup, WA*

Per tablespoon: 49 calories, 13 g carbohydrates, 0.2 g protein, 0 g total fat (0 g saturated), 0 mg cholesterol, 1 mg sodium

Ever on the move, 1960s readers liked easily transported picnic recipes

Sprinkle cheese over the tomato topping; put back in oven until melted

JACK FAGAN

A weekend breakfast treat for your family: serve hot-from-the-oven scones

A SAMPLING FROM
—1967 *to* 1970—

Jerry Anne DiVecchio, now Sunset's senior editor for food and entertaining, wrote a definitive story about Quiche Lorraine in 1965. The concept was readily embraced, spinning off 1967's Caraway Cheese Quiche in Kitchen Cabinet. Even so, we weren't sure everyone knew how to deal with such a tricky French word. "Pronounce it KEESH," we advised.

Perhaps it was safer to serve up familiar—and more easily articulated—favorites like spinach salad and ham loaf. Cornish game hens had moved from the sphere of gourmet foods into the mainstream of the supermarket meat case, though they still seemed a bit more exotic than an everyday chicken.

The scones so popular in today's coffee bars showed up in Kitchen Cabinet as early as 1967, as sugar-sprinkled Buttermilk Scones flavored with a hint of orange.

CARAWAY CHEESE QUICHE

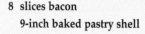

8 slices bacon
   9-inch baked pastry shell
6 ounces kuminost cheese (cumin- and caraway-flavored), shredded
2 green onions, chopped
4 eggs, lightly beaten
1¼ cups milk or half-and-half
1 large firm-ripe tomato
   Salt and pepper

Cook bacon until crisp, drain, and crumble into the pastry shell. Set aside ½ cup of the cheese for topping. Sprinkle remaining cheese and onions in crust. Combine eggs and milk; pour into crust. Bake in a 350°

oven for 35 to 40 minutes, or until custard appears firm when dish is shaken gently.

Meanwhile, peel tomato, cut into ¼-inch thick slices, and cut slices in half. Remove pie from oven, arrange tomato on top, sprinkle lightly with salt and pepper, and then sprinkle with the reserved cheese. Put back in oven until cheese is melted and tomatoes are heated through, about 5 minutes. Serve hot. Makes 6 servings.—*J. E., Seattle (October 1967)*

NOTE: *If you cannot find kuminost cheese, use 1½ cups (about 6 oz.) shredded Swiss cheese plus ¼ teaspoon each caraway seeds and cumin seeds.*

BUTTERMILK SCONES

1⅓ cups all-purpose flour
½ teaspoon *each* baking soda and salt
1 tablespoon sugar
¼ cup butter, margarine, or shortening
2 teaspoons grated orange peel
½ cup buttermilk
   About 1 tablespoon *each* melted butter and sugar

Sift the flour together with the baking soda, salt, and sugar into a bowl. Cut in

the butter with a pastry blender until crumbly. Add the orange peel and buttermilk; stir with a fork until well blended. Turn out on a lightly floured board and knead 5 or 6 times. Pat into a round about ½ inch thick; cut into 6 wedges.

Arrange scones on a buttered baking sheet. Brush with melted butter; sprinkle with sugar. Bake in a 400° oven for about 15 minutes, or until lightly browned. Makes 6.—*H. N., San Francisco (June 1967)*

SPINACH SALAD WITH BACON & APPLE

⅓ cup sliced almonds

¼ cup salad oil or olive oil

3 tablespoons tarragon wine vinegar

⅛ teaspoon salt

Dash of pepper

1 teaspoon sugar

½ teaspoon dry mustard

1 pound fresh spinach, stems removed, leaves rinsed and crisped

3 green onions, thinly sliced

1 red-skinned apple, cored and diced

5 slices bacon, crisply cooked, drained, and crumbled

Toast almonds in a small frying pan over medium heat until golden. Remove from pan; set aside. Stir together oil, vinegar, salt, pepper, sugar, and mustard; set aside. Tear spinach leaves into bite-size pieces and place in a large bowl. Add onions, apple, almonds, and bacon. Stir dressing; pour over salad, mix gently, and serve. Makes 8 servings.—*R. M., Roseburg, OR (March 1970)*

Crisp bacon, diced apple, and toasted almonds enhance fresh spinach salad

CORNISH HENS WITH TOMATOES

2 Cornish game hens (1½ lbs. *each*)

Garlic salt and pepper

1 medium-size onion, chopped

½ pound mushrooms, sliced

3 tablespoons butter or margarine

½ cup dry white wine or chicken broth

2 medium-size tomatoes (about 12 oz. *total*), peeled, seeded, and diced

⅓ cup sour cream or plain yogurt

1 tablespoon flour

Cut hens in half lengthwise. Sprinkle with garlic salt and pepper. Arrange in a 9- by 13-inch baking pan and bake in a 400°

oven for 25 minutes. Meanwhile, in a wide frying pan over medium-high heat, cook onion and mushrooms in butter, stirring often, for 10 minutes. Stir in wine and tomatoes.

Spoon tomato mixture over hens. Reduce oven temperature to 350° and continue to bake until hens are tender (about 15 more minutes). Transfer hens to a platter. Blend sour cream and flour; stir into baking pan. Then stir over medium-high heat until sauce boils and thickens. Serve with hens. Makes 4 servings.—*A. R., Seabeck, WA (October 1970)*

Fresh tomatoes and mushrooms cook with hens, form sauce to serve on top

HAM LOAF WITH ORANGE SAUCE

About 1½ pounds cooked ham

1 large carrot

2 slices firm white bread

2 eggs

2 tablespoons minced onion

1 teaspoon dry mustard

1 can (about 6 oz.) frozen orange juice concentrate, thawed

2 cups water

2 tablespoons cornstarch

⅛ teaspoon *each* ground cinnamon and ground cloves

⅓ cup raisins

Using the fine blade of a food chopper (or food processor), grind the ham (you should have 4 cups); then put the carrot

and bread through the food chopper. In a bowl, combine the ham, carrot, bread, eggs, onion, and dry mustard. Combine orange juice concentrate with water; add ½ cup juice to ham mixture and reserve remaining juice. Blend ham mixture well; press into a 4- by 8-inch loaf pan.

In a small pan, blend cornstarch with reserved orange juice, cinnamon, and cloves. Add raisins and cook, stirring, until thickened. Keep warm.

Bake ham loaf in a 375° oven for 40 to 45 minutes or until loaf feels firm when lightly pressed, basting with some of the orange sauce. Serve sauce with ham loaf. Serves 6.—*H. S., Boonville, CA (April 1970)*

ALICE HARTH

Use leftover ham, ground through food chopper, or cooked ham from market

B·R·E·A·D·S

"When our high school class gave a tea, each of us had to bring refreshments. I made this fruit bread for tiny sandwiches, and all the girls' mothers asked for the recipe," exulted P. M. of Glendale, California in 1939. Kitchen Cabinet contributors have long known that homemade breads win compliments and add interest to the mealtime routine. "Jazz Biscuits pep up any meal, turning an ordinary menu into one guests will long remember," reported another California reader in 1936. • To share these satisfactions today, you can bake lavish Chocolate Chip Scones (page 181), unusual Ginger Biscuits (page 182), or classic Blueberry-Lemon Muffins (page 178)—all "good till the last one is gone," in the words of the cook who created 1938's Sunset Rolls. Or try buttery Cinnamon Sour Cream Coffeecake (page 184), a 1959 recipe with timeless appeal. • Of course, breadbaking isn't all sugar and spice. "There's much written about the nutritive value of wheat germ, but I think more should be said about how good it is," commented a reader in 1939. To find out just how right she was, try our recipe for delicious Wheat Germ Buns (page 189).

BRAN-WHEAT REFRIGERATOR MUFFINS

The batter for these whole-grain muffins can wait in the refrigerator for up to a month, ready to bake as needed. The recipe comes from a fishing lodge in Alaska, where guests welcome a stick-to-the-ribs repast before heading out for a morning on the cold water.

- 2 large shredded wheat biscuits
- 1½ cups boiling water
- 3½ cups all-purpose flour
- 1 tablespoon baking soda
- 1 teaspoon salt
- 1 cup (½ lb.) butter or margarine, at room temperature
- 1½ cups sugar
- 3 large eggs
- 1½ cups buttermilk
- 2½ cups whole bran cereal

Place shredded wheat biscuits in a medium-size bowl. Pour boiling water over biscuits; let stand until cool (about 15 minutes). Meanwhile, in a large bowl, stir together flour, baking soda, and salt; set aside.

In another large bowl, beat butter and sugar with an electric mixer on medium-high speed until creamy. Add eggs, one at a time, beating well after each addition. Beat in shredded wheat–water mixture; add flour mixture and beat until blended. Stir in buttermilk, then bran cereal. (At this point, you may cover airtight and refrigerate for up to 1 month. If desired, transfer batter to a wide-mouth jar before chilling.)

To bake, fill greased or paper-lined 2½-inch muffin cups to the top with batter. Bake in a 400° oven until muffins are browned and a wooden pick inserted in centers comes out clean (20 to 25 minutes). Turn out of pans onto racks; serve warm or at room temperature. Makes about 30 muffins.—*Julie Hack, Yes Bay, AK*

Per muffin: 191 calories, 29 g carbohydrates, 4 g protein, 8 g total fat (4 g saturated), 38 mg cholesterol, 322 mg sodium

SPICY ZUCCHINI BRAN MUFFINS

These distinctive muffins are delicious served warm, spread with butter or whipped cream cheese.

- 2 cups bran flake cereal
- 1 cup shredded zucchini
- ¾ cup milk
- 1 large egg
- ½ cup sugar
- ⅓ cup salad oil
- 1½ cups all-purpose flour
- 2½ teaspoons baking powder
- 1½ teaspoons ground cinnamon
- ½ teaspoon ground ginger

In a large bowl, combine bran cereal, zucchini, milk, egg, sugar, and oil; stir until cereal is moistened.

In a medium-size bowl, stir together flour, baking powder, cinnamon, and ginger. Add flour mixture to zucchini mixture and stir just until dry ingredients are evenly moistened.

Divide batter evenly among 12 well-greased or paper-lined 2½-inch muffin cups. Bake in a 375° oven until muffins are browned and firm to the touch (25 to 30 minutes). Turn out of pans onto racks; serve warm or at room temperature. If made ahead, let cool; then wrap airtight and refrigerate for up to 1 week or freeze for up to 6 months. Makes 12 muffins.—*Maureen W. Valentine, Seattle*

Per muffin: 218 calories, 33 g carbohydrates, 5 g protein, 9 g total fat (2 g saturated), 20 mg cholesterol, 198 mg sodium

CHEESE & BACON CORN MUFFINS

These big muffins go well with chili. Try them alongside Rocky Mountain Chili (page 77) or Chili con Pavo (page 108).

- 8 slices bacon, diced
- 1 cup chopped onion
- 1¼ cups all-purpose flour
- ¾ cup yellow cornmeal
- ⅓ cup sugar
- 3½ teaspoons baking powder
- ½ teaspoon salt
- 2 large eggs
- 1 cup milk
- 3 tablespoons butter or margarine, melted and cooled
- 1¼ cups (about 5 oz.) shredded sharp Cheddar cheese

Cook bacon in a wide frying pan over medium heat until crisp. Remove from pan with a slotted spoon; set aside. Pour off and discard all but 2 tablespoons drippings from pan. Add onion to pan and cook, stirring often, until soft. Remove from heat.

In a large bowl, stir together flour, cornmeal, sugar, baking powder, and salt. In a medium-size bowl, beat eggs, milk, and butter until blended. Add egg mixture to flour mixture and stir just until dry ingredients are evenly moistened. Stir in bacon, onion, and ¾ cup of the cheese.

Divide batter evenly among 16 to 18 greased 2¾- to 3-inch muffin cups, filling cups about two-thirds full. Sprinkle with remaining ½ cup cheese. Bake in a 400° oven until a wooden pick inserted in centers of muffins comes out clean (about 20 minutes). Turn out of pans onto racks; serve warm. Makes 16 to 18 muffins. —*Phyllis Miller, Lynnwood, WA*

Per muffin: 180 calories, 18 g carbohydrates, 6 g protein, 10 g total fat (5 g saturated), 45 mg cholesterol, 319 mg sodium

CRANBERRY-ORANGE MUFFINS

Topped with cinnamon and nuts, these berry-filled muffins are delicious for holiday or weekend breakfasts.

Cinnamon-Nut Topping (recipe follows)
2 cups all-purpose flour
¼ cup sugar
1 tablespoon baking powder
½ teaspoon *each* baking soda and salt
1 large egg
¼ cup salad oil
1 cup orange juice
1 teaspoon grated orange peel
1 cup fresh or frozen cranberries, halved

Prepare Cinnamon-Nut Topping; set aside.

In a large bowl, stir together flour, sugar, baking powder, baking soda, and salt. In a medium-size bowl, beat egg to blend; stir in oil, orange juice, orange peel, and cranberries. Add egg mixture to flour mixture and stir just until dry ingredients are evenly moistened (batter should be lumpy).

Divide batter evenly among 12 greased or paper-lined 2½-inch muffin cups; sprinkle batter evenly with Cinnamon-Nut Topping. Bake in a 375° oven until well browned (about 25 minutes).

Carefully remove muffins from pans and transfer to racks; serve warm or at room temperature. Makes 12 muffins.—*K. C., Westley, CA*

CINNAMON-NUT TOPPING. In a small bowl, stir together ¼ cup firmly packed **brown sugar,** ⅓ cup chopped **walnuts** or almonds, and ½ teaspoon **ground cinnamon.**

Per muffin: 200 calories, 29 g carbohydrates, 3 g protein, 8 g total fat (1 g saturated), 18 mg cholesterol, 285 mg sodium

RASPBERRY-CORNMEAL TEA MUFFINS

Yogurt adds tangy flavor to these golden, raspberry-dotted corn muffins. They're good partners for hot breakfast tea in the morning or for iced tea on a warm afternoon.

1 cup all-purpose flour
⅔ cup yellow cornmeal
⅓ cup sugar
2 teaspoons baking powder
½ teaspoon *each* baking soda and salt
2 large eggs
1 cup vanilla low-fat yogurt
¼ cup salad oil
1 cup fresh raspberries

In a large bowl, stir together flour, cornmeal, sugar, baking powder, baking soda, and salt.

In a medium-size bowl, beat eggs, yogurt, and oil until blended. Add egg mixture to flour mixture and stir just until dry ingredients are evenly moistened. Gently fold in raspberries.

Divide batter equally among 10 greased or paper-lined 2½-inch muffin cups. Bake in a 375° oven until muffins are golden and tops spring back when lightly pressed (20 to 25 minutes). Turn out of pans onto racks; serve warm. If made ahead, let cool; then wrap airtight and hold at room temperature until next day or freeze for up to 6 months. Makes 10 muffins.—*Susan McGrath, Portland*

Per muffin: 202 calories, 28 g carbohydrates, 5 g protein, 8 g total fat (1 g saturated), 44 mg cholesterol, 309 mg sodium

BLUEBERRY-LEMON MUFFINS

Simple blueberry muffins get a bright flavor boost from grated lemon peel.

2 cups all-purpose flour
¾ cup sugar
2 teaspoons baking powder
¼ teaspoon salt
1 large egg
¼ cup salad oil
½ cup milk
1 tablespoon grated lemon peel
1 cup fresh or frozen blueberries

In a large bowl, stir together flour, sugar, baking powder, and salt. In a small bowl, beat egg with oil until blended; then stir in milk and lemon peel. Add egg mixture to flour mixture and stir just until dry ingredients are evenly moistened (batter will be stiff). Gently fold in blueberries.

Divide batter evenly among 12 greased or paper-lined 2½-inch muffin cups. Bake in a 375° oven until muffins are golden (about 20 minutes). Turn out of pans onto racks; serve warm or at room temperature. If made ahead, let cool; then wrap airtight and refrigerate for up to 1 week or freeze for up to 6 months. Makes 12 muffins.—*Rebecca Lowe-Warren, Portland*

Per muffin: 193 calories, 31 g carbohydrates, 3 g protein, 6 g total fat (1 g saturated), 19 mg cholesterol, 149 mg sodium

BAKED CAKE DOUGHNUTS

These nutmeg-scented doughnuts are baked in muffin cups, not fried. Roll them in a spicy cinnamon-sugar coating while they're still hot from the oven.

- 1½ cups all-purpose flour
- ½ cup plus ⅓ cup sugar
- 2 teaspoons baking powder
- ¼ teaspoon *each* salt and ground nutmeg
- 1 large egg
- ½ cup milk
- ⅓ cup plus 3 tablespoons butter or margarine, melted and cooled
- ½ teaspoon vanilla
- 2 tablespoons jelly or marmalade
- ½ teaspoon ground cinnamon

In a large bowl, stir together flour, ½ cup of the sugar, baking powder, salt, and nutmeg. In a medium-size bowl, beat egg, milk, ⅓ cup of the butter, and vanilla until well blended. Add egg mixture to flour mixture; stir just until dry ingredients are evenly moistened.

Divide half the batter equally among 12 greased 2½-inch muffin cups; top batter in each cup with ½ teaspoon of the jelly. Spoon remaining batter equally into cups. Bake in a 400° oven until "doughnuts" are deep golden (18 to 20 minutes). Meanwhile, in a small bowl, mix cinnamon and remaining ⅓ cup sugar.

Carefully turn hot doughnuts out of pans. Brush hot doughnuts with remaining 3 tablespoons butter; roll in cinnamon-sugar mixture to coat. Serve warm or at room temperature. If made ahead, let cool; then wrap airtight and hold at room temperature until next day. Makes 12 doughnuts.—*Barbara Elbing, Palm Desert, CA*

Per doughnut: 212 calories, 29 g carbohydrates, 3 g protein, 10 g total fat (5 g saturated), 41 mg cholesterol, 231 mg sodium

CORNMEAL BREAD

Compared to most cornbreads, this one is almost cakelike—it's exceptionally moist, light, and fine-grained. For a breakfast treat, split and butter the pieces, then toast them under the broiler and spread with honey, marmalade, or strawberry jam.

- 1 cup *each* yellow cornmeal and all-purpose flour
- ½ teaspoon salt
- ½ cup (¼ lb.) butter or margarine
- ⅔ cup sugar
- 2 large eggs
- 1 cup buttermilk
- ½ teaspoon baking soda

In a medium-size bowl, stir together cornmeal, flour, and salt.

Melt butter in a 2- to 3-quart pan pan over low heat. Remove pan from heat and stir in sugar; then add eggs and beat until well blended. In a glass measure, stir together buttermilk and baking soda; stir into butter mixture. Then add flour mixture and stir just until dry ingredients are evenly moistened.

Spread batter evenly in a greased 8-inch-square baking pan. Bake in a 375° oven until bread begins to pull away from sides of pan (about 30 minutes). Makes 8 servings.—*W. S., Kent, WA*

Per serving: 322 calories, 44 g carbohydrates, 6 g protein, 14 g total fat (8 g saturated), 85 mg cholesterol, 387 mg sodium

CHEDDAR CHEESE POPOVERS

Serve these zesty, chili-seasoned popovers hot from the oven, with a bowl of soup or a main-dish salad for lunch or supper.

If you like your popovers especially dry, loosen them from the pans after baking and turn them slightly, so they're sitting at an angle. Then pierce each popover's sides with a thin skewer and let the popovers stand in the turned-off oven (with the oven door slightly ajar) for 8 to 10 minutes.

- 1 cup all-purpose flour
- ½ teaspoon Mexican seasoning (or ¼ teaspoon chili powder and ⅛ teaspoon *each* ground cumin and garlic powder)
- ¼ teaspoon garlic salt
- 1 tablespoon butter or margarine, melted and cooled
- 1 cup milk
- 3 large eggs
- 1 cup (about 4 oz.) shredded sharp Cheddar cheese
- ¼ cup finely chopped ripe olives

In a large bowl, stir together flour, Mexican seasoning, and garlic salt. Add butter, milk, and eggs; beat with an electric mixer on medium-high speed until very smooth, scraping bowl frequently. Beat in cheese and olives.

Divide batter equally among 12 to 14 well-greased ⅓- to ½-cup muffin cups or ovenproof glass custard cups, filling cups one-half to two-thirds full.

Bake on center rack of a 375° oven until well browned and firm to the touch (45 to 50 minutes). Remove from pans and serve hot. Makes 12 to 14 popovers.—*I. R., Sacramento*

Per popover: 127 calories, 9 g carbohydrates, 5 g protein, 8 g total fat (3 g saturated), 63 mg cholesterol, 180 mg sodium

BREAKFAST TEA BREAD

Dense with raisins (nearly a pound and a half of them!) and almonds, this orange-laced bread was created to complement full-flavored breakfast teas—but coffee connoisseurs will appreciate it just as much as tea-sippers do. We suggest using 2 cups each of dark and golden seedless raisins, but you can use 4 cups of one kind if you prefer.

- 2 **cups all-purpose flour**
- 1 **teaspoon baking powder**
- 3 **large eggs**
- ¾ **cup sugar**
- ½ **cup (¼ lb.) butter or margarine, at room temperature**
- 1 **tablespoon finely shredded orange peel**
- 1 **cup sour cream**
- 2 **cups *each* dark raisins and golden raisins**
- ½ **cup chopped almonds**

In a medium-size bowl, stir together flour and baking powder. In a large bowl, beat eggs, sugar, butter, and orange peel until blended. Stir in sour cream. Add flour mixture and beat until well blended. Stir in dark raisins, golden raisins, and almonds.

Spread batter evenly in a greased or nonstick 5- by 9-inch loaf pan; smooth top of batter. Bake in a 325° oven until loaf begins to pull away from sides of pan and a wooden skewer inserted in center comes out clean (1¼ to 1½ hours). Let cool in pan on a rack for about 15 minutes; then turn out onto rack to cool completely. If made ahead, wrap airtight and hold at room temperature for up to 4 days. Cut into thin slices to serve. Makes 1 loaf (about 16 servings).
—*Rebecca Armstrong, Orem, UT*

Per serving: 324 calories, 52 g carbohydrates, 5 g protein, 12 g total fat (6 g saturated), 62 mg cholesterol, 117 mg sodium

FRUITED PUMPKIN BREAD

A bit different from many pumpkin bread recipes, this spicy loaf includes mashed banana for extra fruity flavor. For variety, try substituting chopped dates for some of the walnuts. The bread stays moist and delicious for up to 5 days in the refrigerator—so enjoy one loaf now and keep the other on hand for unexpected guests.

- 3 **cups all-purpose flour**
- 1½ **teaspoons baking soda**
- 1 **teaspoon salt**
- 1 **teaspoon pumpkin pie spice or ground nutmeg**
- ¾ **cup (¼ lb. plus ¼ cup) butter or margarine, at room temperature**
- 1¼ **cups sugar**
- 3 **large eggs**
- ¾ **cup *each* canned pumpkin and mashed ripe banana**
- ½ **to 1 cup chopped walnuts or pecans**

In a large bowl, stir together flour, baking soda, salt, and pumpkin pie spice. In another large bowl, beat butter and sugar with an electric mixer until creamy. Add eggs, one at a time, beating well after each addition; then stir in pumpkin and banana. Add flour mixture and stir just until dry ingredients are evenly moistened. Stir in walnuts.

Spread batter evenly in 2 greased, floured 4- by 8-inch loaf pans. Bake in a 350° oven until a wooden skewer inserted in centers of loaves comes out clean (about 1 hour).

Let bread cool in pans on racks for about 5 minutes; then turn out onto racks to cool completely. If made ahead, wrap cooled loaves airtight and refrigerate for up to 5 days. Makes 2 loaves (10 to 12 servings each).—*J. C., Greenbrae, CA*

Per serving: 213 calories, 28 g carbohydrates, 3 g protein, 10 g total fat (4 g saturated), 46 mg cholesterol, 264 mg sodium

WHOLE WHEAT RAISIN SCONES

Make these wholesome, fragrantly spiced scones for a special weekend breakfast. You might serve them with a crock of Orange Butter (facing page) or sweet Cinnamon Butter (page 185).

- 1 **cup *each* all-purpose flour and whole wheat flour**
- 6 **tablespoons sugar**
- 1 **tablespoon baking powder**
- 1½ **teaspoons ground cinnamon**
- ½ **teaspoon *each* ground nutmeg and salt**
- ⅓ **cup firm butter or margarine, cut into chunks**
- 2 **large eggs, lightly beaten**
- ⅓ **cup milk**
- ½ **cup raisins**

In a large bowl, stir together all-purpose flour, whole wheat flour, 5 tablespoons of the sugar, baking powder, cinnamon, nutmeg, and salt. Cut in butter with a pastry blender or 2 knives (or rub it in with your fingers) until mixture resembles coarse crumbs. Reserve 2 tablespoons of the beaten eggs; add remaining eggs, milk, and raisins to flour mixture. Stir just until dry ingredients are evenly moistened.

Turn dough out onto a lightly floured board and knead about 6 times, or just until dough holds together. Then pat dough into a ¾-inch-thick round. With a sharp knife, cut round into 8 wedges; arrange wedges slightly apart on a greased baking sheet. Brush reserved beaten eggs over scones; then sprinkle with remaining 1 tablespoon sugar. Bake in a 425° oven until browned (18 to 20 minutes). Serve warm. Makes 8 scones.—*K. N., Portland*

Per scone: 272 calories, 41 g carbohydrates, 6 g protein, 10 g total fat (5 g saturated), 75 mg cholesterol, 425 mg sodium

ORANGE-CURRANT SCONES

You bake these currant-dotted, sugar-topped scones in a round cake pan.

Orange Butter (recipe follows)
3 cups all-purpose flour
About ¾ cup sugar
1 teaspoon baking soda
½ teaspoon baking powder
2 teaspoons grated orange peel
½ cup (¼ lb.) firm butter or margarine, cut into chunks
¾ cup dried currants
¾ cup buttermilk

Prepare Orange Butter and set aside.

In a large bowl, stir together flour, ¾ cup of the sugar, baking soda, baking powder, and orange peel. Cut in the ½ cup butter with a pastry blender or 2 knives (or rub it in with your fingers) until mixture resembles fine crumbs. Stir in currants. Add buttermilk and stir just until dry ingredients are evenly moistened.

Turn dough out onto a lightly floured board. Knead 10 times, or just until dough holds together. Pat into a 9-inch round; place in a greased 9-inch-round baking pan. Sprinkle lightly with sugar. Bake in a 400° oven until golden brown (35 to 40 minutes). Turn scone out of pan onto a plate. Cut into 8 wedges; serve warm, with Orange Butter. Makes 8 servings.—*Susan Dalton, San Jose, CA*

ORANGE BUTTER. In a small bowl, beat ½ cup (¼ lb.) **butter** or margarine (at room temperature), 1 teaspoon **grated orange peel,** and 1 tablespoon **powdered sugar** until creamy. Makes about ½ cup.

Per scone: 400 calories, 66 g carbohydrates, 6 g protein, 13 g total fat (7 g saturated), 32 mg cholesterol, 337 mg sodium

Per tablespoon of Orange Butter: 106 calories, 1 g carbohydrates, 0.1 g protein, 12 g total fat (7 g saturated), 31 mg cholesterol, 117 mg sodium

CHOCOLATE CHIP SCONES

It's rare to find any embellishment other than a few plump raisins in a standard English scone—but this recipe departs from tradition by packing in a generous measure of chocolate chips. Serve the scones hot from the oven, when the chocolate is temptingly soft and melting.

2 cups all-purpose flour
¼ cup powdered sugar
1 tablespoon baking powder
6 tablespoons firm butter or margarine, cut into chunks
½ cup semisweet chocolate chips
1 large egg
About ½ cup milk
1 teaspoon granulated sugar

In a large bowl, stir together flour, powdered sugar, and baking powder. Cut in butter with a pastry blender or 2 knives (or rub it in with your fingers) until mixture resembles fine crumbs. Mix in chocolate chips.

Break egg into a glass measure; then add enough milk to make ⅔ cup liquid. Stir to blend egg and milk. Add egg mixture to flour mixture; stir just until dry ingredients are evenly moistened.

Turn dough out onto a lightly floured board and knead 6 to 8 times, or just until dough holds together. Place dough on a greased baking sheet and pat into a 6- by 9-inch rectangle; sprinkle with granulated sugar. Cut dough into six 3-inch squares, then cut each square diagonally in half to make 2 triangles; separate triangles and space at least 1 inch apart. Bake in a 450° oven until golden brown (12 to 15 minutes). Serve warm. Makes 12 scones. —*Donna Henderson, Monmouth, OR*

Per scone: 191 calories, 25 g carbohydrates, 3 g protein, 9 g total fat (5 g saturated), 35 mg cholesterol, 199 mg sodium

SOFT SESAME BISCUITS

These tender little breads are a cross between drop biscuits and muffins.

1 cup *each* all-purpose flour and whole wheat flour
2 tablespoons sugar
1 teaspoon baking soda
¼ teaspoon salt
2 tablespoons sesame seeds
⅓ cup firm butter or margarine, cut into chunks
1 cup buttermilk

In a large bowl, stir together all-purpose flour, whole wheat flour, sugar, baking soda, salt, and 1 tablespoon of the sesame seeds. Cut in butter with a pastry blender or 2 knives (or rub it in with your fingers) until mixture resembles coarse crumbs. Add buttermilk and stir with a fork just until dry ingredients are evenly moistened.

With oiled hands, shape dough into 12 equal balls. Space balls about 1 inch apart on a well-greased baking sheet; then gently press each one to flatten to a thickness of about 1 inch. Sprinkle biscuits evenly with remaining 1 tablespoon sesame seeds. Bake in a 450° oven until biscuits are deep golden brown (12 to 14 minutes). Serve warm. Makes 12 biscuits.—*Chris Petersen, Moscow, ID*

Per biscuit: 147 calories, 19 g carbohydrates, 3 g protein, 7 g total fat (3 g saturated), 14 mg cholesterol, 231 mg sodium

GINGER BISCUITS

A generous quantity of crystallized ginger gives these golden, slightly sweet biscuits their distinctive flavor. Try them with fruit salads or Cool Curry Turkey Salad (page 55).

2 cups all-purpose flour

4 teaspoons baking powder

½ teaspoon salt

¼ cup sugar

6 tablespoons solid vegetable shortening; or 6 tablespoons firm butter or margarine, cut into chunks

½ cup finely chopped crystallized ginger

2 large eggs

About 2 tablespoons milk

About 1 tablespoon butter or margarine, melted; or 1 tablespoon half-and-half

In a large bowl, stir together flour, baking powder, salt, and sugar. Cut in shortening with a pastry blender or 2 knives (or rub it in with your fingers) until mixture resembles coarse crumbs. Stir in ginger. Break eggs into a glass measure; then add enough milk to make ½ cup liquid. Stir to blend eggs and milk. Add egg mixture to flour mixture and stir with a fork just until dry ingredients are evenly moistened.

Turn dough out onto a lightly floured board and knead 4 or 5 times, or just until dough holds together. Roll or pat out dough about ½ inch thick.

Cut out biscuits with a 2-inch biscuit cutter; then arrange biscuits on a greased baking sheet, spacing them about 1½ inches apart. Brush lightly with melted butter and bake in a 425° oven until golden brown (10 to 12 minutes). Serve hot. Makes about 18 biscuits.—*J. H., Menlo Park, CA*

Per biscuit: 144 calories, 20 g carbohydrates, 2 g protein, 6 g total fat (2 g saturated), 26 mg cholesterol, 193 mg sodium

CHEESE BISCUIT STICKS

Flavored with sharp Cheddar cheese and flecked with whole wheat flour, these tender, crisp-crusted biscuit sticks complement tuna, chicken, or turkey salad for lunch or a warm-weather supper.

1 cup *each* all-purpose flour and whole wheat flour

1 tablespoon baking powder

1 teaspoon sugar

½ teaspoon salt

½ cup (¼ lb.) firm butter or margarine, cut into chunks

¾ cup shredded sharp Cheddar cheese

½ cup milk

Poppy seeds or sesame seeds (optional)

In a food processor or a large bowl, whirl or stir together all-purpose flour, whole wheat flour, baking powder, sugar, and salt. Add butter; whirl or rub with your fingers until mixture resembles coarse crumbs. Mix in cheese. Add milk; whirl or stir with a fork just until dry ingredients are evenly moistened.

Turn dough out onto a lightly floured board and knead 8 to 10 times, or just until dough holds together. Shape dough into a ball and set on a greased baking sheet; then pat into an 8-inch round. With a sharp knife, cut round into 1-inch-wide strips. Sprinkle lightly with poppy seeds, if desired.

Bake in a 425° oven until golden brown (25 to 30 minutes). Carefully transfer round to a rack and let cool for about 15 minutes. Serve warm; to serve, cut biscuit sticks apart at lines. Makes 8 servings.—*Judy Taylor, Oakland, CA*

Per serving: 275 calories, 25 g carbohydrates, 7 g protein, 17 g total fat (10 g saturated), 44 mg cholesterol, 522 mg sodium

OATMEAL COFFEE BREAD

To get a headstart on this coffeecake, you can mix the topping and grate the orange peel the night before.

Coconut Topping (recipe follows)

1½ cups all-purpose flour

2 teaspoons baking powder

½ teaspoon salt

6 tablespoons butter or margarine, at room temperature; or 6 tablespoons solid vegetable shortening

¾ cup sugar

2 large eggs

½ cup milk

½ cup quick-cooking rolled oats

1 tablespoon grated orange peel

Prepare Coconut Topping; set aside. In a medium-size bowl, stir together flour, baking powder, and salt. In a large bowl, beat butter and sugar with an electric mixer until creamy. Add eggs, one at a time, beating well after each addition. Stir in milk. Add flour mixture and beat until well blended. Stir in oats and orange peel.

Spoon batter into a greased 9-inch-square baking pan; sprinkle with Coconut Topping. Bake in a 375° oven until a wooden pick inserted in center of cake comes out clean (about 30 minutes). Serve warm or at room temperature. Makes 9 to 12 servings. —*A. M., San Diego, CA*

COCONUT TOPPING. In a small bowl, combine ⅓ cup *each* firmly packed **brown sugar** and **sweetened flaked coconut;** ⅓ cup chopped **walnuts** or pecans; 2 teaspoons **ground cinnamon;** 2 tablespoons **all-purpose flour;** and 2 tablespoons **butter** or margarine (at room temperature). Mix until crumbly.

Per serving: 292 calories, 40 g carbohydrates, 5 g protein, 13 g total fat (7 g saturated), 63 mg cholesterol, 304 mg sodium

BLUEBERRY COFFEECAKE

Dotted with fresh blueberries and topped with buttery, cinnamon-spiced crumbs, this simple cake is good warm or cooled. Top it with whipped cream, if you like.

Crumb Topping (recipe follows)
2 cups all-purpose flour
2 teaspoons baking powder
½ teaspoon salt
¼ cup butter or margarine, at room temperature
¾ cup sugar
1 large egg
½ cup milk
2 cups fresh or frozen blueberries

Prepare Crumb Topping and set aside.

In a medium-size bowl, stir together flour, baking powder, and salt. In a large bowl, beat butter and sugar with an electric mixer until fluffy. Beat in egg; then blend in milk. Add flour mixture and beat until well blended. Gently fold in blueberries.

Spread batter evenly in a greased 9-inch-square baking pan; sprinkle with Crumb Topping. Bake in a 375° oven until cake is golden brown and a wooden pick inserted in center comes out clean (about 45 minutes). Serve warm or at room temperature. Makes 9 to 12 servings.—*J. M., Grass Valley, CA*

CRUMB TOPPING. In a small bowl, stir together ½ cup **sugar,** ½ teaspoon **ground cinnamon,** and ¼ cup **all-purpose flour.** Add ¼ cup firm **butter** or margarine (cut into chunks); cut in butter with a pastry blender or 2 knives (or rub it in with your fingers) until mixture is crumbly.

Per serving: 287 calories, 47 g carbohydrates, 4 g protein, 10 g total fat (6 g saturated), 43 mg cholesterol, 291 mg sodium

CRANBERRY BRUNCH CAKE

Offer wedges of this moist fruit-and-nut cake with morning coffee or as part of a special brunch. Like Cranberry-Orange Muffins (page 178), it's flavored with cinnamon, orange juice, and grated fresh orange peel.

3 cups all-purpose flour
2 teaspoons baking powder
1 teaspoon *each* baking soda and ground cinnamon
½ teaspoon ground ginger
¼ teaspoon ground allspice
1 cup (½ lb.) butter or margarine, at room temperature
2 cups sugar
1 tablespoon grated orange peel
3 large eggs
1 cup orange juice
1½ cups fresh or frozen cranberries
¾ cup chopped walnuts or pecans

In a large bowl, stir together flour, baking powder, baking soda, cinnamon, ginger, and allspice.

In another large bowl, beat butter, sugar, and orange peel with an electric mixer until creamy. Add eggs, one at a time, beating well after each addition. Add flour mixture and orange juice alternately to creamed mixture, blending well after each addition. By hand, stir in cranberries and walnuts.

Spoon batter into a well-greased, floured 10-inch tube pan with a removable bottom. Bake in a 350° oven until a wooden skewer inserted in center comes out clean (about 1 hour). Let cool in pan on a rack for 30 minutes; then remove cake from pan, transfer to a serving plate, and let cool completely. Makes 12 servings.—*C. C., Downey, CA*

Per serving: 469 calories, 63 g carbohydrates, 6 g protein, 22 g total fat (10 g saturated), 95 mg cholesterol, 353 mg sodium

CHOCOLATE NUT COFFEECAKE

Served warm from the oven, this light, even-textured cake is sure to delight chocolate fanciers. It's filled with a crunchy combination of chocolate chips and chopped pecans.

1½ cups sugar
1 teaspoon ground cinnamon
1 cup (about 6 oz.) semisweet chocolate chips
½ cup chopped pecans or walnuts
2 cups all-purpose flour
1½ teaspoons baking powder
1 teaspoon baking soda
½ cup (¼ lb.) butter or margarine, at room temperature
2 large eggs
1 teaspoon vanilla
1 cup sour cream

In a small bowl, mix ½ cup of the sugar, cinnamon, chocolate chips, and pecans; set aside. In a medium-size bowl, stir together flour, baking powder, and baking soda.

In a large bowl, beat butter and remaining 1 cup sugar with an electric mixer until creamy. Add eggs, one at a time, beating well after each addition. Blend in vanilla and sour cream. Add flour mixture and beat until blended.

Spread half the batter in a greased, floured 9- by 13-inch baking pan; sprinkle evenly with half the nut mixture. Spoon remaining batter evenly into pan; sprinkle with remaining nut mixture and press it gently into batter.

Bake in a 350° oven until a wooden pick inserted in center of cake comes out clean (about 35 minutes). Serve warm. Makes 12 to 15 servings.—*M. F., Aloha, OR*

Per serving: 369 calories, 49 g carbohydrates, 4 g protein, 19 g total fat (9 g saturated), 60 mg cholesterol, 252 mg sodium

CINNAMON SOUR CREAM COFFEECAKE

When this recipe first appeared in our pages in 1959, we noted, "September brings an abrupt change in daily schedules for most Western families with school children. And soon the first fall meetings of many organizations will be announced. Our selection of recipes for this busy month includes a delicious coffeecake to start off a morning *kaffee-klatsch*." Topped and filled with cinnamon-spiced walnuts, the rich cake is a long-time favorite for brunches and weekend breakfasts at any time of year.

- ¾ cup finely chopped walnuts
- 2 tablespoons granulated sugar
- 1 teaspoon ground cinnamon
- 2 cups all-purpose flour
- 1½ teaspoons baking powder
- ½ teaspoon baking soda
- 1 cup (½ lb.) butter or margarine, at room temperature
- 1¼ cups granulated sugar
- 2 large eggs
- 1 teaspoon vanilla
- 1 cup sour cream
   Powdered sugar (optional)

In a small bowl, mix walnuts, the 2 tablespoons granulated sugar, and cinnamon; set aside. In a medium-size bowl, stir together flour, baking powder, and baking soda.

In a large bowl, beat butter and the 1¼ cups granulated sugar with an electric mixer until light and fluffy. Add eggs, one at a time, beating well after each addition. Blend in vanilla and sour cream. Add flour mixture and beat until blended (batter will be quite thick).

Sprinkle half the nut mixture evenly over bottom of a well-greased 9-inch tube pan. Spoon half the batter evenly over nut mixture; sprinkle with remaining nut mixture. Then evenly spoon remaining batter into pan. Bake in a 350° oven until a wooden skewer inserted in center of cake comes out clean (50 to 55 minutes). Let cool in pan on a rack for about 15 minutes; then turn out of pan onto a serving plate. Sift powdered sugar over cake, if desired. Makes 8 to 10 servings. —*J. B., San Bernardino, CA*

Per serving: 546 calories, 55 g carbohydrates, 7 g protein, 34 g total fat (17 g saturated), 114 mg cholesterol, 399 mg sodium

CHEESE-GLAZED COFFEECAKE

Cream-puff dough bakes atop a buttery short crust to make this unusual coffeecake. Top it with an orange-scented cream cheese glaze and a sprinkling of sliced almonds.

- 2 cups all-purpose flour
- 1 cup (½ lb.) firm butter or margarine
- 1 cup plus 2 tablespoons water
- 4 large eggs
- ¾ teaspoon almond extract
   Cheese Glaze (recipe follows)
- ½ cup sliced almonds

Place 1 cup of the flour in a medium-size bowl. Dice ½ cup of the butter; add butter to flour and cut it in with a pastry blender or 2 knives (or rub it in with your fingers) until mixture resembles fine crumbs. Sprinkle with 2 tablespoons of the water, then stir with a fork until pastry holds together. Place pastry in a 12-inch pizza pan or on a 12- by 15-inch baking sheet; pat into a 10-inch round.

In a 2- to 3-quart pan, combine remaining 1 cup water and remaining ½ cup butter; bring to a boil over medium heat, stirring until butter is melted. Add remaining 1 cup flour all at once and stir until dough pulls away from sides of pan and forms a ball (about 2 minutes). Remove from heat and let stand for 3 to 5 minutes. Then add eggs, one at a time, beating after each addition until dough is smooth and well blended. Stir in almond extract. Spread dough evenly over pastry round on baking sheet.

Bake in a 400° oven until top of cake is golden brown and looks crisp (about 45 minutes). Let cool in pan on a rack for 10 minutes. Meanwhile, prepare Cheese Glaze.

Drizzle cake with glaze and sprinkle with almonds. Serve warm or at room temperature; to serve, cut into wedges. Makes 10 servings. —*P. U., Darby, MT*

CHEESE GLAZE. In a small bowl, combine 1 small package (about 3 oz.) **cream cheese** (at room temperature), ¾ cup **powdered sugar,** 1 teaspoon **grated orange peel,** and 1 tablespoon **orange juice.** Beat until smooth.

Per serving: 378 calories, 30 g carbohydrates, 7 g protein, 26 g total fat (14 g saturated), 144 mg cholesterol, 239 mg sodium

HEARTY HEALTHY HOTCAKES

When you mention hotcakes, most people think of breakfast. But these light, tender pancakes are just as good for a quick family supper.

GOLDEN SQUASH ROLLS

Banana squash gives these slightly sweet dinner rolls their warm, rich color and moist texture.

About 1 pound banana squash
1 package active dry yeast
¼ cup warm water (about 110°F)
1 cup warm milk (about 110°F)
2 tablespoons butter or margarine, melted and cooled
½ cup sugar
1 teaspoon salt
6¼ to 6¾ cups all-purpose flour

Cut squash into 2-inch squares; peel. Arrange on a steamer rack; cover and steam over 1½ inches boiling water until tender when pierced (15 to 20 minutes). Drain squash and mash until smooth; you need 1 cup. Set aside to cool slightly.

In large bowl, combine yeast and warm water; let stand until yeast is softened (about 5 minutes). Add milk, butter, sugar, salt, and 1 cup of the flour; beat with a heavy-duty mixer or a wooden spoon until smooth. Beat in squash; then beat in 5 to 5½ cups more flour, or enough to make a soft dough.

Turn dough out onto a floured board and knead until smooth and elastic, adding more flour as needed to prevent sticking. Place dough in a greased bowl and turn over to grease top. Cover and let rise in a warm place until doubled (about 1 hour).

Punch dough down and knead briefly on floured board to release air. Then divide dough into 14 equal pieces and shape each into a ball. Arrange rolls, spacing them evenly, in 2 greased 9-inch-round baking pans. Cover and let rise in a warm place until almost doubled (30 to 40 minutes). Then bake in a 400° oven until golden (20 to 25 minutes).

Makes 14 rolls.—*Jennifer Allen, Los Osos, CA*

Per roll: 287 calories, 55 g carbohydrates, 7 g protein, 4 g total fat (2 g saturated), 7 mg cholesterol, 194 mg sodium

WHEAT GERM BUNS

Split these quick-to-make sandwich buns and fill them with beef or turkey burgers, hot off the grill.

2 tablespoons firmly packed brown sugar
1 teaspoon salt
2 packages active dry yeast
About 5 cups all-purpose flour
2 cups milk
¼ cup butter or margarine
2 large eggs
1 cup toasted wheat germ

In a large bowl, stir together sugar, salt, yeast, and 2 cups of the flour. In a small pan, heat milk and butter over medium heat until mixture reaches 115° to 120°F. Stir milk mixture into flour mixture. Add one of the eggs, 1 cup more flour, and wheat germ; beat until well blended. Mix in about 1½ cups more flour, or enough to make a stiff dough.

Turn dough out onto a floured board and knead until smooth (about 10 minutes), adding more flour as needed to prevent sticking. Divide dough into 12 equal pieces and shape each piece into a smooth ball. Arrange buns 3 inches apart on greased baking sheets. Cover and let rise in a warm place until doubled (about 30 minutes).

In a small bowl, beat remaining egg to blend; brush over buns. Bake in a 375° oven until buns are a rich brown (15 to 20 minutes). Makes 12 buns.—*J. B., Point Arena, CA*

Per bun: 322 calories, 49 g carbohydrates, 11 g protein, 9 g total fat (4 g saturated), 51 mg cholesterol, 271 mg sodium

CINNAMON-NUT CRESCENTS

Brush these spicy, nut-filled crescents with a glistening powdered sugar glaze while they're still oven-warm.

1 package active dry yeast
¼ cup warm water (about 110°F)
¾ cup granulated sugar
1 teaspoon ground cinnamon
1 cup chopped walnuts
2 cups all-purpose flour
1 cup (½ lb.) firm butter or margarine
2 large eggs, separated
½ cup powdered sugar
2 tablespoons milk

In a small bowl, combine yeast, warm water, and 1 teaspoon of the granulated sugar; let stand until yeast is softened (about 5 minutes). In another bowl, mix cinnamon, walnuts, and remaining granulated sugar; set aside.

Place flour in a large bowl. Cut in butter with a pastry blender or 2 knives (or rub it in with your fingers) until mixture forms even crumbs. Add egg yolks and yeast mixture; beat until dough forms a smooth ball (3 to 5 minutes). Divide dough into thirds.

Work with one portion of dough at a time. On a floured board, roll each portion into a 12-inch round. Beat egg whites lightly. Brush each round with egg whites and sprinkle with a third of the walnut mixture; then cut round into 8 wedges. Roll up each wedge from wide end toward point; then set rolls about 2 inches apart on greased large baking sheets.

Cover rolls and let rise in a warm place until puffy (about 20 minutes). Bake in a 350° oven until golden (15 to 20 minutes). Blend powdered sugar and milk; brush over warm rolls. Makes 24 rolls.—*L.P., Durango, CO*

Per roll: 184 calories, 18 g carbohydrates, 3 g protein, 12 g total fat (5 g saturated), 39 mg cholesterol, 85 mg sodium

STICKY PECAN ROLLS

After baking these one-rise sweet rolls, invert them so that the tempting caramel-nut topping is on top.

- ¼ teaspoon baking soda
- ¼ cup granulated sugar
- 1 teaspoon salt
- 1 package active dry yeast
- 2½ to 3 cups all-purpose flour
- 1 cup buttermilk
- 3 tablespoons salad oil
- 2 tablespoons water
- ¼ cup butter or margarine, melted
- ½ cup firmly packed brown sugar
- ½ cup pecan halves
- 1 teaspoon ground cinnamon

In a large bowl, stir together baking soda, granulated sugar, salt, yeast, and 1 cup of the flour. In a small pan, heat buttermilk and oil over medium heat until mixture reaches 120° to 130°F. Add oil mixture to flour mixture and beat with an electric mixer on medium speed until smooth (about 2 minutes). Stir in 1½ cups more flour. Turn dough out onto a lightly floured board and knead until smooth and elastic, adding more flour as needed to prevent sticking.

In a small bowl, stir together water, 2 tablespoons of the butter, and ¼ cup of the brown sugar. Divide sugar mixture equally among twelve 2½-inch muffin cups; top equally with pecans.

Roll dough into a 12- by 15-inch rectangle. Brush with remaining 2 tablespoons butter; sprinkle with remaining ¼ cup brown sugar and cinnamon. Roll up dough snugly, jelly roll style, starting with a short end; pinch seam to seal. Cut roll crosswise into 12 slices; place one slice in each muffin cup. Let rise in a warm place until doubled (about 1½ hours).

Bake in a 350° oven until golden (about 25 minutes). Carefully invert pans over a platter; lift off pans. Serve rolls sticky side up. Makes 12 rolls.—*R. W., Seattle*

Per roll: 261 calories, 37 g carbohydrates, 4 g protein, 11 g total fat (3 g saturated), 11 mg cholesterol, 274 mg sodium

KOLACHES

Of Eastern European origin, these plump, sweet breakfast rolls are traditionally filled with apricot or plum jam or preserves.

- 1¼ cups milk
- ⅓ cup butter or margarine
- ⅔ cup sugar
- ½ teaspoon salt
- 1 package active dry yeast
- 2 large eggs
- 5 to 5¼ cups all-purpose flour
  About ½ cup jam or preserves
- 1 large egg yolk
- 1 tablespoon water

In a small pan, heat milk, butter, sugar, and salt over medium heat until mixture reaches 110°F; remove from heat. Pour mixture into a large bowl, stir in yeast, and let stand until yeast is softened (about 5 minutes). Beat in eggs. Using a heavy-duty mixer or a wooden spoon, beat in 4½ cups of the flour. Then turn dough out onto a floured board and knead until smooth and elastic, adding more flour as needed to prevent sticking.

Place dough in a greased bowl and turn over to grease top. Cover and let rise in a warm place until doubled (1½ to 2 hours).

Punch dough down and knead briefly on a floured board to release air. Then roll out dough ½ inch thick and cut into 2- to 2½-inch rounds. Place rounds 2 inches apart on greased baking sheets. Cover and let rise in a warm place until puffy (about 45 minutes).

With your thumbs, make a cavity in center of each roll; fill each with about 1 teaspoon of the jam. In a small bowl, beat egg yolk and water to blend; brush yolk mixture over rolls. Bake in a 350° oven until golden (20 to 25 minutes). Serve warm or at room temperature. Makes 18 to 22 rolls.—*Ellen Hajek, Golden, CO*

Per roll: 220 calories, 38 g carbohydrates, 5 g protein, 6 g total fat (3 g saturated), 42 mg cholesterol, 115 mg sodium

CHOCOLATE BREAD

Both cocoa and chocolate chips go into this sweet bread, making it doubly irresistible to chocolate lovers. While the round, fragrant loaf is still hot, decorate it with a sifting of snowy powdered sugar.

- 1 package active dry yeast
- 1½ cups warm water (about 110°F)
- 2 tablespoons granulated sugar
- ⅓ cup unsweetened cocoa
- 2 tablespoons butter or margarine, at room temperature
- 1 large egg
- ¾ teaspoon salt
- 4 cups all-purpose flour
- 1 cup (about 6 oz.) semisweet chocolate chips
  Powdered sugar

In a large bowl, combine yeast, warm water, and granulated sugar; let stand until yeast is softened (about 5 minutes). Stir in cocoa, butter, egg, and salt. Then add 3 cups of the flour and beat with a heavy-duty mixer or a wooden spoon until dough is very stretchy (about 10 minutes). Stir in chocolate chips.

Sprinkle remaining 1 cup flour on a board; scrape dough out onto flour. Knead 5 or 6 times, or until flour is barely incorporated and you can form dough into a smooth round (about 1 minute). Carefully transfer dough round to a greased large baking sheet. Cover and let rise in a warm place until puffy (about 1 hour). Then bake in a 350° oven until dark brown (about 50 minutes).

Set a paper stencil on hot loaf; rub powdered sugar through a fine strainer over stencil, then lift off stencil. Serve bread hot or warm. Makes 1 loaf (20 to 24 servings).—*Tenia Holland, Salt Lake City*

Per serving: 143 calories, 24 g carbohydrates, 3 g protein, 4 g total fat (2 g saturated), 13 mg cholesterol, 93 mg sodium

GERMAN BUTTERKUCHEN

Streaks of rich, buttery topping marble this almond-topped yeast coffeecake. When the recipe first appeared in 1965, we called it "just right for a late and leisurely breakfast."

- 1½ packages active dry yeast
- 1 teaspoon sugar
- ¼ cup warm water (about 110°F)
- 1 cup milk
- ½ cup sugar
- 1 teaspoon salt
- ¼ cup solid vegetable shortening
- 2 large eggs
- 3¼ cups all-purpose flour
  Buttery Cinnamon Topping (recipe follows)
- ⅓ cup slivered almonds

In a large bowl, combine yeast, the 1 teaspoon sugar, and warm water; let stand until yeast is softened (about 5 minutes).

Meanwhile, in a small pan, heat milk, the ½ cup sugar, salt, and shortening over medium heat until shortening is melted and mixture reaches 110°F; remove from heat.

Stir milk mixture into yeast mixture. Beat in eggs; then gradually add flour, beating with a heavy-duty electric mixer or a wooden spoon until dough is well blended. Spread dough evenly in a greased 9- by 13-inch baking pan. Cover and let rise in a warm place until puffy (about 45 minutes). Meanwhile, prepare Buttery Cinnamon Topping.

Sprinkle topping and almonds evenly over dough; bake in a 375° oven until topping is golden brown and a wooden pick inserted in center of coffeecake comes out clean (about 30 minutes). Cut into squares and serve warm. Makes 12 servings. —*W. P., Honolulu*

BUTTERY CINNAMON TOPPING.
In a medium-size bowl, combine 1 cup **sugar** and ½ teaspoon **ground cinnamon.** Cut ½ cup (¼ lb.) firm **butter** or margarine into chunks; add to sugar mixture and cut in with a pastry blender or 2 knives (or rub in with your fingers) until mixture resembles fine crumbs.

Per serving: 381 calories, 53 g carbohydrates, 6 g protein, 16 g total fat (7 g saturated), 59 mg cholesterol, 291 mg sodium

NUT CRUMB COFFEE BREAD

A crunchy mixture of spiced graham cracker crumbs and nuts—your choice of walnuts, hazelnuts, pecans or almonds—is sprinkled throughout this fragrant pull-apart coffeecake.

- 2 packages active dry yeast
- ½ cup warm water (about 110°F)
- 1 cup milk, scalded and cooled
- 1 cup sugar
- 1 teaspoon salt
- 2 large eggs, lightly beaten
- ¾ cup (¼ lb. plus ¼ cup) butter or margarine, melted and cooled
- 5 cups all-purpose flour
- ⅓ cup graham cracker crumbs
- 1 cup chopped walnuts, hazelnuts, almonds, or pecans
- 1 teaspoon *each* ground cinnamon and grated orange peel

In a small bowl, combine yeast and warm water; let stand until yeast is softened (about 5 minutes).

In a large bowl, stir together milk, ⅔ cup of the sugar, and salt. Then stir in yeast mixture, eggs, ½ cup of the butter, and 2 cups of the flour. Beat with a heavy-duty mixer or a wooden spoon until smooth. Then beat in remaining 3 cups flour to make a smooth, elastic dough. Transfer dough to a greased bowl; cover and let rise in a warm place until doubled (45 minutes to 1 hour).

Meanwhile, in a small bowl, mix graham cracker crumbs, walnuts, cinnamon, orange peel, and remaining ⅓ cup sugar. Pour remaining ¼ cup butter into another small bowl.

Stir dough down. Spoon out walnut-size pieces of dough; roll each in butter. Arrange a third of the balls in a greased 10-inch tube pan with a removable bottom; sprinkle with a third of the crumb mixture. Then arrange half the remaining balls in pan; sprinkle with half the remaining crumb mixture. Top with remaining balls and remaining crumb mixture. Let rise in a warm place until doubled (about 45 minutes).

Bake in a 350° oven until golden brown (about 50 minutes). Let cool in pan for about 10 minutes, then remove from pan and serve warm. Makes 12 servings. —*K. R., Seattle*

Per serving: 463 calories, 62 g carbohydrates, 9 g protein, 20 g total fat (8 g saturated), 69 mg cholesterol, 347 mg sodium

Hot meatballs, served from a shiny chafing dish, made a hit at parties in the 1970s

To serve steak, cut thin, slanting slices diagonally across the grain of the meat

ALICE HARTH

Baked tomatoes with spinach and cheese are good served with chicken and rice

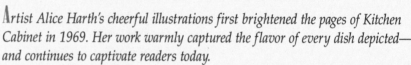

A SAMPLING FROM
1971 to 1975

*A*rtist Alice Harth's cheerful illustrations first brightened the pages of Kitchen Cabinet in 1969. Her work warmly captured the flavor of every dish depicted—and continues to captivate readers today.

The tabletop accessories of the early 1970s are a different matter. The teak board on which we carved Barbecued Flank Steak in 1972 and the chafing dish shown holding appetizer meatballs (at left) have probably long since been relegated to a storage closet or garage sale. Presentation aside, however, these foods are still tempting—as are savory Spinach Baked Tomatoes and cheese-stuffed Beef & Avocado Loaves. Yogurt Pancakes, timely today as we seek lower-fat breakfasts, can be enjoyed even without a 1970s cook-at-the-table griddle. And it doesn't take a casserole with a Scandinavian pedigree to bake Golden Apple Crisp to a bubbling golden brown.

BARBECUED FLANK STEAK

½ cup soy sauce
1 large clove garlic, minced or pressed
1 teaspoon ground ginger
2 tablespoons *each* firmly packed brown sugar, lemon juice, and salad oil
1 tablespoon dehydrated minced onion
¼ teaspoon pepper
1 flank steak (about 1½ lbs.)

In a shallow dish (just large enough to hold steak), stir together soy sauce, garlic, ginger, sugar, lemon juice, oil, onion, and pepper. Add steak and turn to coat with marinade. Cover and refrigerate for at least 6 hours or until next day, turning steak over 3 or 4 times.

Lift steak from marinade and drain briefly (discard marinade). Place steak on a grill 4 to 6 inches above a solid bed of hot coals. Cook, turning once, until browned on both sides and done to your liking; cut to test (10 to 12 minutes for medium-rare). To serve, cut steak across the grain into thin slanting slices. Makes 4 servings.
—*J. W., San Diego, CA (May 1972)*

SPINACH BAKED TOMATOES

8 tomato halves, peeled
Garlic salt and seasoned pepper
½ cup finely chopped onion
3 tablespoons melted butter
1 package (about 10 oz.) frozen chopped spinach
⅓ cup crushed bread stuffing mix
1 egg, lightly beaten
2 tablespoons grated Parmesan cheese.

Arrange the tomatoes in a greased shallow baking pan. Sprinkle with garlic salt and seasoned pepper. In a medium-sized frying pan, sauté the onion in butter for about 5 minutes. Add the spinach; heat and break it apart as it cooks until spinach is tender and the liquid is almost evaporated.

Remove from heat and stir in the stuffing mix and egg. Mound spinach mixture on tomatoes. Sprinkle with cheese and bake, uncovered, in a 350° oven for about 15 minutes, or until heated through. Makes 4 to 8 servings.—*J. B., Stockton, CA (September 1971)*

EEF & AVOCADO LOAVES

ncase cheese-stuffed avocado halves in round beef, then bake briefly.

¼ **pounds lean ground beef**
⅓ **cup fine dry bread crumbs**
1 **cup tomato-based chili sauce**
1 **egg**
1 **small onion, finely chopped**
½ **teaspoon salt**
¼ **teaspoon pepper**
1 **tablespoon Worcestershire**
2 **small avocados**
1 **tablespoon lemon juice**
¾ **cup shredded jack cheese**
¼ **cup canned diced green chiles**

lix together the beef, crumbs, ½ cup of

the chili sauce, egg, onion, salt, pepper, and Worcestershire. Divide mixture into 8 equal portions and flatten each into an oval patty about 5 inches long. Pit, peel, and halve avocados; rub with lemon juice. Combine cheese and 2 tablespoons of the chiles; stuff evenly into avocado halves and place each, cheese side down, on a beef patty. Top with remaining patties and pinch together to enclose avocado. Arrange, flat side down, in a shallow baking pan.

Bake in a 375° oven for 15 minutes or until meat is barely pink when slashed. Combine remaining chili sauce with remaining chiles; heat until bubbly and serve with meat loaves. Serves 4.—*S. M., Mission Viejo, CA (July 1975)*

Place avocado half on a beef patty, top with another, and press together to seal

OGURT PANCAKES

rve these pancakes with butter or with ore yogurt or sour cream and fresh fruit ich as peaches or strawberries.

1 **tablespoon sugar**
1 **teaspoon *each* baking powder and baking soda**
½ **teaspoon salt**
½ **cups all-purpose flour**
4 **eggs, lightly beaten**
1 **cup unflavored yogurt**
Butter or margarine (optional)

Yogurt, flavored yogurt, or sour cream (optional)
Sweetened fresh fruit

In a bowl, combine the sugar, baking powder, baking soda, salt, and flour; add the eggs and 1 cup yogurt and mix until smooth. Bake pancakes on a moderately hot greased griddle until nicely browned on both sides. Serve with butter and yogurt, if you wish, and your choice of fruit. Makes about 1 dozen 4-inch pancakes.—*N. P., Malibu, CA (June 1972)*

Tangy flavored pancakes call for topping of strawberries or other fresh fruits

OLDEN APPLE CRISP

About 4 or 5 medium-sized Golden Delicious apples
⅓ **cup apricot nectar or orange juice**
¼ **cup granulated sugar**
½ **cup brown sugar, firmly packed**
¾ **teaspoon ground cinnamon**
¼ **teaspoon salt**
¾ **cup all-purpose flour**
¼ **cup butter or margarine**

el and core apples and cut them into ices about ½ inch thick to make 6 cups iced apples. Turn them into a well-but- red 8-inch-square baking dish or other

shallow 2-quart baking dish. Combine the apricot nectar with granulated sugar; pour over apples. Mix the brown sugar, cinnamon, salt, and flour until well blended. Cut in butter with a pastry blender or 2 knives until particles are about the size of small peas. Squeeze small handfuls of the crumb mixture together firmly, then crumble evenly over apples into coarse chunks.

Bake, uncovered, in a 375° oven until the topping is browned and the apples tender, about 40 minutes. Serve warm or chilled. Makes 6 to 8 servings.—*M. D., Bellevue, WA (February 1972)*

Golden Delicious apples with extra fruit flavor and pebbly crumb topping

D·E·S·S·E·R·T·S

Two friends came to call, and I served them this original and easily prepared dessert. Their exclamation was, 'Why don't you give this recipe to Sunset Magazine? They will honestly appreciate it.' So here it is," a Fresno reader wrote us in 1936. This impulse to share something delectable has motivated many a dessert contribution to Kitchen Cabinet. Submitting a recipe for the now-classic cookies called Dream Bars in 1934, the contributor noted, "I gave a large party last fall, and 26 guests took home this recipe!" • Among the sweet pleasures in this chapter is a dessert from 1929, Sunset's first year of publication: Lemon Cake Pie (page 208). This venerable favorite still inspires variations using the West's home-grown citrus fruits; one example is Orange Pudding Cake (page 210) from 1990. • Other Western fruits also figure prominently in our treasured desserts. Orange Chiffon Cake with Straw-berry Sauce (page 203), Italian Plum Pie (page 207), Oregon Blueberry Cobbler (page 212), and Pears Fandango (page 214) are just a small sampling.

CHOCOLATE CHIP OATMEAL CRISPIES

"If you are not fond of chocolate," our editors commented when this recipe first appeared in a 1958 *Kitchen Cabinet*, "you can substitute seedless raisins or pitted chopped dates." Not fond of chocolate! Today, the chocolate chips seem the most compelling reason to bake these crunchy cookies.

- 1½ cups all-purpose flour
- 1 teaspoon baking soda
- ½ teaspoon salt
- ½ cup (¼ lb.) butter or margarine, at room temperature
- ½ cup solid vegetable shortening
- 1 cup *each* granulated sugar and firmly packed brown sugar
- 2 large eggs
- 1 teaspoon vanilla
- 3 cups quick-cooking rolled oats
- 1 cup (about 6 oz.) semisweet chocolate chips
- ½ cup coarsely chopped walnuts or pecans

In a medium-size bowl, stir together flour, baking soda, and salt. In a large bowl, beat butter, shortening, granulated sugar, and brown sugar with an electric mixer until light and fluffy. Add eggs, one at a time, beating well after each addition. Beat in vanilla.

Stir in flour mixture; then mix in oats, chocolate chips, and walnuts until evenly blended.

Drop heaping teaspoonfuls of dough onto lightly greased baking sheets, spacing cookies about 1 inch apart. Bake in a 350° oven until cookies are golden brown (12 to 15 minutes). Transfer cookies to racks to cool. Makes about 80 cookies. —R. A. W., Seattle

Per cookie: 81 calories, 11 g carbohydrates, 1 g protein, 4 g total fat (2 g saturated), 8 mg cholesterol, 48 mg sodium

PISTACHIO LACE COOKIES

A festive addition to a plate of Christmas sweets, these crisp, pistachio-studded wafers spread to lacelike fragility as they bake.

- ¼ cup butter or margarine
- 6 tablespoons firmly packed brown sugar
- 2 tablespoons light corn syrup
- ¼ cup all-purpose flour
- 1 teaspoon vanilla
- 1 cup shelled salted pistachio nuts

Melt butter in a 1- to 1½-quart pan over medium heat. Remove from heat and stir in sugar, corn syrup, flour, vanilla, and pistachios.

Grease and lightly flour 2 nonstick 12- by 15-inch baking sheets. On each sheet, drop three 1-tablespoon mounds of batter, spacing mounds well apart. Push nuts slightly apart with a spoon.

Bake in a 350° oven until cookies are bubbly and rich golden brown (about 10 minutes; if using one oven, switch positions of baking sheets after 5 minutes). Remove from oven and let stand just until cookies are firm enough to ease free when a slender spatula is slipped beneath them (about 2 minutes). If cookies are too soft, they'll pull apart when lifted; if too hard, they'll break (return them to oven to soften again). Transfer baked cookies to racks to cool. Repeat to bake remaining batter.

If made ahead, place cooled cookies in a rigid-sided container and cover airtight; hold at room temperature for up to 2 days or freeze for up to 1 month. Makes about 14 cookies.—*Carole Van Brocklin, Port Angeles, WA*

Per cookie: 152 calories, 14 g carbohydrates, 2 g protein, 11 g total fat (3 g saturated), 9 mg cholesterol, 139 mg sodium

PEANUT BLOSSOM COOKIES

A chocolate candy kiss crowns each of these rich, sugar-coated peanut butter cookies. Be sure to unwrap the kisses before you start to bake, since you'll need to place them on hot-from-the-oven cookies to soften the chocolate.

- 1¾ cups all-purpose flour
- 1 teaspoon baking soda
- ½ teaspoon salt
- ½ cup solid vegetable shortening
- ¼ cup peanut butter
- ½ cup granulated sugar
- ⅓ cup firmly packed brown sugar
- 1 large egg
- 1 teaspoon vanilla
- Granulated sugar
- About 72 chocolate kisses, unwrapped

In a medium-size bowl, stir together flour, baking soda, and salt. In a large bowl, beat shortening, peanut butter, the ½ cup granulated sugar, and brown sugar with an electric mixer until fluffy. Beat in egg and vanilla; stir in flour mixture until well blended.

Shape scant teaspoonfuls of dough into balls; roll each in granulated sugar to coat lightly. Arrange balls slightly apart on greased baking sheets. Bake in a 350° oven until cookies just begin to brown (8 to 10 minutes).

Remove cookies from oven; top each with a chocolate kiss, pressing down until cookie cracks around edge. Return to oven and continue to bake until chocolate is soft (3 to 5 more minutes). Transfer to racks to cool. Makes about 72 cookies.—*K. E., San Jose, CA*

Per cookie: 71 calories, 8 g carbohydrates, 1 g protein, 4 g total fat (2 g saturated), 4 mg cholesterol, 47 mg sodium

CHOCOLATE PINWHEEL COOKIES

Fans of peanut butter and chocolate won't be able to get enough of these pretty refrigerator cookies. To create the pinwheel pattern, you roll a peanut butter dough around melted dark chocolate.

1¼ cups all-purpose flour

½ teaspoon *each* baking soda, salt, and ground cinnamon

½ cup (¼ lb.) butter or margarine, at room temperature

½ cup creamy peanut butter

½ cup *each* granulated sugar and firmly packed brown sugar

1 large egg

1 cup (about 6 oz.) semisweet chocolate chips

In a medium-size bowl, stir together flour, baking soda, salt, and cinnamon. In a large bowl, beat butter, peanut butter, granulated sugar, and brown sugar with an electric mixer until light and creamy. Beat in egg; add flour mixture and stir until well blended. Wrap dough tightly in plastic wrap and refrigerate until firm (about 2 hours).

Place chocolate chips in the top of a double boiler over simmering water; or place in a small, heavy pan over very low heat. Stir occasionally until chocolate is melted and smooth. Remove from heat; let cool slightly.

On a sheet of wax paper, pat dough into a 12-inch square; even up sides. Spread chocolate evenly over dough to within ½ inch of edges. Roll up tightly, jelly roll style; cut roll in half crosswise, wrap each half in plastic wrap, and refrigerate until firm (at least 2 hours) or until next day.

Remove one roll from refrigerator at a time. Cut each roll into ¼-inch-thick slices; place slices ½ inch apart on ungreased baking sheets. Bake in a 375° oven until cookies are lightly browned (8 to 10 minutes). Let cookies cool slightly on baking sheets; then transfer to racks to cool completely. Makes about 48 cookies. —C. C., *Lakewood, CA*

Per cookie: 80 calories, 10 g carbohydrates, 1 g protein, 4 g total fat (2 g saturated), 10 mg cholesterol, 70 mg sodium

MOLASSES CRUNCH COOKIES

For an afternoon or evening snack, bring on a basket of molasses-flavored crisps to accompany glasses of milk or tangy apple cider.

1 cup all-purpose flour

½ teaspoon baking soda

¼ teaspoon salt (optional)

½ cup chopped walnuts

½ cup (¼ lb.) butter or margarine, at room temperature

6 tablespoons *each* firmly packed brown sugar and dark molasses

1 large egg

½ teaspoon vanilla

In a medium-size bowl, stir together flour, baking soda, salt (if used), and walnuts. In a large bowl, beat butter, sugar, molasses, egg, and vanilla with an electric mixer on high speed until light and fluffy. With mixer on low speed, thoroughly blend in flour mixture.

Drop rounded teaspoonfuls of dough onto well-greased baking sheets, spacing cookies about 1½ inches apart (cookies spread as they bake). Bake in a 350° oven until cookies are slightly darker brown at edges (8 to 10 minutes). Transfer to racks to cool; cookies crisp as they cool. If made ahead, wrap airtight and hold at room temperature for up to 3 days or freeze for up to 1 month. Makes about 48 cookies. —*Linda Twitchell, Bellingham, WA*

Per cookie: 53 calories, 5 g carbohydrates, 0.6 g protein, 3 g total fat (1 g saturated), 10 mg cholesterol, 42 mg sodium

BUTTERY LEMON BARS

Long-time favorites for potlucks and parties, these rich bars feature a tangy lemon custard baked atop a buttery cookie crust.

1 cup (½ lb.) butter or margarine, at room temperature

½ cup powdered sugar

2⅓ cups all-purpose flour

4 large eggs

2 cups granulated sugar

1 teaspoon grated lemon peel

6 tablespoons lemon juice

1 teaspoon baking powder

3 tablespoons powdered sugar

In a large bowl, beat butter and the ½ cup powdered sugar until fluffy. Add 2 cups of the flour; beat until well blended. Spread dough evenly over bottom of a well-greased 9- by 13-inch baking pan. Bake in a 350° oven for 20 minutes.

Meanwhile, in a medium-size bowl, beat eggs with an electric mixer until blended. Gradually add granulated sugar, beating until mixture is thick and well blended. Add lemon peel, lemon juice, remaining ⅓ cup flour, and baking powder; beat until thoroughly blended.

Pour lemon mixture over hot baked crust; continue to bake until topping is pale gold (15 to 20 more

minutes). Remove from oven and sprinkle evenly with the 3 tablespoons powdered sugar; let cool in pan on a rack. To serve, cut into bars or squares. Makes about 20 cookies.
—R. S., Newport Beach, CA

Per cookie: 249 calories, 36 g carbohydrates, 3 g protein, 11 g total fat (6 g saturated), 67 mg cholesterol, 139 mg sodium

GRANDMA PETERSON'S PEPPERNODER

Crunchy and not too sweet, these tiny traditional holiday cookies store well—a good thing, since the recipe makes 480 of them! Potato starch is sold in the gourmet or ethnic foods section of supermarkets and health food stores.

- ½ cup (¼ lb.) butter or margarine, at room temperature
- 1⅔ cups sugar
- 4 large eggs
- 1 teaspoon baking soda
- 1 teaspoon ground cardamom, ground mace, or ground nutmeg
- ½ teaspoon ground ginger
- 3½ cups all-purpose flour
- 1 package (about 1 lb.) potato starch

In a large bowl, beat butter, sugar, and eggs until well blended. Add baking soda, cardamom, and ginger; beat until blended. Stir in flour and potato starch to make a dry, crumbly dough.

Turn dough out onto a board and knead until smooth. Divide dough into 16 equal pieces. On board, gently roll each piece into a ½-inch-thick rope about 15 inches long. Cut rope into ½-inch-thick slices. Arrange slices about ½ inch apart, cut sides down, on lightly greased baking sheets. Bake in a 375° oven until cookies are light brown on bottoms (about 14 minutes). Transfer to board to cool. Store cooled cookies airtight at room temperature for up to 2 weeks.

Makes about 40 dozen cookies.
—Helen M. Peterson, Hemet, CA

Per cookie: 13 calories, 2 g carbohydrates, 0.1 g protein, 0.4 g total fat (0.1 g saturated), 2 mg cholesterol, 7 mg sodium

GINGER SHORTBREAD WEDGES

Present slender triangles of spiced brown-sugar shortbread with hot tea and fresh kumquats or tangerines.

- 2 cups all-purpose flour
- 1 cup firmly packed brown sugar
- 1 tablespoon ground ginger
- 1 cup (½ lb.) firm butter or margarine, cut into chunks

In a food processor or a large bowl, whirl or stir together flour, sugar, and ginger. Add butter; whirl or rub with your fingers until mixture resembles coarse crumbs. Press and squeeze mixture together with your hands.

Place dough in a 9- or 10-inch-round baking pan (preferably one with a removable bottom). With your fingers, press dough into an even layer. Press tines of a fork around edge of dough to form a decorative border; then prick surface of dough all over.

Bake in a 325° oven until golden brown (1 hour to 1 hour and 10 minutes). Then remove shortbread from oven and cut into 16 wedges. Let cool in pan on a rack until warm (about 25 minutes); then loosen cookies around pan edge and remove pan rim (or carefully turn cookies out of pan). Let cool. If made ahead, wrap airtight and hold at room temperature for up to 5 days or freeze for up to 1 month. Makes 16 cookies.—*Patt Hudler, Loleta, CA*

Per cookie: 211 calories, 26 g carbohydrates, 2 g protein, 12 g total fat (7 g saturated), 31 mg cholesterol, 123 mg sodium

SWEDISH CHOCOLATE BARS

Moist, rich, and crunchy with almonds, these thin bar cookies taste much like brownies.

- ½ cup (¼ lb.) butter or margarine
- 1½ ounces unsweetened chocolate
- 2 large eggs, at room temperature
- 1 cup granulated sugar
- ½ cup finely chopped almonds
- ⅓ cup all-purpose flour
  Powdered sugar

In a small, heavy pan, combine butter and chocolate. Place over very low heat until butter is melted; then stir to blend butter and chocolate smoothly. Remove from heat; let cool slightly.

In a medium-size bowl, beat eggs and granulated sugar with an electric mixer until mixture is thick and fluffy. Add chocolate-butter mixture; beat until blended. Add almonds and flour and stir until well blended.

Spread batter in a well-greased 9- by 13-inch baking pan. Bake in a 400° oven until center springs back when lightly pressed (18 to 20 minutes). Let cool in pan on a rack; then sprinkle lightly with powdered sugar. To serve, cut into bars. Makes about 24 cookies.—*B.H., Portola Valley, CA*

Per cookie: 108 calories, 11 g carbohydrates, 1 g protein, 7 g total fat (3 g saturated), 28 mg cholesterol, 51 mg sodium

PUMPKIN BARS

These spicy, cakelike bars are spread with a thin orange glaze while still warm from the oven. They're delicious for an afternoon or after-school snack, with good hot coffee or frosty-cold milk.

1½ cups all-purpose flour

1 teaspoon ground cinnamon

½ teaspoon *each* ground ginger, ground allspice, and baking soda

½ cup (¼ lb.) butter or margarine, at room temperature

1 cup firmly packed brown sugar

1 large egg

½ cup canned pumpkin

½ cup chopped pitted dates or raisins

½ cup chopped walnuts, pecans, or hazelnuts

Orange Glaze (recipe follows)

In a medium-size bowl, stir together flour, cinnamon, ginger, allspice, and baking soda. In a large bowl, beat butter and sugar with an electric mixer until creamy. Beat in egg, then pumpkin. Add flour mixture and beat until well blended. Stir in dates and walnuts.

Spread batter evenly in a greased shallow 10- by 15-inch baking pan. Bake in a 350° oven until cake begins to pull away from sides of pan (16 to 18 minutes). Meanwhile, prepare Orange Glaze.

Spread warm cake with glaze; let cool in pan on a rack. To serve, cut into bars or squares. Makes about 36 cookies.—*M. M., Santa Ana, CA*

ORANGE GLAZE. In a small bowl, stir together 1 cup **powdered sugar** and 5 teaspoons **frozen orange juice concentrate,** thawed. (Or blend sugar with 1 teaspoon grated orange peel and 1 tablespoon orange juice.)

Per cookie: 102 calories, 16 g carbohydrates, 1 g protein, 4 g total fat (2 g saturated), 13 mg cholesterol, 51 mg sodium

WHITE & DARK CHOCOLATE BROWNIES

These dark, chewy brownies are temptingly studded with white chocolate chips. Chill the chips before adding them to the batter; that way, they'll still look like distinct polka dots when the cookies are done.

¾ cup all-purpose flour

¼ teaspoon baking soda

¼ teaspoon salt (optional)

⅓ cup butter or margarine

¾ cup sugar

2 tablespoons water

1 cup (about 6 oz.) semisweet chocolate chips

1 teaspoon vanilla

2 large eggs

1 cup (about 6 oz.) white chocolate chips, chilled

In a small bowl, stir together flour, baking soda, and salt (if used).

In a 2- to 3-quart pan, combine butter, sugar, and water. Bring to a boil over high heat, stirring constantly. Remove from heat and add semisweet chocolate chips and vanilla; stir until chocolate is melted and mixture is smooth. Add eggs, one at a time, beating well after each addition. Stir in flour mixture. Let batter cool to room temperature (10 to 15 minutes); then stir in white chocolate chips.

Spread batter in a greased 8- or 9-inch-square baking pan. Bake in a 350° oven until sides are firm and center springs back when lightly pressed (35 to 40 minutes). Let cool in pan on a rack. Serve warm or cool; to serve, cut into bars. If made ahead, cover and hold at room temperature until next day. Makes about 12 brownies.—*Mary B. Brock, Grass Valley, CA*

Per brownie: 285 calories, 37 g carbohydrates, 3 g protein, 14 g total fat (9 g saturated), 49 mg cholesterol, 107 mg sodium

CHOCOLATE MINT STICKS

A mint-flavored buttercream frosting is sandwiched between a brownie and a chocolate topping in these super-delicious bars. For Valentine's Day, you might tint the frosting a delicate pink and cut the chilled cookies into heart shapes.

½ cup (¼ lb.) plus 1 tablespoon butter or margarine

3 ounces unsweetened chocolate

2 large eggs

1 cup sugar

½ teaspoon peppermint extract

½ cup *each* chopped walnuts and all-purpose flour

Mint Frosting (recipe follows)

In a small, heavy pan, combine ½ cup of the butter and 2 ounces of the chocolate. Place pan over very low heat until butter is melted; then stir to blend butter and chocolate smoothly. Remove from heat and let cool slightly.

In a medium-size bowl, beat eggs to blend. Stir in chocolate mixture, sugar, peppermint extract, walnuts, and flour.

Spread batter evenly in a greased 9- by 13-inch baking pan and bake in a 350° oven until center springs back when lightly pressed (about 20 minutes) Let cool in pan on a rack for 30 minutes. Meanwhile, prepare Mint Frosting.

Spread cooled brownies with Mint Frosting. Refrigerate for 5 minutes. Place remaining 1 tablespoon butter and remaining 1 ounce chocolate in a small, heavy pan. Place pan over very low heat until butter is melted; then stir to blend butter and chocolate smoothly.

Brush chocolate mixture over frosting; refrigerate until chocolate is firm. To serve, cut into small bars. Makes about 54 brownies.—*K. E., Eugene, OR*

MINT FROSTING. In a small bowl, combine 3 tablespoons **butter** or margarine (at room temperature), 1½ tablespoons **milk,** 1 teaspoon **peppermint extract,** ⅛ teaspoon **green food coloring,** and 1½ cups **powdered sugar.** Beat until smooth and fluffy.

Per brownie: 74 calories, 9 g carbohydrates, 0.7 g protein, 4 g total fat (2 g saturated), 15 mg cholesterol, 31 mg sodium

ALMOND-CARAMEL BARS

Surprise the brown-baggers in your family by tucking in one of these cookies with the usual lunchtime fare. Chewy and easy to make, they're topped with a rich caramel-nut glaze.

- ¾ cup all-purpose flour
- ½ teaspoon baking powder
- ¼ teaspoon salt
- 2 large eggs
- ½ cup granulated sugar
- ¾ cup chopped almonds
- ¾ cup firmly packed brown sugar
- 2 tablespoons butter or margarine
- 1 tablespoon milk

In a medium-size bowl, combine flour, baking powder, salt, eggs, granulated sugar, ½ cup of the almonds, and ½ cup of the brown sugar; beat until well blended. Spread batter evenly in a greased 9-inch-square baking pan. Bake in a 350° oven until a wooden pick inserted in center comes out clean (about 20 minutes).

Meanwhile, melt butter in a small pan over low heat. Stir in remaining ¼ cup almonds, remaining ¼ cup brown sugar, and milk. Remove pan from heat.

Spread almond-sugar mixture evenly over hot baked cookies. Broil about 4 inches below heat until topping is bubbly all over and golden brown (about 2 minutes). Let cool in pan on a rack. To serve, cut into bars. Makes about 24 cookies.—*L. G., Bremerton, WA*

Per cookie: 97 calories, 15 g carbohydrates, 2 g protein, 4 g total fat (1 g saturated), 20 mg cholesterol, 53 mg sodium

HAND-PAINTED CHRISTMAS COOKIES

Get out the fanciful Christmas cutters to make these almond-frosted cookies. To add your personal touch, paint a pattern on each cookie with undiluted food coloring (be sure to rinse your paintbrush thoroughly between colors).

- 1 cup (½ lb.) butter or margarine, at room temperature
- 1½ cups sugar
- 2 large eggs
- 1 teaspoon almond extract
- ½ teaspoon baking soda
- 3 cups all-purpose flour
  Almond Frosting (recipe follows)
  Food coloring

In a large bowl, beat butter and sugar with an electric mixer until fluffy. Add eggs, one at a time, beating well after each addition. Beat in almond extract. Stir in baking soda; then stir in flour until well blended. Divide dough into 4 equal portions; wrap each portion tightly in plastic wrap and refrigerate until firm (at least 2½ hours) or for up to 3 days.

On a floured board, roll out dough, one portion at a time, to a thickness of ³⁄₁₆ inch. Cut out with small or medium-size cookie cutters. Arrange cookies 1 inch apart on ungreased baking sheets. Bake in a 350° oven until golden (about 12 minutes). Transfer to racks to cool.

Prepare Almond Frosting. Dip tops of cookies in frosting; then return to racks and let stand until frosting is dry (1½ to 2 hours). Using fine paintbrushes, decorate cookies with undiluted food coloring; let stand until food coloring is dry (about 15 minutes). If made ahead, store airtight at room temperature for up to 4 days. Makes about 60 small cookies.—*Diane Boyer, Napa, CA*

ALMOND FROSTING. In a large bowl, beat 3 large **egg whites** with an electric mixer on high speed until frothy. Add 1½ teaspoons **almond extract** and 3½ cups sifted **powdered sugar;** beat until smooth.

NOTE: If you prefer not to use a frosting containing raw egg whites, you may substitute a simple powdered sugar glaze (it won't look as opaque as the frosting above).

Per cookie: 97 calories, 16 g carbohydrates, 1 g protein, 3 g total fat (2 g saturated), 15 mg cholesterol, 47 mg sodium

Lemon Tea Cake

You can bake this lemon-drenched cake in either a fluted tube pan or a loaf pan. It's a treat with a cup of afternoon tea, and delightful for dessert with a topping of sweetened sliced strawberries.

- 1⅔ cups all-purpose flour
- 1 teaspoon baking powder
- ½ teaspoon salt
- ½ cup (¼ lb.) butter or margarine, at room temperature
- 1 cup sugar
- 1 teaspoon vanilla
- 1 tablespoon grated lemon peel
- 2 large eggs
- ½ cup milk
- ½ cup chopped walnuts or pecans
- Lemon Syrup (recipe follows)

In a medium-size bowl, stir together flour, baking powder, and salt.

In a large bowl, beat butter and sugar with an electric mixer until creamy; beat in vanilla and lemon peel. Add eggs, one at a time, beating well after each addition. Add flour mixture to butter mixture alternately with milk, beating until smooth after each addition. Stir in walnuts.

Spoon batter into a greased, floured 7- to 8-cup tube pan or loaf pan. Bake in a 350° oven until cake is golden brown on top and a wooden skewer inserted in center comes out clean (45 to 55 minutes).

Meanwhile, prepare Lemon Syrup and set aside.

With skewer, pierce hot cake all over. Spoon Lemon Syrup evenly over cake. Let cake cool in pan on a rack for 5 to 10 minutes; then loosen edge of cake from pan and carefully turn out onto rack to cool completely. Makes 8 to 10 servings. —*M. J., Bellevue, WA*

LEMON SYRUP. In a small bowl, combine 3 tablespoons *each* **sugar** and **lemon juice;** stir until sugar is dissolved.

Per serving: 358 calories, 47 g carbohydrates, 5 g protein, 17 g total fat (8 g saturated), 77 mg cholesterol, 313 mg sodium

Chocolate Applesauce Cake

This cake has the moist, firm texture typical of applesauce cakes, but spices and chocolate make it different from the usual. It's delicious plain, but if you'd like to dress it up a bit, top it with a dusting of powdered sugar or a simple buttercream frosting.

- 1¾ cups all-purpose flour
- 3 tablespoons unsweetened cocoa
- 1 teaspoon *each* baking soda and ground cinnamon
- ½ teaspoon salt
- ¼ teaspoon *each* ground nutmeg and ground cloves
- ½ cup solid vegetable shortening
- 1 cup firmly packed brown sugar
- 1 large egg
- 1½ cups canned applesauce
- 1 cup chopped walnuts (optional)

In a medium-size bowl, stir together flour, cocoa, baking soda, cinnamon, salt, nutmeg, and cloves. In a large bowl, beat shortening and sugar with an electric mixer until light and fluffy. Beat in egg; then stir in applesauce. Add flour mixture and beat until well blended. Stir in walnuts (if used).

Spread batter evenly in a well-greased 9-inch-square baking pan. Bake in a 350° oven until a wooden pick inserted in center comes out clean (35 to 40 minutes). Let cool in pan on a rack. Makes 9 servings. —*K. B., Lake Oswego, OR*

Per serving: 335 calories, 52 g carbohydrates, 4 g protein, 13 g total fat (3 g saturated), 24 mg cholesterol, 290 mg sodium

Caramel Apple Cake

While this speedy spice cake is hot from the oven, you saturate it with a buttery caramel topping.

- 2 cups all-purpose flour
- 1 tablespoon baking powder
- 2 teaspoons ground cinnamon
- ½ teaspoon salt
- 1 cup firmly packed brown sugar
- ½ cup salad oil
- 1 tablespoon vanilla
- 2 large eggs
- 2 medium-size tart apples (about 12 oz. *total*), peeled, cored, and coarsely chopped
- Caramel Topping (recipe follows)

In a medium-size bowl, stir together flour, baking powder, cinnamon, and salt. In a large bowl, beat sugar, oil, and vanilla with an electric mixer until blended. Add eggs, one at a time, beating well after each addition. Add flour mixture and beat just until blended. Stir in apples.

Spread batter evenly in a greased 9-inch-square baking pan. Bake in a 350° oven until center of cake springs back when lightly pressed (30 to 40 minutes).

When cake is almost done, prepare Caramel Topping. Set hot cake (in pan) on a rack. Pierce cake all over with a fork; slowly and evenly pour Caramel Topping over cake. Serve cake warm or at room temperature. Makes 9 servings.—*Barbara Keenan, Fort Morgan, CO*

CARAMEL TOPPING. In a small pan, combine ½ cup firmly packed **brown sugar,** ¼ cup **butter** or margarine, and ¼ cup **whipping cream.** Bring to a boil; then reduce heat and simmer, stirring, for 5 minutes. Remove from heat and stir in 1 teaspoon **vanilla.** Use hot or warm.

Per serving: 458 calories, 63 g carbohydrates, 4 g protein, 21 g total fat (6 g saturated), 68 mg cholesterol, 372 mg sodium

APRICOT BRANDY POUND CAKE

Flavored with apricot brandy and a hint of lemon and almond, this moist cake is an ideal autumn dessert.

- 3 cups all-purpose flour
- ½ teaspoon baking soda
- 1 cup (½ lb.) butter or margarine, at room temperature
- 2½ cups sugar
- 6 large eggs
- 1 cup reduced-fat or regular sour cream
- ½ cup apricot brandy or orange-flavored liqueur
- 1 teaspoon vanilla
- ½ teaspoon lemon extract
- ¼ teaspoon almond extract

In a large bowl, stir together flour and baking soda. In another large bowl, beat butter with an electric mixer until creamy. Gradually add sugar, beating until mixture is light and fluffy. Add eggs, one at a time, beating well after each addition. Add sour cream, brandy, vanilla, lemon extract, and almond extract; beat until well blended. Gradually add flour mixture, beating until well blended.

Spoon batter into a well-greased, floured 10-inch (3-quart) tube pan. Bake in a 325° oven until a wooden skewer inserted in center of cake comes out clean (1¼ to 1½ hours). Let cool in pan on a rack for 10 min-utes; then carefully turn out onto rack to cool completely. Makes 16 to 18 servings.—*Carmela Meely, Walnut Creek, CA*

Per serving: 349 calories, 48 g carbohydrates, 6 g protein, 15 g total fat (8 g saturated), 109 mg cholesterol, 178 mg sodium

SPICY CARROT CAKE

Baked in a tube pan, this homey cake is so moist and richly flavored that it needs no frosting.

- 2½ cups all-purpose flour
- 1½ teaspoons *each* baking soda and ground cinnamon
- 1 teaspoon ground nutmeg
- ½ teaspoon salt
- 1 cup (½ lb.) butter or margarine, at room temperature
- 2 cups sugar
- 4 large eggs
- 1 teaspoon vanilla
- 1½ cups finely shredded carrots
- ¼ cup buttermilk
- ¾ cup chopped walnuts

In a medium-size bowl, stir together flour, baking soda, cinnamon, nut-meg, and salt. In a large bowl, beat butter and sugar with an electric mixer until creamy. Add eggs, one at a time, beating well after each addi-tion. Stir in vanilla and carrots. Add flour mixture to butter mixture alter-nately with buttermilk, beating well after each addition. Stir in walnuts.

Spoon batter into a greased, floured 10-inch (3-quart) tube pan. Bake in a 350° oven until a wooden skewer inserted in center of cake comes out clean (about 1 hour). Let cool in pan on a rack for 10 minutes; then turn out onto rack to cool com-pletely. Makes about 12 servings. —*L. M., Arcadia, CA*

Per serving: 451 calories, 57 g carbohydrates, 6 g protein, 23 g total fat (11 g saturated), 112 mg cho-lesterol, 445 mg sodium

SOUR CREAM POUND CAKE

Simply elegant, this rich cake is a favorite accompaniment for summer fruits such as sweet cherries or lightly sweetened raspberries or straw-berries. In fall and winter, serve thin slices with an after-dinner sip of port.

- 6 large eggs, separated
- 2½ cups granulated sugar
- 1 cup (½ lb.) butter or margarine, at room temperature
- ½ teaspoon ground mace or ground nutmeg
- ¼ teaspoon baking soda
- 3 cups cake flour
- 1 cup sour cream
  Powdered sugar (optional)

In a large bowl, beat egg whites with an electric mixer on high speed until frothy. Gradually add ½ cup of the granulated sugar, beating just until whites hold soft, moist peaks. Set aside.

In another large bowl, beat butter and remaining 2 cups granulated sugar until creamy. Add egg yolks, one at a time, beating well after each addition. Blend in mace and baking soda. Add flour to butter mixture alternately with sour cream, adding about a third of each at a time; beat until smooth after each addition. Fold egg whites into batter.

Spoon batter into a greased, floured 10-inch (3-quart) tube pan. Bake in a 300° oven until a wooden skewer inserted in center of cake comes out clean (about 1½ hours). Let cool in pan on a rack for 5 min-utes; then carefully turn out onto rack to cool completely. If desired, sift powdered sugar over cake just before serving. Makes about 16 servings. —*Ethel Riddle, Santa Cruz, CA*

Per serving: 361 calories, 48 g carbohydrates, 5 g protein, 17 g total fat (10 g saturated), 117 mg cho-lesterol, 174 mg sodium

Black Bottom Cupcakes

As these cocoa cupcakes bake, the chocolate chips in the cream cheese filling sink to the bottom.

Chocolate Chip Filling (recipe follows)

1½ cups all-purpose flour

1 cup sugar

¼ cup unsweetened cocoa

1 teaspoon baking soda

½ teaspoon salt

1 cup water

5 tablespoons salad oil

1 tablespoon cider vinegar

1 teaspoon vanilla

About ⅓ cup finely chopped walnuts

Prepare Chocolate Chip Filling; set aside.

In a large bowl, stir together flour, sugar, cocoa, baking soda, and salt. In a medium-size bowl, stir together water, oil, vinegar, and vanilla. Gradually add oil mixture to flour mixture, stirring until well blended.

Divide batter evenly among 18 paper-lined 2½-inch muffin cups. Top batter in each cup with 1 heaping tablespoon of the Chocolate Chip Filling and 1 scant teaspoon of the walnuts. Bake in a 350° oven until tops of cupcakes spring back when lightly pressed (about 25 minutes). Let cool in pans on racks for about 15 minutes; then remove from pans and transfer to racks to cool completely. Makes 18 cupcakes.—S. D., Selah, WA

CHOCOLATE CHIP FILLING. In a bowl, beat 1 large package (about 8 oz.) **cream cheese** (at room temperature), 1 large **egg**, and ⅓ cup **sugar** until smooth. Stir in 1 cup (about 6 oz.) **semisweet chocolate chips.**

Per cupcake: 239 calories, 30 g carbohydrates, 3 g protein, 13 g total fat (5 g saturated), 26 mg cholesterol, 173 mg sodium

Chocolate Torte

Red raspberry jam and a glossy chocolate glaze top this dense, fudgy cake. If you like, decorate the dessert with pecan halves.

½ cup light corn syrup

4 ounces unsweetened chocolate, coarsely chopped

½ cup *each* all-purpose flour and finely chopped pecans

½ teaspoon *each* baking powder and ground cinnamon

3 large eggs, separated

¾ cup sugar

½ cup (¼ lb.) butter or margarine, at room temperature

Dark Chocolate Glaze (recipe follows)

½ cup raspberry jam

In a 1- to 1½-quart pan, heat corn syrup over medium heat, stirring, until hot. Add chocolate and remove pan from heat; stir until chocolate is melted and mixture is smooth. Let cool slightly.

In a small bowl, stir together flour, pecans, baking powder, and cinnamon. In a deep medium-size bowl, beat egg whites with an electric mixer on high speed until frothy. Gradually add ½ cup of the sugar, beating until whites hold soft, distinct peaks.

In a large bowl, beat butter and remaining ¼ cup sugar with electric mixer until creamy. Add egg yolks, one at a time, beating well after each addition. Beat in chocolate mixture; add flour mixture and beat until well blended. Stir about a fourth of the egg whites into batter; gently fold in remaining whites just until blended.

Spread batter evenly in a greased, floured 9-inch spring-form pan. Bake in a 350° oven until center of cake feels firm when lightly pressed (about 30 minutes). Let cool in pan on a rack; then remove pan rim and place cake on a serving plate.

Prepare Dark Chocolate Glaze. Spread jam evenly over top of cake; then drizzle warm glaze over top and sides. If made ahead, cover and refrigerate for up to 2 days. Makes 10 to 12 servings.—*Roxanne Chan, Albany, CA*

DARK CHOCOLATE GLAZE. In a 1- to 1½-quart pan, heat ¼ cup **light corn syrup** over medium heat, stirring, until hot. Add 4 ounces **semisweet chocolate,** chopped; remove pan from heat and stir until chocolate is melted and mixture is smooth. Use warm.

Per serving: 407 calories, 55 g carbohydrates, 4 g protein, 22 g total fat (11 g saturated), 81 mg cholesterol, 164 mg sodium

Picnic Brownie Cakes

Bake these brownie cupcakes for the minimum time if you like a creamier center, for the maximum time if you prefer a cakelike texture.

1 cup (½ lb.) butter or margarine

4 ounces unsweetened chocolate

2 cups sugar

4 large eggs

1 teaspoon vanilla

1 cup all-purpose flour

1 cup chopped walnuts

18 walnut halves or ⅓ cup coarsely chopped walnuts

In a heavy 2- to 3-quart pan, combine butter and chocolate. Place over very low heat until butter is melted; then stir to blend butter and chocolate smoothly. Remove from heat and stir in sugar. Add eggs, one at a time, beating well after each addition. Stir in vanilla; then add flour and beat until blended. Stir in the 1 cup chopped walnuts.

Divide batter evenly among 18 paper-lined 2½-inch muffin cups. Place 1 walnut half or 1 scant teaspoon chopped walnuts atop batter in each muffin cup.

Bake in a 350° oven until tops of cakes are crackly-looking and lighter in color (23 to 28 minutes); tops should feel firm, but interiors of cakes should be moist. Let cool in pans on racks for about 15 minutes (cakes will settle slightly), then remove from pans and transfer to racks to cool completely. Makes 18 cupcakes.
—*Karen Prescott, Clatskanie, OR*

Per cupcake: 306 calories, 31 g carbohydrates, 4 g protein, 20 g total fat (9 g saturated), 75 mg cholesterol, 120 mg sodium

CHOCOLATE CREAM TORTE

For a festive occasion, bring on this luxurious freezer torte. A smooth chocolate–cream cheese filling tops a crisp, granola-nut crust.

Granola Crust (recipe follows)
1 cup (about 6 oz.) semisweet chocolate chips
2 tablespoons sugar
1 large package (about 8 oz.) cream cheese, at room temperature
⅓ cup milk
1 cup whipping cream

Prepare Granola Crust; set aside.

Reserve 2 tablespoons of the chocolate chips. In a 2- to 3-quart pan, combine remaining chocolate chips and sugar. Place over very low heat; stir occasionally until chocolate is melted and mixture is smooth. Remove from heat and let cool.

In a large bowl, beat cream cheese and milk with an electric mixer until fluffy. Blend in chocolate mixture. Slowly beat in whipping cream, then beat until mixture holds soft peaks. Spread cheese mixture evenly over Granola Crust; sprinkle with the reserved 2 tablespoons chocolate chips.

Freeze torte until firm (at least 4 hours) before serving. If made ahead, wrap frozen torte airtight and freeze for up to 2 weeks. Let stand at room temperature for 15 to 30 minutes before cutting. Makes 8 to 10 servings.—*Susan Cameron, Portland*

GRANOLA CRUST. Melt 2 tablespoons **butter** or margarine in a wide frying pan over medium-high heat. Add 6 tablespoons **sugar** and cook, stirring, until bubbly. Add 1¼ cups **granola cereal with nuts;** stir until sugar just begins to lightly caramelize (about 5 minutes). Spread mixture in a 9-inch spring-form pan or 9-inch-round baking pan with a removable bottom. Let cool.

Per serving: 399 calories, 36 g carbohydrates, 5 g protein, 28 g total fat (16 g saturated), 65 mg cholesterol, 120 mg sodium

ORANGE CHIFFON CAKE WITH STRAWBERRY SAUCE

In making a chiffon cake, the secret of success is to use a straight-sided, non-fluted tube pan. Serve the light, fine-textured cake in wedges, with an orange-flavored fresh berry sauce.

2¼ cups cake flour
1½ cups sugar
1 tablespoon baking powder
1 teaspoon salt
½ cup salad oil
6 large egg yolks
¾ cup orange juice
2 tablespoons grated orange peel
1 cup egg whites (about 8 large egg whites)
½ teaspoon cream of tartar
Strawberry Sauce (recipe follows)

In a large bowl, stir together flour, 1 cup of the sugar, baking powder, and salt. Add oil, egg yolks, orange juice, and orange peel; beat until smooth and well blended.

In another large bowl, combine egg whites and cream of tartar; beat with an electric mixer on high speed until whites hold soft peaks. Gradually add remaining ½ cup sugar, beating until whites hold stiff peaks. Gently fold batter into whites.

Spoon batter into an ungreased straight-sided 10-inch tube pan (preferably one with a removable bottom). Bake in a 325° oven until cake is browned on top and a wooden skewer inserted in center comes out clean (about 1 hour and 10 minutes). Invert cake onto a funnel and let cool. Meanwhile, prepare Strawberry Sauce.

Carefully loosen sides of cake from pan; remove cake from pan and place on a serving plate. Serve with Strawberry Sauce. Makes 12 to 14 servings.—*I. H., Saratoga, CA*

STRAWBERRY SAUCE. In a 2½-quart pan, stir together ½ cup **sugar** and 1½ tablespoons **cornstarch;** then stir in 1 cup **orange juice** and ¼ cup **orange-flavored liqueur** (or ¼ cup more orange juice). Bring to a boil; boil, stirring, for 1 minute. Remove from heat and stir in 6 cups hulled, sliced **fresh strawberries.** Let cool. Makes about 6½ cups.

Per serving of cake: 277 calories, 40 g carbohydrates, 5 g protein, 11 g total fat (2 g saturated), 98 mg cholesterol, 317 mg sodium

Per ½ cup of Strawberry Sauce: 76 calories, 17 g carbohydrates, 0.6 g protein, 0.3 g total fat (0 g saturated), 0 mg cholesterol, 1 mg sodium

RICOTTA CHEESECAKE

Delicious topped with fresh berries, this cheesecake features a lemon-scented ricotta filling. For the crust, use any crisp lemon-flavored cookies.

Lemon Crust (recipe follows)
3   large eggs
3   cups ricotta cheese
⅔   cup sugar
⅓   cup sour cream
⅓   cup cornstarch
1   teaspoon baking powder
1   teaspoon vanilla
3   tablespoons butter or margarine, melted and cooled
2   teaspoons grated lemon peel
½   cup raisins (optional)

Prepare Lemon Crust; set aside.

In a blender or food processor, combine eggs, ricotta cheese, sugar, and sour cream; whirl until smooth. Blend cornstarch and baking powder; add to cheese mixture along with vanilla, butter, and lemon peel. Whirl until smooth, scraping down sides of container as needed. Stir in raisins (if used).

Spoon filling into Lemon Crust. Bake in a 325° oven until center of cheesecake appears set when pan is gently shaken (about 1 hour). Let cool in pan on a rack; then cover and refrigerate. Makes 10 to 12 servings.
—J. L., Los Gatos, CA

LEMON CRUST. In a small bowl, stir together 1½ cups **lemon cookie crumbs** or vanilla wafer crumbs and 2½ tablespoons **butter** or margarine, melted. Press over bottom and sides of a 9-inch spring-form pan. Bake in a 350° oven for 6 minutes. Let cool on a rack.

Per serving: 314 calories, 26 g carbohydrates, 10 g protein, 19 g total fat (11 g saturated), 111 mg cholesterol, 215 mg sodium

PUMPKIN CHEESECAKE

If you like both pumpkin pie and cheesecake, you'll want to try this creamy dessert, perfect for Thanksgiving—or any other festive fall dinner. Decorate the cake with pecans and puffs of whipped cream.

1¾ cups graham cracker crumbs
2   tablespoons granulated sugar
3   tablespoons butter or margarine, melted
2   large packages (about 8 oz. *each*) cream cheese, at room temperature
¾   cup firmly packed brown sugar
1   can (about 1 lb.) pumpkin
2   teaspoons pumpkin pie spice
2   large eggs
    Sweetened whipped cream
    Pecan halves

In a medium-size bowl, stir together graham cracker crumbs, granulated sugar, and butter. Press mixture over bottom and about 1 inch up sides of a 9-inch spring-form pan. Bake in a 350° oven for 10 minutes. Let cool on a rack.

In a large bowl, beat cream cheese and brown sugar with an electric mixer until blended. Stir in pumpkin and pumpkin pie spice. Add eggs, one at a time, beating well after each addition.

Pour pumpkin mixture into crust. Bake in a 350° oven until center of cheesecake barely jiggles when pan is gently shaken (about 50 minutes). Let cool in pan on a rack. Then remove pan rim; cover cheesecake lightly and refrigerate until cold (at least 3 hours) or until next day. Before serving, top cheesecake with whipped cream and pecan halves. Makes 8 to 10 servings.—*Chantal M. Irvin, Gallup, NM*

Per serving: 418 calories, 44 g carbohydrates, 7 g protein, 24 g total fat (14 g saturated), 113 mg cholesterol, 352 mg sodium

FLAKY PASTRY

This recipe makes enough for two double-crust pies or four pie shells. It freezes well, so you might want to keep a few baked crusts in your freezer, ready to fill with fresh fruit any time.

3   cups all-purpose flour
1   teaspoon salt
1¼ cups solid vegetable shortening
1   large egg
1   tablespoon distilled white vinegar
¼   cup cold water

In a large bowl, stir together flour and salt. Cut in shortening with a pastry blender or 2 knives (or rub it in with your fingers) until mixture resembles coarse crumbs. In a small bowl, beat egg, vinegar, and water to blend well. Drizzle egg mixture over flour mixture and mix lightly until all flour is moistened and pastry holds together in a ball (add few more drops of water, if needed). Divide pastry into 4 equal portions. On a lightly floured board, roll each portion into an 11½-inch round.

To make baked pie shells, fit each pastry round into a 9-inch pie pan; trim and flute edge. Prick bottoms of pastry shells all over with a fork. Bake in a 425° oven until nicely browned (10 to 12 minutes). Let cool on racks. If made ahead, wrap cooled shells airtight and freeze for up to 6 months. Makes four 9-inch pie shells.—*C. P., Portland*

Per pie shell: 946 calories, 76 g carbohydrates, 12 g protein, 66 g total fat (17 g saturated), 53 mg cholesterol, 568 mg sodium

ROSY APPLE PIE

Fresh rhubarb joins the apples in this pie, bringing a tart, refreshing taste of early spring to a year-round dessert favorite.

- 1 cup granulated sugar
- 2 tablespoons quick-cooking tapioca
- ½ teaspoon ground mace or ground nutmeg
- 4 cups peeled, sliced tart apples
- 2 cups thinly sliced rhubarb
  Pastry for a single-crust 9-inch pie
- ½ cup *each* all-purpose flour and firmly packed brown sugar
- 1 teaspoon ground cinnamon
- ⅓ cup firm butter or margarine, cut into chunks
  Vanilla ice cream (optional)

In a large bowl, stir together granulated sugar, tapioca, and mace. Gently mix in apples and rhubarb; set aside.

On a lightly floured board, roll pastry into an 11½-inch round; fit into a 9-inch pie pan. Trim and flute edge; make edge fairly high to keep in fruit juices during baking.

Spoon apple mixture into pastry shell. In a small bowl, stir together flour, brown sugar, and cinnamon. Cut in butter with a pastry blender or 2 knives (or rub it in with your fingers) until mixture resembles coarse crumbs; sprinkle crumb mixture evenly over pie.

Bake in a 375° oven until filling is bubbly, apples are tender when pierced, and topping is browned (45 to 55 minutes). Serve warm or cool; top with ice cream, if desired. Makes 6 to 8 servings.—*M. S., Seattle*

Per serving: 469 calories, 75 g carbohydrates, 3 g protein, 19 g total fat (8 g saturated), 31 mg cholesterol, 191 mg sodium

BLUEBERRY-APPLE DEEP-DISH PIE

Topped with a tender cream cheese pastry and baked in a shallow casserole, this two-fruit pie will remind you of old-fashioned cobbler.

Cream Cheese Pastry (recipe follows)
- ⅔ cup sugar
- 3 tablespoons quick-cooking tapioca
- 3 cups peeled, sliced apples
- 2 cups fresh blueberries
- 1 tablespoon lemon juice
  About 2 teaspoons milk

Prepare Cream Cheese Pastry.

In a shallow 2-quart casserole, stir together sugar and tapioca. Gently mix in apples, blueberries, and lemon juice.

Measure dimensions of casserole at top. Then, on a floured board, roll out pastry slightly larger than casserole; place pastry atop fruit mixture in casserole. Fold pastry under, flush with casserole rim; flute edge against rim. Cut a few slits in top of pastry; brush pastry with milk. Bake in a 400° oven until crust is richly browned (about 40 minutes). Serve warm or cool. Makes 8 servings.
—*Carmela Meely, Walnut Creek, CA*

CREAM CHEESE PASTRY. In a food processor or a medium-size bowl, whirl or beat together 6 tablespoons **butter** or margarine (at room temperature) and 1 small package (about 3 oz.) **cream cheese** (at room temperature) until smooth. Add ¾ cup **all-purpose flour;** whirl or beat until incorporated. With your hands, shape pastry into a flattened ball; wrap airtight and refrigerate for at least 2 hours or until next day.

Per serving: 281 calories, 41 g carbohydrates, 3 g protein, 13 g total fat (8 g saturated), 35 mg cholesterol, 140 mg sodium

SHREDDED APPLE PIE

There's nothing wrong with traditional apple pie—but when you're in the mood for a different interpretation, turn to this unusual recipe. The fruit is shredded, not sliced, and flavored with lemon and orange instead of the usual spices.

- 1½ teaspoons grated lemon peel
- 1 tablespoon grated orange peel
- ¼ cup orange juice
- 2 teaspoons lemon juice
- 1½ tablespoons flour
- 1½ cups sugar
- 4 cups peeled, shredded tart apples
  Pastry for a double-crust 9-inch pie
- 2 eggs, well beaten
  Whipped cream (optional)

In a large bowl, mix lemon peel, orange peel, orange juice, and lemon juice. Mix flour and sugar; blend into juice-peel mixture. Gently mix in apples; set aside.

Divide pastry in half. On a lightly floured board, roll one portion of pastry into an 11½-inch round; fit into a 9-inch pie pan.

Stir eggs into apple mixture; then spoon apple mixture into pastry-lined pan. Roll out remaining pastry and place on pie; trim and flute edge, then pierce top with a fork in several places. (Or, if desired, cut pastry for top crust into strips and make a lattice top.)

Bake in a 450° oven for 15 minutes. Then reduce oven temperature to 350° and continue to bake until filling is bubbly and crust is golden brown (about 30 more minutes). Serve warm or cool; top with whipped cream, if desired. Makes 6 to 8 servings.—*J. A., Modesto, CA*

Per serving: 505 calories, 77 g carbohydrates, 5 g protein, 21 g total fat (5 g saturated), 76 mg cholesterol, 181 mg sodium

CHEESECAKE APPLE TORTE

Here's a handsome dessert that combines the best of two favorites—cheesecake and apple pie.

- ½ cup (¼ lb.) butter or margarine, at room temperature
- ⅓ cup plus ½ cup sugar
- 1 teaspoon vanilla
- 1 cup all-purpose flour
- 1 large package (about 8 oz.) cream cheese, at room temperature
- 1 large egg
- ½ cup raisins
- 1 teaspoon ground cinnamon
- ½ teaspoon grated lemon peel
- 2 cups ¼-inch-thick slices of peeled Granny Smith apples

In a medium-size bowl, beat butter, ⅓ cup of the sugar, and vanilla until fluffy. Add flour; stir until dough holds together.

Spread dough evenly over bottom and 1½ inches up sides of a 9-inch spring-form pan or 9-inch-round baking pan with a removable bottom. Bake in a 350° oven until golden (about 20 minutes).

In another medium-size bowl, beat cream cheese, ¼ cup of the sugar, and egg until smooth. Spread cheese mixture over bottom of baked crust; sprinkle with raisins. In a large bowl, stir together remaining ¼ cup sugar, cinnamon, and lemon peel; gently mix in apples. Then arrange apple slices, slightly overlapping, over raisins.

Bake until apple slices are tender when pierced and filling appears set in center when pan is gently shaken (about 40 minutes). Let cool on a rack for at least 30 minutes before serving. Makes 8 servings.—*Angie Berberian, Fresno, CA*

Per serving: 397 calories, 46 g carbohydrates, 5 g protein, 22 g total fat (14 g saturated), 89 mg cholesterol, 211 mg sodium

CRANBERRY–APPLE PIE

This festive pie is served with a hot wine sauce that enhances both the apples and the berries in the filling.

- Pastry for a double-crust 9-inch pie
- 1 cup sugar
- 2 tablespoons all-purpose flour
- 6 medium-size tart apples (about 2¼ lbs. *total*), peeled, cored, and thinly sliced
- 1 cup fresh cranberries, coarsely chopped
- 1 tablespoon butter or margarine
- Wine Sauce (recipe follows)

Divide pastry in half. On a lightly floured board, roll one portion of pastry into an 11½-inch round; fit into a 9-inch pie pan.

In a small bowl, stir together sugar and flour. Sprinkle half the sugar mixture over bottom of pastry-lined pan. Lightly mix apples and cranberries; mound fruit mixture over sugar mixture. Sprinkle with remaining sugar mixture and dot with butter. Roll out remaining pastry and place on pie; trim and flute edge, then pierce top with a fork in several places. Bake in a 425° oven until filling is bubbly and crust is golden brown (about 45 minutes).

Meanwhile, prepare Wine Sauce. Serve pie warm, with sauce to add to taste. Makes 6 to 8 servings.—*P. T., Hollywood, CA*

WINE SAUCE. In a 1- to 1½-quart pan, combine ½ cup **sugar**, 1 tablespoon **cornstarch**, ½ teaspoon **ground cinnamon**, ¹⁄₁₆ teaspoon **salt**, and 1 teaspoon **grated orange peel.** Stir until well blended. Gradually stir in ½ cup *each* **water** and **cream sherry** (or 1 cup orange juice) and 1 tablespoon **lemon juice.** Bring to a boil over medium-high heat, stirring; then boil, stirring, until sauce is clear and thickened. Add 1 tablespoon **butter** or margarine and stir until melted. Serve hot. Makes about 1¼ cups.

Per serving of pie: 482 calories, 72 g carbohydrates, 4 g protein, 21 g total fat (6 g saturated), 20 mg cholesterol, 179 mg sodium

Per tablespoon of Wine Sauce: 36 calories, 6 g carbohydrates, 0 g protein, 1 g total fat (0.4 g saturated), 2 mg cholesterol, 13 mg sodium

APPLE PASTRY SQUARES

Rows of glossy apple slices baked atop a buttery crust make an easy-to-serve dessert for a crowd.

- ½ cup water
- 2¼ cups sugar
- 8 large tart apples (about 4 lbs. *total*), peeled, cored, and cut into ½-inch-thick slices
- 1 teaspoon *each* grated lemon peel and ground cinnamon
- ⅛ teaspoon ground nutmeg
- 2 cups all-purpose flour
- ¾ cup (¼ lb. plus ¼ cup) firm butter or margarine, cut into chunks
- 2 large egg yolks

In a wide 3½- to 5-quart pan, stir together water and 2 cups of the sugar. Bring to a boil, stirring until sugar is dissolved. Add half the apple slices and cook, stirring, until apples are glossy (about 6 minutes). Remove apples from pan with a slotted spoon; set aside. Add remaining apples and cook, stirring, until glossy (about 6 minutes). Return first batch of apples to pan; then stir in lemon peel, cinnamon, and nutmeg. Remove from heat.

In a large bowl, stir together flour and remaining ¼ cup sugar. Cut in butter with a pastry blender or 2 knives (or rub it in with your fingers) until mixture resembles fine crumbs. Add egg yolks and mix with your fingers until dough forms a smooth ball. Press dough firmly and evenly over bottom and up sides of a shallow 10- by 15-inch baking pan. Bake in a 300° oven for 25 minutes.

Arrange apple slices evenly over crust. Drizzle with any syrup left in apple cooking pan. Continue to bake until apples are tender when pierced and crust is lightly browned (about 20 more minutes). Makes about 16 servings.—C. R., Las Vegas

Per serving: 305 calories, 54 g carbohydrates, 2 g protein, 10 g total fat (6 g saturated), 50 mg cholesterol, 89 mg sodium

ITALIAN PLUM PIE

A touch of orange peel accents the flavor of prune plums in this lattice-topped pie. You'll find the distinctive-tasting small, oval plums in markets in September.

- 2 **pounds Italian (prune) plums**
- 1¼ **cups sugar**
- ⅛ **teaspoon *each* salt and ground cinnamon**
- 2 **teaspoons grated orange peel**
- ¼ **cup quick-cooking tapioca**
  Pastry for a double-crust 9-inch pie
- 2 **tablespoons butter or margarine**

Cut plums into quarters or sixths; remove and discard pits. You should have 4 cups plums. In a large bowl, stir together sugar, salt, cinnamon, orange peel, and tapioca. Gently mix in plums, then set aside.

Divide pastry in half. On a lightly floured board, roll one portion of pastry into an 11½-inch round; fit

into a 9-inch pie pan. Spoon plum mixture into pastry-lined pan; dot with butter. Roll out remaining pastry and cut into strips; weave into a lattice top for pie. Trim and flute edge. Bake in a 400° oven until filling is bubbly all over and crust is nicely browned (30 to 35 minutes). Serve warm or cool. Makes 6 to 8 servings. —D. K., Palo Alto, CA

Per serving: 550 calories, 87 g carbohydrates, 4 g protein, 22 g total fat (7 g saturated), 24 mg cholesterol, 263 mg sodium

CRUNCHY WALNUT PIE

The West's plentiful walnuts are at their best in this version of a classic nut pie. It's best if made a day ahead.

  Pastry for a single-crust 9-inch pie
- 3 **large eggs**
- ½ **cup firmly packed brown sugar**
- 1 **cup light corn syrup**
- ¼ **teaspoon salt**
- 1 **teaspoon *each* ground cinnamon and vanilla**
- ¼ **cup butter or margarine, melted and cooled**
- 1 **cup walnut halves or pieces**

On a lightly floured board, roll pastry into an 11½-inch round; fit into a 9-inch pie pan. Trim and flute edge.

In a large bowl, beat eggs, sugar, corn syrup, salt, cinnamon, vanilla, and butter until well blended. Stir in walnuts. Pour mixture into pastry shell. Bake on lowest rack of a 375° oven until filling jiggles only slightly in center when pan is gently shaken (about 50 minutes). Let cool on a rack for at least 2 hours before serving. For best flavor, bake pie a day ahead and let cool completely; then cover with foil and hold at room temperature until serving time. Makes 6 to 8 servings.—J. G., Saratoga, CA

Per serving: 529 calories, 66 g carbohydrates, 7 g protein, 29 g total fat (8 g saturated), 116 mg cholesterol, 317 mg sodium

STRAWBERRY & CHEESE TART

Arrange halved fresh strawberries in a circular pattern atop this pretty tart.

  Butter Pastry (recipe follows)
- 2 **small packages (about 3 oz. *each*) cream cheese, at room temperature**
- 5 **cups hulled, halved fresh strawberries**
- 1 **cup sugar**
- 3 **tablespoons cornstarch**
- 1 **cup water**
  Few drops of red food coloring (optional)

Prepare Butter Pastry. Press pastry evenly over bottom and up sides of an 11-inch tart pan with a removable bottom. Bake in a 300° oven until golden (about 30 minutes). Let cool on a rack.

Spread cream cheese over bottom of crust; arrange 4 cups of the strawberries atop cheese. In a small bowl, mash remaining 1 cup strawberries. In a 1- to 2-quart pan, combine sugar and cornstarch. Blend in mashed berries, water, and food coloring (if used). Bring to a boil, stirring; then boil, stirring, until glaze is thick and clear (about 1 minute). Spoon hot glaze over strawberries in crust. Refrigerate until set (about 2 hours) or for up to 6 hours before serving. Makes 8 servings.—E. P., Ashland, OR

BUTTER PASTRY. In a food processor or a large bowl, whirl or stir together 1⅓ cups **all-purpose flour** and 3 tablespoons **sugar**. Add ½ cup (¼ lb.) firm **butter** or margarine (cut into chunks). Whirl or rub with your fingers until mixture resembles coarse crumbs. Blend in 1 large **egg yolk.** With your hands, shape dough into a smooth ball.

Per serving: 414 calories, 55 g carbohydrates, 5 g protein, 20 g total fat (12 g saturated), 81 mg cholesterol, 183 mg sodium

CRISP-CRUST PEACH PIE

A crunchy cornmeal crust distinguishes this creamy peach pie.

Cornmeal Pastry (recipe follows)
1 cup sugar
½ cup all-purpose flour
1 teaspoon ground cinnamon
¼ teaspoon *each* salt and ground nutmeg
1 cup whipping cream
4 cups peeled, sliced peaches

Prepare Cornmeal Pastry. Place pastry between 2 sheets of wax paper and roll into an 11½-inch round. Peel off top paper; invert pastry round into a 9-inch pie pan. Peel off remaining paper; gently fit pastry into pan. Trim and flute edge; prick bottom of pastry shell all over with a fork. Bake in a 450° oven for 10 minutes.

Meanwhile, in a medium-size bowl, stir together sugar, flour, cinnamon, salt, and nutmeg. Add cream and stir until smooth.

Reduce oven temperature to 400°. Arrange peaches evenly in hot crust; pour cream mixture evenly over peaches. Bake until filling appears set in center when pan is gently shaken (about 40 minutes). Let cool on a rack; then refrigerate for at least 2 hours or up to 6 hours before serving. Makes 6 to 8 servings. —K. P., Vail, AZ

CORNMEAL PASTRY. In a medium-size bowl, stir together ¾ cup **all-purpose flour,** ½ cup **yellow cornmeal,** and ½ teaspoon **salt.** Cut in ⅓ cup **solid vegetable shortening** with a pastry blender or 2 knives (or rub it in with your fingers) until mixture resembles coarse crumbs. Mix in ¼ cup **cold water,** 1 tablespoon at a time. Shape pastry into a ball.

Per serving: 456 calories, 65 g carbohydrates, 5 g protein, 21 g total fat (9 g saturated), 38 mg cholesterol, 246 mg sodium

BLUEBERRY PEACH PIE

Filled with juicy fresh peaches and blueberries and topped with macaroon crumbs, this pie has a buttery crust that requires no rolling—you just press it into the pan.

⅔ cup sugar
¼ cup quick-cooking tapioca
¼ teaspoon *each* grated lemon peel and ground cinnamon
5 medium-size peaches (1½ to 1¾ lbs. *total*), peeled, pitted, and sliced
2 cups fresh blueberries
1 tablespoon lemon juice
Lemon Butter Pastry (recipe follows)
2 tablespoons butter or margarine
1 cup crisp macaroon cookie crumbs

In a large bowl, stir together sugar, tapioca, lemon peel, and cinnamon. Gently mix in peaches, blueberries, and lemon juice. Let stand for 15 minutes.

Meanwhile, prepare Lemon Butter Pastry. Press pastry evenly over bottom and up sides of a 9-inch pie pan; flute edge. Bake in a 300° oven for 15 minutes.

Increase oven temperature to 350°. Spoon peach mixture into crust; dot with butter and sprinkle with cookie crumbs. Bake until topping is browned (about 35 minutes). Serve warm or cool. Makes 6 to 8 servings. —L. G., Bremerton, WA

LEMON BUTTER PASTRY. In a medium-size bowl, stir together 1½ cups **all-purpose flour,** 3 tablespoons **sugar,** and ¼ teaspoon **grated lemon peel.** Add ¼ cup firm **butter** or margarine (cut into chunks). Cut in butter with a pastry blender or 2 knives (or rub it in with your fingers) until mixture resembles fine crumbs. Add 2 large **egg yolks;** mix well.

With your hands, shape pastry into a smooth ball.

Per serving: 461 calories, 81 g carbohydrates, 5 g protein, 14 g total fat (9 g saturated), 87 mg cholesterol, 185 mg sodium

LEMON CAKE PIE

Here's an old, old favorite. As it bakes, a cakelike topping forms over the sweet-tart lemon filling.

Pastry for a single-crust 9-inch pie
1½ cups sugar
2 tablespoons butter or margarine, melted and cooled
⅓ cup all-purpose flour
¼ teaspoon salt
½ teaspoon grated lemon peel
5 tablespoons lemon juice
3 large eggs, separated
1¼ cups milk

On a lightly floured board, roll pastry into an 11½-inch round; fit into a 9-inch pie pan. Trim and flute edge.

In a large bowl, stir together sugar and butter; then blend in flour, salt, lemon peel, and lemon juice. In a small bowl, beat egg yolks to blend; then stir in milk. Stir egg mixture into lemon mixture until smoothly blended.

In a medium-size bowl, beat egg whites with an electric mixer on high speed until they hold stiff, moist peaks; gently fold egg whites into lemon mixture.

Pour filling into pastry shell. Bake on lowest rack of a 375° oven until filling is richly browned on top and center feels set when lightly pressed (45 to 55 minutes). Let cool on a rack. Serve at room temperature. If made ahead, refrigerate for up to 6 hours. Makes 6 to 8 servings.—E. J. S., Vancouver, WA

Per serving: 412 calories, 61 g carbohydrates, 6 g protein, 16 g total fat (6 g saturated), 114 mg cholesterol, 243 mg sodium

MACAROON BAKED PEACHES

Now that fresh peaches from South America are available in winter, you won't have to wait until midsummer to make this almond-accented dessert.

About 7 large ripe peaches (2½ to 3 lbs. *total*)
Lemon juice
6 crisp macaroon cookies, coarsely crushed
⅓ cup chopped almonds
1 large egg white
1 tablespoon sugar
¼ teaspoon almond extract
¼ cup sweetened shredded coconut
½ cup orange juice
1 cup whipping cream (optional)

Peel, halve, and pit peaches. Brush peach halves with lemon juice to prevent discoloration. Place 12 of the peach halves, cut side up, in a 7- by 11-inch baking dish. Chop enough of the remaining peach halves to make ½ cup; place chopped peaches in a bowl and lightly mix in cookie crumbs and almonds.

In a small bowl, beat egg white with an electric mixer on high speed until frothy; gradually add sugar and almond extract, beating until mixture holds stiff peaks. Fold egg white mixture into crumb mixture; then spoon mixture equally into peach halves. Sprinkle with coconut. Pour orange juice around peaches in baking dish.

Bake in a 400° oven until topping is lightly browned and peaches are heated through (about 20 minutes). Serve warm or cool. If desired, top with cream (unwhipped, or whipped and sweetened). Makes 6 to 8 servings.—*L. F., Portland*

Per serving: 208 calories, 36 g carbohydrates, 4 g protein, 7 g total fat (3 g saturated), 0 mg cholesterol, 67 mg sodium

QUICK SUNDAE SAUCE

Blend chocolate syrup, sour cream, and peanut butter to make this quick, rich dessert sauce. If you like, sprinkle the sauce with chopped peanuts or crushed peanut brittle after spooning it over your favorite ice cream.

1 cup purchased chocolate syrup
⅔ cup sour cream
1 teaspoon vanilla
½ cup peanut butter

In a blender or food processor, whirl chocolate syrup, sour cream, vanilla, and peanut butter until smoothly blended. (Or combine ingredients in a large bowl and beat with an electric mixer to blend.)

To serve, pour sauce into the top of a double boiler or into a bowl set over hot (not boiling) water. Let stand until sauce is barely warm to the touch. If made ahead, cover and refrigerate for up to 1 week. Before serving, let stand at room temperature for 1 hour; then warm as directed above. Makes about 2⅓ cups. —*J. B., Bellingham, WA*

Per tablespoon: 48 calories, 6 g carbohydrates, 1 g protein, 3 g total fat (1 g saturated), 2 mg cholesterol, 26 mg sodium

CHOCOLATE DOUBLE-DIP STRAWBERRIES

Big, sweet berries coated in both semisweet and white chocolate will look and taste best if served within a few hours after dipping.

12 large fresh strawberries with stems (*each* 2 to 2½ inches wide)
¾ cup semisweet chocolate chips
½ cup white chocolate chips or chopped white chocolate

Rinse strawberries; do not remove stems. Let drain on paper towels.

Place semisweet chocolate in the top of a double boiler or in a bowl set over hot (not simmering) water. Stir occasionally until chocolate is smoothly melted (about 8 minutes); remove from hot water. Or place chocolate in a microwave-safe bowl; microwave on HIGH (100%) for 5 seconds at a time until melted, stirring after each 5 seconds.

Dip each strawberry, tip first, into semisweet chocolate, rotating berry to coat about two-thirds of the way up. Set strawberries well apart on a wax paper–lined 12- by 15-inch baking sheet. (Or imbed wooden picks well apart in plastic foam; then impale each berry, tip up, on a wooden pick.) Refrigerate until chocolate is firm (about 15 minutes).

In another pan or bowl, melt white chocolate as directed above for semisweet chocolate. Dip each strawberry, tip first, into white chocolate, rotating berry to coat about half of the dark chocolate at the strawberry tip. Refrigerate for at least 10 minutes or up to 8 hours before serving. To eat, hold berries by the stem. Makes 12 strawberries.—*Heather Sager, Carlsbad, CA*

Per strawberry: 107 calories, 14 g carbohydrates, 1 g protein, 6 g total fat (4 g saturated), 0.1 mg cholesterol, 10 mg sodium

APPLE-FILLED CRÊPES

Serve these crêpes for dessert; or try them for brunch, with sausages.

  Dessert Crêpes (recipe follows)
5 tablespoons butter or margarine, melted
4 cups peeled, thinly sliced apples
7 tablespoons sugar
1½ teaspoons ground cinnamon

Prepare Dessert Crêpes and set aside.

Heat 1 tablespoon of the butter in a wide frying pan over medium-high heat; stir in apples, ¼ cup of the sugar, and ½ teaspoon of the cinnamon. Stir often until apples are soft (6 to 8 minutes). Remove from heat.

Fill crêpes equally with apple filling; roll up to enclose filling. Arrange rolled crêpes, seam side down, in a 7-by 11-inch baking dish. In a small bowl, mix remaining 3 tablespoons sugar and remaining 1 teaspoon cinnamon; sprinkle over crêpes. Drizzle with remaining ¼ cup butter. Bake in a 350° oven until crêpes are heated through and lightly browned (about 15 minutes). Makes 6 servings.
—M. E., Renton, WA

DESSERT CRÊPES. In a blender or food processor, combine 3 large **eggs,** 6 tablespoons **all-purpose flour,** ½ teaspoon **salt,** 1 tablespoon **sugar,** ¾ cup **milk,** and 1½ teaspoons melted **butter** or margarine. Whirl until smooth.

Heat a 6- to 7-inch crêpe pan or other flat-bottomed frying pan over medium-high heat. Add ½ teaspoon **butter** or magarine and swirl to coat pan surface. Stir batter and pour about 3 tablespoons into pan, quickly tilting pan so batter coats pan bottom. Cook until surface of crêpe feels dry and edge is lightly browned. Turn crêpe over with a spatula and cook until browned on other side. Turn out onto a plate. Repeat to cook remaining batter, using ½ teaspoon **butter** or margarine for each crêpe and stacking crêpes as made. You should have 6 crêpes.

Per serving: 302 calories, 36 g carbohydrates, 5 g protein, 16 g total fat (9 g saturated), 144 mg cholesterol, 356 mg sodium

MEXICAN CHOCOLATE ICE CREAM

You'll find round, cinnamon-scented cakes of sweet Mexican chocolate in Hispanic markets and well-stocked supermarkets.

2 cakes (about 3½ oz. *each*) **Mexican chocolate, chopped (or 7 oz. semi-sweet chocolate, chopped, plus 1 teaspoon ground cinnamon)**
¾ **cup sugar**
4 **cups milk or half-and-half**
2 **large eggs, beaten**
2 **teaspoons vanilla**

Place Mexican chocolate (or semisweet chocolate and cinnamon) in a 2- to 3-quart pan. Set pan over lowest heat; when chocolate begins to soften, stir until smoothly melted. Stir in sugar, milk, and eggs. Increase heat to medium-low and cook, stirring, until mixture coats the back of a metal spoon in an even, velvety layer (20 to 30 minutes). Remove from heat; stir in vanilla. Let cool; then cover and refrigerate until cold (at least 3 hours) or until next day.

Pour chocolate mixture into container of a 1½-quart or larger ice cream maker. Freeze according to manufacturer's directions until firm. If made ahead, store in freezer in an airtight container for up to 2 weeks. Makes 10 servings (about ½ cup *each*).—*Marilyn Swartz, Los Angeles*

Per serving: 231 calories, 33 g carbohydrates, 5 g protein, 10 g total fat (6 g saturated), 56 mg cholesterol, 63 mg sodium

PEARS FANDANGO

Ice cream topped with hot fresh fruit sauce is always a treat for dessert. Here's a spectacular combination you can make all year round; use winter pears during the cold-weather months, luscious tropical mangoes when they're plentiful and economical throughout the summer.

1 tablespoon butter or margarine
4 large ripe pears such as Anjou, Bosc, or Comice (about 2 lbs. *total*), peeled, cored, and thinly sliced
¼ cup firmly packed light brown sugar
¼ cup rum, orange-flavored liqueur, or thawed frozen orange juice concentrate
1 teaspoon grated lemon peel
3 tablespoons lemon juice
1½ pints vanilla ice cream or vanilla frozen yogurt

Melt butter in a wide frying pan over medium heat. Add pears and cook, stirring occasionally, until lightly browned (about 20 minutes). Stir in sugar, rum, lemon peel, and lemon juice. Bring to a boil over high heat; then boil, stirring often, until sauce is thick enough to cling lightly to fruit (2 to 3 minutes). Keep warm.

Divide ice cream among 6 individual bowls; spoon pears and sauce equally over ice cream and serve immediately. Makes 6 servings.
—*Adrienne Sweeney, Kaneohe, HI*

Per serving: 289 calories, 46 g carbohydrates, 3 g protein, 10 g total fat (6 g saturated), 34 mg cholesterol, 78 mg sodium

MANGOES FANDANGO

Follow directions for **Pears Fandango,** but omit pears and use 2 large ripe **mangoes** (about 2 lbs. *total*). Peel mangoes and cut fruit from pits in chunks; then proceed as directed above. Makes 6 servings.

Per serving: 275 calories, 43 g carbohydrates, 3 g protein, 9 g total fat (6 g saturated), 34 mg cholesterol, 80 mg sodium

SUMMER BERRY ICE CREAM

When you make this frozen dessert, you can choose from a variety of ripe, juicy purple berries. For a pretty presentation, reserve a few of the whole berries to garnish scoops of the smooth crimson ice cream—then add a sprig of fresh mint to each serving.

- 6 cups fresh boysenberries, blackberries, or ollallieberries
- 2 to 2½ cups sugar
- 4 cups whipping cream
  Rock salt
  Ice

Place berries in a 4- to 6-quart pan. Cook over medium heat, stirring, just until berries are soft (about 5 minutes). With the back of a wooden spoon, rub berries through a wire strainer; discard seeds.

Measure berry purée; you should have 2 to 2½ cups. In a large bowl, combine purée with an equal amount of sugar. Blend in cream.

Pour mixture into container of a 1-gallon ice- and salt-cooled ice cream maker; secure dasher and lid. Pack around ice cream container with 1 part rock salt to 8 parts ice. Crank until dasher is hard to turn. (Or pour berry mixture into container of a 2-quart or larger electric ice cream maker; freeze acording to manufacturer's directions until ice cream is softly frozen.)

Serve ice cream. Or, for a firmer texture, remove dasher, cover ice cream with plastic wrap, and replace lid; freeze until firm. (Or freeze in an airtight container in freezer for up to 6 weeks.) Makes 16 servings (about ½ cup *each*).—*Ruth Hallanger, Oxnard, CA*

Per serving: 308 calories, 36 g carbohydrates, 2 g protein, 19 g total fat (12 g saturated), 66 mg cholesterol, 21 mg sodium

LEMON FROZEN YOGURT

This dessert has the most pleasing texture if served slightly soft. If you like, accompany each serving with a crisp, spicy gingersnap or two.

- 4 cups vanilla low-fat yogurt
- 4 teaspoons grated lemon peel
- ¼ cup lemon juice
- ¼ cup light corn syrup
  Thin lemon slices
  Gingersnaps (optional)

In a 9- or 10-inch-square metal pan, stir together yogurt, lemon peel, lemon juice, and corn syrup. Cover airtight and freeze until firm (at least 6 hours) or for up to 3 weeks.

Break frozen yogurt mixture into large chunks (if necessary, let stand at room temperature until soft enough to break up). Whirl chunks in a food processor or beat with an electric mixer until a smooth-textured slush forms. Return slush to pan; cover and freeze until slightly firmer (about 30 minutes) or for up to 3 hours.

Spoon frozen yogurt into chilled bowls; garnish with lemon slices. Serve with gingersnaps, if desired. Makes 6 to 8 servings.—*Christina McCarroll, Los Altos, CA*

Per serving: 146 calories, 28 g carbohydrates, 6 g protein, 2 g total fat (1 g saturated), 6 mg cholesterol, 102 mg sodium

ORANGE SHERBET CUPS

Bits of marmalade add an intriguing sweetness and texture to fresh orange sherbet served in hollowed-out orange shells.

- 7 large oranges (3½ to 4½ lbs. *total*)
- ⅓ cup honey
- ⅔ cup orange marmalade
- 2 cups half-and-half
- ¼ cup orange-flavored liqueur or orange juice
  Mint sprigs

Grate enough peel (colored part only) from one of the oranges to make 1 tablespoon. Cut top third from remaining 6 oranges. Squeeze juice from all 7 oranges; set juice aside. Then scrape out and discard pulp from the 6 orange shells (both tops and bottoms) so they can be used as serving containers. Cover; set aside.

In a blender or food processor, combine grated orange peel, 2 cups of the orange juice, honey, marmalade, half-and-half, and liqueur. Whirl until well blended; then pour into a 9- by 13-inch metal pan and freeze until firm (at least 4 hours).

Break mixture into large chunks (if necessary, let stand at room temperature until soft enough to break up). Whirl chunks in a food processor or beat with an electric mixer until a smooth-textured slush forms. Return slush to pan and freeze until firm (about 1 hour).

Mound sherbet in bottom pieces of orange shells; cover tightly and freeze until firm (at least 1 hour) or for up to 2 weeks. Before serving, cover each orange shell with its top, if desired. Garnish with mint sprigs. Makes 6 servings.—*M. D., Morro Bay, CA*

Per serving: 349 calories, 62 g carbohydrates, 4 g protein, 10 g total fat (6 g saturated), 30 mg cholesterol, 55 mg sodium

CHRONOLOGICAL INDEX

Chafing dish crab (12/71), 128
Chocolate applesauce cake (1/71), 200
Cumin cabbage & sausages (3/71), 90
Fruited sweet potato casserole (11/71), 150
Ginger biscuits (5/71), 182
Pecan crunch pear pie (9/71), 209
Spicy carrot cake (11/71), 201
Spinach baked tomatoes (9/71), 192
Tomato fried rice (7/71), 162

1972
Barbecued flank steak (5/72), 192
Beef & vegetable supper soup (10/72), 29
Blueberry peach pie (7/72), 208
Chicken with crunchy rice (6/72), 107
Fruited pumpkin bread (11/72), 180
Golden apple crisp (2/72), 193
Leafy bean soup (3/72), 26
Minted tuna salad (5/72), 57
Oven-fried chicken & spareribs (4/72), 105
Simmered corned beef (6/72), 73
Summer slaw (7/72), 41
Swiss chard bisque (9/72), 24
Yogurt pancakes (6/72), 193

1973
Brown rice & vegetable sauté (6/73), 138
Chocolate nut coffeecake (1/73), 183
Crisp spinach salad (11/73), 39
Ground beef patties with lemon sauce (2/73), 79
Pork & apple sauté (3/73), 83
Red cherry pudding pie (2/73), 211
Rhubarb oat crumble (5/73), 212

1974
Beef & mushroom bake (5/74), 79
Cheese-topped eggplant casserole (5/74), 159
Cottage cheese pan rolls (6/74), 188
Crusty potato cups (3/74), 147
Oregon blueberry cobbler (7/74), 212
Oven-barbecued spareribs (3/74), 83
Veal & artichoke stew (12/74), 91

1975
Beef & avocado loaves (7/75), 193
Beef & barley soup (10/75), 29
Crumb-topped baked onions (12/75), 154
Crunchy potato salad (5/75), 48
Crunchy walnut pie (10/75), 207
Island meatballs (4/75), 78
Lamb & brown rice pilaf (5/75), 87
Lemon tea cake (5/75), 200
Mexican oyster stew (2/75), 35
Oatmeal yeast bread (3/75), 187
Pork & sauerkraut soup (11/75), 30
Posh squash (8/75), 157
South-of-the-border brunch eggs (6/75), 61
Sweet-sour chile sauce (9/75), 167

1976
Buttery lemon bars (2/76), 196
Chilled broccoli cheese salad (10/76), 46
Chilled vegetable salad platter (7/76), 45
Chunky apple pancakes (2/76), 185
Crisp-crust peach pie (8/76), 208

Company veal sauté (12/76), 91
Cranberry-orange muffins (12/76), 178
Gold Country special (11/76), 64
Italian sausage & bean soup (1/76), 30
Pork chops with rhubarb dressing (5/76), 81
Ricotta cheesecake (4/76), 204
Salmon Florentine (7/76), 118
Sautéed sesame fish (10/76), 121
Shrimp appetizer quiches (5/76), 15
Slivered chicken & walnuts (6/76), 102
Sticky pecan rolls (4/76), 190
Super simple white bread (10/76), 186
Tuna noodle salad (8/76), 52

1977
Bacon-stuffed trout (5/77),115
Cheddar cheese popovers (10/77), 179
Korean beef strips (6/77), 72
Lemon-mint lamb meatballs (3/77), 88
Oven sweet & sour pork (10/77), 84
Roast pork with soy-garlic baste (2/77), 82
Rocky Mountain chili (9/77), 77
Spinach soufflé (4/77), 66

1978
Bulgur Mexicana (10/78), 140
Cheesy caraway potatoes (2/78), 149
Cinnamon swirl loaf (6/78), 186
Curried rice salad (8/78), 51
Easy bean dip olé (11/78), 9
Herbed mushrooms (6/78), 155
Macaroon baked peaches (8/78), 213
New Mexico marinated bell pepper strips (8/78), 169
Orange chiffon cake with strawberry sauce (4/78), 203
Orange sherbet cups (7/78), 215
Rocky Mountain raclette (7/78), 149
Savory mushroom tarts (3/78), 15
Sweet potato puff ramekins (11/78), 150
Swordfish steaks with mushrooms (8/78), 125
Veal stroganoff (10/78), 91
Yogurt chicken with oranges (2/78), 102

1979
Avocadowiches (1/79), 143
Baked chicken with garlic spaghetti (10/79), 96
Black bottom cupcakes (3/79), 202
Butter-basted crab (2/79), 129
Chocolate mint sticks (5/79), 198
Italian sausage–stuffed mushrooms (6/79), 16
Leek & ham quiche (4/79), 67
Oven-baked turkey legs (11/79), 108
Puget Sound steamed clams (10/79), 130
Romaine salad with creamy garlic dressing (4/79), 40
Salsa chicken with cheese (3/79), 100
Sicilian ricotta frittata (8/79), 63
Two-way baked potatoes (10/79), 148
Vegetable-topped fish fillets (9/79), 119

1980
Almond-caramel bars (5/80), 199
Beef satay with peanut sauce (5/80), 72
Cheesy chestnut tidbits (5/80), 14
Foolproof soufflé squares (12/80), 66
Frosted zucchini or potato rounds (3/80), 147
Minted potato salad (7/80), 49
Plum-glazed chicken (5/80), 95
Quick sole & shrimp casserole (4/80), 124
Rosy apple teacup salads (11/80), 43
Summer squash relish (8/80), 170
Tarragon-marinated vegetable platter (4/80), 45

1981
Asparagus spears with egg dressing (4/81), 152
Bacon & egg burritos (2/81), 64
Baked pork chops with herb stuffing (3/81), 80
Caesar-style vegetable salad (10/81), 44
Chile cheese fish stacks (10/81), 120
Cinnamon-nut crescents (8/81), 189
Fall fruit platter (11/81), 42
Fresh pineapple crisp (1/81), 211
Green & orange salad (3/81), 40
Salad Italiano with basil dressing (9/81), 39
Tomato cheese stacks (9/81), 152
Tuna carbonara (11/81), 125
Whole wheat raisin scones (1/81), 180
Zucchini-cheese appetizer squares (6/81), 13

1982
Baked apples & carrots (3/82), 155
Bit o'emerald soup (3/82), 25
Chicken & apple sauté (4/82), 101
Chunky salsa (6/82), 167
Confetti coleslaw (5/82), 41
Cornish hens with wild rice stuffing (3/82), 110
Crispy oven-fried chicken for a dozen (5/82), 99
Greek scrambled eggs (6/82), 61
Hot stuffed tomatoes (8/82), 152
Ravioli & cabbage soup (10/82), 29
Salmon grill diable (7/82), 117
Strawberry & cheese tart (4/82), 207
Sweet & sour baked beans (7/82), 161
Tandoori chicken (9/82), 107
Turkey-grape salad (8/82), 56
Wheat germ buns (9/82), 189

1983
Apple cider stew (10/83), 76
Cheese-glazed coffeecake (2/83), 184
Eggplant crêpes (8/83), 67
Garden gazpacho (8/83), 21
Ginger & lime butter (6/83), 168
Grandma Peterson's peppernoder (12/83), 197
Hangtown fry (9/83), 130
Hashed brown zucchini (9/83), 158
Hawaiian honey chicken (3/83), 98
Orange-date relish (10/83), 171
Oregonian chili (9/83), 109
Oven lamb shank stew (1/83), 87
Turkey barley soup (11/83), 32
Walnut chard crêpes (5/83), 66
Wine-braised chuck roast (2/83), 74

1984
Asparagus chicken stir-fry (4/84), 100
Baked marinated eggplant (9/84), 159
Blueberry-lemon muffins (8/84), 178
Chiles rellenos meatballs (6/84), 78
Cinnamon-apple Dutch baby (8/84), 65
Colorado bean soup (3/84), 26
Cool curry turkey salad (7/84), 55
Cranberry brunch cake (11/84), 183
Garlic chicken & grapes (12/84), 106
Golden squash rolls (10/84), 189
Halibut with vegetable crest (7/84), 122
Lemon-mustard roast lamb (10/84), 86
Pumpkin cheesecake (11/84), 204
Quick refrigerator cucumber chips (6/84), 170
Ranchero soufflé (11/84), 65
Sesame flank steak (5/84), 71
Soft New Mexican vegetable tacos (3/84), 142
Spiced lamb-stuffed peppers (9/84), 88
Summer berry ice cream (6/84), 215
Zucchini omelets (9/84), 62

1985
Broiled avocado salad (11/85), 57
Caramel apple cake (11/85), 200
Cheese & bacon corn muffins (2/85), 177
Cheese & bacon in a bread boat (9/85), 14
Chicken ratatouille (5/85), 104
Chicken salad with sesame dressing (6/85), 54
Chocolate bread pudding (10/85), 210
Grilled soy-lemon halibut (9/85), 122
Hot & sour beef with cucumber (7/85), 75
Hungarian cabbage rolls (10/85), 79
Jayne's Chinese chicken (7/85), 96
Jayne's Chinese duck (7/85), 96
Jicama-pea salad (5/85), 47
Kolaches (3/85), 190
Marinated mushrooms (8/85), 13
Picnic brownie cakes (6/85), 202
Pigs in a quilt (6/85), 90
Roasted onion spread (5/85), 11
Sesame-ginger steamed mussels (3/85), 131
Spring asparagus spread (4/85), 10
Toasted cabbage with noodles (4/85), 151
Tri-mustard tomato salad (8/85), 44

1986
Almond pilaf with sherry (10/86), 161
Broiled fish Dijon (8/86), 121
Cabbage-paprika stroganoff (1/86), 76
Cheese crackers (11/86), 16
Chicken & avocado salad (12/86), 54
Chicken pasta Italiano (8/86), 103
Chili con queso (9/86), 9
Chinese chicken & shrimp soup (4/86), 33
Chocolate cream torte (5/86), 203